NISSAN | ALTIMA
2007-10 REPAIR MANUAL

Deleted

P9-CDV-297

**Covers U.S. and Canadian models of Nissan Altima
2007 through 2010**

Does not include information specific to hybrid models

by Tim Imhoff

CHILTON *Automotive Books*

PUBLISHED BY **HAYNES NORTH AMERICA, Inc.**

Manufactured in USA
©2011 Haynes North America, Inc.
ISBN-13: 978-1-56392-907-6
ISBN-10: 1-56392-907-4
Library of Congress Control Number 2011921366

Haynes Publishing Group
Sparkford Nr Yeovil
Somerset BA22 7JJ England

Haynes North America, Inc
861 Lawrence Drive
Newbury Park
California 91320 USA

ABCDE
FGHIJ
KLMNO
PQRST

Contents

Photographer and mechanic with a 2009 Nissan Altima

ACKNOWLEDGEMENTS

Wiring diagrams originated by Valley Forge Technical Information Services.

While every attempt is made to ensure that the information in this manual is correct, no liability can be accepted by the authors or publishers for loss, damage or injury caused by any errors in, or omissions from, the information given.

About this manual

ITS PURPOSE

The purpose of this manual is to help you get the best value from your vehicle. It can do so in several ways. It can help you decide what work must be done, even if you choose to have it done by a dealer service department or a repair shop; it provides information and procedures for routine maintenance and servicing; and it offers diagnostic and repair procedures to follow when trouble occurs.

We hope you use the manual to tackle the work yourself. For many simpler jobs, doing it yourself may be quicker than arranging an appointment to get the vehicle into a shop and making the trips to leave it and pick it up. More importantly, a lot of money can be saved by avoiding the expense the shop must pass on to you to cover its labor and overhead costs. An added benefit is the sense of satisfaction and accomplishment that you feel after doing the job yourself.

USING THE MANUAL

The manual is divided into Chapters. Each Chapter is divided into numbered Sections. Each Section consists of consecutively numbered paragraphs.

At the beginning of each numbered Section you will be referred to any illustrations which apply to the procedures in that Section. The reference numbers used in illustration captions pinpoint the pertinent Section and the Step within that Section. That is, illustration 3.2 means the illustration refers to Section 3 and Step (or paragraph) 2 within that Section.

Procedures, once described in the text, are not normally repeated. When it's necessary to refer to another Chapter, the reference will be given as Chapter and Section number. Cross references given without use of the word "Chapter" apply to Sections and/or paragraphs in the same Chapter. For example, "see Section 8" means in the same Chapter.

References to the left or right side of the vehicle assume you are sitting in the driver's seat, facing forward.

Even though we have prepared this manual with extreme care, neither the publisher nor the author can accept responsibility for any errors in, or omissions from, the information given.

➡NOTE

A *Note* provides information necessary to properly complete a procedure or information which will make the procedure easier to understand.

✳✳ CAUTION

A *Caution* provides a special procedure or special steps which must be taken while completing the procedure where the Caution is found. Not heeding a Caution can result in damage to the assembly being worked on.

✳✳ WARNING

A *Warning* provides a special procedure or special steps which must be taken while completing the procedure where the Warning is found. Not heeding a Warning can result in personal injury.

Introduction

The Nissan Altima is available in two-door coupe and four-door sedan body styles.

The transversely-mounted 2.5L four-cylinder engine or 3.5L V6 engine used in these models are equipped with a sequential multi-port electronic fuel injection system.

The engine transmits power to the front wheels through either a six-speed manual transaxle or a continuously variable automatic transaxle (CVT) via independent driveaxles.

The Altima has a steel uni-body and four-wheel independent suspension. The rack-and-pinion steering unit is mounted behind the engine. It has power assist as standard equipment.

All models are equipped with power assisted front and rear disc brakes. An anti-lock braking system is standard equipment on some models.

Vehicle identification numbers

Modifications are a continuing and unpublicized process in vehicle manufacturing. Since spare parts manuals and lists are compiled on a numerical basis, the individual vehicle numbers are essential to correctly identify the component required.

VEHICLE IDENTIFICATION NUMBER (VIN)

This very important identification number is located on a plate attached to the dashboard inside the windshield on the driver's side of the vehicle (see illustration). The VIN also appears on the Vehicle Certificate of Title and Registration. It contains information such as where and when the vehicle was manufactured, the model year and the body style.

VIN ENGINE AND MODEL YEAR CODES

Two particularly important pieces of information found in the VIN are the engine code and the model year code. Counting from the left, the engine code letter designation is the 4th character and the model year code designation is the 10th character.

On the models covered by this manual the engine codes are:

A   QR25DE 2.5L DOHC
B   VQ35DE 3.5L DOHC

On the models covered by this manual the model year codes are:

7   2007
8   2008
9   2009
A   2010

The Vehicle Identification Number (VIN) is visible through the driver's side of the windshield

The Manufacturer's Certification label is affixed to the drivers side door post

The Engine Identification Number is stamped on the front side of the engine block, near the transaxle (2.4L engine shown)

The transaxle ID number is located on top of the transaxle bellhousing (manual transaxle shown)

MANUFACTURER'S CERTIFICATION REGULATION LABEL

The manufacturer's Certification Regulation label is attached to the driver's side door post (see illustration). The label contains the name of the manufacturer, the month and year of production, the Gross Vehicle Weight Rating (GVWR), the Gross Axle Weight Rating (GAWR) and the certification statement.

ENGINE IDENTIFICATION NUMBERS

On four-cylinder models, the engine code number can be found on a pad on the front (radiator) side of the cylinder block, near the transaxle (see illustration). On V6 models, the engine code number is located at the left end (driver's side) of the engine, just above the transaxle bellhousing.

TRANSAXLE IDENTIFICATION NUMBERS

The transaxle identification number is stamped on top of the bellhousing (see illustration).

VEHICLE EMISSIONS CONTROL INFORMATION (VECI) LABEL

The emissions control information label is found on the bottom side of the hood. This label contains information on the emissions control equipment installed on the vehicle, as well as a vacuum diagram (see illustration).

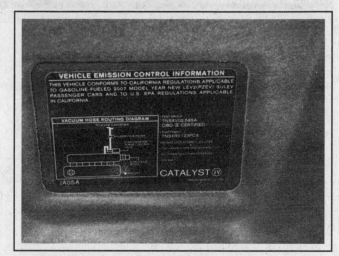

The Vehicle Emissions Control Information (VECI) label is located on the bottom side of the hood

Recall information

Vehicle recalls are carried out by the manufacturer in the rare event of a possible safety-related defect. The vehicle's registered owner is contacted at the address on file at the Department of Motor Vehicles and given the details of the recall. Remedial work is carried out free of charge at a dealer service department.

If you are the new owner of a used vehicle which was subject to a recall and you want to be sure that the work has been carried out, it's best to contact a dealer service department and ask about your individual vehicle - you'll need to furnish them your Vehicle Identification Number (VIN).

The table below is based on information provided by the National Highway Traffic Safety Administration (NHTSA), the body which oversees vehicle recalls in the United States. The recall database is updated constantly. For the latest information on vehicle recalls, check the NHTSA website at www.nhtsa.gov, or call the NHTSA hotline at 1-888-327-4236.

Recall date	Recall campaign number	Model(s) affected	Concern
JUN 21, 2007	07V267000	2007 Altima	On certain vehicles, if a sufficiently hot object enters the air filter housing through the engine fresh air system and contacts the engine air filter, the flammability characteristics of the air filter material are such that the filter may ignite.
DEC 28, 2007	07V599000	2008 Altima	On certain vehicles that have had the Body Control Module (BCM) replaced during service at a dealership, the tire pressure monitoring system (TPMS) may have been inadvertently deactivated due to an issue with the dealer service software. If the TPMS is turned off, it would not alert the driver to a decrease in the tire pressure as designed.
JUL 31, 2008	08V363000	2008 Altima	The left side front suspension transverse link (control arm) bolt may not have been tightened to specification. This could cause the bolt to come loose while the vehicle is being driven.
SEP 15, 2008	08V464000	2009 Altima	On some models equipped with 16-inch alloy wheels, some of these wheels may not have been manufactured to specification. This could cause lug nuts to come loose.

Recall date	Recall campaign number	Model(s) affected	Concern
OCT 07, 2008	08V521000	2007 and 2008 Altima	On some models, the passenger airbag may have a problem that could cause it not to deploy.
SEP 16, 2009	09V358000	2009 and 2010 Altima	Some models may have upper front strut insulators that were manufactured out of specification, causing a potential for the strut insulator to crack.
MAY 07, 2010	10V193000	2010 Altima	Some models may have front side members that were not welded to specification.
SEP 10, 2010	10V401000	2008 Altima	Models that were equipped with a Garmin Nuvi Model 750 navigation system may have batteries in that system that could overheat and cause a fire

Buying parts

Replacement parts are available from many sources, which generally fall into one of two categories - authorized dealer parts departments and independent retail auto parts stores. Our advice concerning these parts is as follows:

Retail auto parts stores: Good auto parts stores will stock frequently needed components which wear out relatively fast, such as clutch components, exhaust systems, brake parts, tune-up parts, etc. These stores often supply new or reconditioned parts on an exchange basis, which can save a considerable amount of money. Discount auto parts stores are often very good places to buy materials and parts needed for general vehicle maintenance such as oil, grease, filters, spark plugs, belts, touch-up paint, bulbs, etc. They also usually sell tools and general accessories, have convenient hours, charge lower prices and can often be found not far from home.

Authorized dealer parts department: This is the best source for parts which are unique to the vehicle and not generally available elsewhere (such as major engine parts, transmission parts, trim pieces, etc.).

Warranty information: If the vehicle is still covered under warranty, be sure that any replacement parts purchased - regardless of the source - do not invalidate the warranty!

To be sure of obtaining the correct parts, have engine and chassis numbers available and, if possible, take the old parts along for positive identification.

MAINTENANCE TECHNIQUES

There are a number of techniques involved in maintenance and repair that will be referred to throughout this manual. Application of these techniques will enable the home mechanic to be more efficient, better organized and capable of performing the various tasks properly, which will ensure that the repair job is thorough and complete.

Fasteners

Fasteners are nuts, bolts, studs and screws used to hold two or more parts together. There are a few things to keep in mind when working with fasteners. Almost all of them use a locking device of some type, either a lockwasher, locknut, locking tab or thread adhesive. All threaded fasteners should be clean and straight, with undamaged threads and undamaged corners on the hex head where the wrench fits. Develop the habit of replacing all damaged nuts and bolts with new ones. Special locknuts with nylon or fiber inserts can only be used once. If they are removed, they lose their locking ability and must be replaced with new ones.

Rusted nuts and bolts should be treated with a penetrating fluid to ease removal and prevent breakage. Some mechanics use turpentine in a spout-type oil can, which works quite well. After applying the rust penetrant, let it work for a few minutes before trying to loosen the nut or bolt. Badly rusted fasteners may have to be chiseled or sawed off or removed with a special nut breaker, available at tool stores.

If a bolt or stud breaks off in an assembly, it can be drilled and removed with a special tool commonly available for this purpose. Most automotive machine shops can perform this task, as well as other repair procedures, such as the repair of threaded holes that have been stripped out.

Flat washers and lockwashers, when removed from an assembly, should always be replaced exactly as removed. Replace any damaged washers with new ones. Never use a lockwasher on any soft metal surface (such as aluminum), thin sheet metal or plastic.

Fastener sizes

For a number of reasons, automobile manufacturers are making wider and wider use of metric fasteners. Therefore, it is important to be able to tell the difference between standard (sometimes called U.S. or SAE) and metric hardware, since they cannot be interchanged.

All bolts, whether standard or metric, are sized according to diameter, thread pitch and length. For example, a standard 1/2 - 13 x 1 bolt is 1/2 inch in diameter, has 13 threads per inch and is 1 inch long. An M12 - 1.75 x 25 metric bolt is 12 mm in diameter, has a thread pitch of 1.75 mm (the distance between threads) and is 25 mm long. The two bolts are nearly identical, and easily confused, but they are not interchangeable.

In addition to the differences in diameter, thread pitch and length, metric and standard bolts can also be distinguished by examining the bolt heads. To begin with, the distance across the flats on a standard bolt head is measured in inches, while the same dimension on a metric bolt is sized in millimeters (the same is true for nuts). As a result, a standard wrench should not be used on a metric bolt and a metric wrench should not be used on a standard bolt. Also, most standard bolts have slashes radiating out from the center of the head to denote the grade or strength of the bolt, which is an indication of the amount of torque that can be applied to it. The greater the number of slashes, the greater the strength of the bolt. Grades 0 through 5 are commonly used on automobiles. Metric bolts have a property class (grade) number, rather than a slash, molded into their heads to indicate bolt strength. In this case, the higher the number, the stronger the bolt. Property class numbers 8.8, 9.8 and 10.9 are commonly used on automobiles.

Strength markings can also be used to distinguish standard hex nuts from metric hex nuts. Many standard nuts have dots stamped into one side, while metric nuts are marked with a number. The greater the number of dots, or the higher the number, the greater the strength of the nut.

Metric studs are also marked on their ends according to property class (grade). Larger studs are numbered (the same as metric bolts), while smaller studs carry a geometric code to denote grade.

It should be noted that many fasteners, especially Grades 0 through 2, have no distinguishing marks on them. When such is the case, the only way to determine whether it is standard or metric is to measure the thread pitch or compare it to a known fastener of the same size.

Standard fasteners are often referred to as SAE, as opposed to metric. However, it should be noted that SAE technically refers to a non-metric fine thread fastener only. Coarse thread non-metric fasteners are referred to as USS sizes.

Since fasteners of the same size (both standard and metric) may have different strength ratings, be sure to reinstall any bolts, studs or nuts removed from your vehicle in their original locations. Also, when replacing a fastener with a new one, make sure that the new one has a strength rating equal to or greater than the original.

Tightening sequences and procedures

Most threaded fasteners should be tightened to a specific torque value (torque is the twisting force applied to a threaded component such as a nut or bolt). Overtightening the fastener can weaken it and cause it to break, while undertightening can cause it to eventually come loose. Bolts, screws and studs, depending on the material they are made of and their thread diameters, have specific torque values, many of which are noted in the Specifications at the end of each Chapter. Be sure to follow the torque recommendations closely. For fasteners not assigned a specific torque, a general torque value chart is presented here as a guide. These torque values are for dry (unlubricated) fasteners threaded into steel or cast iron (not aluminum). As was previously mentioned, the size and grade of a fastener determine the amount of torque that can safely be applied to it. The figures listed here are approximate for Grade 2 and Grade 3 fasteners. Higher grades can tolerate higher torque values.

Fasteners laid out in a pattern, such as cylinder head bolts, oil pan bolts, differential cover bolts, etc., must be loosened or tightened in sequence to avoid warping the component. This sequence will normally be shown in the appropriate Chapter. If a specific pattern is not given, the following procedures can be used to prevent warping.

Initially, the bolts or nuts should be assembled finger-tight only. Next, they should be tightened one full turn each, in a criss-cross or diagonal pattern. After each one has been tightened one full turn, return to the first one and tighten them all one-half turn, following the same

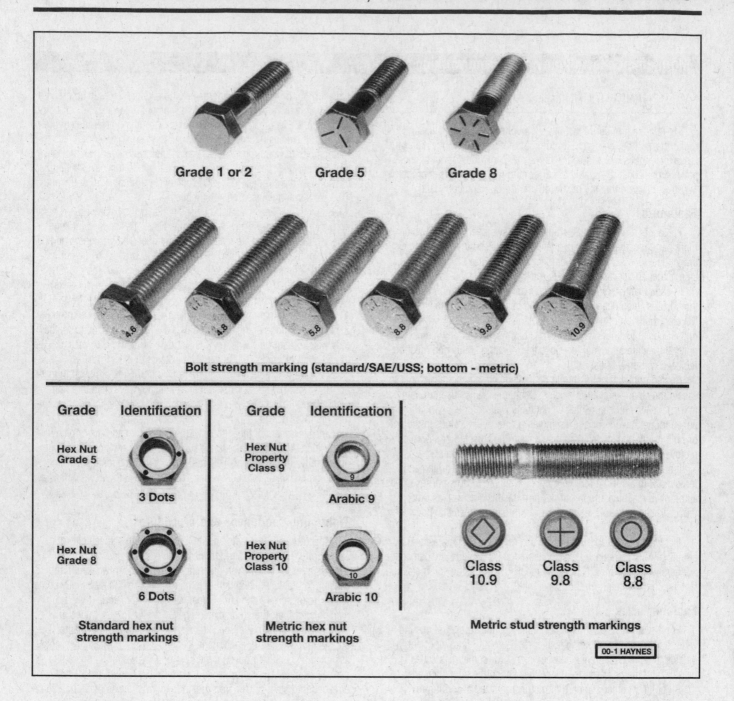

Grade 1 or 2   Grade 5   Grade 8

Bolt strength marking (standard/SAE/USS; bottom - metric)

Grade	Identification
Hex Nut Grade 5	3 Dots
Hex Nut Grade 8	6 Dots

Standard hex nut strength markings

Grade	Identification
Hex Nut Property Class 9	Arabic 9
Hex Nut Property Class 10	Arabic 10

Metric hex nut strength markings

Class 10.9   Class 9.8   Class 8.8

Metric stud strength markings

00-1 HAYNES

pattern. Finally, tighten each of them one-quarter turn at a time until each fastener has been tightened to the proper torque. To loosen and remove the fasteners, the procedure would be reversed.

Component disassembly

Component disassembly should be done with care and purpose to help ensure that the parts go back together properly. Always keep track of the sequence in which parts are removed. Make note of special characteristics or marks on parts that can be installed more than one way, such as a grooved thrust washer on a shaft. It is a good idea to lay the disassembled parts out on a clean surface in the order that they were removed. It may also be helpful to make sketches or take instant photos of components before removal.

When removing fasteners from a component, keep track of their locations. Sometimes threading a bolt back in a part, or putting the washers and nut back on a stud, can prevent mix-ups later. If nuts and bolts cannot be returned to their original locations, they should be kept in a compartmented box or a series of small boxes. A cupcake or muffin tin is ideal for this purpose, since each cavity can hold the bolts and nuts from a particular area (i.e. oil pan bolts, valve cover bolts, engine

Metric thread sizes	Ft-lbs	Nm
M-6	6 to 9	9 to 12
M-8	14 to 21	19 to 28
M-10	28 to 40	38 to 54
M-12	50 to 71	68 to 96
M-14	80 to 140	109 to 154

Pipe thread sizes		
1/8	5 to 8	7 to 10
1/4	12 to 18	17 to 24
3/8	22 to 33	30 to 44
1/2	25 to 35	34 to 47

U.S. thread sizes		
1/4 - 20	6 to 9	9 to 12
5/16 - 18	12 to 18	17 to 24
5/16 - 24	14 to 20	19 to 27
3/8 - 16	22 to 32	30 to 43
3/8 - 24	27 to 38	37 to 51
7/16 - 14	40 to 55	55 to 74
7/16 - 20	40 to 60	55 to 81
1/2 - 13	55 to 80	75 to 108

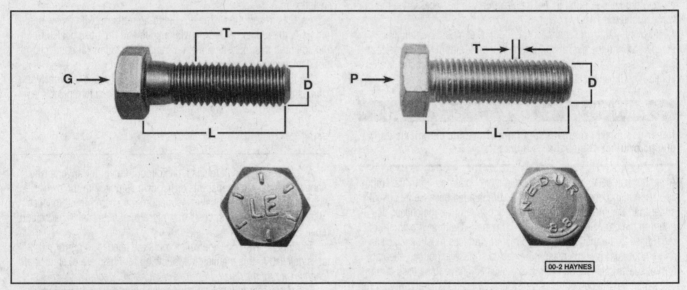

Standard (SAE and USS) bolt dimensions/grade marks

G   Grade marks (bolt strength)
L   Length (in inches)
T   Thread pitch (number of threads per inch)
D   Nominal diameter (in inches)

Metric bolt dimensions/grade marks

P   Property class (bolt strength)
L   Length (in millimeters)
T   Thread pitch (distance between threads in millimeters)
D   Diameter

mount bolts, etc.). A pan of this type is especially helpful when working on assemblies with very small parts, such as the carburetor, alternator, valve train or interior dash and trim pieces. The cavities can be marked with paint or tape to identify the contents.

Whenever wiring looms, harnesses or connectors are separated, it is a good idea to identify the two halves with numbered pieces of masking tape so they can be easily reconnected.

Gasket sealing surfaces

Throughout any vehicle, gaskets are used to seal the mating surfaces between two parts and keep lubricants, fluids, vacuum or pressure contained in an assembly.

Many times these gaskets are coated with a liquid or paste-type gasket sealing compound before assembly. Age, heat and pressure can sometimes cause the two parts to stick together so tightly that they are very difficult to separate. Often, the assembly can be loosened by striking it with a soft-face hammer near the mating surfaces. A regular hammer can be used if a block of wood is placed between the hammer and the part. Do not hammer on cast parts or parts that could be easily damaged. With any particularly stubborn part, always recheck to make sure that every fastener has been removed.

Avoid using a screwdriver or bar to pry apart an assembly, as they

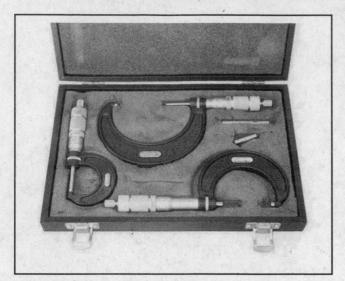

Micrometer set

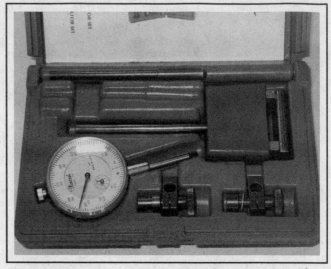

Dial indicator set

can easily mar the gasket sealing surfaces of the parts, which must remain smooth. If prying is absolutely necessary, use an old broom handle, but keep in mind that extra clean up will be necessary if the wood splinters.

After the parts are separated, the old gasket must be carefully scraped off and the gasket surfaces cleaned. Stubborn gasket material can be soaked with rust penetrant or treated with a special chemical to soften it so it can be easily scraped off.

✸✸ CAUTION:

Never use gasket removal solutions or caustic chemicals on plastic or other composite components.

A scraper can be fashioned from a piece of copper tubing by flattening and sharpening one end. Copper is recommended because it is usually softer than the surfaces to be scraped, which reduces the chance of gouging the part. Some gaskets can be removed with a wire brush, but regardless of the method used, the mating surfaces must be left clean and smooth. If for some reason the gasket surface is gouged, then a gasket sealer thick enough to fill scratches will have to be used during reassembly of the components. For most applications, a non-drying (or semi-drying) gasket sealer should be used.

Hose removal tips

✸✸ WARNING:

If the vehicle is equipped with air conditioning, do not disconnect any of the A/C hoses without first having the system depressurized by a dealer service department or a service station.

Hose removal precautions closely parallel gasket removal precautions. Avoid scratching or gouging the surface that the hose mates against or the connection may leak. This is especially true for radiator hoses. Because of various chemical reactions, the rubber in hoses can bond itself to the metal spigot that the hose fits over. To remove a hose, first loosen the hose clamps that secure it to the spigot. Then, with slip-joint pliers, grab the hose at the clamp and rotate it around the spigot. Work it back and forth until it is completely free, then pull it off. Silicone or other lubricants will ease removal if they can be applied between the hose and the outside of the spigot. Apply the same lubricant to the inside of the hose and the outside of the spigot to simplify installation.

As a last resort (and if the hose is to be replaced with a new one anyway), the rubber can be slit with a knife and the hose peeled from the spigot. If this must be done, be careful that the metal connection is not damaged.

If a hose clamp is broken or damaged, do not reuse it. Wire-type clamps usually weaken with age, so it is a good idea to replace them with screw-type clamps whenever a hose is removed.

TOOLS

A selection of good tools is a basic requirement for anyone who plans to maintain and repair his or her own vehicle. For the owner who has few tools, the initial investment might seem high, but when compared to the spiraling costs of professional auto maintenance and repair, it is a wise one.

To help the owner decide which tools are needed to perform the tasks detailed in this manual, the following tool lists are offered: *Maintenance and minor repair, Repair/overhaul* and *Special.*

The newcomer to practical mechanics should start off with the *maintenance and minor repair* tool kit, which is adequate for the simpler jobs performed on a vehicle. Then, as confidence and experience grow, the owner can tackle more difficult tasks, buying additional tools as they are needed. Eventually the basic kit will be expanded into the *repair and overhaul* tool set. Over a period of time, the experienced do-it-yourselfer will assemble a tool set complete enough for most repair and overhaul procedures and will add tools from the special category when it is felt that the expense is justified by the frequency of use.

Maintenance and minor repair tool kit

The tools in this list should be considered the minimum required for performance of routine maintenance, servicing and minor repair work. We recommend the purchase of combination wrenches (box-end and open-end combined in one wrench). While more expensive than open end wrenches, they offer the advantages of both types of wrench.

Combination wrench set (1/4-inch to 1 inch or 6 mm to 19 mm)
Adjustable wrench, 8 inch
Spark plug wrench with rubber insert

Spark plug gap adjusting tool
Feeler gauge set
Brake bleeder wrench
Standard screwdriver (5/16-inch x 6 inch)
Phillips screwdriver (No. 2 x 6 inch)
Combination pliers - 6 inch
Hacksaw and assortment of blades
Tire pressure gauge
Grease gun

Oil can
Fine emery cloth
Wire brush
Battery post and cable cleaning tool
Oil filter wrench
Funnel (medium size)
Safety goggles
Jackstands (2)
Drain pan

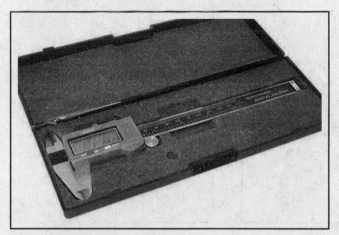

Dial caliper

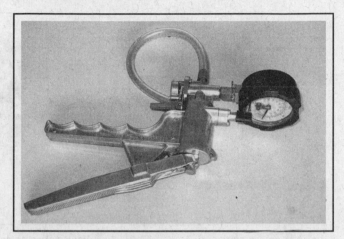

Hand-operated vacuum pump

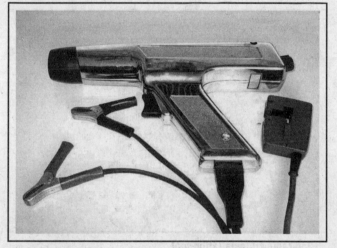

Timing light

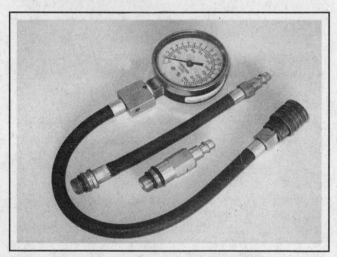

Compression gauge with spark plug hole adapter

Damper/steering wheel puller

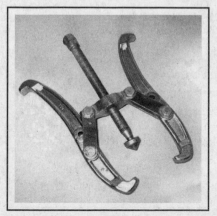

General purpose puller

Hydraulic lifter removal tool

➡**Note: If basic tune-ups are going to be part of routine maintenance, it will be necessary to purchase a good quality stroboscopic timing light and combination tachometer/dwell meter. Although they are included in the list of special tools, it is mentioned here because they are absolutely necessary for tuning most vehicles properly.**

Repair and overhaul tool set

These tools are essential for anyone who plans to perform major repairs and are in addition to those in the maintenance and minor repair tool kit. Included is a comprehensive set of sockets which, though expensive, are invaluable because of their versatility, especially when various extensions and drives are available. We recommend the 1/2-inch drive over the 3/8-inch drive. Although the larger drive is bulky and more expensive, it has the capacity of accepting a very wide range of large sockets. Ideally, however, the mechanic should have a 3/8-inch drive set and a 1/2-inch drive set.

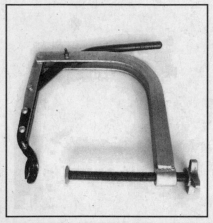

Valve spring compressor

Valve spring compressor

Ridge reamer

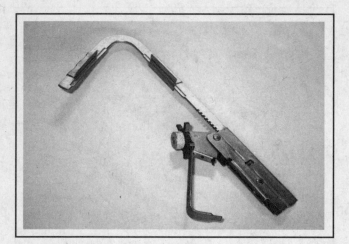

Piston ring groove cleaning tool

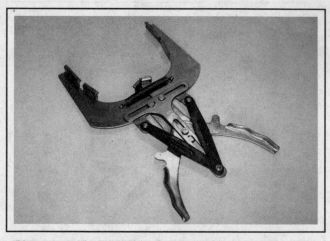

Ring removal/installation tool

Ring compressor

Cylinder hone

Brake hold-down spring tool

Torque angle gauge

Clutch plate alignment tool

Socket set(s)
Reversible ratchet
Extension - 10 inch
Universal joint
Torque wrench (same size drive as sockets)
Ball peen hammer - 8 ounce
Soft-face hammer (plastic/rubber)
Standard screwdriver (1/4-inch x 6 inch)
Standard screwdriver (stubby - 5/16-inch)
Phillips screwdriver (No. 3 x 8 inch)
Phillips screwdriver (stubby - No. 2)
Pliers - vise grip
Pliers - lineman's
Pliers - needle nose
Pliers - snap-ring (internal and external)
Cold chisel - 1/2-inch
Scribe
Scraper (made from flattened copper tubing)
Centerpunch
Pin punches (1/16, 1/8, 3/16-inch)
Steel rule/straightedge - 12 inch
Allen wrench set (1/8 to 3/8-inch or 4 mm to 10 mm)
A selection of files
Wire brush (large)
Jackstands (second set)
Jack (scissor or hydraulic type)

➡**Note: Another tool which is often useful is an electric drill with a chuck capacity of 3/8-inch and a set of good quality drill bits.**

Special tools

The tools in this list include those which are not used regularly, are expensive to buy, or which need to be used in accordance with their manufacturer's instructions. Unless these tools will be used frequently, it is not very economical to purchase many of them. A consideration would be to split the cost and use between yourself and a friend or friends. In addition, most of these tools can be obtained from a tool rental shop on a temporary basis.

This list primarily contains only those tools and instruments widely available to the public, and not those special tools produced by the vehicle manufacturer for distribution to dealer service departments. Occasionally, references to the manufacturer's special tools are included in the text of this manual. Generally, an alternative method of doing the job without the special tool is offered. However, sometimes

there is no alternative to their use. Where this is the case, and the tool cannot be purchased or borrowed, the work should be turned over to the dealer service department or an automotive repair shop.

Valve spring compressor
Piston ring groove cleaning tool
Piston ring compressor
Piston ring installation tool
Cylinder compression gauge
Cylinder ridge reamer
Cylinder surfacing hone
Cylinder bore gauge
Micrometers and/or dial calipers
Hydraulic lifter removal tool
Balljoint separator
Universal-type puller
Impact screwdriver
Dial indicator set
Stroboscopic timing light (inductive pick-up)
Hand operated vacuum/pressure pump
Tachometer/dwell meter
Universal electrical multimeter
Cable hoist
Brake spring removal and installation tools
Floor jack

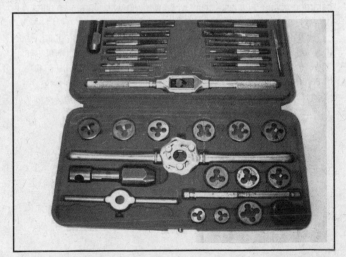

Tap and die set

Buying tools

For the do-it-yourselfer who is just starting to get involved in vehicle maintenance and repair, there are a number of options available when purchasing tools. If maintenance and minor repair is the extent of the work to be done, the purchase of individual tools is satisfactory. If, on the other hand, extensive work is planned, it would be a good idea to purchase a modest tool set from one of the large retail chain stores. A set can usually be bought at a substantial savings over the individual tool prices, and they often come with a tool box. As additional tools are needed, add-on sets, individual tools and a larger tool box can be purchased to expand the tool selection. Building a tool set gradually allows the cost of the tools to be spread over a longer period of time and gives the mechanic the freedom to choose only those tools that will actually be used.

Tool stores will often be the only source of some of the special tools that are needed, but regardless of where tools are bought, try to avoid cheap ones, especially when buying screwdrivers and sockets, because they won't last very long. The expense involved in replacing cheap tools will eventually be greater than the initial cost of quality tools.

Care and maintenance of tools

Good tools are expensive, so it makes sense to treat them with respect. Keep them clean and in usable condition and store them properly when not in use. Always wipe off any dirt, grease or metal chips before putting them away. Never leave tools lying around in the work area. Upon completion of a job, always check closely under the hood for tools that may have been left there so they won't get lost during a test drive.

Some tools, such as screwdrivers, pliers, wrenches and sockets, can be hung on a panel mounted on the garage or workshop wall, while others should be kept in a tool box or tray. Measuring instruments, gauges, meters, etc. must be carefully stored where they cannot be damaged by weather or impact from other tools.

When tools are used with care and stored properly, they will last a very long time. Even with the best of care, though, tools will wear out if used frequently. When a tool is damaged or worn out, replace it. Subsequent jobs will be safer and more enjoyable if you do.

HOW TO REPAIR DAMAGED THREADS

Sometimes, the internal threads of a nut or bolt hole can become stripped, usually from overtightening. Stripping threads is an all-too-common occurrence, especially when working with aluminum parts, because aluminum is so soft that it easily strips out.

Usually, external or internal threads are only partially stripped. After they've been cleaned up with a tap or die, they'll still work. Sometimes, however, threads are badly damaged. When this happens, you've got three choices:

1) *Drill and tap the hole to the next suitable oversize and install a larger diameter bolt, screw or stud.*

2) *Drill and tap the hole to accept a threaded plug, then drill and tap the plug to the original screw size. You can also buy a plug already threaded to the original size. Then you simply drill a hole to the specified size, then run the threaded plug into the hole with a bolt and jam nut. Once the plug is fully seated, remove the jam nut and bolt.*

3) *The third method uses a patented thread repair kit like Heli-Coil or Slimsert. These easy-to-use kits are designed to repair damaged threads in straight-through holes and blind holes. Both are available as kits which can handle a variety of sizes and thread patterns. Drill the hole, then tap it with the special included tap. Install the Heli-Coil and the hole is back to its original diameter and thread pitch.*

Regardless of which method you use, be sure to proceed calmly and carefully. A little impatience or carelessness during one of these relatively simple procedures can ruin your whole day's work and cost you a bundle if you wreck an expensive part.

WORKING FACILITIES

Not to be overlooked when discussing tools is the workshop. If anything more than routine maintenance is to be carried out, some sort of suitable work area is essential.

It is understood, and appreciated, that many home mechanics do not have a good workshop or garage available, and end up removing an engine or doing major repairs outside. It is recommended, however, that the overhaul or repair be completed under the cover of a roof.

A clean, flat workbench or table of comfortable working height is an absolute necessity. The workbench should be equipped with a vise that has a jaw opening of at least four inches.

As mentioned previously, some clean, dry storage space is also required for tools, as well as the lubricants, fluids, cleaning solvents, etc. which soon become necessary.

Sometimes waste oil and fluids, drained from the engine or cooling system during normal maintenance or repairs, present a disposal problem. To avoid pouring them on the ground or into a sewage system, pour the used fluids into large containers, seal them with caps and take them to an authorized disposal site or recycling center. Plastic jugs, such as old antifreeze containers, are ideal for this purpose.

Always keep a supply of old newspapers and clean rags available. Old towels are excellent for mopping up spills. Many mechanics use rolls of paper towels for most work because they are readily available and disposable. To help keep the area under the vehicle clean, a large cardboard box can be cut open and flattened to protect the garage or shop floor.

Whenever working over a painted surface, such as when leaning over a fender to service something under the hood, always cover it with an old blanket or bedspread to protect the finish. Vinyl covered pads, made especially for this purpose, are available at auto parts stores.

Jacking and towing

JACKING

The vehicle should be on level ground. Place the shift lever in Park, if you have an automatic, or Reverse if you have a manual transaxle. Block the wheel diagonally opposite the wheel being changed. Set the parking brake.

The jack fits over the rocker panel flange (there are two jacking points on each side of the vehicle, indicated by a notch in the rocker panel flange)

Remove the spare tire and jack from stowage. Remove the wheel cover and trim ring (if so equipped) with the tapered end of the lug nut wrench by inserting and twisting the handle and then prying against the back of the wheel cover. Loosen the wheel lug nuts about 1/4-to-1/2 turn each.

Place the scissors-type jack under the side of the vehicle and adjust the jack height until it fits in the notch in the vertical rocker panel flange nearest the wheel to be changed. There is a front and rear jacking point on each side of the vehicle (see illustration).

Turn the jack handle clockwise until the tire clears the ground. Remove the lug nuts and pull the wheel off. Replace it with the spare.

Install the lug nuts with the beveled edges facing in. Tighten them snugly. Don't attempt to tighten them completely until the vehicle is lowered or it could slip off the jack. Turn the jack handle counterclockwise to lower the vehicle. Remove the jack and tighten the lug nuts in a diagonal pattern.

Install the cover (and trim ring, if used) and be sure it's snapped into place all the way around.

Stow the tire, jack and wrench. Unblock the wheels.

TOWING

As a general rule, the vehicle should be towed with the front (drive) wheels off the ground. If they can't be raised, place them on a dolly. The intelligent key must be in its slot in the instrument panel and the starter button display must be in the ACC position to unlock the steering column lock.

Models with a manual transaxle can be towed with all four wheels on the ground (such as behind a motorhome) provided that every 500 miles the engine is started and allowed to idle for two minutes to circulate the transaxle lubricant.

Equipment specifically designed for towing should be used. It should be attached to the main structural members of the vehicle, not the bumpers or brackets.

Safety is a major consideration when towing and all applicable state and local laws must be obeyed. A safety chain system must be used at all times.

Booster battery (jump) starting

Observe the following precautions when using a booster battery to start a vehicle:

a) *Before connecting the booster battery, make sure the ignition switch is in the Off position.*

b) *Turn off the lights, heater and other electrical loads.*

c) *Your eyes should be shielded. Safety goggles are a good idea.*

d) *Make sure the booster battery is the same voltage as the dead one in the vehicle.*

e) *The two vehicles MUST NOT TOUCH each other.*

f) *Make sure the transmission is in Neutral (manual) or Park (automatic).*

g) *If the booster battery is not a maintenance-free type, remove the vent caps and lay a cloth over the vent holes.*

Connect the red jumper cable to the positive (+) terminals of each battery.

Connect one end of the black cable to the negative (-) terminal of the booster battery. The other end of this cable should be connected to a good ground on the engine block (see illustration). Make sure the cable will not come into contact with the fan, drivebelts or other moving parts of the engine.

Start the engine using the booster battery, then, with the engine running at idle speed, disconnect the jumper cables in the reverse order of connection.

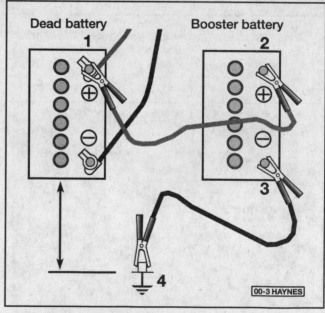

Make the booster battery cable connections in the numerical order shown (note that the negative cable of the booster battery is NOT attached to the negative terminal of the dead battery)

Automotive chemicals and lubricants

A number of automotive chemicals and lubricants are available for use during vehicle maintenance and repair. They include a wide variety of products ranging from cleaning solvents and degreasers to lubricants and protective sprays for rubber, plastic and vinyl.

CLEANERS

Carburetor cleaner and choke cleaner is a strong solvent for gum, varnish and carbon. Most carburetor cleaners leave a dry-type lubricant film which will not harden or gum up. Because of this film it is not recommended for use on electrical components.

Brake system cleaner is used to remove brake dust, grease and brake fluid from the brake system, where clean surfaces are absolutely necessary. It leaves no residue and often eliminates brake squeal caused by contaminants.

Electrical cleaner removes oxidation, corrosion and carbon deposits from electrical contacts, restoring full current flow. It can also be used to clean spark plugs, carburetor jets, voltage regulators and other parts where an oil-free surface is desired.

Demoisturants remove water and moisture from electrical components such as alternators, voltage regulators, electrical connectors and fuse blocks. They are non-conductive and non-corrosive.

Degreasers are heavy-duty solvents used to remove grease from the outside of the engine and from chassis components. They can be sprayed or brushed on and, depending on the type, are rinsed off either with water or solvent.

LUBRICANTS

Motor oil is the lubricant formulated for use in engines. It normally contains a wide variety of additives to prevent corrosion and reduce foaming and wear. Motor oil comes in various weights (viscosity ratings) from 0 to 50. The recommended weight of the oil depends on the season, temperature and the demands on the engine. Light oil is used in cold climates and under light load conditions. Heavy oil is used in hot climates and where high loads are encountered. Multi-viscosity oils are designed to have characteristics of both light and heavy oils and are available in a number of weights from 0W-20 to 20W-50.

Gear oil is designed to be used in differentials, manual transmissions and other areas where high-temperature lubrication is required.

Chassis and wheel bearing grease is a heavy grease used where increased loads and friction are encountered, such as for wheel bearings, ball-joints, tie-rod ends and universal joints.

High-temperature wheel bearing grease is designed to withstand the extreme temperatures encountered by wheel bearings in disc brake equipped vehicles. It usually contains molybdenum disulfide (moly), which is a dry-type lubricant.

White grease is a heavy grease for metal-to-metal applications where water is a problem. White grease stays soft under both low and high temperatures (usually from -100 to +190-degrees F), and will not wash off or dilute in the presence of water.

Assembly lube is a special extreme pressure lubricant, usually containing moly, used to lubricate high-load parts (such as main and rod bearings and cam lobes) for initial start-up of a new engine. The assembly lube lubricates the parts without being squeezed out or washed away until the engine oiling system begins to function.

Silicone lubricants are used to protect rubber, plastic, vinyl and nylon parts.

Graphite lubricants are used where oils cannot be used due to contamination problems, such as in locks. The dry graphite will lubricate metal parts while remaining uncontaminated by dirt, water, oil or acids. It is electrically conductive and will not foul electrical contacts in locks such as the ignition switch.

Moly penetrants loosen and lubricate frozen, rusted and corroded fasteners and prevent future rusting or freezing.

Heat-sink grease is a special electrically non-conductive grease that is used for mounting electronic ignition modules where it is essential that heat is transferred away from the module.

SEALANTS

RTV sealant is one of the most widely used gasket compounds. Made from silicone, RTV is air curing, it seals, bonds, waterproofs, fills surface irregularities, remains flexible, doesn't shrink, is relatively easy to remove, and is used as a supplementary sealer with almost all low and medium temperature gaskets.

Anaerobic sealant is much like RTV in that it can be used either to seal gaskets or to form gaskets by itself. It remains flexible, is solvent resistant and fills surface imperfections. The difference between an anaerobic sealant and an RTV-type sealant is in the curing. RTV cures when exposed to air, while an anaerobic sealant cures only in the absence of air. This means that an anaerobic sealant cures only after the assembly of parts, sealing them together.

Thread and pipe sealant is used for sealing hydraulic and pneumatic fittings and vacuum lines. It is usually made from a Teflon compound, and comes in a spray, a paint-on liquid and as a wrap-around tape.

CHEMICALS

Anti-seize compound prevents seizing, galling, cold welding, rust and corrosion in fasteners. High-temperature anti-seize, usually made with copper and graphite lubricants, is used for exhaust system and exhaust manifold bolts.

Anaerobic locking compounds are used to keep fasteners from vibrating or working loose and cure only after installation, in the absence of air. Medium strength locking compound is used for small nuts, bolts and screws that may be removed later. High-strength locking compound is for large nuts, bolts and studs which aren't removed on a regular basis.

Oil additives range from viscosity index improvers to chemical treatments that claim to reduce internal engine friction. It should be noted that most oil manufacturers caution against using additives with their oils.

Gas additives perform several functions, depending on their chemical makeup. They usually contain solvents that help dissolve gum and varnish that build up on carburetor, fuel injection and intake parts. They also serve to break down carbon deposits that form on the inside surfaces of the combustion chambers. Some additives contain upper cylinder lubricants for valves and piston rings, and others contain chemicals to remove condensation from the gas tank.

MISCELLANEOUS

Brake fluid is specially formulated hydraulic fluid that can withstand the heat and pressure encountered in brake systems. Care must be taken so this fluid does not come in contact with painted surfaces or plastics. An opened container should always be resealed to prevent contamination by water or dirt.

Weatherstrip adhesive is used to bond weatherstripping around doors, windows and trunk lids. It is sometimes used to attach trim pieces.

Undercoating is a petroleum-based, tar-like substance that is designed to protect metal surfaces on the underside of the vehicle from corrosion. It also acts as a sound-deadening agent by insulating the bottom of the vehicle.

Waxes and polishes are used to help protect painted and plated surfaces from the weather. Different types of paint may require the use of different types of wax and polish. Some polishes utilize a chemical or abrasive cleaner to help remove the top layer of oxidized (dull) paint on older vehicles. In recent years many non-wax polishes that contain a wide variety of chemicals such as polymers and silicones have been introduced. These non-wax polishes are usually easier to apply and last longer than conventional waxes and polishes.

CONVERSION FACTORS

LENGTH (distance)

Inches (in)	X 25.4	= Millimeters (mm)	X 0.0394	= Inches (in)
Feet (ft)	X 0.305	= Meters (m)	X 3.281	= Feet (ft)
Miles	X 1.609	= Kilometers (km)	X 0.621	= Miles

VOLUME (capacity)

Cubic inches (cu in; in³)	X 16.387	= Cubic centimeters (cc; cm³)	X 0.061	= Cubic inches (cu in; in³)
Imperial pints (Imp pt)	X 0.568	= Liters (l)	X 1.76	= Imperial pints (Imp pt)
Imperial quarts (Imp qt)	X 1.137	= Liters (l)	X 0.88	= Imperial quarts (Imp qt)
Imperial quarts (Imp qt)	X 1.201	= US quarts (US qt)	X 0.833	= Imperial quarts (Imp qt)
US quarts (US qt)	X 0.946	= Liters (l)	X 1.057	= US quarts (US qt)
Imperial gallons (Imp gal)	X 4.546	= Liters (l)	X 0.22	= Imperial gallons (Imp gal)
Imperial gallons (Imp gal)	X 1.201	= US gallons (US gal)	X 0.833	= Imperial gallons (Imp gal)
US gallons (US gal)	X 3.785	= Liters (l)	X 0.264	= US gallons (US gal)

MASS (weight)

Ounces (oz)	X 28.35	= Grams (g)	X 0.035	= Ounces (oz)
Pounds (lb)	X 0.454	= Kilograms (kg)	X 2.205	= Pounds (lb)

FORCE

Ounces-force (ozf; oz)	X 0.278	= Newtons (N)	X 3.6	= Ounces-force (ozf; oz)
Pounds-force (lbf; lb)	X 4.448	= Newtons (N)	X 0.225	= Pounds-force (lbf; lb)
Newtons (N)	X 0.1	= Kilograms-force (kgf; kg)	X 9.81	= Newtons (N)

PRESSURE

Pounds-force per square inch (psi; lbf/in²; lb/in²)	X 0.070	= Kilograms-force per square centimeter (kgf/cm²; kg/cm²)	X 14.223	= Pounds-force per square inch (psi; lbf/in²; lb/in²)
Pounds-force per square inch (psi; lbf/in²; lb/in²)	X 0.068	= Atmospheres (atm)	X 14.696	= Pounds-force per square inch (psi; lbf/in²; lb/in²)
Pounds-force per square inch (psi; lbf/in²; lb/in²)	X 0.069	= Bars	X 14.5	= Pounds-force per square inch (psi; lbf/in²; lb/in²)
Pounds-force per square inch (psi; lbf/in²; lb/in²)	X 6.895	= Kilopascals (kPa)	X 0.145	= Pounds-force per square inch (psi; lbf/in²; lb/in²)
Kilopascals (kPa)	X 0.01	= Kilograms-force per square centimeter (kgf/cm²; kg/cm²)	X 98.1	= Kilopascals (kPa)

TORQUE (moment of force)

Pounds-force inches (lbf in; lb in)	X 1.152	= Kilograms-force centimeter (kgf cm; kg cm)	X 0.868	= Pounds-force inches (lbf in; lb in)
Pounds-force inches (lbf in; lb in)	X 0.113	= Newton meters (Nm)	X 8.85	= Pounds-force inches (lbf in; lb in)
Pounds-force inches (lbf in; lb in)	X 0.083	= Pounds-force feet (lbf ft; lb ft)	X 12	= Pounds-force inches (lbf in; lb in)
Pounds-force feet (lbf ft; lb ft)	X 0.138	= Kilograms-force meters (kgf m; kg m)	X 7.233	= Pounds-force feet (lbf ft; lb ft)
Pounds-force feet (lbf ft; lb ft)	X 1.356	= Newton meters (Nm)	X 0.738	= Pounds-force feet (lbf ft; lb ft)
Newton meters (Nm)	X 0.102	= Kilograms-force meters (kgf m; kg m)	X 9.804	= Newton meters (Nm)

VACUUM

Inches mercury (in. Hg)	X 3.377	= Kilopascals (kPa)	X 0.2961	= Inches mercury
Inches mercury (in. Hg)	X 25.4	= Millimeters mercury (mm Hg)	X 0.0394	= Inches mercury

POWER

Horsepower (hp)	X 745.7	= Watts (W)	X 0.0013	= Horsepower (hp)

VELOCITY (speed)

Miles per hour (miles/hr; mph)	X 1.609	= Kilometers per hour (km/hr; kph)	X 0.621	= Miles per hour (miles/hr; mph)

FUEL CONSUMPTION *

Miles per gallon, Imperial (mpg)	X 0.354	= Kilometers per liter (km/l)	X 2.825	= Miles per gallon, Imperial (mpg)
Miles per gallon, US (mpg)	X 0.425	= Kilometers per liter (km/l)	X 2.352	= Miles per gallon, US (mpg)

TEMPERATURE

Degrees Fahrenheit = (°C x 1.8) + 32   Degrees Celsius (Degrees Centigrade; °C) = (°F - 32) x 0.56

*It is common practice to convert from miles per gallon (mpg) to liters/100 kilometers (l/100km), where mpg (Imperial) x l/100 km = 282 and mpg (US) x l/100 km = 235

FRACTION/DECIMAL/MILLIMETER EQUIVALENTS

DECIMALS TO MILLIMETERS

Decimal	mm	Decimal	mm
0.001	0.0254	0.500	12.7000
0.002	0.0508	0.510	12.9540
0.003	0.0762	0.520	13.2080
0.004	0.1016	0.530	13.4620
0.005	0.1270	0.540	13.7160
0.006	0.1524	0.550	13.9700
0.007	0.1778	0.560	14.2240
0.008	0.2032	0.570	14.4780
0.009	0.2286	0.580	14.7320
		0.590	14.9860
0.010	0.2540		
0.020	0.5080		
0.030	0.7620		
0.040	1.0160	0.600	15.2400
0.050	1.2700	0.610	15.4940
0.060	1.5240	0.620	15.7480
0.070	1.7780	0.630	16.0020
0.080	2.0320	0.640	16.2560
0.090	2.2860	0.650	16.5100
		0.660	16.7640
0.100	2.5400	0.670	17.0180
0.110	2.7940	0.680	17.2720
0.120	3.0480	0.690	17.5260
0.130	3.3020		
0.140	3.5560		
0.150	3.8100	0.700	17.7800
0.160	4.0640	0.710	18.0340
0.170	4.3180	0.720	18.2880
0.180	4.5720	0.730	18.5420
0.190	4.8260	0.740	18.7960
		0.750	19.0500
0.200	5.0800	0.760	19.3040
0.210	5.3340	0.770	19.5580
0.220	5.5880	0.780	19.8120
0.230	5.8420	0.790	20.0660
0.240	6.0960		
0.250	6.3500		
0.260	6.6040	0.800	20.3200
0.270	6.8580	0.810	20.5740
0.280	7.1120	0.820	21.8280
0.290	7.3660	0.830	21.0820
		0.840	21.3360
0.300	7.6200	0.850	21.5900
0.310	7.8740	0.860	21.8440
0.320	8.1280	0.870	22.0980
0.330	8.3820	0.880	22.3520
0.340	8.6360	0.890	22.6060
0.350	8.8900		
0.360	9.1440		
0.370	9.3980		
0.380	9.6520		
0.390	9.9060		
		0.900	22.8600
0.400	10.1600	0.910	23.1140
0.410	10.4140	0.920	23.3680
0.420	10.6680	0.930	23.6220
0.430	10.9220	0.940	23.8760
0.440	11.1760	0.950	24.1300
0.450	11.4300	0.960	24.3840
0.460	11.6840	0.970	24.6380
0.470	11.9380	0.980	24.8920
0.480	12.1920	0.990	25.1460
0.490	12.4460	1.000	25.4000

FRACTIONS TO DECIMALS TO MILLIMETERS

Fraction	Decimal	mm	Fraction	Decimal	mm
1/64	0.0156	0.3969	33/64	0.5156	13.0969
1/32	0.0312	0.7938	17/32	0.5312	13.4938
3/64	0.0469	1.1906	35/64	0.5469	13.8906
1/16	0.0625	1.5875	9/16	0.5625	14.2875
5/64	0.0781	1.9844	37/64	0.5781	14.6844
3/32	0.0938	2.3812	19/32	0.5938	15.0812
7/64	0.1094	2.7781	39/64	0.6094	15.4781
1/8	0.1250	3.1750	5/8	0.6250	15.8750
9/64	0.1406	3.5719	41/64	0.6406	16.2719
5/32	0.1562	3.9688	21/32	0.6562	16.6688
11/64	0.1719	4.3656	43/64	0.6719	17.0656
3/16	0.1875	4.7625	11/16	0.6875	17.4625
13/64	0.2031	5.1594	45/64	0.7031	17.8594
7/32	0.2188	5.5562	23/32	0.7188	18.2562
15/64	0.2344	5.9531	47/64	0.7344	18.6531
1/4	0.2500	6.3500	3/4	0.7500	19.0500
17/64	0.2656	6.7469	49/64	0.7656	19.4469
9/32	0.2812	7.1438	25/32	0.7812	19.8438
19/64	0.2969	7.5406	51/64	0.7969	20.2406
5/16	0.3125	7.9375	13/16	0.8125	20.6375
21/64	0.3281	8.3344	53/64	0.8281	21.0344
11/32	0.3438	8.7312	27/32	0.8438	21.4312
23/64	0.3594	9.1281	55/64	0.8594	21.8281
3/8	0.3750	9.5250	7/8	0.8750	22.2250
25/64	0.3906	9.9219	57/64	0.8906	22.6219
13/32	0.4062	10.3188	29/32	0.9062	23.0188
27/64	0.4219	10.7156	59/64	0.9219	23.4156
7/16	0.4375	11.1125	15/16	0.9375	23.8125
29/64	0.4531	11.5094	61/64	0.9531	24.2094
15/32	0.4688	11.9062	31/32	0.9688	24.6062
31/64	0.4844	12.3031	63/64	0.9844	25.0031
1/2	0.5000	12.7000	1	1.0000	25.4000

Safety first!

Regardless of how enthusiastic you may be about getting on with the job at hand, take the time to ensure that your safety is not jeopardized. A moment's lack of attention can result in an accident, as can failure to observe certain simple safety precautions. The possibility of an accident will always exist, and the following points should not be considered a comprehensive list of all dangers. Rather, they are intended to make you aware of the risks and to encourage a safety conscious approach to all work you carry out on your vehicle.

ESSENTIAL DOS AND DON'TS

DON'T rely on a jack when working under the vehicle. Always use approved jackstands to support the weight of the vehicle and place them under the recommended lift or support points.

DON'T attempt to loosen extremely tight fasteners (i.e. wheel lug nuts) while the vehicle is on a jack - it may fall.

DON'T start the engine without first making sure that the transmission is in Neutral (or Park where applicable) and the parking brake is set.

DON'T remove the radiator cap from a hot cooling system - let it cool or cover it with a cloth and release the pressure gradually.

DON'T attempt to drain the engine oil until you are sure it has cooled to the point that it will not burn you.

DON'T touch any part of the engine or exhaust system until it has cooled sufficiently to avoid burns.

DON'T siphon toxic liquids such as gasoline, antifreeze and brake fluid by mouth, or allow them to remain on your skin.

DON'T inhale brake lining dust - it is potentially hazardous (see Asbestos below).

DON'T allow spilled oil or grease to remain on the floor - wipe it up before someone slips on it.

DON'T use loose fitting wrenches or other tools which may slip and cause injury.

DON'T push on wrenches when loosening or tightening nuts or bolts. Always try to pull the wrench toward you. If the situation calls for pushing the wrench away, push with an open hand to avoid scraped knuckles if the wrench should slip.

DON'T attempt to lift a heavy component alone - get someone to help you.

DON'T rush or take unsafe shortcuts to finish a job.

DON'T allow children or animals in or around the vehicle while you are working on it.

DO wear eye protection when using power tools such as a drill, sander, bench grinder, etc. and when working under a vehicle.

DO keep loose clothing and long hair well out of the way of moving parts.

DO make sure that any hoist used has a safe working load rating adequate for the job.

DO get someone to check on you periodically when working alone on a vehicle.

DO carry out work in a logical sequence and make sure that everything is correctly assembled and tightened.

DO keep chemicals and fluids tightly capped and out of the reach of children and pets.

DO remember that your vehicle's safety affects that of yourself and others. If in doubt on any point, get professional advice.

STEERING, SUSPENSION AND BRAKES

These systems are essential to driving safety, so make sure you have a qualified shop or individual check your work. Also, compressed suspension springs can cause injury if released suddenly - be sure to use a spring compressor.

AIRBAGS

Airbags are explosive devices that can CAUSE injury if they deploy while you're working on the vehicle. Follow the manufacturer's instructions to disable the airbag whenever you're working in the vicinity of airbag components.

ASBESTOS

Certain friction, insulating, sealing, and other products - such as brake linings, brake bands, clutch linings, torque converters, gaskets, etc. - may contain asbestos or other hazardous friction material. Extreme care must be taken to avoid inhalation of dust from such products, since it is hazardous to health. If in doubt, assume that they do contain asbestos.

FIRE

Remember at all times that gasoline is highly flammable. Never smoke or have any kind of open flame around when working on a vehicle. But the risk does not end there. A spark caused by an electrical short circuit, by two metal surfaces contacting each other, or even by static electricity built up in your body under certain conditions, can ignite gasoline vapors, which in a confined space are highly explosive. Do not, under any circumstances, use gasoline for cleaning parts. Use an approved safety solvent.

Always disconnect the battery ground (-) cable at the battery before working on any part of the fuel system or electrical system. Never risk spilling fuel on a hot engine or exhaust component. It is strongly recommended that a fire extinguisher suitable for use on fuel and electrical fires be kept handy in the garage or workshop at all times. Never try to extinguish a fuel or electrical fire with water.

FUMES

Certain fumes are highly toxic and can quickly cause unconsciousness and even death if inhaled to any extent. Gasoline vapor falls into this category, as do the vapors from some cleaning solvents. Any draining or pouring of such volatile fluids should be done in a well ventilated area.

When using cleaning fluids and solvents, read the instructions on the container carefully. Never use materials from unmarked containers.

Never run the engine in an enclosed space, such as a garage. Exhaust fumes contain carbon monoxide, which is extremely poisonous. If you need to run the engine, always do so in the open air, or at least have the rear of the vehicle outside the work area.

THE BATTERY

Never create a spark or allow a bare light bulb near a battery. They normally give off a certain amount of hydrogen gas, which is highly explosive.

Always disconnect the battery ground (-) cable at the battery before working on the fuel or electrical systems.

If possible, loosen the filler caps or cover when charging the battery from an external source (this does not apply to sealed or maintenance-free batteries). Do not charge at an excessive rate or the battery may burst.

Take care when adding water to a non maintenance-free battery and when carrying a battery. The electrolyte, even when diluted, is very corrosive and should not be allowed to contact clothing or skin.

Always wear eye protection when cleaning the battery to prevent the caustic deposits from entering your eyes.

HOUSEHOLD CURRENT

When using an electric power tool, inspection light, etc., which operates on household current, always make sure that the tool is correctly connected to its plug and that, where necessary, it is properly grounded. Do not use such items in damp conditions and, again, do not create a spark or apply excessive heat in the vicinity of fuel or fuel vapor.

SECONDARY IGNITION SYSTEM VOLTAGE

A severe electric shock can result from touching certain parts of the ignition system (such as the spark plug wires) when the engine is running or being cranked, particularly if components are damp or the insulation is defective. In the case of an electronic ignition system, the secondary system voltage is much higher and could prove fatal.

HYDROFLUORIC ACID

This extremely corrosive acid is formed when certain types of synthetic rubber, found in some O-rings, oil seals, fuel hoses, etc. are exposed to temperatures above 750-degrees F (400-degrees C). The rubber changes into a charred or sticky substance containing the acid. *Once formed, the acid remains dangerous for years. If it gets onto the skin, it may be necessary to amputate the limb concerned.*

When dealing with a vehicle which has suffered a fire, or with components salvaged from such a vehicle, wear protective gloves and discard them after use.

Troubleshooting

CONTENTS

This section provides an easy reference guide to the more common problems which may occur during the operation of your vehicle. These problems and their possible causes are grouped under headings denoting various components or systems, such as Engine, Cooling system, etc. They also refer you to the chapter and/or section which deals with the problem.

Remember that successful troubleshooting is not a mysterious black art practiced only by professional mechanics. It is simply the result of the right knowledge combined with an intelligent, systematic approach to the problem. Always work by a process of elimination, starting with the simplest solution and working through to the most complex - and never overlook the obvious. Anyone can run the gas tank dry or leave the lights on overnight, so don't assume that you are exempt from such oversights.

Finally, always establish a clear idea of why a problem has occurred and take steps to ensure that it doesn't happen again. If the electrical system fails because of a poor connection, check the other connections in the system to make sure that they don't fail as well. If a particular fuse continues to blow, find out why - don't just replace one fuse after another. Remember, failure of a small component can often be indicative of potential failure or incorrect functioning of a more important component or system.

ENGINE

1   Engine will not rotate when attempting to start

1   Battery terminal connections loose or corroded (Chapter 1).
2   Battery discharged or faulty (Chapter 1).
3   Automatic transaxle not completely engaged in Park (Chapter 7) or clutch pedal not completely depressed (Chapter 8).
4   Broken, loose or disconnected wiring in the starting circuit (Chapters 5 and 12).
5   Starter motor pinion jammed in flywheel ring gear (Chapter 5).
6   Starter solenoid faulty (Chapter 5).
7   Starter motor faulty (Chapter 5).
8   Ignition switch faulty (Chapter 12).
9   Starter pinion or flywheel teeth worn or broken (Chapter 5).
10 Faulty Body Control Module (BCM) or Intelligent Power Distribution Module (IPDM) (see Chapter 12).

2   Engine rotates but will not start

1   Fuel tank empty.
2   Battery discharged (engine rotates slowly) (Chapter 5).
3   Battery terminal connections loose or corroded (Chapter 1).
4   Leaking fuel injector(s), faulty fuel pump, pressure regulator, etc. (Chapter 4).
5   Broken timing chain (Chapter 2).
6   Ignition system problem (Chapter 5).
7   Worn, faulty or incorrectly gapped spark plugs (Chapter 1).
8   Broken, loose or disconnected wiring in the starting circuit (Chapter 5).
9   Loose distributor is changing ignition timing (Chapter 5).
10 Defective MAF sensor (see Chapter 6).

3   Engine hard to start when cold

1   Battery discharged or low (Chapter 1).
2   Malfunctioning fuel system (Chapter 4).
3   Faulty coolant temperature sensor or intake air temperature sensor (Chapter 6).
4   Injector(s) leaking (Chapter 4).
5   Faulty ignition system (Chapter 5).
6   Defective MAF sensor (see Chapter 6).

4   Engine hard to start when hot

1   Air filter clogged (Chapter 1).
2   Fuel not reaching the fuel injection system (Chapter 4).
3   Corroded battery connections, especially ground (Chapter 1).
4   Faulty coolant temperature sensor or intake air temperature sensor (Chapter 6).

5   Starter motor noisy or excessively rough in engagement

1   Pinion or flywheel gear teeth worn or broken (Chapter 5).
2   Starter motor mounting bolts loose or missing (Chapter 5).

6   Engine starts but stops immediately

1   Insufficient fuel reaching the fuel injector(s) (Chapters 1 and 4).
2   Vacuum leak at the gasket between the intake manifold/plenum and throttle body (Chapters 1 and 4).

7   Oil puddle under engine

1   Oil pan gasket and/or oil pan drain bolt washer leaking (Chapter 2).
2   Oil pressure sending unit leaking (Chapter 2).
3   Valve cover leaking (Chapter 2).
4   Engine oil seals leaking (Chapter 2).
5   Oil pump housing leaking (Chapter 2).

8   Engine lopes while idling or idles erratically

1   Vacuum leakage (Chapters 2 and 4).
2   Leaking EGR valve (Chapter 6).
3   Air filter clogged (Chapter 1).
4   Fuel pump not delivering sufficient fuel to the fuel injection system (Chapter 4).
5   Leaking head gasket (Chapter 2).
6   Timing chain and/or sprockets worn (Chapter 2).
7   Camshaft lobes worn (Chapter 2).

9   Engine misses at idle speed

1   Spark plugs worn or not gapped properly (Chapter 1).
2   Vacuum leaks (Chapters 2 and 4).
3   Uneven or low compression (Chapter 2).
4   Problem with the fuel injection system (Chapter 4).
5   Faulty ignition coils (Chapter 5).

10 Engine misses throughout driving speed range

1 Fuel filter clogged and/or impurities in the fuel system (Chapter 1).
2 Low fuel output at the fuel injector(s) (Chapter 4).
3 Faulty or incorrectly gapped spark plugs (Chapter 1).
4 Faulty ignition coils (Chapter 5).
5 Faulty emission system components (Chapter 6).
6 Low or uneven cylinder compression pressures (Chapter 2).
7 Vacuum leak in fuel injection system, throttle body, intake manifold, IAC/AAC valve or vacuum hoses (Chapter 4).

11 Engine stumbles on acceleration

1 Spark plugs fouled (Chapter 1).
2 Problem with fuel injection system (Chapter 4).
3 Fuel filter clogged (Chapters 1 and 4).
4 Intake manifold air leak (Chapters 2 and 4).
5 EGR system malfunction (Chapter 6).

12 Engine surges while holding accelerator steady

1 Intake air leak (Chapter 4).
2 Fuel pump or fuel pressure regulator faulty (Chapter 4).
3 Problem with fuel injection system (Chapter 4).
4 Problem with the emissions control system (Chapter 6).

13 Engine stalls

1 Fuel filter clogged and/or water and impurities in the fuel system (Chapters 1 and 4).
2 Faulty emissions system components (Chapter 6).
3 Faulty or incorrectly gapped spark plugs (Chapter 1).
4 Vacuum leak in the fuel injection system, intake manifold or vacuum hoses (Chapters 2 and 4).
5 Valve clearances incorrectly set (Chapter 1).

14 Engine lacks power

1 Faulty or incorrectly gapped spark plugs (Chapter 1).
2 Problem with the fuel injection system (Chapter 4).
3 Plugged air filter (Chapter 1).
4 Brakes binding (Chapter 9).
5 Automatic transaxle fluid level incorrect (Chapter 1).
6 Clutch slipping (Chapter 8).
7 Fuel filter clogged and/or impurities in the fuel system (Chapters 1 and 4).
8 Emission control system not functioning properly (Chapter 6).
9 Low or uneven cylinder compression pressures (Chapter 2).
10 Obstructed exhaust system (Chapters 2 and 4).

15 Engine backfires

1 Emission control system not functioning properly (Chapter 6).
2 Problem with the fuel injection system (Chapter 4).
3 Vacuum leak at fuel injector(s), intake manifold or vacuum hoses (Chapters 2 and 4).
4 Valve clearances incorrectly set and/or valves sticking (Chapter 1).

16 Pinging or knocking engine sounds during acceleration or uphill

1 Incorrect grade of fuel.
2 Fuel injection system faulty (Chapter 4).
3 Improper or damaged spark plugs (Chapter 1).
4 Malfunctioning knock sensor (Chapter 6).
5 Vacuum leak (Chapters 2 and 4).

17 Engine runs with oil pressure light on

1 Low oil level (Chapter 1).
2 Idle rpm below specification (Chapter 1).
3 Short in wiring circuit (Chapter 12).
4 Faulty oil pressure sender (Chapter 2C).
5 Worn engine bearings and/or oil pump (Chapter 2).

18 Engine continues to run after switching off

Faulty ignition switch (Chapter 12), Powertrain Control Module (PCM) (Chapter 6), or Body Control Module (BCM).

ENGINE ELECTRICAL SYSTEM

19 Battery will not hold a charge

1 Alternator drivebelt defective or not adjusted properly (Chapter 1).
2 Battery electrolyte level low (Chapter 1).
3 Battery terminals loose or corroded (Chapter 1).
4 Alternator not charging properly (Chapter 5).
5 Loose, broken or faulty wiring in the charging circuit (Chapter 5).
6 Short in vehicle wiring (Chapter 12).
7 Internally defective battery (Chapters 1 and 5).

20 Alternator light fails to go out

1 Faulty alternator or charging circuit (Chapter 5).
2 Alternator drivebelt defective or out of adjustment (Chapter 1).
3 Alternator voltage regulator inoperative (Chapter 5).

21 Alternator light fails to come on when key is turned on

1 Warning light bulb defective (Chapter 12).
2 Fault in the instrument cluster, dash wiring or bulb holder (Chapter 12).

FUEL SYSTEM

22 Excessive fuel consumption

1 Dirty or clogged air filter element (Chapter 1).
2 Emissions system not functioning properly (Chapter 6).
3 Fuel injection system not functioning properly (Chapter 4).
4 Low tire pressure or incorrect tire size (Chapter 1).

23 Fuel leakage and/or fuel odor

1 Leaking fuel feed or return line (Chapters 1 and 4).
2 Tank overfilled.
3 Problem with fuel injection system (Chapter 4).

COOLING SYSTEM

24 Overheating

1 Insufficient coolant in system (Chapter 1).
2 Water pump drivebelt defective or out of adjustment (Chapter 1).
3 Radiator core blocked or grille restricted (Chapter 3).
4 Thermostat faulty (Chapter 3).
5 Electric coolant fan inoperative or blades broken (Chapter 3).
6 Radiator cap not maintaining proper pressure (Chapter 3).

25 Overcooling

Faulty thermostat (Chapter 3).

26 External coolant leakage

1 Deteriorated/damaged hoses; loose clamps (Chapters 1 and 3).
2 Water pump defective (Chapter 3).
3 Leakage from radiator core or coolant reservoir bottle (Chapter 3).
4 Engine drain or water jacket core plugs leaking.

27 Internal coolant leakage

1 Leaking cylinder head gasket (Chapter 2).
2 Cracked cylinder bore or cylinder head (Chapter 2).

28 Coolant loss

1 Too much coolant in system (Chapter 1).
2 Coolant boiling away because of overheating (Chapter 3).
3 Internal or external leakage (Chapter 3).
4 Faulty radiator cap (Chapter 3).

29 Poor coolant circulation

1 Inoperative water pump (Chapter 3).
2 Restriction in cooling system (Chapters 1 and 3).
3 Water pump drivebelt defective/out of adjustment (Chapter 1).
4 Thermostat sticking (Chapter 3).

CLUTCH

30 Pedal travels to floor - no pressure or very little resistance

1 Hydraulic release system leaking or air in the system (Chapter 8).
2 Broken release bearing or fork (Chapter 8).

31 Unable to select gears

1 Faulty transaxle (Chapter 7).
2 Faulty clutch disc or pressure plate (Chapter 8).
3 Faulty release lever or release bearing (Chapter 8).
4 Faulty shift lever assembly or cable(s) (Chapter 8).

32 Clutch slips (engine speed increases with no increase in vehicle speed)

1 Clutch plate worn (Chapter 8).
2 Clutch plate is oil soaked by leaking rear main seal (Chapter 8).
3 Warped pressure plate or flywheel (Chapter 8).
4 Weak diaphragm spring in pressure plate (Chapter 8).
5 Piston stuck in bore of clutch release cylinder, preventing clutch from fully engaging (Chapter 8).

33 Grabbing (chattering) as clutch is engaged

1 Oil on clutch plate lining, burned or glazed facings (Chapter 8).
2 Worn or loose engine or transaxle mounts (Chapters 2 and 7).
3 Worn splines on clutch plate hub (Chapter 8).
4 Warped pressure plate or flywheel (Chapter 8).
5 Burned or smeared resin on flywheel or pressure plate (Chapter 8).

34 Transaxle rattling (clicking)

1 Release bearing defective (Chapter 8).
2 Internal transaxle problem.

35 Noise in clutch area

Faulty bearing (Chapter 8).

36 Clutch pedal stays on floor

1 Defective release cylinder (Chapter 8).
2 Hydraulic release system leaking or air in the system (Chapter 8).

37 High pedal effort

1 Piston binding in bore of release cylinder (Chapter 8).
2 Pressure plate faulty (Chapter 8).

MANUAL TRANSAXLE

38 Knocking noise at low speeds

1 Worn driveaxle constant velocity (CV) joints (Chapter 8).
2 Worn side gear shaft counterbore in differential case (Chapter 7A).*

39 Noise most pronounced when turning

Differential gear noise (Chapter 7A).*

40 Clunk on acceleration or deceleration

1 Loose engine or transaxle mounts (Chapters 2 and 7A).
2 Worn differential pinion shaft in case.*
3 Worn side gear shaft counterbore in differential case (Chapter 7A).*
4 Worn or damaged driveaxle inboard CV joints (Chapter 8).

41 Clicking noise in turns

Worn or damaged outboard CV joint (Chapter 8).

42 Vibration

1 Rough wheel bearing (Chapter 10).
2 Damaged driveaxle (Chapter 8).
3 Out of round tires.
4 Tire out of balance.
5 Worn CV joint (Chapter 8).

43 Noisy in neutral with engine running

1 Damaged input gear bearing (Chapter 7A).*
2 Damaged clutch release bearing (Chapter 8).

44 Noisy in one particular gear

1 Damaged or worn constant mesh gears (Chapter 7A).*
2 Damaged or worn synchronizers (Chapter 7A).*
3 Bent reverse fork (Chapter 7A).*
4 Damaged fourth speed gear or output gear (Chapter 7A).*
5 Worn or damaged reverse idler gear or idler bushing (Chapter 7A).*

45 Noisy in all gears

1 Insufficient lubricant (Chapter 7A).
2 Damaged or worn bearings (Chapter 7A).*
3 Worn or damaged input gear shaft and/or output gear shaft (Chapter 7A).*

46 Slips out of gear

1 Worn or improperly adjusted linkage (Chapter 7A).
2 Shift linkage does not work freely, binds (Chapter 7A).
3 Input gear bearing retainer broken or loose (Chapter 7A).*
4 Worn shift fork (Chapter 7A).*

47 Leaks lubricant

1 Side gear shaft seals worn (Chapter 7A.
2 Excessive amount of lubricant in transaxle (Chapter 1).
3 Loose or broken input gear shaft bearing retainer (Chapter 7A).*
4 Input gear bearing retainer O-ring and/or lip seal damaged (Chapter 7A).*
5 Shifter shaft seal leaking (Chapter 7A).

48 Hard to shift

Shift cable(s) worn (Chapter 7A).

Although the corrective action necessary to remedy the symptoms described is beyond the scope of this manual, the above information should be helpful in isolating the cause of the condition so that the owner can communicate clearly with a professional mechanic.

AUTOMATIC TRANSAXLE

Note: Due to the complexity of the automatic transaxle, it is difficult for the home mechanic to properly diagnose and service this component. For problems other than the following, the vehicle should be taken to a dealer or transaxle shop.

49 Fluid leakage

1 Automatic transaxle fluid is a deep red color. Fluid leaks should not be confused with engine oil, which can easily be blown onto the transaxle by air flow.
2 To pinpoint a leak, first remove all built-up dirt and grime from the transaxle housing with degreasing agents and/or steam cleaning. Then drive the vehicle at low speeds so air flow will not blow the leak far from its source. Raise the vehicle and determine where the leak is coming from. Common areas of leakage are:

 a) *Pan*
 b) *Dipstick tube*
 c) *Transaxle oil lines*
 d) *Speed sensor (Chapter 7)*
 e) *Driveaxle oil seals (Chapter 7).*

50 Transaxle fluid brown or has a burned smell

Transaxle fluid overheated (Chapter 1).

51 General shift mechanism problems

1 Chapter 7, Part B, deals with checking and adjusting the shift cable on automatic transaxles. Common problems which may be attributed to poorly adjusted cable are:

 a) *Engine starting in gears other than Park or Neutral.*
 b) *Indicator on shifter pointing to a gear other than the one actually being used.*
 c) *Vehicle moves when in Park.*

2 Refer to Chapter 7B for the shift cable adjustment procedure.

52 Transaxle will not downshift with accelerator pedal pressed to the floor

The transaxle is electronically controlled. This type of problem - which is caused by a malfunction in the control unit, a sensor or solenoid, or the circuit itself - is beyond the scope of this book. Take the vehicle to a dealer service department or a competent automatic transmission shop.

53 Engine will start in gears other than Park or Neutral

Neutral start switch out of adjustment or malfunctioning (Chapter 7B).

54 Transaxle slips, is noisy or has no drive in forward or reverse gears

There are many probable causes for the above problems, but the home mechanic should be concerned with only one possibility - fluid level. Before taking the vehicle to a repair shop, check the level and condition of the fluid as described in Chapter 1. Correct the fluid level as necessary or change the fluid if needed. If the problem persists, have a professional diagnose the cause.

DRIVEAXLES

55 Clicking noise in turns

Worn or damaged outboard CV joint (Chapter 8).

56 Shudder or vibration during acceleration

1 Excessive toe-in (Chapter 10).
2 Worn or damaged inboard or outboard CV joints (Chapter 8).
3 Sticking inboard CV joint assembly (Chapter 8).

57 Vibration at highway speeds

1 Out of balance front wheels and/or tires.
2 Out of round front tires.
3 Worn CV joint(s) (Chapter 8).

BRAKES

➡ **Note: Before assuming that a brake problem exists, make sure that:**

a) The tires are in good condition and properly inflated (Chapter 1).
b) The front end alignment is correct (Chapter 10).
c) The vehicle is not loaded with weight in an unequal manner.

58 Vehicle pulls to one side during braking

1 Incorrect tire pressures (Chapter 1).
2 Front end out of alignment (have the front end aligned).
3 Front, or rear, tire sizes not matched to one another.
4 Restricted brake lines or hoses (Chapter 9).
5 Malfunctioning caliper assembly (Chapter 9).
6 Loose suspension parts (Chapter 10).
7 Loose calipers (Chapter 9).
8 Excessive wear of brake pad material or disc on one side.

59 Noise (high-pitched squeal when the brakes are applied)

Front and/or rear disc brake pads worn out. The noise comes from the wear sensor rubbing against the disc (does not apply to all vehicles). Replace pads with new ones immediately (Chapter 9).

60 Brake roughness or chatter (pedal pulsates)

1 Excessive lateral runout (Chapter 9).
2 Uneven pad wear (Chapter 9).
3 Defective disc (Chapter 9).

61 Excessive brake pedal effort required to stop vehicle

1 Malfunctioning power brake booster (Chapter 9).
2 Partial system failure (Chapter 9).
3 Excessively worn pads (Chapter 9).
4 Piston in caliper stuck or sluggish (Chapter 9).
5 Brake pads contaminated with brake fluid, oil or grease (Chapter 9).
6 Brake disc grooved and/or glazed (Chapter 1).
7 New pads installed and not yet seated. It will take a while for the new material to seat against the disc.

62 Excessive brake pedal travel

1 Partial brake system failure (Chapter 9).
2 Insufficient fluid in master cylinder (Chapters 1 and 9).
3 Air trapped in system (Chapters 1 and 9).

63 Dragging brakes

1 Incorrect adjustment of brake light switch (Chapter 9).
2 Master cylinder pistons not returning correctly (Chapter 9).
3 Restricted brakes lines or hoses (Chapters 1 and 9).
4 Incorrect parking brake adjustment (Chapter 9).

64 Grabbing or uneven braking action

1 Malfunction of proportioning valve (Chapter 9).
2 Binding brake pedal mechanism (Chapter 9).

65 Brake pedal feels spongy when depressed

1 Air in hydraulic lines (Chapter 9).
2 Master cylinder mounting bolts loose (Chapter 9).
3 Master cylinder defective (Chapter 9).

66 Brake pedal travels to the floor with little resistance

1 Little or no fluid in the master cylinder reservoir caused by leaking caliper piston(s) (Chapter 9).
2 Loose, damaged or disconnected brake lines (Chapter 9).

67 Parking brake does not hold

Parking brake improperly adjusted (Chapter 9).

SUSPENSION AND STEERING SYSTEMS

➡**Note: Before attempting to diagnose the suspension and steering systems, perform the following preliminary checks:**

  a) *Tires for wrong pressure and uneven wear.*
  b) *Steering universal joints from the column to the rack and pinion for loose connectors or wear.*
  c) *Front and rear suspension and the rack-and-pinion assembly for loose or damaged parts.*
  d) *Out-of-round or out-of-balance tires, bent rims and loose and/or rough wheel bearings.*

68 Vehicle pulls to one side

1 Mismatched or uneven tires.
2 Broken or sagging springs (Chapter 10).
3 Wheel alignment out-of-specifications.
4 Front brake dragging (Chapter 9).

69 Abnormal or excessive tire wear

1 Wheel alignment out-of-specifications (Chapter 10).
2 Sagging or broken springs (Chapter 10).
3 Tire out-of-balance.
4 Worn strut damper (Chapter 10).
5 Overloaded vehicle.
6 Tires not rotated regularly.

70 Wheel makes a thumping noise

1 Blister or bump on tire.
2 Improper strut damper action (Chapter 10).

71 Shimmy, shake or vibration

1 Tire or wheel out-of-balance or out-of-round.
2 Worn wheel bearings (Chapters 1, 8 and 10).
3 Worn tie-rod ends (Chapter 10).
4 Worn lower balljoints (Chapters 1 and 10).
5 Excessive wheel runout.
6 Blister or bump on tire.

72 Hard steering

1 Lack of lubrication at balljoints or tie-rod ends (Chapter 10).
2 Front wheel alignment out-of-specifications.
3 Low tire pressure(s) (Chapter 1).

73 Poor returnability of steering to center

1 Worn balljoints or tie-rod ends (Chapter 10).
2 Binding in balljoints (Chapter 10).
3 Binding in steering column (Chapter 10).
4 Worn steering gear assembly (Chapter 10).
5 Front wheel alignment out-of-specifications.

74 Abnormal noise at the front end

1 Worn balljoints or tie-rod ends (Chapter 10).
2 Damaged strut mounting (Chapter 10).
3 Worn control arm bushings or tie-rod ends (Chapter 10).
4 Loose stabilizer bar (Chapter 10).
5 Loose wheel nuts.
6 Loose suspension bolts (Chapter 10)

75 Wander or poor steering stability

1 Mismatched or uneven tires.
2 Worn balljoints or tie-rod ends (Chapter 10).
3 Worn strut assemblies (Chapter 10).
4 Loose stabilizer bar (Chapter 10).
5 Broken or sagging springs (Chapter 10).
6 Wheels out of alignment.

76 Erratic steering when braking

1 Wheel bearings worn (Chapter 10).
2 Broken or sagging springs (Chapter 10).
3 Leaking caliper (Chapter 9).
4 Warped brake discs (Chapter 9).

77 Excessive pitching and/or rolling around corners or during braking

1 Loose stabilizer bar (Chapter 10).
2 Worn strut dampers or mountings (Chapter 10).
3 Broken or sagging springs (Chapter 10).
4 Overloaded vehicle.

78 Suspension bottoms

1 Overloaded vehicle.
2 Worn strut dampers or springs (Chapter 10).

79 Cupped tires

1 Front wheel or rear wheel alignment out-of-specifications.
2 Worn strut dampers (Chapter 10).
3 Wheel bearings worn (Chapter 10).
4 Excessive tire or wheel runout.
5 Worn balljoints (Chapter 10).

80 Excessive tire wear on outside edge

1 Inflation pressures incorrect (Chapter 1).
2 Excessive speed in turns.
3 Front end alignment incorrect (excessive toe-in). Have professionally aligned.
4 Suspension arm bent (Chapter 10).

81 Excessive tire wear on inside edge

1 Inflation pressures incorrect (Chapter 1).
2 Front end alignment incorrect (toe-out). Have professionally aligned.
3 Loose or damaged steering components (Chapter 10).

82   Tire tread worn in one place

1   Tires out-of-balance.
2   Damaged or buckled wheel. Inspect and replace if necessary.
3   Defective tire (Chapter 1).

83   Excessive play or looseness in steering system

1   Wheel bearing(s) worn (Chapter 10).
2   Tie-rod end loose (Chapter 10).
3   Steering gear loose (Chapter 10).
4   Worn or loose steering intermediate shaft (Chapter 10).

84   Rattling or clicking noise in steering gear

1   Steering gear loose (Chapter 10).
2   Steering gear defective.

1

TUNE-UP
AND ROUTINE
MAINTENANCE

Section

Reference to other Chapters

1 Nissan Altima maintenance schedule

The maintenance intervals in this manual are provided with the assumption that you, not the dealer, will be doing the work. These are the minimum maintenance intervals recommended by the factory for vehicles that are driven daily. If you wish to keep your vehicle in peak condition at all times, you may wish to perform some of these procedures even more often. Because frequent maintenance enhances the efficiency, performance and resale value of your car, we encourage you to do so. If you drive in dusty areas, tow a trailer, idle or drive at low speeds for extended periods or drive for short distances (less than four miles) in below freezing temperatures, shorter intervals are also recommended.

When your vehicle is new, it should be serviced by a factory authorized dealer service department to protect the factory warranty. In many cases, the initial maintenance check is done at no cost to the owner.

EVERY 250 MILES OR WEEKLY, WHICHEVER COMES FIRST

Check the engine oil level (Section 4)
Check the engine coolant level (Section 4)
Check the windshield washer fluid level (Section 4)
Check the battery electrolyte (Section 4)
Check the brake fluid level (Section 4)
Check the clutch fluid level (Section 4)
Check the tires and tire pressures (Section 5)

EVERY 3000 MILES OR 3 MONTHS, WHICHEVER COMES FIRST

All items listed above plus:
Check the power steering fluid level (Section 6)
Check the automatic transaxle fluid level (Section 7)
Change the engine oil and oil filter (Section 8)

EVERY 7500 MILES OR 6 MONTHS, WHICHEVER COMES FIRST

Inspect and replace if necessary the windshield wiper blades (Section 9)
Check and service the battery (Section 10)
Check the engine drivebelt (Section 11)
Inspect and replace if necessary all underhood hoses (Section 12)
Check the cooling system (Section 13)
Rotate the tires (Section 14)

EVERY 15,000 MILES OR 12 MONTHS, WHICHEVER COMES FIRST

All items listed above plus:
Inspect the brake system (Section 15)*

Replace the cabin air filter (Section 16)
Inspect the fuel system (Section 18)
Check the manual transaxle lubricant level (Section 19)
Inspect the suspension and steering components (Section 20)
Inspect the exhaust system (Section 21)
Check the driveaxle boots (Section 22)

EVERY 30,000 MILES OR 24 MONTHS, WHICHEVER COMES FIRST

All items listed above plus:
Replace the air filter (Section 17)
Service the cooling system (drain, flush and refill) (Section 24)
Inspect the evaporative emissions control system (Section 25)
Check and replace if necessary the PCV valve (Section 28)

EVERY 60,000 MILES OR 48 MONTHS, WHICHEVER COMES FIRST

Change the automatic transaxle fluid (Section 26)**
Change the manual transaxle lubricant (Section 27)**
Check (and adjust if noisy) the valve clearance (Section 29)

EVERY 105,000 MILES OR 72 MONTHS, WHICHEVER COMES FIRST

Replace the spark plugs (Section 23)
* This item is affected by "severe" operating conditions as described below. If your vehicle is operated under "severe" conditions, perform all maintenance indicated with an asterisk (*) at half the indicated intervals. Severe conditions are indicated if you mainly operate your vehicle under one or more of the following conditions:
  Operating in dusty areas
  Towing a trailer
  Idling for extended periods and/or low speed operation
  Operating when outside temperatures remain below freezing and when most trips are less than 4 miles
** If operated under one or more of the following conditions, change the, manual or automatic transmission fluid and differential lubricant every 30,000 miles:
  In heavy city traffic where the outside temperature regularly reaches 90-degrees F (32-degrees C) or higher
  In hilly or mountainous terrain
  Frequent trailer pulling

Typical engine compartment components - four-cylinder model shown

1	Brake fluid reservoir	5	Automatic transaxle fluid level dipstick	9	Coolant reservoir
2	Air filter housing	6	Engine oil dipstick	10	Oil fill cap
3	Battery	7	Radiator cap	11	Power steering fluid reservoir
4	Fuse/relay box	8	Windshield washer fluid reservoir		

Typical engine compartment underside components

1	Engine oil drain plug	4	Balljoint	6	Brake caliper
2	Driveaxle inner joint and boot	5	Lower control arm	7	Exhaust pipe
3	Tie-rod end				

Typical rear underside components

1	Subframe	3	Stabilizer bar bracket	5	Fuel tank
2	Muffler	4	Suspension lower control arm		

2 Introduction

This Chapter is designed to help the home mechanic maintain the Nissan Altima for peak performance, economy, safety and long life.

Included in this Chapter is a master maintenance schedule, followed by Sections dealing specifically with each item on the schedule. Visual checks, adjustments, component replacement and other helpful items are included. Refer to the accompanying illustrations of the engine compartment and the underside of the vehicle for the location of various components.

Servicing your Altima in accordance with the mileage/time maintenance schedule and the following Sections will provide it with a planned maintenance program that should result in a long and reliable service life. This is a comprehensive plan, so maintaining some items but not others at the specified service intervals will not produce the same results.

As you service your Altima, you will discover that many of the procedures can, and should, be grouped together because of the nature of the particular procedure you're performing or because of the close

proximity of two otherwise unrelated components to one another.

For example, if the vehicle is raised for any reason, you should inspect the exhaust, suspension, steering and fuel systems while you're under the vehicle. When you're rotating the tires, it makes good sense to check the brakes and wheel bearings since the wheels are already removed.

Finally, let's suppose you have to borrow or rent a torque wrench. Even if you only need to tighten the spark plugs, you might as well check the torque of as many critical fasteners as time allows.

The first step of this maintenance program is to prepare yourself before the actual work begins. Read through all Sections pertinent to the procedures you're planning to do, then make a list of and gather together all the parts and tools you will need to do the job. If it looks as if you might run into problems during a particular segment of some procedure, seek advice from your local auto parts stores or dealer service department.

3 Tune-up general information

The term tune-up is used in this manual to represent a combination of individual operations rather than one specific procedure.

If, from the time the vehicle is new, the routine maintenance schedule is followed closely and frequent checks are made of fluid levels and high wear items, as suggested throughout this manual, the engine will be kept in relatively good running condition and the need for additional work will be minimized.

More likely than not, however, there will be times when the engine is running poorly due to lack of regular maintenance. This is even more likely if a used vehicle, which has not received regular and frequent maintenance checks, is purchased. In such cases, an engine tune-up will be needed outside of the regular routine maintenance intervals.

The first step in any tune-up or engine diagnosis to help correct a poor running engine would be a cylinder compression check. A check of the engine compression (see Chapter 2C) will give valuable information regarding the overall performance of many internal components and should be used as a basis for tune-up and repair procedures. If, for instance, a compression check indicates serious internal engine wear, a conventional tune-up will not help the running condition of the engine and would be a waste of time and money.

The following series of operations are those most often needed to

bring a generally poor running engine back into a proper state of tune.

MINOR TUNE-UP

Check all engine related fluids (Section 4)
Clean, inspect and test the battery (Section 10)
Check the drivebelts (Section 11)
Check all underhood hoses (Section 12)
Check the cooling system (Section 13)
Check the air filter (Section 17)
Replace the spark plugs (Section 23)

MAJOR TUNE-UP

All items listed under Minor tune-up, plus . . .
Replace the air filter (Section 17)
Check the fuel system (Section 18)
Check the charging system (Chapter 5)
Check the ignition system (Chapter 5)

4 Fluid level checks (every 250 miles or weekly)

1 Fluids are an essential part of the lubrication, cooling, brake, clutch and other systems. Because these fluids gradually become depleted and/or contaminated during normal operation of the vehicle, they must be periodically replenished. See *Recommended lubricants and fluids* and *Capacities* in this Chapter's Specifications before adding fluid to any of the following components.

➡Note: The vehicle must be on level ground before fluid levels can be checked.

ENGINE OIL

▶ **Refer to illustrations 4.2a, 4.2b, 4.4, 4.6a and 4.6b**

2 The engine oil level is checked with a dipstick located at the front of the engine (see illustrations).

3 The oil level should be checked before the vehicle has been driven, or about 5 minutes after the engine has been shut off. If the oil

4.2a Engine oil dipstick location - four-cylinder engine

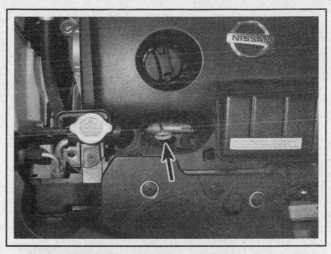

4.2b Engine oil dipstick location - V6 engine

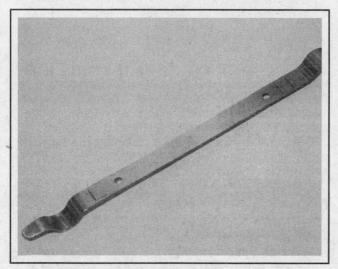

4.4 The oil level should be at or near the H mark - if it isn't, add enough oil to bring the level to near the H mark

4.6a Oil filler cap location - four-cylinder engine

is checked immediately after driving the vehicle, some of the oil will remain in the upper engine components, producing an inaccurate reading on the dipstick.

4   Pull the dipstick out and wipe all the oil from the end with a clean rag or paper towel. Insert the clean dipstick all the way back in and pull it out again. Observe the oil at the end of the dipstick; the level should be between the L and H marks (see illustration).

5   It takes about one quart of oil to raise the level from the L mark to the H mark on the dipstick. Do not allow the level to drop below the L mark or oil starvation may cause engine damage. Conversely, overfilling the engine (adding oil above the H mark) may cause oil fouled spark plugs, oil leaks or oil seal failures.

6   Wipe the area around the filler cap, then remove the cap from the valve cover to add oil (see illustrations). Use a funnel to prevent spills. After adding the oil, install the filler cap hand tight. Start the engine and look carefully for any small leaks around the oil filter or drain plug. Stop the engine and check the oil level again after it has had sufficient time to drain from the upper block and cylinder head galleys.

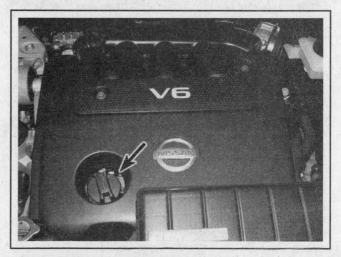

4.6b Oil filler cap location - V6 engine

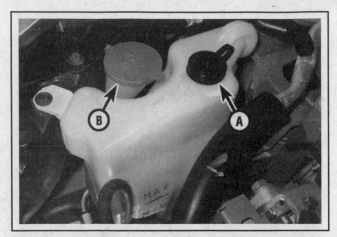

4.8 Don't confuse the coolant reservoir (A) with the windshield washer fluid container (B) - add coolant to bring the level near the MAX mark on the reservoir

7   Checking the oil level is an important preventive maintenance step. A continually dropping oil level indicates oil leakage through damaged seals, from loose connections, or past worn rings or valve guides. If the oil looks milky in color or has water droplets in it, a cylinder head gasket may be leaking. The cylinder head should be checked immediately. The condition of the oil should also be checked. Each time you check the oil level, slide your thumb and index finger up the dipstick before wiping off the oil. If you see small dirt or metal particles clinging to the dipstick, the oil should be changed (see Section 8).

ENGINE COOLANT

▶ **Refer to illustration 4.8**

✻ WARNING:

Do not allow antifreeze to come in contact with your skin or painted surfaces of the vehicle. Flush contaminated areas immediately with plenty of water. Don't store new coolant or leave old coolant lying around where it's accessible to children or pets - they're attracted by its sweet smell and may drink it. Ingestion of even a small amount of coolant can be fatal! Wipe up garage floor and drip pan spills immediately. Keep antifreeze containers covered and repair cooling system leaks as soon as they're noticed.

8   All vehicles covered by this manual are equipped with a pressurized coolant recovery system. A white coolant reservoir located in the right front corner of the engine compartment is connected by a hose to the base of the coolant filler cap (see illustration). If the coolant gets too hot during engine operation, coolant can escape through the relief valve in the filler cap, then through a connecting hose into the reservoir. As the engine cools, the coolant is automatically drawn back into the cooling system to maintain the correct level.

9   The coolant level should be checked regularly. It must be between the Max and Min lines on the tank. The level will vary with the temperature of the engine. When the engine is cold, the coolant level should be at or slightly above the Min mark on the tank. Once the engine has warmed up, the level should be at or near the Max mark. If it isn't, allow the fluid in the tank to cool, then remove the cap from the reservoir and add coolant to bring the level up to the Max line. Use only ethylene/

glycol type coolant and water in the mixture ratio recommended by your owner's manual. Do not use supplemental inhibitor additives. If only a small amount of coolant is required to bring the system up to the proper level, water can be used. However, repeated additions of water will dilute the recommended antifreeze and water solution. In order to maintain the proper ratio of antifreeze and water, it is advisable to top up the coolant level with the correct mixture. Refer to your owner's manual for the recommended ratio.

10 If the coolant level drops within a short time after replenishment, there may be a leak in the system. Inspect the radiator, hoses, engine coolant filler cap, drain plugs, air bleeder plugs and water pump. If no leak is evident, have the radiator cap pressure tested by your dealer.

✻ WARNING:

Never remove the radiator cap or the coolant recovery reservoir cap when the engine is running or has just been shut down, because the cooling system is hot. Escaping steam and scalding liquid could cause serious injury.

11 If it is necessary to open the radiator cap, wait until the system has cooled completely, then wrap a thick cloth around the cap and turn it to the first stop. If any steam escapes, wait until the system has cooled further, then remove the cap.

12 When checking the coolant level, always note its condition. It should be relatively clear. If it is brown or rust colored, the system should be drained, flushed and refilled. Even if the coolant appears to be normal, the corrosion inhibitors wear out with use, so it must be replaced at the specified intervals.

13 Do not allow antifreeze to come in contact with your skin or painted surfaces of the vehicle. Flush contacted areas immediately with plenty of water.

WINDSHIELD WASHER FLUID

14 Fluid for the windshield washer system is stored in a plastic reservoir which is located on the right side of the engine compartment adjacent to the coolant reservoir (see illustration 4.8). In milder climates, plain water can be used to top up the reservoir, but the reservoir should be kept no more than two-thirds full to allow for expansion should the water freeze. In colder climates, the use of a specially designed windshield washer fluid, available at your dealer and any auto parts store, will help lower the freezing point of the fluid. Mix the solution with water in accordance with the manufacturer's directions on the container. Do not use regular antifreeze. It will damage the vehicle's paint.

BATTERY ELECTROLYTE

▶ **Refer to illustration 4.15**

15 On models not equipped with a sealed battery, check the electrolyte level (see illustration) of all six battery cells. It must be between the upper and lower levels. If the level is low, remove the filler/vent cap and add distilled water. Install and securely re-tighten the cap.

✻ CAUTION:

Overfilling the cells may cause electrolyte to spill over during periods of heavy charging, causing corrosion or damage.

BRAKE AND CLUTCH FLUIDS

▶ **Refer to illustration 4.17**

16 The brake master cylinder is mounted on the front of the power booster unit in the engine compartment. The hydraulic clutch master cylinder used on manual transaxle vehicles is located next to the brake master cylinder.

17 To check the fluid level of the brake and clutch master cylinders, simply look at the MAX and MIN marks on the reservoir (see illustration). The level should be within the specified distance from the maximum fill line.

18 If the level is low, wipe the top of the reservoir cover with a clean rag to prevent contamination of the brake system before lifting the cover.

19 Add only the specified brake fluid to the brake and clutch reservoirs (refer to *Recommended lubricants and fluids* in this Chapter's Specifications or your owner's manual). Mixing different types of brake fluid can damage the system. Fill the brake master cylinder reservoir only to the MAX line.

> ❊❊ **WARNING:**
>
> **Use caution when filling either reservoir - brake fluid can harm your eyes and damage painted surfaces. Do not use brake fluid that has been opened for more than one year or has been left open. Brake fluid absorbs moisture from the air. Excess moisture can cause a dangerous loss of braking.**

20 While the reservoir cap is removed, inspect the master cylinder reservoir for contamination. If deposits, dirt particles or water droplets are present, the system should be drained and refilled.

21 After filling the reservoir to the proper level, make sure the lid is properly seated to prevent fluid leakage and/or system pressure loss.

22 The fluid in the brake master cylinder will drop slightly as the brake pads at each wheel wear down during normal operation. If either master cylinder requires repeated replenishing to keep it at the proper level, this is an indication of leakage in the brake or clutch system, which should be corrected immediately. If the brake system shows an indication of leakage check all brake lines and connections, along with the calipers, wheel cylinders and booster (see Section 15 for more

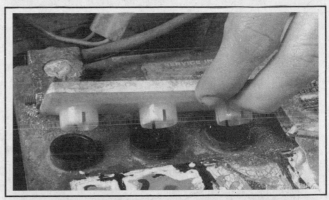

4.15 Remove the cell caps to check the water level in the battery - if the level is low, add distilled water only

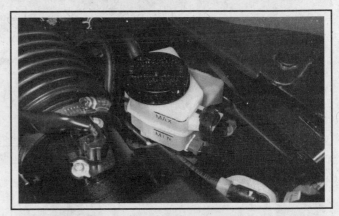

4.17 The brake fluid level should be kept between the MIN and MAX marks on the translucent plastic reservoir

information). If the hydraulic clutch system shows an indication of leakage check all clutch lines and connections, along with the clutch slave cylinder (see Chapter 8 for more information).

23 If, upon checking the brake or clutch master cylinder fluid level, you discover one or both reservoirs empty or nearly empty, the systems should be bled (see Chapter 9).

5 Tire and tire pressure checks (every 250 miles or weekly)

▶ **Refer to illustrations 5.2, 5.3, 5.4a, 5.4b and 5.8**

1 Periodic inspection of the tires may spare you from the inconvenience of being stranded with a flat tire. It can also provide you with vital information regarding possible problems in the steering and suspension systems before major damage occurs.

2 Normal tread wear can be monitored with a simple, inexpensive device known as a tread depth indicator (see illustration). When the tread depth reaches the specified minimum, replace the tire(s).

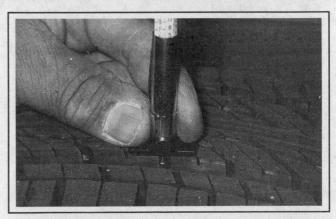

5.2 A tire tread depth indicator should be used to monitor tire wear - they are available at auto parts stores and service stations and cost very little

5.3 This chart will help you determine the condition of your tires, the probable cause(s) of abnormal wear and the corrective action necessary

UNDERINFLATION

CUPPING

OVERINFLATION

INCORRECT TOE-IN OR EXTREME CAMBER

Cupping may be caused by:
- Underinflation and/or mechanical irregularities such as out-of-balance condition of wheel and/or tire, and bent or damaged wheel.
- Loose or worn steering tie-rod or steering idler arm.
- Loose, damaged or worn front suspension parts.

FEATHERING DUE TO MISALIGNMENT

5.4a If a tire loses air on a steady basis, check the valve core first to make sure it's snug (special inexpensive wrenches are commonly available at auto parts stores)

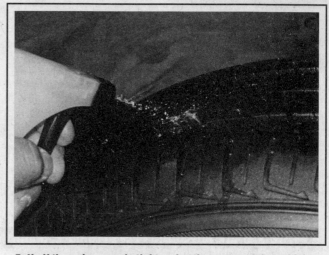

5.4b If the valve core is tight, raise the corner of the vehicle with the low tire and spray a soapy water solution onto the tread as the tire is turned slowly - slow leaks will cause small bubbles to appear

3   Note any abnormal tread wear (see illustration). Tread pattern irregularities such as cupping, flat spots and more wear on one side than the other are indications of front end alignment and/or balance problems. If any of these conditions are noted, take the vehicle to a tire shop or service station to correct the problem.

4   Look closely for cuts, punctures and embedded nails or tacks. Sometimes a tire will hold its air pressure for a short time or leak down very slowly even after a nail has embedded itself into the tread. If a slow leak persists, check the valve stem core to make sure it is tight (see illustration). Examine the tread for an object that may have embedded itself into the tire or for a plug that may have begun to leak (radial tire punctures are repaired with a plug that is installed in a puncture). If a puncture is suspected, it can be easily verified by spraying a solution of soapy water onto the puncture area (see illustration). The soapy solution will bubble if there is a leak. Unless the puncture is inordinately large, a tire shop or gas station can usually repair the punctured tire.

5   Carefully inspect the inner sidewall of each tire for evidence of brake fluid leakage. If you see any, inspect the brakes immediately.

6   Correct tire air pressure adds miles to the lifespan of the tires, improves mileage and enhances overall ride quality. Tire pressure cannot be accurately estimated by looking at a tire, particularly if it is a radial. A tire pressure gauge is therefore essential. Keep an accurate gauge in the glove box. The pressure gauges fitted to the nozzles of air hoses at gas stations are often inaccurate.

7   Always check tire pressure when the tires are cold. "Cold" in this case, means the vehicle has not been driven over a mile in the three hours preceding a tire pressure check. A pressure rise of four to eight pounds is not uncommon once the tires are warm.

8   Unscrew the valve cap protruding from the wheel or hubcap and push the gauge firmly onto the valve (see illustration). Note the reading on the gauge and compare this figure to the recommended tire pressure shown on the tire placard on the left door. Be sure to reinstall the valve cap to keep dirt and moisture out of the valve stem mechanism. Check all four tires and, if necessary, add enough air to bring them up to the recommended pressure levels.

9   Don't forget to keep the spare tire inflated to the specified pressure (consult your owner's manual). Note that the air pressure specified for the compact spare is significantly higher than the pressure of the regular tires.

5.8 To extend the life of your tires, check the air pressure at least once a week with an accurate gauge (don't forget the spare!)

6   Power steering fluid level check (every 3000 miles or 3 months)

▶ Refer to illustration 6.1

1   To check the fluid level in the reservoir, simply look at the MIN and MAX on the side of the reservoir (see illustration). The level should be within the specified distance from the maximum fill line. Use the HOT range at fluid temperatures of 122 to 176 degrees F. Use the COLD range at fluid temperatures of 32 to 86 degrees F. At no time should the fluid level drop below the minimum mark on the reservoir.

2   If additional fluid is required, use a clean rag to wipe off the reservoir cap and area around the cap. This will prevent any foreign matter from entering the reservoir during the check.

3   Unscrew the top cap and pour the specified type directly into the reservoir, using a funnel to prevent spills. Install the cap and tighten securely.

4   If the reservoir requires frequent fluid additions, all power steering hoses, hose connections, the power steering pump and the rack and pinion assembly should be carefully checked for leaks

6.1 The power steering fluid reservoir is mounted at the rear of the engine compartment on the passenger's side

7   Automatic transaxle fluid level check (every 3000 miles or 3 months)

▶ Refer to illustrations 7.4a and 7.4b

1   The level of the automatic transaxle fluid should be carefully maintained. Low fluid level can lead to slipping or loss of drive, while overfilling can cause foaming, loss of fluid and transaxle damage.

2   The transaxle fluid level should only be checked when the transaxle is hot (at its normal operating temperature). If the vehicle has just been driven over 10 miles (15 miles in a frigid climate), and the

fluid temperature is 160 to 175-degrees F, the transaxle is hot.

✳✳ CAUTION:

If the vehicle has just been driven for a long time at high speed or in city traffic in hot weather, or if it has been pulling a trailer, an accurate fluid level reading cannot be obtained. Allow the fluid to cool down for about 30 minutes.

7.4a The automatic transaxle dipstick is located in a tube which extends forward from the transaxle - press the tab on the dipstick to release the lock

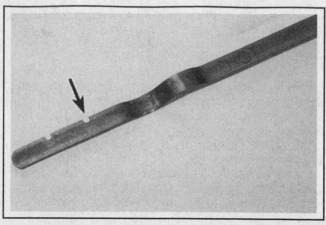

7.4b Check the automatic transaxle fluid with the engine idling at operating temperature and the gear selector in Park, then add fluid to bring the level near the upper notch

3   If the vehicle has not been driven, park the vehicle on level ground, set the parking brake, then start the engine and bring it to operating temperature. While the engine is idling, depress the brake pedal and move the selector lever through all the gear ranges, beginning and ending in Park.

4   With the engine still idling, remove the dipstick from its tube (see illustration). Check the level of the fluid on the dipstick (see illustration) and note its condition.

5   Wipe the fluid from the dipstick with a clean rag and reinsert it back into the filler tube until the cap seats.

➡**Note: When inserting the dipstick, rotate it 1/2-turn so the tab on the cap doesn't lock into place when the dipstick is fully inserted.**

6   Pull the dipstick out again and note the fluid level. If the level is at the low side of the range, add the specified automatic transaxle fluid through the dipstick tube with a funnel.

❈❈ **CAUTION:**

This vehicle uses a special fluid designed specifically for the Nissan CVT transaxle. Don't use another fluid or damage may occur. See this Chapter's Specifications.

7   Add just enough of the recommended fluid to fill the transaxle to the proper level. It takes about one pint to raise the level from the low mark to the high mark when the fluid is hot, so add the fluid a little at a time and keep checking the level until it is correct. Once the fluid level is correct, reinstall the dipstick with the locking tab oriented correctly, making sure it locks into place.

8   The condition of the fluid should also be checked along with the level. If the fluid at the end of the dipstick is black or a dark reddish brown color, or if it emits a burned smell, the fluid should be changed (see Section 26). If you are in doubt about the condition of the fluid, purchase some new fluid and compare the two for color and smell.

8   Engine oil and oil filter change (every 3000 miles or 3 months)

◗ **Refer to illustrations 8.2, 8.5, 8.10 and 8.12**

1   Frequent oil changes are the best preventive maintenance the home mechanic can give the engine, because aging oil becomes diluted and contaminated, which leads to premature engine wear.

2   Make sure that you have all the necessary tools before you begin this procedure (see illustration). You should also have plenty of rags or newspapers handy for mopping up any spills.

3   Park the vehicle on a level spot. Start the engine and allow it to reach its normal operating temperature (the needle on the temperature gauge should be at least above the bottom mark). Warm oil and contaminates will flow out more easily. Turn off the engine when it's warmed up. Remove the filler cap in the valve cover.

4   Raise the vehicle and support it securely on jackstands.

❈❈ **WARNING:**

To avoid personal injury, never get beneath the vehicle when it is supported by only by a jack. The jack provided with your vehicle is designed solely for raising the vehicle to remove and replace the wheels. Always use jackstands to support the vehi-

cle when it becomes necessary to place your body underneath the vehicle.

5   Being careful not to touch the hot exhaust components, place the drain pan under the drain plug in the bottom of the pan and remove the plug (see illustration). You may want to wear gloves while unscrewing the plug the final few turns if the engine is really hot.

6   Allow the old oil to drain into the pan. It may be necessary to move the pan farther under the engine as the oil flow slows to a trickle. Inspect the old oil for the presence of metal shavings and chips.

7   After all the oil has drained, wipe off the drain plug with a clean rag. Even minute metal particles clinging to the plug would immediately contaminate the new oil.

8   Clean the area around the drain plug opening, reinstall the plug and tighten it to the torque listed in this Chapter's Specifications.

9   Move the drain pan into position under the oil filter.

10 Loosen the oil filter by turning it counterclockwise with the filter wrench (see illustration). Any standard filter wrench should work. Once the filter is loose, use your hands to unscrew it from the block. Just as the filter is detached from the block, immediately tilt the open end up to

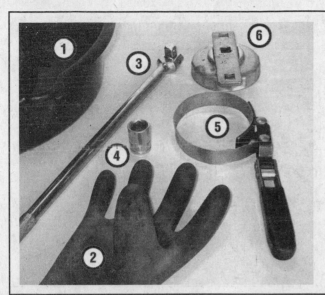

8.2 These tools are required when changing the engine oil and filter

1 **Drain pan** - It should be fairly shallow in depth, but wide in order to prevent spills

2 **Rubber gloves** - When removing the drain plug and filter, it is inevitable that you will get oil on your hands (the gloves will prevent burns)

3 **Breaker bar** - Sometimes the oil drain plug is pretty tight and a long breaker bar is needed to loosen it

4 **Socket** - To be used with the breaker bar or a ratchet (must be the correct size to fit the drain plug)

5 **Filter wrench** - This is a metal band-type wrench, which requires clearance around the filter to be effective

6 **Filter wrench** - This type fits on the bottom of the filter and can be turned with a ratchet or breaker bar (different size wrenches are available for different types of filters)

8.5 Use a proper size box-end wrench or socket to remove the oil drain plug and avoid rounding it off

8.10 The oil filter is located on the right end of the engine. Use an oil filter wrench for removal; DO NOT use the wrench to tighten the new filter (four-cylinder model shown)

8.12 Lubricate the oil filter gasket with clean engine oil before installing the filter on the engine

prevent the oil inside the filter from spilling out.

❊❊ WARNING:

The engine exhaust manifold may still be hot, so be careful.

11 With a clean rag, wipe off the oil filter mounting surface. Make sure that none of the old gasket remains stuck to the mounting surface. It can be removed with a scraper if necessary.

12 Compare the old filter with the new one to make sure they are the same type. Smear some engine oil on the rubber gasket of the new filter and screw it into place (see illustration). Because over-tightening the filter will damage the gasket, do not use a filter wrench to tighten the filter. Tighten it by hand until the gasket contacts the seating surface. Then seat the filter by giving it an additional 3/4-turn.

13 Remove all tools, rags, etc. from under the vehicle, being careful not to spill the oil in the drain pan, then lower the vehicle.

14 Remove the filler cap and add new oil to the engine. Use a spout or funnel to prevent oil from spilling onto the top of the engine. Pour four quarts of fresh oil into the engine. Wait a few minutes to allow the

oil to drain into the pan, then check the level on the oil dipstick (see Section 4 if necessary). If the oil level is at or near the H mark, install the filler cap hand tight, start the engine and allow the new oil to circulate.

15 Allow the engine to run for about a minute. While the engine is running, look under the vehicle and check for leaks at the oil pan drain plug and around the oil filter. If either is leaking, stop the engine and tighten the plug or filter slightly.

16 Wait a few minutes to allow the oil to trickle down into the pan, then recheck the level on the dipstick and, if necessary, add enough oil to bring the level to the H mark.

17 During the first few trips after an oil change, make it a point to check frequently for leaks and proper oil level.

18 The old oil drained from the engine cannot be reused in its present state and should be disposed of. Check with your local auto parts store, disposal facility or environmental agency to see if they will accept the oil for recycling. After the oil has cooled it can be drained into a container (capped plastic jugs, topped bottles, milk cartons, etc.) for transport to one of these disposal sites. Don't dispose of the oil by pouring it on the ground or down a drain!

9 Windshield wiper blade inspection and replacement (every 7500 miles or 6 months)

▶ **Refer to illustrations 9.3, 9.5 and 9.6**

1   The windshield wiper and blade assembly should be inspected periodically for damage, loose components and cracked or worn blade elements.

2   Road film can build up on the wiper blades and affect their efficiency, so they should be washed regularly with a mild detergent solution.

3   The action of the wiping mechanism can loosen bolts, nuts and fasteners, so they should be checked and tightened, as necessary (see illustration), at the same time the wiper blades are checked.

4   If the wiper blade elements are cracked, worn or warped, or no longer clean adequately, they should be replaced with new ones.

5   Lift the arm assembly away from the glass for clearance, press on the release lever, then slide the wiper blade assembly out of the hook in the end of the arm (see illustration).

6   Use needle-nose pliers to compress the blade element, then slide the element out of the frame and discard it (see illustration).

7   Installation is the reverse of removal.

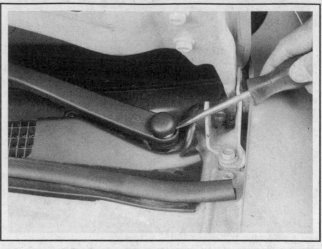

9.3 Gently pry off the trim cap and check the tightness of the wiper arm retaining nut

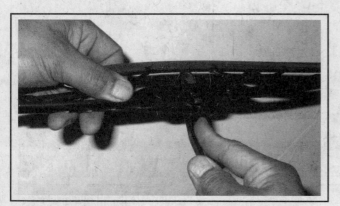

9.5 Press on the release tab and push the blade assembly down out of the hook in the arm

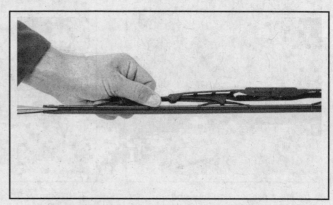

9.6 Use needle-nose pliers to compress the rubber element, then slide the element out - slide the new element in and lock the blade assembly fingers into the notches of the wiper element

10 Battery check, maintenance and charging (every 7500 miles or 6 months)

▶ **Refer to illustrations 10.1, 10.6a, 10.6b, 10.7a and 10.7b**

❊❊ WARNING:

Certain precautions must be followed when checking and servicing the battery. Hydrogen gas, which is highly flammable, is always present in the battery cells, so keep lighted tobacco and all other open flames and sparks away from the battery. The electrolyte inside the battery is actually dilute sulfuric acid, which will cause injury if splashed on your skin or in your eyes. It will also ruin clothes and painted surfaces. When removing the battery cables, always detach the negative cable first and hook it up last!

1   A routine preventive maintenance program for the battery in your vehicle is the only way to ensure quick and reliable starts. But before performing any battery maintenance, make sure that you have the proper equipment necessary to work safely around the battery (see illustration).

2   There are also several precautions that should be taken whenever battery maintenance is performed. Before servicing the battery, always turn the engine and all accessories off and disconnect the cable from the negative terminal of the battery.

3   The battery produces hydrogen gas, which is both flammable and explosive. Never create a spark, smoke or light a match around the battery. Always charge the battery in a ventilated area.

4   Electrolyte contains poisonous and corrosive sulfuric acid. Do not allow it to get in your eyes, on your skin or on your clothes. Never ingest it. Wear protective safety glasses when working near the battery. Keep children away from the battery.

5   Note the external condition of the battery. If the positive terminal and cable clamp on your vehicle's battery is equipped with a rubber protector, make sure it isn't torn or damaged. It should completely cover the terminal. Look for any corroded or loose connections, cracks in the case or cover or loose hold-down clamps. Also check the entire length of each cable for cracks and frayed conductors.

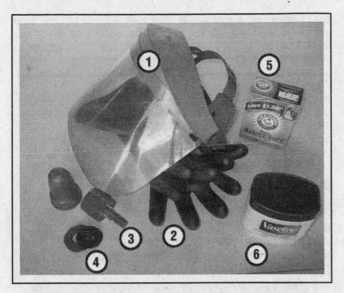

10.1 Tools and materials required for battery maintenance

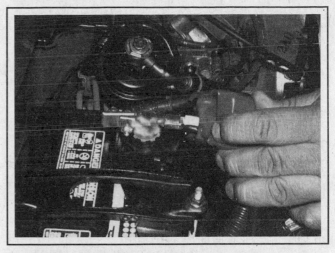

10.6a Battery terminal corrosion usually appears as light, fluffy powder

1   Face shield/safety goggles - When removing corrosion with a brush, the acidic particles can easily fly up into your eyes

2   Rubber gloves - Another safety item to consider when servicing the battery; remember that's acid inside the battery

3   Battery post/cable cleaner - This wire brush cleaning tool will remove all traces of corrosion from the battery posts and cable clamps

4   Treated felt washers - Placing one of these on each post, directly under the cable clamps, will help prevent corrosion

5   Baking soda - A solution of baking soda and water can be used to neutralize corrosion

6   Petroleum jelly - A layer of this on the battery posts will help prevent corrosion

6   If corrosion, which looks like white, fluffy deposits (see illustration) is evident, particularly around the terminals, the battery should be removed for cleaning. Loosen the cable clamp bolts with a wrench, being careful to remove the ground cable first, and slide them off the terminals (see illustration). Then disconnect the hold-down clamp bolt and nut, remove the clamp and lift the battery from the engine compartment.

7   Clean the cable clamps thoroughly with a battery brush or a terminal cleaner and a solution of warm water and baking soda (see illustration). Wash the terminals and the top of the battery case with the same solution but make sure that the solution doesn't get into the battery. When cleaning the cables, terminals and battery top, wear safety goggles and rubber gloves to prevent any solution from coming in contact with your eyes or hands. Wear old clothes too - even diluted, sulfuric acid splashed onto clothes will burn holes in them. If the terminals have been extensively corroded, clean them up with a terminal cleaner (see illustration). Thoroughly wash all cleaned areas with plain water.

10.6b Removing a cable from the battery post with a wrench - sometimes special battery pliers are required for this procedure if corrosion has caused deterioration of the nut hex (always remove the ground cable first and hook it up last!)

10.7a When cleaning the cable clamps, all corrosion must be removed (the inside of the clamp is tapered to match the taper on the post, so don't remove too much material)

10.7b Regardless of the type of tool used to clean the battery posts, a clean, shiny surface should be the result

8   Make sure the battery tray is in good condition and the hold-down clamp bolt or nut is tight. If the battery is removed from the tray, make sure no parts remain in the bottom of the tray when the battery is reinstalled. When reinstalling the hold-down clamp bolt or nut, do not over-tighten it.

9   Information on removing and installing the battery can be found in Chapter 5. Information on jump starting can be found at the front of this manual.

CLEANING

10   Corrosion on the hold-down components, battery case and surrounding areas can be removed with a solution of water and baking soda. Thoroughly rinse all cleaned areas with plain water.

11   Any metal parts of the vehicle damaged by corrosion should be covered with a zinc-based primer, then painted.

CHARGING

✲✲ WARNING:

When batteries are being charged, hydrogen gas, which is very explosive and flammable, is produced. Do not smoke or allow open flames near a charging or a recently charged battery. Wear eye protection when near the battery during charging. Also, make sure the charger is unplugged before connecting or disconnecting the battery from the charger.

12   Slow-rate charging is the best way to restore a battery that's discharged to the point where it will not start the engine. It's also a good way to maintain the battery charge in a vehicle that's only driven a few miles between starts. Maintaining the battery charge is particularly important in the winter when the battery must work harder to start the engine and electrical accessories that drain the battery are in greater use.

13   It's best to use a one or two-amp battery charger (sometimes called a "trickle" charger). They are the safest and put the least strain on the battery. They are also the least expensive. For a faster charge, you can use a higher amperage charger, but don't use one rated more than 1/10th the amp/hour rating of the battery. Rapid boost charges that claim to restore the power of the battery in one to two hours are hardest on the battery and can damage batteries not in good condition. This type of charging should only be used in emergency situations.

14   The average time necessary to charge a battery should be listed in the instructions that come with the charger. As a general rule, a trickle charger will charge a battery in 12 to 16 hours.

11 Drivebelt check (every 7500 miles or 6 months) and replacement

CHECK

▶ **Refer to illustrations 11.3 and 11.4**

1   These models are use a serpentine drivebelt with a tensioner (automatic adjuster). The good condition and proper tension of the belt is critical to the operation of the engine. Because of their composition and the high stresses to which they are subjected, drivebelts stretch and deteriorate as they get older. They must therefore be periodically inspected.

2   The serpentine drivebelt transmits power to all the accessories.

3   With the engine off, open the hood and locate the drivebelt. With a flashlight, check each belt for separation of the adhesive rubber on both sides of the core, core separation from the belt side, a severed core, separation of the ribs from the adhesive rubber, cracking or separation of the ribs, and torn or worn ribs or cracks in the inner ridges of the ribs (see illustration). Also check for fraying and glazing, which gives the belt a shiny appearance. Both sides of the belt should be inspected, which means you will have to twist the belt to check the underside. Use your fingers to feel the belt where you can't see it. If any of the above conditions are evident, replace the belt (see Steps 5 through 7).

4   Check the drivebelt indicator for excessive stretch (see illustration). If the drivebelt indicator is out of limit, replace the drivebelt (see Steps 5 through 7).

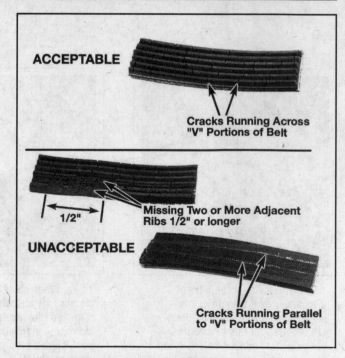

11.3 Here are some of the more common problems associated with drivebelts (check the belts very carefully to prevent an untimely breakdown)

11.4 If the indicator notch (A) on the moveable part of the tensioner passes the stationary mark (B) on the tensioner body, the drivebelt has stretched beyond its limit and should be replaced (four-cylinder engine shown)

11.7 Release the tension using a wrench, then insert a drill bit or rod to lock the tensioner in place (four-cylinder engine)

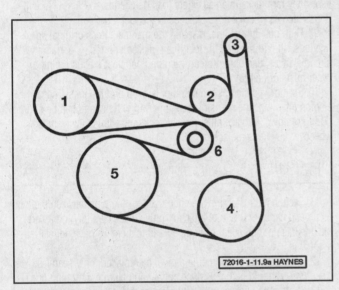

11.9a Drivebelt routing diagram - four-cylinder engine

1	Power steering pump	4	Air conditioning compressor
2	Water pump	5	Crankshaft pulley
3	Alternator	6	Tensioner pulley

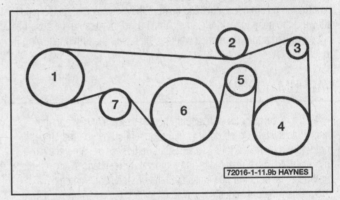

11.9b Drivebelt routing diagram - V6 engine

1	Power steering pump	5	Idler pulley
2	Idler pulley	6	Crankshaft pulley
3	Alternator	7	Tensioner pulley
4	Air conditioning compressor		

✳✳ CAUTION:

Do not loosen the drivebelt tensioner pulley bolt or it will be necessary to replace the entire tensioner with a new one. The tensioner can be locked in position by inserting a drill bit or other metal rod into the lock holes (see illustration).

8 Remove the drivebelt from the tensioner and all accessories.

9 Install the new drivebelt, making sure that it's properly routed (see illustrations).

10 Reconnect the battery and perform the necessary re-learn procedures (see Chapter 5).

TENSIONER REPLACEMENT

11 Remove the drivebelt (see Steps 5 through 8).

12 Remove the drivebelt tensioner mounting bolts.

13 Installation is the reverse of removal. Tighten the tensioner mounting fasteners to the torque listed in this Chapter's Specifications.

DRIVEBELT REPLACEMENT

▸ **Refer to illustrations 11.7, 11.9a and 11.9b**

5 Disconnect the cable from the negative terminal of the battery (see Chapter 5).

6 Loosen the right front wheel lug nuts. Raise the vehicle and support it securely on jackstands. Remove the right inner fender splash shield.

7 Rotate the belt tensioner clockwise using a wrench on the pulley bolt to release tension on the drivebelt.

12 Underhood hose check and replacement (every 7500 miles or 6 months)

✳✳ CAUTION:

Replacement of air conditioning hoses must be left to a dealer service department or air conditioning shop that has the equipment to depressurize the system safely. Never remove air conditioning components or hoses until the system has been depressurized.

GENERAL

1   High temperatures in the engine compartment can cause the deterioration of the rubber and plastic hoses used for engine, accessory and emission systems operation. Periodic inspection should be made for cracks, loose clamps, material hardening and leaks.

2   Information specific to the cooling system hoses can be found in Section 13.

3   Some, but not all, hoses are secured to the fittings with clamps. Where clamps are used, check to be sure they haven't lost their tension, allowing the hose to leak. If clamps aren't used, make sure the hose has not expanded and/or hardened where it slips over the fitting, allowing it to leak.

VACUUM HOSES

4   It's quite common for vacuum hoses, especially those in the emissions system, to be color coded or identified by colored stripes molded into them. Various systems require hoses with different wall thickness, collapse resistance and temperature resistance. When replacing hoses, be sure the new ones are made of the same material.

5   Often the only effective way to check a hose is to remove it completely from the vehicle. If more than one hose is removed, be sure to label the hoses and fittings to ensure correct installation.

6   When checking vacuum hoses, be sure to include any plastic T-fittings in the check. Inspect the fittings for cracks and the hose where it fits over the fitting for distortion, which could cause leakage.

7   A small piece of vacuum hose (1/4-inch inside diameter) can be used as a stethoscope to detect vacuum leaks. Hold one end of the hose to your ear and probe around vacuum hoses and fittings, listening for the hissing sound characteristic of a vacuum leak.

✳✳ WARNING:

When probing with the vacuum hose stethoscope, be very careful not to come into contact with moving engine components such as the drivebelts, cooling fan, etc.

FUEL HOSE

✳✳ WARNING:

There are certain precautions which must be taken when inspecting or servicing fuel system components. Work in a well ventilated area and do not allow open flames (cigarettes, appliance pilot lights, etc.) or bare light bulbs near the work area. Mop up any spills immediately and do not store fuel-soaked rags where they could ignite.

8   Check all rubber fuel lines for deterioration and chafing. Check especially for cracks in areas where the hose bends and just before fittings, such as where a hose attaches to the fuel filter.

9   High quality fuel line, meeting the manufacturer's original specifications, should be used for fuel line replacement. Never, under any circumstances, use unreinforced vacuum line, clear plastic tubing or water hose for fuel lines.

10   Spring-type clamps are commonly used on fuel lines. These clamps often lose their tension over a period of time, and can be sprung during removal. Replace all spring-type clamps with screw clamps whenever a hose is replaced.

METAL LINES

11   Sections of metal line are often used for fuel line between the fuel pump and carburetor or fuel injection unit. Check carefully to be sure the line has not been bent or crimped and that cracks have not started in the line.

12   If a section of metal fuel line must be replaced, only seamless steel tubing should be used, since copper and aluminum tubing don't have the strength necessary to withstand normal engine vibration.

13   Check the metal brake lines where they enter the master cylinder and brake proportioning unit (if used) for cracks in the lines or loose fittings. Any sign of brake fluid leakage calls for an immediate thorough inspection of the brake system.

13 Cooling system check (every 7500 miles or 6 months)

◆ **Refer to illustration 13.4**

1   Many major engine failures can be attributed to a faulty cooling system. If the vehicle is equipped with an automatic transaxle, the cooling system also cools the transaxle fluid and thus plays an important role in prolonging transaxle life.

2   The cooling system should be checked with the engine cold. Do this before the vehicle is driven for the day or after the engine has been shut off for at least three hours.

3   Remove the radiator cap by turning it to the left until it reaches

a stop. If you hear a hissing sound (indicating there is still pressure in the system), wait until it stops. Now press down on the cap with the palm of your hand and continue turning to the left until the cap can be removed. Thoroughly clean the cap, inside and out, with clean water. Also clean the filler neck on the radiator. All traces of corrosion should be removed. The coolant inside the radiator should be relatively transparent. If it's rust colored, the system should be drained and refilled (see Section 24). If the coolant level isn't up to the top, add additional antifreeze/coolant mixture (see Section 4).

Check for a chafed area that could fail prematurely.

Check for a soft area indicating the hose has deteriorated inside.

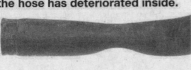

Overtightening the clamp on a hardened hose will damage the hose and cause a leak.

Check each hose for swelling and oil-soaked ends. Cracks and breaks can be located by squeezing the hose

13.4 Hoses, like drivebelts, have a habit of failing at the worst possible time - to prevent the inconvenience of a blown radiator or heater hose, inspect them carefully as shown here

4   Carefully check the large upper and lower radiator hoses along with the smaller diameter heater hoses which run from the engine to the firewall. Inspect each hose along its entire length, replacing any hose which is cracked, swollen or shows signs of deterioration. Cracks may become more apparent if the hose is squeezed (see illustration). Regardless of condition, it's a good idea to replace hoses with new ones every two years.

5   Make sure that all hose connections are tight. A leak in the cooling system will usually show up as white or rust colored deposits on the areas adjoining the leak. If wire-type clamps are used at the ends of the hoses, it may be a good idea to replace them with more secure screw-type clamps.

6   Use compressed air or a soft brush to remove bugs, leaves, etc. from the front of the radiator or air conditioning condenser. Be careful not to damage the delicate cooling fins or cut yourself on them.

7   Every other inspection, or at the first indication of cooling system problems, have the cap and system pressure tested. If you don't have a pressure tester, most gas stations and repair shops will do this for a minimal charge.

14 Tire rotation (every 7500 miles or 6 months)

♦ **Refer to illustration 14.2**

1   The tires should be rotated at the specified intervals and whenever uneven wear is noticed. Since the vehicle will be raised and the tires removed anyway, check the brakes (see Section 15) at this time.

2   Radial tires must be rotated in a specific pattern (see illustration).

3   Refer to the information in *Jacking and towing* at the front of this manual for the proper procedures to follow when raising the vehicle and changing a tire. If the brakes are to be checked, do not apply the parking brake as stated. Make sure the tires are blocked to prevent the vehicle from rolling.

4   Preferably, the entire vehicle should be raised at the same time. This can be done on a hoist or by jacking up each corner and then lowering the vehicle onto jackstands placed under the frame rails. Always use four jackstands and make sure the vehicle is firmly supported.

5   After rotation, check and adjust the tire pressures as necessary and be sure to check the lug nut tightness.

6   For further information on the wheels and tires, refer to Chapter 10.

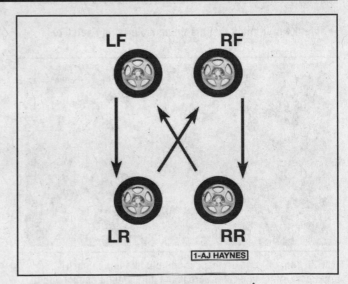

14.2 The recommended tire rotation pattern for these vehicles

15 Brake check (every 15,000 miles or 12 months)

✳✳ WARNING:

The dust created by the brake system is harmful to your health. Never blow it out with compressed air and don't inhale any of it. An approved filtering mask should be worn when working on the brakes. Do not, under any circumstances, use petroleum-based solvents to clean brake parts. Use brake system cleaner only! Try to use non-asbestos replacement parts whenever possible.

➡Note: For detailed photographs of the brake system, refer to Chapter 9.

1   In addition to the specified intervals, the brakes should be inspected every time the wheels are removed or whenever a defect is suspected. Any of the following symptoms could indicate a potential brake system defect: The vehicle pulls to one side when the brake pedal is depressed; the brakes make squealing or dragging noises when applied; brake pedal travel is excessive; the pedal pulsates; brake fluid leaks, usually onto the inside of the tire or wheel.

2   The disc brake pads have built-in wear indicators which should make a high pitched squealing or scraping noise when they are worn to the replacement point. When you hear this noise, replace the pads immediately or expensive damage to the discs can result.

3   Loosen the wheel lug nuts.

4   Raise the vehicle and place it securely on jackstands.

5   Remove the wheels (see *Jacking and towing* at the front of this book, or your owner's manual, if necessary).

DISC BRAKES

▸ **Refer to illustrations 15.6 and 15.11**

6   There are two pads (an outer and an inner) in each caliper. The pads are visible through inspection holes in each caliper (see illustration).

7   Check the pad thickness by looking at each end of the caliper and through the inspection hole in the caliper body. If the lining material is less than the thickness listed in this Chapter's Specifications, replace the pads.

➡Note: Keep in mind that the lining material is riveted or

bonded to a metal backing plate and the metal portion is not included in this measurement.

8   If it is difficult to determine the exact thickness of the remaining pad material by the above method, or if you are at all concerned about the condition of the pads, remove the caliper(s), then remove the pads from the calipers for further inspection (see Chapter 9).

9   Once the pads are removed from the calipers, clean them with brake cleaner and re-measure them with a ruler or a vernier caliper.

10   Measure the disc thickness with a micrometer to make sure that it still has service life remaining. If any disc is thinner than the specified minimum thickness, replace it (see Chapter 9). Even if the disc has service life remaining, check its condition. Look for scoring, gouging and burned spots. If these conditions exist, remove the disc and have it resurfaced (see Chapter 9).

11   Before installing the wheels, check all brake lines and hoses for damage, wear, deformation, cracks, corrosion, leakage, bends and twists, particularly in the vicinity of the rubber hoses at the calipers (see illustration). Check the clamps for tightness and the connections for leakage. Make sure that all hoses and lines are clear of sharp edges, moving parts and the exhaust system. If any of the above conditions are noted, repair, reroute or replace the lines and/or fittings as necessary (see Chapter 9).

BRAKE BOOSTER CHECK

12   Sit in the driver's seat and perform the following sequence of tests.

13   With the brake fully depressed, start the engine - the pedal should move down a little when the engine starts.

14   With the engine running, depress the brake pedal several times - the travel distance should not change.

15   Depress the brake, stop the engine and hold the pedal in for about 30 seconds - the pedal should neither sink nor rise.

16   Restart the engine, run it for about a minute and turn it off. Then firmly depress the brake several times - the pedal travel should decrease with each application.

17   If your brakes do not operate as described above when the preceding tests are performed, the brake booster is either in need of repair or has failed. Refer to Chapter 9 for the removal procedure.

15.6 You will find an inspection hole like this in each caliper - placing a ruler across the hole should enable you to determine the thickness of remaining pad material for both inner and outer pads

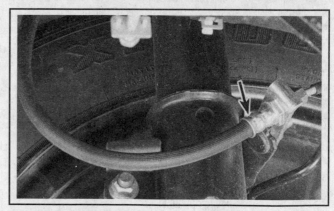

15.11 Check along the brake hoses and at each fitting for deterioration and cracks

PARKING BRAKE

18 Actuate the parking brake with a normal amount of force and count the number of clicks. The adjustment should be within the specified number of clicks listed in Chapter 9 Specifications. If you hear more or fewer clicks, adjust the parking brake (see Chapter 9).

19 An alternative method of checking the parking brake is to park the vehicle on a steep hill with the parking brake set and the transaxle in Neutral (be sure to stay in the vehicle during this check!). If the parking brake cannot prevent the vehicle from rolling, it is in need of adjustment (see Chapter 9).

16 Cabin air filter replacement (every 15,000 miles or 12 months)

1 The cabin air filter is located behind the center console and the glove box.

➡ **Note: Not all models have cabin air filters.**

2 Remove the glove box assembly (see Chapter 11).

3 Remove the right side trim panel from the center console (see Chapter 11).

4 Remove the cabin air filter cover by releasing the tab at its lower edge.

5 Slide the cabin filter from the blower assembly.

6 Installation is the reverse of removal.

17 Air filter check and replacement (every 30,000 miles or 12 months)

▸ **Refer to illustrations 17.1a and 17.1b**

1 The air filter is located inside the air filter housing at the left (driver's) side of the engine compartment. To remove the air filter, release the spring clips that secure the two halves of the housing together, then separate the halves and remove the air filter element (see illustrations).

2 Inspect the outer surface of the filter element. If it is dirty, replace it. If it is only moderately dusty, it can be reused by blowing it clean from the back to the front surface with compressed air. Because it is a pleated paper type filter, it cannot be washed or oiled. If it cannot be cleaned satisfactorily with compressed air, discard and replace it. While the cover is off, be careful not to drop anything down into the housing.

✳✳ **CAUTION:**

Never drive the vehicle with the air cleaner removed. Excessive engine wear could result and backfiring could even cause a fire under the hood.

3 Wipe out the inside of the air filter housing.

4 Place the new filter into the housing, making sure it seats properly.

5 Reassemble the housing halves and snap the clips into place.

17.1a Detach the clips (arrows) and separate the halves of the air filter housing . . .

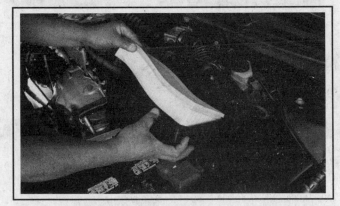

17.1b . . . then remove the air filter

18 Fuel system check (every 15,000 miles or 12 months)

▸ **Refer to illustrations 18.5 and 18.6**

✳✳ **WARNING:**

Gasoline is extremely flammable, so take extra precautions when you work on any part of the fuel system. Don't smoke or allow open flames or bare light bulbs near the work area, and don't work in a garage where a gas-type appliance (such as a water heater or clothes dryer) is present. Since gasoline is car-cinogenic, wear fuel-resistant gloves when there's a possibility of being exposed to fuel, and, if you spill any fuel on your skin, rinse it off immediately with soap and water. Mop up any spills immediately and do not store fuel-soaked rags where they could ignite. The fuel system is under constant pressure, so, if any fuel lines are to be disconnected, the fuel pressure in the system must be relieved first (see Chapter 4 for more information). When you perform any kind of work on the fuel system, wear safety glasses and have a Class B type fire extinguisher on hand.

1   If you smell gasoline while driving or after the vehicle has been sitting in the sun, inspect the fuel system immediately.

2   Remove the gas cap and inspect it for damage and corrosion. The gasket should have an unbroken sealing imprint. If the gasket is damaged or corroded, remove it and install a new one.

3   Inspect the fuel feed and return lines for cracks. Make sure the threaded flare nut type connectors (which secure the metal fuel lines to the fuel injection system) and the clamps (which secure the hoses to the in-line fuel filter) are tight.

4   Since some components of the fuel system - the fuel tank and part of the fuel feed and return lines, for example - are underneath the vehicle, they can be inspected more easily with the vehicle raised on a hoist. If that's not possible, raise the vehicle and support it securely on jackstands.

5   With the vehicle raised and safely supported, inspect the gas tank and filler neck for punctures, cracks and other damage. The connection between the filler neck and the tank is particularly critical. Sometimes a rubber filler neck will leak because of loose clamps or deteriorated rubber (see illustration). These are problems a home mechanic can usually rectify.

✳✳ WARNING:

Do not, under any circumstances, try to repair a fuel tank (except rubber components). A welding torch or any open flame can easily cause fuel vapors inside the tank to explode.

6   Carefully check all rubber hoses and metal lines leading away from the fuel tank (see illustration). Check for loose connections, deteriorated hoses, crimped lines and other damage. Carefully inspect the lines from the tank to the fuel injection system. Repair or replace damaged sections as necessary (see Chapter 4).

18.5 Inspect the fuel filler hoses for cracks and make sure the clamps are tight

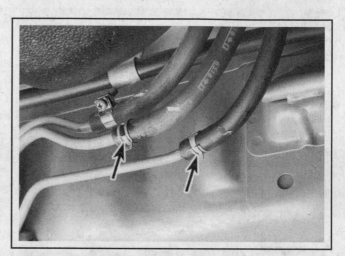

18.6 Carefully inspect fuel line clamps for loss of tension which can result in leaking fuel lines

19 Manual transaxle lubricant level check (every 15,000 miles or 12 months)

▶ **Refer to illustration 19.1**

1   The manual transaxle does not have a dipstick. To check the fluid level, raise the vehicle and support it securely on jackstands. Remove the fill plug (located at the rear of the clutch housing). Use a measuring stick to check the level of the fluid from the top of the transaxle housing (see illustration). The level should be at 2.4 to 2.6 inches for four-cylinder models, or 2.6 to 2.8 inches for V6 models.

2   If the transaxle needs more fluid, use a funnel or gear oil pump to add more fluid to the transaxle. Re-check the level and add more fluid, if necessary.

3   Install the fill plug. Drive the vehicle a short distance, then check for leaks.

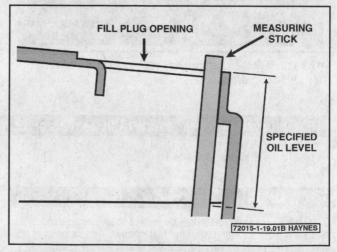

19.1 Insert a measuring stick into the fill hole of the manual transaxle to measure the lubricant level

20 Steering and suspension check (every 15,000 miles or 12 months)

➡**Note: For detailed illustrations of the steering and suspension components, refer to Chapter 10.**

WITH THE WHEELS ON THE GROUND

▶ **Refer to illustration 20.1**

1   With the vehicle stopped and the front wheels pointed straight ahead, rock the steering wheel gently back and forth. If freeplay (see illustration) is excessive, a front wheel bearing, main shaft yoke, intermediate shaft yoke, lower arm balljoint or steering system joint is worn or the steering gear is out of adjustment or broken. Refer to Chapter 10 for the appropriate repair procedure.

2   Other symptoms, such as excessive vehicle body movement over rough roads, swaying (leaning) around corners and binding as the steering wheel is turned, may indicate faulty steering and/or suspension components.

3   Check the shock absorbers by pushing down and releasing the vehicle several times at each corner. If the vehicle does not come back to a level position within one or two bounces, the shocks/struts are worn and must be replaced. When bouncing the vehicle up and down, listen for squeaks and noises from the suspension components.

UNDER THE VEHICLE

▶ **Refer to illustrations 20.6a and 20.6b**

4   Raise the vehicle with a floor jack and support it securely on jackstands. See *Jacking and towing* at the front of this book for proper jacking points.

5   Check the tires for irregular wear patterns and proper inflation. See Section 5 in this Chapter for information regarding tire wear.

6   Inspect the universal joint between the steering shaft and the steering gear housing. Check the steering gear housing for grease leakage. Make sure that the boots are not damaged and that the boot clamps

are not loose (see illustration). Check the steering linkage for looseness or damage. Check the tie-rod ends for excessive play. Look for loose bolts, broken or disconnected parts and deteriorated rubber bushings on all suspension and steering components (see illustration). While an assistant turns the steering wheel from side to side, check the steering components for free movement, chafing and binding. If the steering components do not seem to be reacting with the movement of the steering wheel, try to determine where the slack is located.

7   Check the balljoints by moving each lower arm up and down with a pry bar to ensure that its balljoint has no play. If any balljoint does have play, replace it. See Chapter 10 for the front balljoint replacement procedure.

8   Inspect the balljoint boots for damage and leaking grease. Replace the balljoints with new ones if they are damaged (see Chapter 10).

20.1 Steering wheel freeplay is the amount of travel between an initial steering input and the point at which the front wheels begin to turn (indicated by a slight resistance)

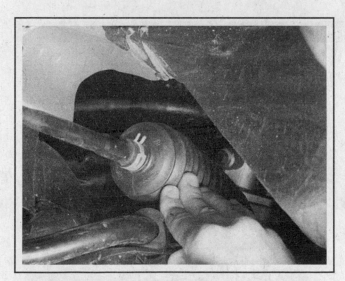

20.6a Check the steering gear boots for cracks and leaking steering fluid

20.6b Check the stabilizer bar bushings for deterioration at the front and the rear of the vehicle

21 Exhaust system check (every 15,000 miles or 12 months)

▶ **Refer to illustrations 21.2 and 21.4**

1   With the engine cold (at least three hours after the vehicle has been driven), check the complete exhaust system from its starting point at the engine to the end of the tailpipe. This should be done on a hoist where unrestricted access is available.

2   Check the pipes and connections for evidence of leaks (see illustration), severe corrosion or damage. Make sure that all brackets and hangers are in good condition and tight.

3   At the same time, inspect the underside of the body for holes, corrosion, open seams, etc. which may allow exhaust gases to enter the passenger compartment. Seal all body openings with silicone or body putty.

4   Rattles and other noises can often be traced to the exhaust system, especially the mounts and hangers (see illustration). Try to move the pipes, muffler and catalytic converter. If the components can come in contact with the body or suspension parts, secure the exhaust system with new mounts.

5   Check the running condition of the engine by inspecting inside the end of the tailpipe. The exhaust deposits here are an indication of engine state-of-tune. If the pipe is black and sooty or coated with white deposits, the engine is in need of a tune-up, including a thorough fuel system inspection.

21.2 Check the flange connections for exhaust leaks - also check that the retaining nuts are securely tightened

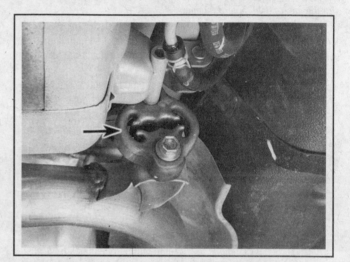

21.4 Check the exhaust system hangers for damage and cracks

22 Driveaxle boot check (every 15,000 miles or 12 months)

▶ **Refer to illustration 22.2**

1   The driveaxle boots are very important because they prevent dirt, water and foreign material from entering and damaging the constant velocity (CV) joints.

2   Inspect the boots for tears and cracks as well as loose clamps (see illustration). If there is any evidence of cracks or leaking lubricant, they must be replaced as described in Chapter 8.

22.2 Check the driveaxle boot for cracks or leaking grease

23 Spark plug check and replacement (every 105,000 miles or 72 months)

▶ Refer to illustrations 23.1, 23.4a and 23.4b

1   Spark plug replacement requires a spark plug socket and extension which fits onto a ratchet. This socket is lined with a rubber grommet to protect the porcelain insulator of the spark plug and to hold the plug while you remove it. You will also need a wire-type feeler gauge to check and adjust the spark plug gap and a torque wrench to tighten the new plugs to the specified torque (see illustration).

2   If you are replacing the plugs, purchase the new plugs, adjust them to the proper gap and then replace each plug one at a time.

3   Inspect each of the new plugs for defects. If there are any signs of cracks in the porcelain insulator of a plug, don't use it.

4   Check the electrode gaps of the new plugs. Check the gap by inserting the wire gauge of the proper thickness between the electrodes at the tip of the plug (see illustration). The gap between the electrodes should be identical to that listed in this Chapter's Specifications. If the gap is incorrect, use the notched adjuster on the feeler gauge body to bend the curved side electrode slightly (see illustration).

5   If the side electrode is not exactly over the center electrode, use the notched adjuster to align them.

❋❋ CAUTION:

If the gap of a new plug must be adjusted, bend only the base of the ground electrode - do not touch the tip.

REMOVAL

4-cylinder engine

▶ Refer to illustration 23.7

6   Remove the ignition coils (see Chapter 5).
7   Remove the spark plugs (see illustration).
8   If compressed air is available, blow any dirt or foreign material away from the spark plug area before proceeding (a common bicycle

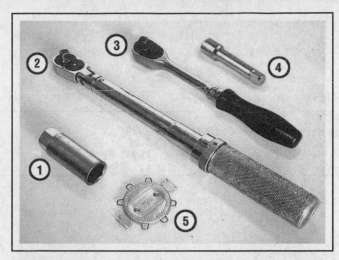

23.1 Tools required for changing spark plugs

1   **Spark plug socket** - This will have special padding inside to protect the spark plug porcelain insulator
2   **Torque wrench** - Although not mandatory, use of this tool is the best way to ensure that the plugs are tightened properly
3   **Ratchet** - Standard hand tool to fit the plug socket
4   **Extension** - Depending on model and accessories, you may need special extensions and universal joints to reach one or more of the plugs
5   **Spark plug gap gauge** - This gauge for checking the gap comes in a variety of styles. Make sure the gap for your engine is included

pump will also work).

V6 engine

9   Remove the upper intake manifold (see Chapter 2B) and the ignition coils (see Chapter 5).
10 Remove the spark plugs (see illustration 23.7).

23.4a Spark plug manufacturers recommend using a wire-type gauge when checking the gap - if the wire does not slide between the electrodes with a slight drag, adjustment is required

23.4b To change the gap, bend the side electrode only, as indicated by the arrows, and be very careful not to crack or chip the porcelain insulator surrounding the center electrode

23.7 Use a spark plug socket with a ratchet and an extension to remove the spark plugs

All engines

▶ **Refer to illustration 23.11**

11 Whether you are replacing the plugs at this time or intend to reuse the old plugs, compare the spark plug to those shown in this chart to get an indication of the general running condition of the engine. (see illustration)

INSTALLATION

▶ **Refer to illustrations 23.12a and 23.12b**

12 Prior to installation, apply a coat of anti-seize compound to the plug threads (see illustration). It's often difficult to insert spark plugs into their holes without cross-threading them. To avoid this possibility, fit a short piece of snug-fitting rubber hose over the end of the spark plug (see illustration). The flexible hose acts as a universal joint to help align the plug with the plug hole. Should the plug begin to cross-thread, the hose will slip on the spark plug, preventing thread damage. Tighten the plug to the torque listed in this Chapter's Specifications.

13 Follow the above procedure for the remaining spark plugs.

14 After replacing all the plugs, install the ignition coils (see Chapter 5).

A **normally worn** spark plug should have light tan or gray deposits on the firing tip.

A **carbon fouled** plug, identified by soft, sooty, black deposits, may indicate an improperly tuned vehicle. Check the air cleaner, ignition components and engine control system.

An **oil fouled** spark plug indicates an engine with worn piston rings and/or bad valve seals allowing excessive oil to enter the chamber.

This spark plug has been **left in the engine too long,** as evidenced by the extreme gap- Plugs with such an extreme gap can cause misfiring and stumbling accompanied by a noticeable lack of power.

A **physically damaged** spark plug may be evidence of severe detonation in that cylinder. Watch that cylinder carefully between services, as a continued detonation will not only damage the plug, but could also damage the engine.

A **bridged or almost bridged** spark plug, identified by a build up between the electrodes caused by excessive carbon or oil build-up on the plug.

23.11 Inspect the spark plug to determine engine running conditions

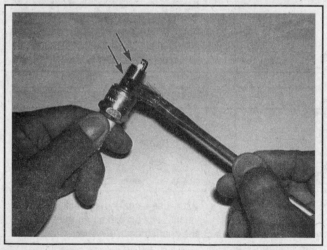

23.12a Apply a coat of anti-seize compound to the spark plug threads, being careful not to get any near the lower threads

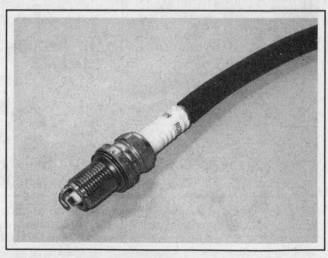

23.12b A length of snug-fitting rubber hose will save time and prevent damaged threads when installing the spark plugs

24 Cooling system servicing (draining, flushing and refilling) (every 30,000 miles or 24 months)

✳✳ WARNING:

Do not allow engine coolant (antifreeze) to come in contact with your skin or painted surfaces of the vehicle. Rinse off spills immediately with plenty of water. Antifreeze is highly toxic if ingested. Never leave antifreeze laying around in an open container or in puddles on the floor; children and pets are attracted by It's sweet smell and may drink it. Check with local authorities about disposing of used antifreeze. Many communities have collection centers which will see that antifreeze is disposed of safely.

1   Periodically, the cooling system should be drained, flushed and refilled to replenish the antifreeze mixture and prevent formation of rust and corrosion, which can impair the performance of the cooling system and cause engine damage. When the cooling system is serviced, all hoses and the radiator cap should be checked and replaced if necessary.

DRAINING

▶ **Refer to illustrations 24.4 and 24.5**

2   Apply the parking brake and block the wheels. If the vehicle has just been driven, wait several hours to allow the engine to cool down before beginning this procedure.

3   Remove the radiator cap.

4   Move a large container under the radiator drain to catch the coolant. Then using a large screwdriver, open the radiator drain plug and direct the coolant into the container (see illustration).

5   After the coolant stops flowing out of the radiator, move the container under the engine block drain plug(s) (see illustration).

➡ **Note: Four-cylinder models have one engine block drain plug, V6 models have two drain plugs, one on each side of the engine block.**

Remove the plug(s) and allow the coolant in the block to drain.

6   While the coolant is draining, check the condition of the radiator hoses, heater hoses and clamps (refer to Section 12 if necessary).

7   Replace any damaged clamps or hoses (see Chapter 3).

FLUSHING

8   Once the system is completely drained, flush the radiator with fresh water from a garden hose until water runs clear at the drain. The flushing action of the water will remove sediments from the radiator but will not remove rust and scale from the engine and cooling tube surfaces.

9   These deposits can be removed by the chemical action of a cleaner. Follow the procedure outlined in the manufacturer's instructions. If the radiator is severely corroded, damaged or leaking, it should be removed (see Chapter 3) and taken to a radiator repair shop.

10   Remove the overflow hose from the coolant recovery reservoir. Drain the reservoir and flush it with clean water, then reconnect the hose.

REFILLING

11   Close and tighten the radiator drain. Install and tighten the engine block drain plug(s).

12   Make sure the heater temperature control is in the maximum heat position.

13   Slowly refill the radiator with a 50/50 mixture of water and antifreeze until coolant reaches the lip on the radiator filler neck. Add coolant to the reservoir up to the lower mark.

14   Leave the radiator cap off and run the engine in a well-ventilated area until the thermostat opens (coolant will begin flowing through the radiator and the upper radiator hose will become hot).

15   Rev the engine to apporoximately 2500 rpm for ten seconds, then let it idle; do this a few times.

16   Turn the engine off and let it cool. Add more coolant mixture to bring the level back up to the lip on the radiator filler neck.

17   Squeeze the upper radiator hose to expel air, then add more coolant mixture if necessary. Replace the radiator cap.

18   Start the engine, allow it to reach normal operating temperature and check for leaks.

24.4 The radiator drain fitting is located at the bottom of the radiator

24.5 After draining the radiator, be sure to fully drain the cooling system by removing the engine block drain plug (four-cylinder engine shown)

25 Evaporative emissions control system check (every 30,000 miles or 24 months)

1   The function of the evaporative emissions control system is to draw fuel vapors from the gas tank and fuel system, store them in a charcoal canister, then burn them during normal engine operation.

2   The most common symptom of a fault in the evaporative emissions system is a strong fuel odor in the engine compartment. If a fuel odor is detected, inspect the charcoal canister, located at the front of the engine compartment. Check the canister and all hoses for damage and deterioration.

3   The evaporative emissions control system is explained in more detail in Chapter 6.

26 Automatic transaxle fluid change (every 60,000 miles or 48 months)

➥Note: Failure to use the correct fluid will damage the transaxle and void the warranty.

1   At the specified time intervals, the automatic transaxle fluid should be drained and replaced.

2   Before beginning work, purchase the specified transaxle fluid (see *Recommended fluids and lubricants* and *Capacities* in this Chapter's Specifications).

3   Other tools necessary for this job include jackstands to support the vehicle in a raised position, a wrench, a large drain pan, newspapers and clean rags.

4   The fluid should be drained after the vehicle has been driven and brought to operating temperature. Hot fluid is more effective than cold fluid at removing built up sediment.

✶✶ WARNING:

Fluid temperature can exceed 350-degrees F in a hot transaxle. Wear protective gloves.

5   Raise the vehicle and place it on jackstands. Put the transaxle in Park and turn off the engine.

6   Move the necessary equipment under the vehicle, being careful not to touch any of the hot exhaust components.

2007 AND 2008 FOUR-CYLINDER MODELS

7   Place the drain pan under the drain plug and remove the drain plug. Be sure the drain pan is in position, as fluid will come out with some force. Once the fluid is drained, reinstall the drain plug securely.

2009 AND LATER FOUR-CYLINDER MODELS AND ALL V6.MODELS

▶ **Refer to illustration 26.8**

8   Disconnect the transaxle fluid cooler line that exits the radiator from the pipe that leads to the transaxle (see illustration). Direct the hose into a drain pan.

9   Remove the dipstick and put a funnel in the tube. Open several quarts of transaxle fluid and set them nearby.

26.8 Follow this hose from the right (driver's) side of the radiator to the pipe, then disconnect the hose from the pipe and direct the end of the hose into a drain pan (2009 and later four-cylinder models and all V6 models)

10 Start the engine and allow it to idle.

11 Observe the fluid coming out of the radiator/cooler while slowly adding new fluid. When the fluid coming out becomes clear, shut off the engine.

12 Connect the transaxle cooler line.

ALL MODELS

13 Lower the vehicle.

14 With the engine off, add new fluid to the transaxle through the dipstick tube (see Section 7). Use a funnel to prevent spills. It is best to add a little fluid at a time, checking the level with the dipstick. Allow the fluid time to drain into the pan.

15 Start the engine and shift the selector into all positions from Park through Low then shift into Park and apply the parking brake.

16 With the engine idling, check the fluid level. Add fluid, a little at a time, until it's up to the Cool level on the dipstick.

27 Manual transaxle lubricant change (every 60,000 miles or 48 months)

1 At the specified time intervals, the manual transaxle lubricant should be drained and replaced.

2 Before beginning work, purchase the specified transaxle lubricant (see *Recommended fluids and lubricants* and *Capacities* in this Chapter's Specifications).

3 Other tools necessary for this job include jackstands to support the vehicle in a raised position, 3/8-inch drive ratchet, a drain pan capable of holding at least four quarts, newspapers and clean rags.

4 Remove the check/fill plug from the top of the transaxle (to the rear of the clutch housing, near the firewall), then remove the drain plug and allow the old oil to drain into the pan.

5 Reinstall the drain plug securely.

6 Add new fluid using a funnel. Refer to Section 19 for information about setting the fluid level to the proper height.

7 Install the check/fill plug.

28 Positive Crankcase Ventilation (PCV) valve check and replacement (every 30,000 miles or 24 months)

▶ **Refer to illustrations 28.1a and 28.1b**

1 Remove the engine cover, then locate the PCV valve on the valve cover (see illustrations).

2 Disconnect the hose, then remove the PCV valve.

3 With the engine idling at normal operating temperature, place your finger over the end of the valve. If there's no vacuum at the valve, check for a plugged hose or valve. Replace any plugged or deteriorated hoses.

4 When purchasing a replacement PCV valve, make sure it's for your particular vehicle and engine size. Compare the old valve with the new one to make sure they're the same.

5 Installation is the reverse of removal.

28.1a PCV valve location - four-cylinder engine

28.1b PCV valve location - V6 engine

29 Valve clearance check and adjustment (every 60,000 miles or 48 months)

▶ **Refer to illustrations 29.6a, 29.6b, 29.6c, 29.7a, 29.7b, 29.8 and 29.10**

➡**Note: The manufacturer recommends adjusting the valve clearance at the specified interval only if the valve train is making excessive noise.**

1 Disconnect the cable from the negative terminal of the battery (see Chapter 5).

2 Remove the valve cover(s) (see Chapter 2A or 2B).

3 On manual transaxle vehicles, set the parking brake and place the transaxle in the neutral position.

4 Remove the spark plugs (see Section 23).

5 Position the number 1 piston at TDC on the compression stroke and align the timing marks (see Chapter 2A or 2B).

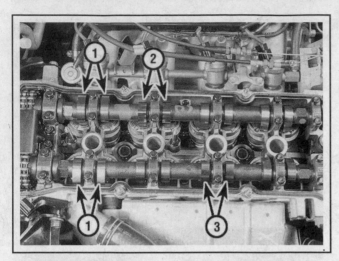

29.6a On four-cylinder engines, when the no. 1 piston is at TDC on the compression stroke, the valve clearance for the no. 1 and no. 3 cylinder exhaust valves and the no. 1 and no. 2 cylinder intake valves can be measured

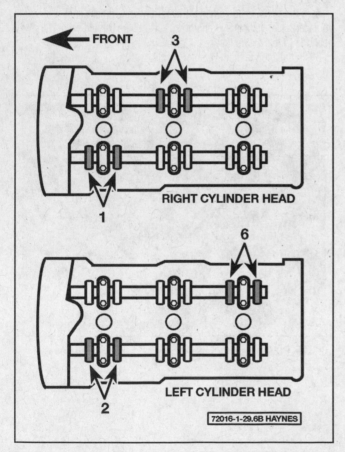

29.6b On V6 engines, when the no. 1 piston is at TDC on the compression stroke, the valve clearance for the no. 1 and no. 6 cylinder intake valves and the no. 2 and no. 3 cylinder exhaust valves can be measured

6   Measure the clearance of the indicated valves with a feeler gauge (see illustrations). Record each measurement and compare your measurements with the desired valve clearance found in this Chapter's Specifications. Note which are out of specification; this data will be used later to determine the required lifter.

7   On four-cylinder engines, turn the crankshaft one complete revolution and realign the timing marks. On V6 engines, turn the crankshaft 240 degrees (2/3-turn). Measure and record the clearances of the valves (see illustrations).

8   On V6 engines only, rotate the crankshaft an additional 240 degrees and perform the same operation for the remaining valves (see illustration).

9   These engines don't use valve adjusting shims. If a clearance is out of specification, the lifter must be replaced with a new lifter that has a different thickness head to correct the clearance. Refer to Chapter 2 and remove the camshafts to access the lifters.

10 Mark the lifters that are to be replaced, and record which valve they came from. Measure the thickness of the center of the lifter with a micrometer (see illustration). To calculate the correct thickness of a replacement lifter that will place the valve clearance within the specified value, use the following formula:

$$N = T + A - V$$

N = thickness of the new lifter
T = thickness of the old lifter
A = valve clearance measured
V = desired valve clearance (see this Chapter's Specifications)

11 Select a lifter with a thickness as close as possible to the valve clearance calculated. Lifters are marked on the underside as to their size.

12 Mark the new lifters as to their destination, lubricate them with engine assembly lube and install them. After replacing the lifters, refer to Chapter 2A or 2B and install the camshaft(s).

13 The remainder of installation is the reverse of removal. Reconnect the battery and perform the necessary re-learn procedures (see Chapter 5).

29.6c You will feel drag as you pull the feeler gauge if the adjustment is correct

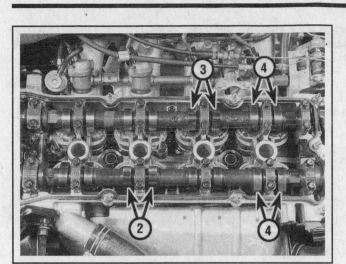

29.7a On four-cylinder engines, when the no. 4 piston is at TDC on the compression stroke, the valve clearances for the no. 2 and no. 4 cylinder exhaust valves and the no. 3 and no. 4 cylinder intake valves can be measured

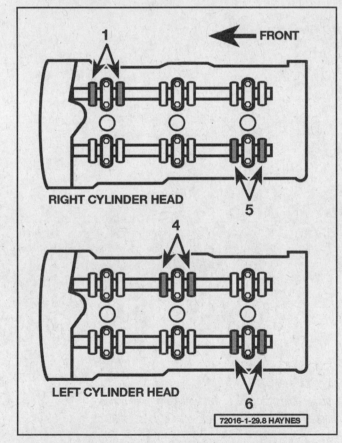

29.8 On V6 engines, after checking the valves indicated in illustration 29.7b, turn the crankshaft an additional 240 degrees (2/3 turn) clockwise and check the valve clearances for the no. 4 and no. 5 cylinder intake valves and the no. 1 and no. 6 cylinder exhaust valves can be measured

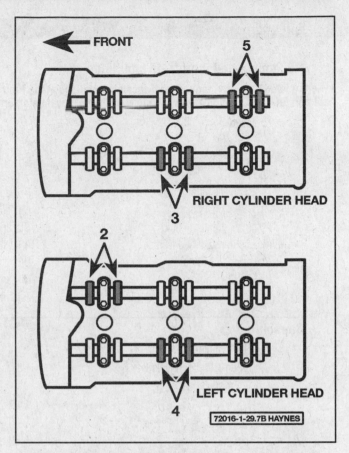

29.7b On V6 engines, after checking the valves indicated in illustration 29.6b, turn the crankshaft 240 degrees (2/3 turn) clockwise and check the valve clearances for the no. 2 and no. 3 cylinder intake valves and the no. 4 and no. 5 cylinder exhaust valves can be measured

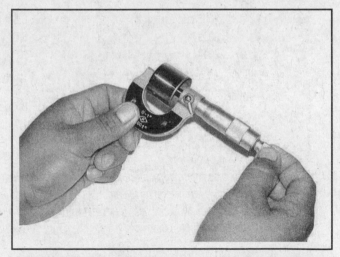

29.10 Measure the lifter thickness with a micrometer

Specifications

Recommended lubricants and fluids

➡Note: Listed here are manufacturer recommendations at the time this manual was written. Manufacturers occasionally upgrade their fluid and lubricant specifications, so check with your local auto parts store for current recommendations.

Engine oil	
Type	API "certified for gasoline engines"
Viscosity	SAE 5W-30
Fuel	
Four-cylinder models	Unleaded gasoline, 87 octane or higher
V6 models	Unleaded gasoline, 91 octane or higher
Automatic transaxle fluid	Nissan CVT fluid NS-2
Manual transaxle lubricant	API GL-4 75W-85 gear oil
Brake and clutch fluid	DOT 3 brake fluid or equivalent
Power steering fluid	Nissan PSF power steering fluid or DEXRON VI automatic transmission fluid

Capacities*

Engine oil (including filter)	
Four-cylinder models	4.8 quarts
V6 models	
2007	4.5 quarts
2008 and 2009	4.8 quarts
2010	5.1 quarts
Coolant (including reservoir tank)	
Four-cylinder models	
2008 and earlier	6.4 quarts
2009	8 quarts
2010	8.1 quarts
V6 models	
2008 and earlier	6.8 quarts
2009	8.6
2010	9.5
Automatic transaxle**	
Four-cylinder models	
2009 and earlier models	8.7 quarts
2010 models	7.7 quarts
V6 models	10.7 quarts
Manual transaxle	Up to 3.7 pints

*All capacities approximate. Add as necessary to bring up to appropriate level.

**The best way to determine the amount of fluid to add during a routine fluid change is to measure the amount drained. Additionally, on 2009 and later four-cylinder models and all V6 models, the fluid changing procedure will require 30 to 50-percent more fluid than what is listed here (refer to Section 26).

Ignition system

Spark plugs	
Four-cylinder engine	
2009 and earlier	
Type	NGK DILKAR6A-11 or equivalent
Gap	0.043 inch

Four-cylinder engine (continued)
    2010
        Type   Denso FXE22HR-11 or equivalent
        Gap   0.043 inch
V6 engine
    2008 and earlier
        Type   Denso FXE20HR-11 or equivalent
        Gap   0.043 inch
    2009 and later
        Type   Denso FXE22HR-11 or equivalent
        Gap   0.043 inch
Firing order
    Four-cylinder engine   1-3-4-2
    V6 engine   1-2-3-4-5-6

2.5L four-cylinder engine

72015-1-specs HAYNES

3.5L V6 engine

72015-1-specs HAYNES

Cylinder locations

Valve clearance (engine cold)

Four-cylinder engine
    Intake valves   0.009 to 0.013 inch
    Exhaust valves   0.010 to 0.013 inch
V6 engine
    Intake valves   0.010 to 0.013 inch
    Exhaust valves   0.011 to 0.015 inch

Cooling system

Thermostat starts to open
    Four-cylinder models   177 to 182-degrees F
    V6 models   180-degrees F

Brakes

Disc brake pad lining thickness (minimum)
    Front   0.08 inch
    Rear   0.04 inch
Brake pedal   See Chapter 9
Parking brake adjustment   See Chapter 9

Suspension and steering

Steering wheel freeplay limit	1-3/8 inches
Balljoint allowable movement	0 inch

Torque specifications	Ft-lbs
Engine oil drain plug	25
Automatic transaxle drain plug	25
Drivebelt tensioner mounting bolts	18
Manual transaxle drain plug	25
Manual transaxle fill plug	39
Spark plugs	14 to 22
Wheel lug nuts	83

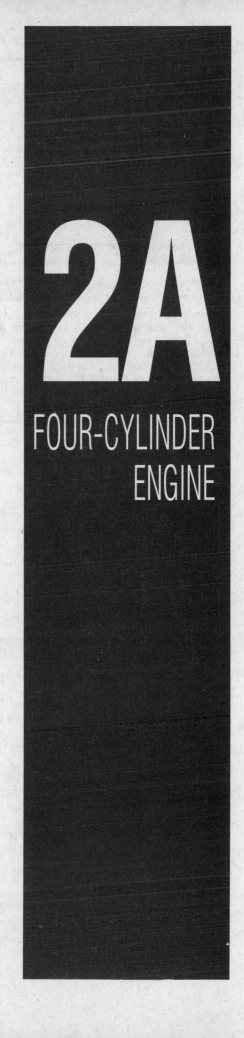

2A

FOUR-CYLINDER ENGINE

Section

Reference to other Chapters

1 General information

This Part of Chapter 2 is devoted to in-vehicle repair procedures for the four-cylinder engine. Information concerning engine removal and installation and engine overhaul can be found in Part C of this Chapter. The following repair procedures are based on the assumption that the engine is installed in the vehicle. If the engine has been removed from the vehicle and mounted on a stand, many of the steps outlined in this Part of Chapter 2 will not apply.

2 Repair operations possible with the engine in the vehicle

✳✳ WARNING:

The models covered by this manual are equipped with a Supplemental Restraint System (SRS), more commonly known as airbags. Always disarm the airbag system before working in the vicinity of any airbag system component to avoid the possibility of accidental deployment of the airbag, which could cause personal injury (see Chapter 12). Do not use a memory saving device to preserve the PCM's memory when working on or near airbag system components.

Many major repair operations can be accomplished without removing the engine from the vehicle.

Clean the engine compartment and the exterior of the engine with some type of degreaser before any work is done. It will make the job easier and help keep dirt out of the internal areas of the engine.

Depending on the components involved, it may be helpful to remove the hood to improve access to the engine as repairs are performed (refer to Chapter 11 if necessary). Cover the fenders to prevent damage to the paint. Special pads are available, but an old bedspread or blanket will also work.

If vacuum, exhaust, oil or coolant leaks develop, indicating a need for gasket or seal replacement, the repairs can generally be made with the engine in the vehicle. The intake and exhaust manifold gaskets, oil pan gasket, crankshaft oil seals and cylinder head gasket are all accessible with the engine in place.

Exterior engine components, such as the intake and exhaust manifolds, the oil pan, the oil pump, the water pump, the starter motor, the alternator, and the fuel system components can be removed for repair with the engine in place.

Since the cylinder head can be removed without pulling the engine, camshaft and valve component servicing can also be accomplished with the engine in the vehicle. Replacement of the timing chain and sprockets is also possible with the engine in the vehicle.

In extreme cases caused by a lack of necessary equipment, repair or replacement of piston rings, pistons, connecting rods and rod bearings is possible with the engine in the vehicle. However, this practice is not recommended because of the cleaning and preparation work that must be done to the components involved.

3 Top Dead Center (TDC) for number one piston - locating

▶ **Refer to illustrations 3.6 and 3.8**

1   Top Dead Center (TDC) is the highest point in the cylinder that each piston reaches as it travels up-and-down when the crankshaft turns. Each piston reaches TDC on the compression stroke and again on the exhaust stroke, but TDC generally refers to piston position on the compression stroke.

2   Positioning the number one piston at TDC is an essential part of many procedures, such as camshaft, timing chain or distributor removal.

3   Before beginning this procedure, be sure to place the transmission in Park or Neutral and apply the parking brake or block the rear wheels. If method b) or c) in the next Step will be used to rotate the engine, disable the fuel system by removing the fuel pump fuse (see Chapter 4, Section 2). Remove the spark plugs (see Chapter 1).

4   In order to bring any piston to TDC, the crankshaft must be turned using one of the methods outlined below. When looking at the front of the engine (timing chain end), normal crankshaft rotation is clockwise.

   a) *The preferred method is to turn the crankshaft with a socket and ratchet attached to the bolt threaded into the front of the crankshaft.*

   b) *A remote starter switch, which may save some time, can also be used. Follow the instructions included with the switch. Once the piston is close to TDC, use a socket and ratchet as described in the previous paragraph.*

   c) *If an assistant is available to turn the ignition switch to the Start position in short bursts, you can get the piston close to TDC without a remote starter switch. Make sure your assistant is out of the vehicle, away from the ignition switch, then use a socket and ratchet as described in Paragraph a) to complete the procedure.*

5   Install a compression pressure gauge in the number one spark plug hole (see Chapter 2C). It should be a gauge with a screw-in fitting and a hose at least six inches long.

6   Remove the inner fender splash shield (see illustration). Rotate the crankshaft using one of the methods described above while observing for pressure on the compression gauge. The moment the gauge shows pressure indicates that the number one cylinder has begun the compression stroke.

7   Once the compression stroke has begun, TDC for the compression stroke is reached by bringing the piston to the top of the cylinder.

8   Continue turning the crankshaft until the TDC notch in the crank-

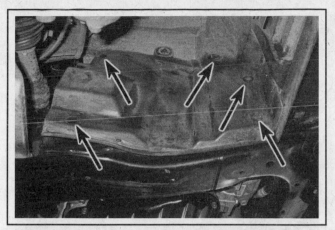

3.6 Remove the right inner fender splash shield retainers to access the crankshaft pulley

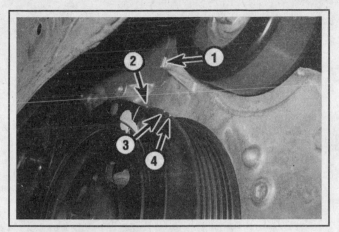

3.8 Top Dead Center (TDC) details

1	Pointer on timing chain cover	3	10-degrees BTDC
2	TDC mark	4	15-degrees BTDC

shaft damper is aligned with the pointer on the timing chain cover (see illustration). At this point, the number one cylinder is at TDC on the compression stroke. If the marks are aligned but there was no compression, the piston was on the exhaust stroke. Continue rotating the crankshaft 360-degrees (1-turn).

➡**Note: If a compression gauge is not available, you can simply place a blunt object (such as the end of a screwdriver handle) over the spark plug hole and listen for compression as the**

engine is rotated. Once compression at the No. 1 spark plug hole is noted, the remainder of the Step is the same.

9   After the number one piston has been positioned at TDC on the compression stroke, TDC for any of the remaining cylinders can be located by turning the crankshaft 180-degrees and following the firing order (refer to the Specifications). For example, rotating the engine 180-degrees past TDC #1 will put the engine at TDC compression for cylinder #3.

4   Valve cover - removal and installation

REMOVAL

▶ **Refer to illustrations 4.5a, 4.5b and 4.10**

1   Disconnect the cable from the negative terminal of the battery (see Chapter 5).
2   Remove the engine cover and the front air inlet duct.

3   Remove the engine blow-by hose.
4   Remove the power steering fluid reservoir and move it out of the way.
5   Support the engine from below using a block of wood on a floor jack or from above using an engine support fixture. Remove the right top engine mount components that interfere with the valve cover (see illustrations).

4.5a With the engine supported securely from below, remove these mounts

4.5b Disconnect the ground wires and remove the upper engine support bracket for access to the valve cover bolts

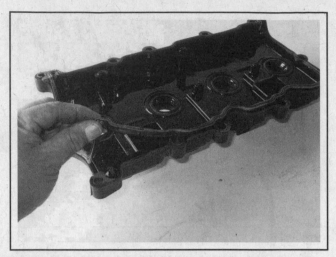

4.10 Remove the gasket from the cover and install a new one

4.12 Apply a bead of RTV sealant to these inside corners to avoid leaks

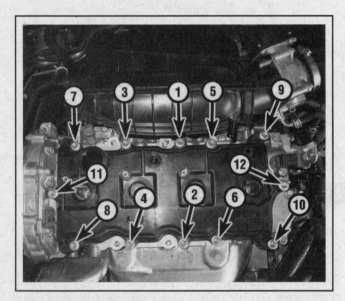

4.13 Valve cover bolt tightening sequence

6   Disconnect the PCV hose.

7   Remove the ignition coils (see Chapter 5).

8   Disconnect the electrical connectors from the fuel injectors. Move the injector wiring harness aside.

9   Remove the bolts around the cover's perimeter in the order opposite the tightening sequence (see illustration 4.13). Loosen the bolts starting at the ends and work toward the center. If the cover is stuck to the cylinder head, bump the end with a wood block and a hammer to jar it loose. If that doesn't work, try to slip a flexible putty knife between the cylinder head and cover to break the seal.

✳✳ CAUTION:

Don't pry at the cover or housing-to-cylinder head joint or damage to the sealing surfaces may occur, leading to oil leaks after the cover is reinstalled.

10 Remove the gasket from the valve cover (see illustration).

INSTALLATION

♦ **Refer to illustrations 4.12 and 4.13**

11 The mating surfaces of the valve cover and cylinder head must be clean when the cover is installed. Use a gasket scraper to remove all traces of sealant from the areas shown in illustration 4.12, then clean the mating surfaces with lacquer thinner or acetone. If there's residue or oil on the mating surfaces when the cover is installed, oil leaks may develop.

✳✳ CAUTION:

Use care when scraping the soft aluminum of the cylinder head or the plastic valve cover. It is soft, and deep scratches may lead to oil leaks.

12 Install the valve cover with a new gasket. Apply RTV sealant to the indicated areas (see illustration).

13 Tighten the bolts in the indicated sequence to the torque listed in this Chapter's Specifications (see illustration).

14 The remainder of installation is the reverse of the removal procedure.

15 Reconnect the battery and perform the necessary re-learn procedures (see Chapter 5).

5   Intake manifold - removal and installation

✳✳ **WARNING:**

The engine must be completely cool before beginning this procedure.

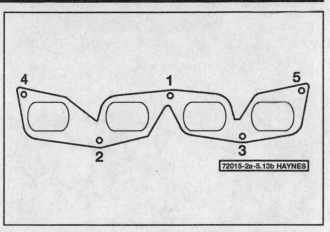

5.12 Intake manifold bolt tightening sequence - re-torque bolt 1 after finishing

REMOVAL

1   Relieve the fuel system pressure (see Chapter 4).

2   Disconnect the cable from the negative terminal of the battery (see Chapter 5).

3   Remove the cowl cover (see Chapter 11) and the fender support brace.

4   Remove the blow-by hose and the intake air ducts.

5   Label and detach the PCV hose, brake booster hose, throttle control actuator, the EVAP hose and the purge control solenoid. Clamp off then disconnect the coolant hoses connected to the throttle body.

6   Remove the fuel rail and injectors from the manifold adapter (see Chapter 4).

7   Remove the intake manifold collector mounting nuts and bolts. Start with the end bolts and work toward the center bolt in the reverse of the tightening sequence (see illustration 5.12).

8   Remove the intake manifold collector and the intake manifold adapter from the cylinder head.

INSTALLATION

▸ **Refer to illustration 5.12**

9   Use a scraper to remove all traces of old gasket material and

sealant from the manifold and cylinder head, then clean the mating surfaces with brake system cleaner.

10 Install a new gasket, then position the intake manifold adapter on the cylinder head studs.

11 Install a new gasket, then position the intake manifold collector on the lower intake manifold adapter and install the nuts/bolts.

12 Tighten the nuts/bolts to the torque listed in this Chapter's Specifications. Follow the recommended tightening sequence (see illustration). Re-torque bolt number one when you're done with number 5.

13 Install the remaining parts in the reverse order of removal.

14 Reconnect the battery and perform the necessary re-learn procedures (see Chapter 5).

6   Exhaust manifold - removal and installation

✳✳ **WARNING:**

The engine must be completely cool before beginning this procedure.

REMOVAL

▸ **Refer to illustration 6.7**

1   Disconnect the cable from the negative terminal of the battery (see Chapter 5).

2   Block the rear wheels and set the parking brake. Loosen the lug nuts of the right front wheel. Raise the front of the vehicle and support it securely on jackstands. Remove the right front wheel.

3   Remove the engine splash shields.

4   Remove the right inner fender splash shield (see Chapter 11), then remove the drivebelt (see Chapter 1).

5   Remove the alternator (see Chapter 5).

6   Disconnect the electrical connector from the oxygen sensor (see Chapter 6).

7   Remove the heat shield from the exhaust manifold (see illustration).

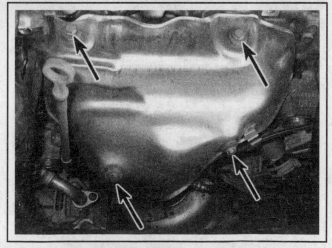

6.7 Remove the exhaust manifold heat shield bolts

8   Disconnect the exhaust pipe from the exhaust manifold.

➡ **Note: Applying penetrating oil to the exhaust manifold fasteners may make removing the nuts/bolts easier.**

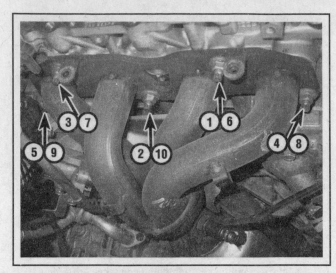

6.14 Each exhaust manifold nut must be tightened twice in this sequence

9   Remove the exhaust manifold brace.

10 Remove the exhaust manifold-to-cylinder head nuts, working from the outside toward the middle, and detach the manifold and gasket.

INSTALLATION

▸ **Refer to illustration 6.14**

11 Use a scraper to remove all traces of old gasket material and carbon deposits from the exhaust manifold and cylinder head mating surfaces.

12 Position the new exhaust manifold gasket over the cylinder head studs.

13 Install the manifold and thread the mounting nuts into place.

14 Working in the correct sequences, tighten the nuts to the torque listed in this Chapter's Specifications (see illustration).

15 Reinstall the remaining parts in the reverse order of removal. Use anti-seize lubricant on the exhaust pipe studs.

16 Reconnect the battery and perform the necessary re-learn procedures (see Chapter 5).

7   Crankshaft front oil seal - replacement

▸ **Refer to illustrations 7.5, 7.6, 7.8 and 7.9**

1   Loosen the lug nuts of the right front wheel. Raise the vehicle and support it securely on jackstands. Remove the right front wheel.

2   Remove the right inner wheel well (see Chapter 11).

3   Remove the drivebelts (see Chapter 1).

4   Remove the crankshaft pulley bolt. If necessary, have an assistant hold the crankshaft from turning by wedging a screwdriver in the flywheel/driveplate teeth through the access hole.

5   Use a puller to remove the pulley from the crankshaft (see illustration).

6   Use a seal-puller tool, or wrap the tip of a screwdriver with tape, to pry out the seal, being careful not to damage the seal bore or scratch the surface of the crankshaft snout (see illustration).

7   Clean the bore in the timing chain cover and coat the outer edge of the new seal with engine oil or multi-purpose grease. Also lubricate the seal lips.

8   Using a seal driver or a socket with an outside diameter slightly smaller than the outside diameter of the seal, carefully drive the new seal into place (see illustration). Make sure it's installed squarely and driven in to the same depth as the original. Check the seal after installation to make sure the garter spring didn't pop out of place.

✳✳ CAUTION:

Be sure to use the proper adapter on the end of the crankshaft to prevent damage to the threads or end of the crankshaft. Also, the jaws of the puller must bolt to the hub of the pulley or grasp the hub of the pulley, not the outer diameter.

✳✳ CAUTION:

The oil seal lip goes toward the engine, and the dust seal lip toward the pulley.

7.5 Remove the pulley from the crankshaft using a puller

7.6 Use a seal puller or screwdriver, with the tip wrapped in tape, to pry the seal out of the timing chain cover

7.8 Drive the new seal squarely into the timing chain cover with a seal driver or a large socket

7.9 It's best to use a pulley installation tool to press the crankshaft pulley into place

9   Reinstall the crankshaft pulley and drivebelt (see illustration). Tighten the crankshaft pulley bolt to the torque listed in this Chap-ter's Specifications.

10 Run the engine and check for oil leaks.

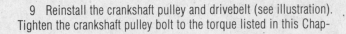

8   Timing chain/balance shaft chain and sprockets - removal, inspection and installation

✳✳ WARNING:

The engine must be completely cool before beginning this pro-cedure.

✳✳ CAUTION:

The timing system is complex. Severe engine damage will occur if you make any mistakes. Do not attempt this procedure unless you are highly experienced with this type of repair. If you are at all unsure of your abilities, consult an expert. Double-check all your work and be sure everything is correct before you attempt to start the engine.

➡Note: The manufacturer recommends that the engine be removed for this procedure. This Section describes servicing the timing chain assembly with the engine in the vehicle, however it is usually easier to remove the engine first. See Chapter 2C for more information on engine removal. If you choose to remove the engine for this procedure, ignore the steps which don't apply.

REMOVAL

▶ Refer to illustration 8.11

1   Relieve the fuel system pressure (see Chapter 4).

2   Position the engine at TDC for cylinder number one (see Sec-tion 3). Disconnect the cable from the negative terminal of the battery (see Chapter 5).

3   Remove the coolant reservoir.

4   Remove the alternator and bracket (see Chapter 5).

5   Remove the valve cover (see Section 4).

6   Support the engine from above with an engine hoist or an engine support fixture.

7   Remove the oil pan and strainer (see Section 12).

8   Disconnect the electrical connector for the Intake Valve Timing (IVT) control solenoid.

9   Remove the bolts retaining the IVT/camshaft sprocket cover to the timing chain main cover. Remove the cover.

➡Note: Use a sharp tool to cut the RTV sealant securing the cover. Remove the bolts in the reverse of the tightening sequence (see illustration 8.33).

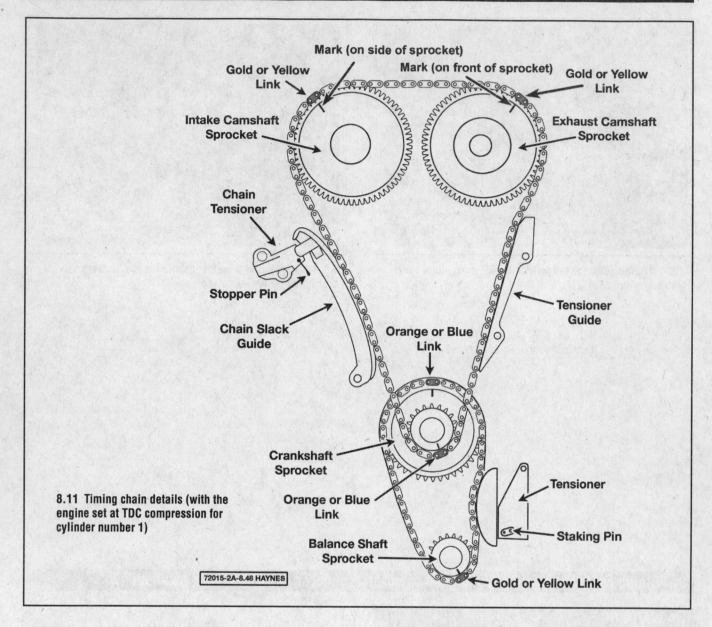

8.11 Timing chain details (with the engine set at TDC compression for cylinder number 1)

72015-2A-8.48 HAYNES

10 Remove the upper chain guide from between the two camshaft sprockets.

11 Check the positions of the camshaft sprockets. They should be aligned at TDC number 1 (see illustration).

12 Remove the crankshaft pulley (see Section 7). Don't allow the crankshaft to turn while removing the bolt.

13 Remove the timing chain cover. Follow the reverse of the tightening sequence to remove the bolts (see illustration 8.32).

14 Using the tip of a screwdriver, push down on the tensioner plunger and insert a stopper pin of the correct diameter into the hole on the tensioner. Once the tensioner is locked in the retracted position, remove the bolts and the tensioner from the front of the engine.

15 Remove the timing chain.

16 Use an open-end wrench on the hex of the camshaft to hold the camshaft as you unbolt the camshaft sprocket bolts. If the chain is being removed for removal of the camshafts or cylinder head only, skip the remainder of this removal procedure.

17 Remove the timing chain tensioner, the tensioner guide, and the oil pump drive spacer.

18 Remove the balance shaft chain. Lift the tensioner lever up to release the ratchet claw mechanism on the balance shaft chain tensioner.

19 Pull the tensioner sleeve in and hold the sleeve stationary, then install a staking pin into the lever to lock the lever with the tensioner sleeve.

20 Remove the balance shaft tensioner bolts and the tensioner.

21 Remove the balance shaft chain and the crankshaft sprocket.

22 Remove the balance shaft unit mounting bolts. Follow the reverse of the tightening sequence (see illustration 8.24).

INSPECTION

23 Inspect the camshaft, idler and crankshaft sprockets for wear of the teeth and keyways. Inspect the chains for cracks or excessive wear of the rollers. Inspect the facing of the chain guides for excessive wear.

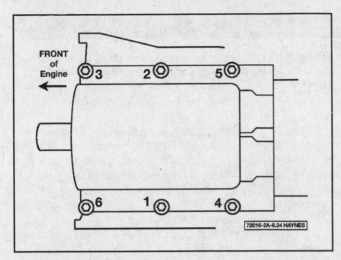

8.24 Bolt tightening sequence for the balance shaft assembly

INSTALLATION

▶ **Refer to illustrations 8.24, 8.32 and 8.33**

24 Install the balance shaft unit using new bolts, then tighten the bolts to the torque listed in this Chapter's Specifications following the proper sequence (see illustration).

25 Install the crankshaft sprocket and the balance shaft chain. Make sure the colored links on the balance shaft chain align with the mating marks on the crankshaft sprocket and the balance shaft sprocket.

26 Install the balance shaft tensioner bolts and the tensioner. The bolt hole positions may have changed since the tensioner was removed. The chain guide and the tensioner move freely with the staking pin as the pivot. First align and tighten the two chain tensioner bolts and move the tensioner to match the bolt holes.

27 Double-check the balance shaft chain alignment marks. Repeat the procedure if the alignment marks are incorrect. Release the staking pin from the tensioner to apply tension to the balance shaft chain.

28 Install the timing chain, aligning the colored links with the mating marks on the camshaft and crankshaft sprockets (see illustration 8.11).

29 Install the timing chain guide and chain slack guide. Tighten the bolts to the torque listed in this Chapter's Specifications.

30 Install the timing chain tensioner and release the stopper pin. Double-check the timing chain alignment marks, and if they are incorrect, repeat the procedure. Tighten the sprocket bolts to the torque listed in this Chapter's Specifications.

31 Apply a bead of RTV sealant to the mating surfaces around the perimeter of the timing chain cover, as well as around the bolt hole in the center (bolt no. 11 in illustration 8.32).

32 Install the timing chain cover. Tighten the cover bolts in the correct sequence (see illustration) and to the torque listed in this Chapter's Specifications.

33 Apply a bead of RTV sealant to the mating surfaces around the perimeter of the IVT/camshaft sprocket cover. Install the cover and tighten the bolts, in the correct sequence, to the torque listed in this Chapter's Specifications (see illustration).

34 The remainder of the installation is the reverse of the disassembly sequence.

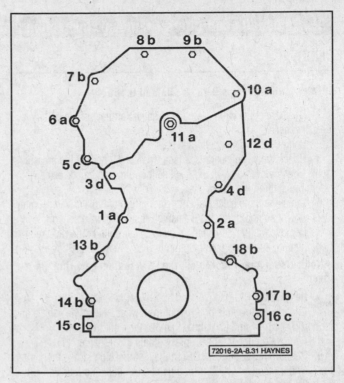

8.32 Timing chain main cover bolt tightening sequence; the letters refer to bolt lengths (bolts of different lengths have different torque values, as noted in this Chapter's Specifications)

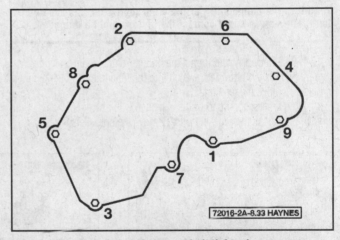

8.33 IVT/camshaft sprocket cover bolt tightening sequence

✳✳ CAUTION:

Before starting the engine, carefully rotate the crankshaft by hand through at least two full revolutions (use a socket and breaker bar on the crankshaft pulley center bolt). If you feel any resistance, STOP! There is something wrong - most likely valves are contacting the pistons. You must find the problem before proceeding.

35 Reconnect the battery and perform the necessary re-learn procedures (see Chapter 5).

9 Camshafts and lifters - removal, inspection and installation

REMOVAL

▶ **Refer to illustrations 9.13, 9.16a and 9.16b**

1   Disconnect the cable from the negative terminal of the battery (see Chapter 5).

2   Remove the valve cover (see Section 4).

3   Check the valve clearances (see Chapter 1). Record the measurements; if any valves are out of specification, they can be corrected before reinstalling the camshafts.

4   Disconnect the electrical connectors from the Intake Valve Timing (IVT) control solenoid and the Camshaft Position (CMP) sensor.

5   Remove the IVT/camshaft sprocket cover bolts in the reverse of the tightening sequence (see illustration 8.33). Remove the cover.

➡**Note: Use a sharp tool to cut the RTV sealant securing the cover.**

6   Remove the CMP sensor and its bracket (see Chapter 6).

7   Loosen the lug nuts of the right front wheel. Raise the vehicle and support it securely on jackstands. Remove the right front wheel.

8   Remove the inner fender splash shield (see Chapter 11).

9   Position the engine at TDC on the compression stroke for number one cylinder (see Section 3). Using paint or an indelible marker, mark the links of the timing chain that correspond to the timing marks on the camshaft sprockets (see illustration 8.11).

※※ **CAUTION:**

Don't turn the camshaft(s) or the crankshaft after this has been done. The valves could contact the pistons and be damaged.

10   Use a screwdriver to retract the plunger of the chain tensioner, then insert a drill bit or Allen wrench into the hole to secure the plunger in place. Remove the tensioner.

11   Hold the hexagon part of the camshaft with a wrench, then remove the camshaft sprocket bolts. Remove the sprockets.

➡**Note: It isn't necessary to maintain tension on the timing chain; the timing chain won't separate from the crankshaft sprocket.**

12   Remove the upper timing chain guide through the timing chain cover.

13   Before removing the camshafts, use a dial indicator to check camshaft endplay (see illustration). Mount the dial indicator so the gauge tip can be placed at the end of the camshaft. Move the camshaft all the way to the rear and zero the dial indicator. Next, use a screwdriver to pry it all the way forward. If the endplay (the total amount of movement) exceeds the limit listed in this Chapter's Specifications, replace the camshaft and/or cylinder head.

14   Loosen the camshaft bearing caps in the reverse of the tightening sequence (see illustrations 9.23b).

※※ **CAUTION:**

Keep the caps in order. They must go back in the same locations from which they were removed.

15   Remove the bearing caps and lift the camshafts straight up and out.

16   Pull the lifters straight up and store them in numbered plastic bags or a marked box (see illustrations).

INSPECTION

▶ **Refer to illustrations 9.18a, 9.18b, 9.19a, and 9.19b**

17   Visually examine the camshaft lobes, journals, bearing caps and lifters. Check for score marks, pitting and evidence of overheating (blue, discolored areas). If wear is excessive or damage is evident, the component will have to be replaced.

18   Using a micrometer, measure camshaft journal diameter and lobe height (see illustrations), and compare your measurements to this

9.13 With a dial indicator in place, pry the camshaft forward and back to check the camshaft endplay

9.16a Pull the lifters straight up to remove them

9.16b The lifters can be stored in individually-marked plastic bags, or in a divided, marked box like this one

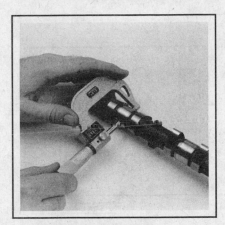

9.18a Measure each journal diameter with a micrometer (if any journal measures less than the specified limit, replace the camshaft)

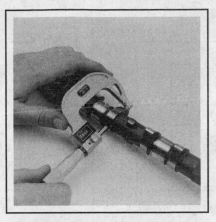

9.18b Measure the lobe heights - if any lobe height is less than the minimum listed in this Chapter's Specifications, replace the camshaft

9.19a Place a strip of Plastigage under each camshaft bearing cap and tighten the caps to Specifications

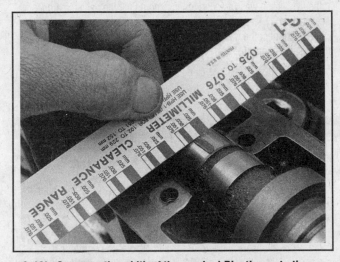

9.19b Compare the width of the crushed Plastigage to the scale on the envelope to determine the oil clearance

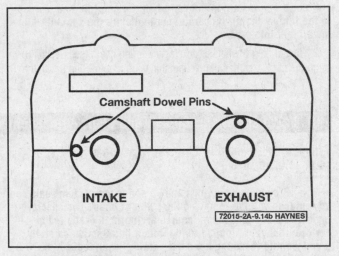

9.22 Correct positions of the dowel pins for camshaft installation

Chapter's Specifications. If the lobe height is less than the minimum allowable, the camshaft is worn and must be replaced.

19 Check the oil clearance for each camshaft journal as follows:

a) *Clean the bearing caps and the camshaft journals with brake system cleaner.*

b) *Carefully lay the camshafts in place in the cylinder head. DON'T use any lubrication.*

c) *Lay a strip of Plastigage on each journal.*

d) *Install the bearing caps with the arrows pointing toward the front (timing chain end) of the engine.*

e) *Tighten the bolts in sequence (see illustration 9.23b) to the torque listed in this Chapter's Specifications in 1/4-turn increments.*

✳✳ CAUTION:

Don't turn the camshaft while the Plastigage is in place.

f) *Remove the bolts, in the proper sequence, and detach the bearing caps.*

g) *Compare the width of the crushed Plastigage (at it's widest point) to the scale on the Plastigage envelope (see illustrations).*

h) *If the clearance is greater than specified, replace the camshaft and/or cylinder head.*

20 Scrape off the Plastigage with your fingernail or the edge of a credit card - don't scratch or nick the journals or bearing caps.

INSTALLATION

◆ **Refer to illustrations 9.22, 9.23a and 9.23b**

21 Apply moly-based engine assembly lubricant to the camshaft lobes and journals.

22 Install the camshafts in their original positions at TDC.

➡**Note: The camshaft dowel pins must face the 12 o'clock position (exhaust camshaft) and 9 o'clock position (intake camshaft) (see illustration).**

23 Apply a 1/8-inch bead of RTV sealant to the mating surface of the timing chain cover. Install the bearing caps and bolts and tighten

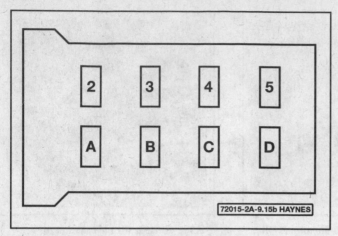

9.23a Camshaft bearing cap designations

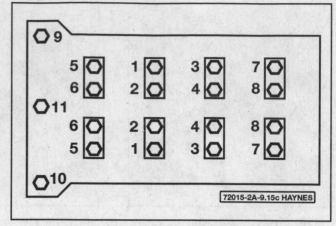

9.23b Camshaft bearing cap bolt tightening sequence

them in sequence (see illustrations) to the torque listed in this Chapter's Specifications.

➡ **Note: When installing the no. 1 bearing cap (the one closest to the timing chain), be careful not to disturb the sealant while lowering it into place.**

24 Install the camshaft sprockets and timing chain (see Section 8). Align the marks on the timing chain that you made in Step 9 with the timing marks on the camshaft spockets

25 The remainder of installation is the reverse of removal. If any part of the valve train was replaced, check and adjust the valve clearance (see Chapter 1).

26 Reconnect the battery and perform the necessary re-learn procedures (see Chapter 5).

---

10 Valve springs, retainers and seals - replacement

◆ Refer to illustrations 10.1, 10.2a, 10.2b, 10.3, 10.4, 10.7, 10.8, 10.9, 10.10 and 10.11

➡ Note: Broken valve springs and defective valve stem seals can be replaced without removing the cylinder head. Two special tools and a compressed air source are normally required to perform this operation, so read through this Section carefully. If you want to leave the head on, obtain Nissan tools J-26336-B and J-26336-20. They are available from specialty automotive tool suppliers, but they are expensive. It may also be possible to modify another type of spring compressor to work by means of welding and fabrication. Verify the availability of the correct spring compressor before beginning the job. If you can't get the special tools, then you'll have to remove the heads and use a C-clamp type valve spring compressor.

1 Remove the cylinder head (see Section 11), or refer to Chapter 2B, Section 5 for information on removing the valve springs with the cylinder head in place (see illustration).

2 With the cylinder head on a sturdy workbench, use a large, clamp-type valve spring compressor and adapter to compress each valve spring (see illustrations). Make sure the bottom section of the tool is located under the valve which spring is being removed, and compress the spring just enough to remove the keepers with a magnet or small pliers.

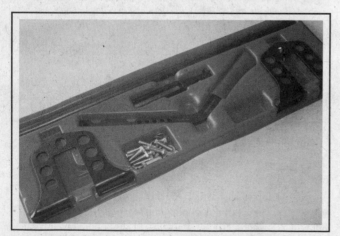

10.1 This is an example of the special valve spring compressor that must be used to avoid having to remove the head

10.2a Compress the valve spring and remove the keepers with needle-nose pliers or a magnet

10.2b Because of the tight quarters, a spring compressor must be used with an adapter that has windows in the side to access the keepers

10.3 Remove the retainer and valve spring

10.4 Remove the valve stem seal with needle-nose pliers

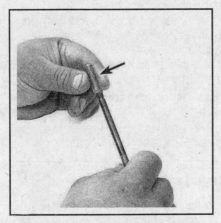

10.7 Slip a plastic sleeve over the valve stem to protect the new seal during installation

10.8 Lubricate the new seal and slip it onto the valve, past the protector

10.9 Tap the new seals down onto the valve guide with a deep socket

3   Pull the valve spring out with its retainer (see illustration).

4   Remove the old valve stem oil seal with pliers (see illustration).

5   Remove the valve and inspect the valve stem for damage. Rotate the valve in the guide and check the end for eccentric movement, which would indicate that the valve is bent.

6   Move the valve up-and-down in the guide and make sure it doesn't bind. If the valve stem binds, either the valve is bent or the guide is damaged. In either case, the cylinder head will require repair.

7   Lubricate the valve stem with engine oil and install it in the cylinder head. A plastic seal protector that slips over the valve stem is usually provided with the seals (see illustration). This protects the new seal from being torn as it passes over the keeper grooves in the valve. If you don't have the seal protector, apply a few wraps of cellulose tape around the valve stem instead.

8   Lubricate the new seal with multi-purpose grease and push it down over the valve stem by hand (see illustration). When it is down against the guide, remove the plastic protector or tape from the valve stem.

9   Use a deep socket of the appropriate size to lightly tap the new seal down against the top of the valve guide (see illustration).

10   Install the spring in position over the valve, with the retainer in place (see illustration).

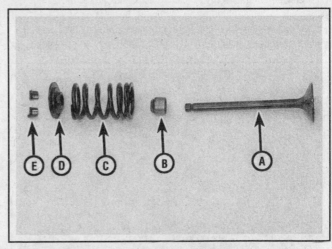

10.10 Arrangement of valve components

A   Valve
B   Valve stem seal
C   Valve spring
D   Retainer
E   Keepers

10.11 Apply a small dab of grease to each keeper before installation to retain them in place on the valve stem until the spring is released

11 Compress the valve spring and retainer and carefully position the keepers in the groove. Apply a small dab of grease to the inside of each keeper to retain it in place if necessary (see illustration) and insert them with needle-nose pliers.

12 Remove the pressure from the spring tool and make sure the keepers are seated.

13 Reinstall the lifters and camshafts (see Section 9).

14 The remainder of installation is the reverse of removal.

15 Start the engine, then check for oil leaks and unusual sounds coming from the valve cover area.

11 Cylinder head - removal and installation

✳✳ WARNING:

The engine must be completely cool before beginning this procedure.

REMOVAL

▶ **Refer to illustration 11.9**

1 Relieve the fuel system pressure (see Chapter 4). Position the engine at TDC compression for cylinder no. 1 (see Section 3), then disconnect the cable from the negative terminal of the battery (see Chapter 5).

2 Drain the coolant (see Chapter 1).

3 Remove the timing chain (see Section 8).

4 Remove the camshafts (see Section 9).

5 Remove the exhaust manifold (see Section 6).

6 Remove the intake manifold (see Section 5).

7 Label and remove any remaining items attached to the cylinder head, such as coolant fittings, tubes, cables, hoses or wiring harnesses.

8 Using a breaker bar and the appropriate-sized hex bit, loosen the cylinder head bolts in 1/4-turn increments until they can be removed by hand. Loosen the bolts in reverse of the tightening sequence (see illustration 11.19) to avoid warping or cracking the cylinder head.

9 Lift the cylinder head off the engine block. If it's stuck, very carefully pry up at the transmission end, beyond the gasket surface, at a casting protrusion (see illustration).

10 Remove all external components from the cylinder head to allow for thorough cleaning and inspection.

➡ **Note: See Chapter 2 Part C for cylinder head servicing procedures.**

INSTALLATION

▶ **Refer to illustrations 11.12, 11.15 and 11.19**

11 The mating surfaces of the cylinder head and block must be perfectly clean when the cylinder head is installed.

12 Use a gasket scraper to remove all traces of carbon and old gasket material (see illustration), then clean the mating surfaces with lacquer thinner or acetone. If there's oil on the mating surfaces when the cylinder head is installed, the gasket may not seal correctly and leaks could develop. When working on the block, stuff the cylinders with clean shop rags to keep out debris. Use a vacuum cleaner to remove material that falls into the cylinders.

11.9 Pry under the cylinder head under casting protrusions only - do not pry between mating surfaces

11.12 Remove all traces of old gasket material - the cylinder head and block mating surfaces must be perfectly clean to ensure a good gasket seal

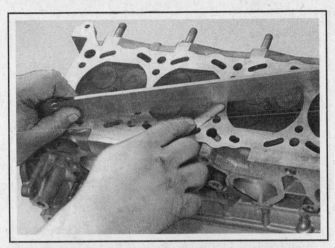

11.15 Check the cylinder head gasket surface for warpage by trying to insert a feeler gauge under the straightedge. See this Chapter's Specifications for the maximum warpage allowed and use a feeler gauge of that thickness

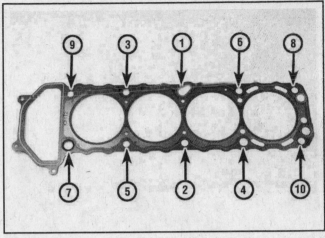

11.19 Cylinder head bolt TIGHTENING sequence

13 Check the block and cylinder head mating surfaces for nicks, deep scratches and other damage. If damage is slight, it can be removed with a fine file; if it's excessive, machining may be the only alternative.

14 Use a tap of the correct size to chase the threads in the cylinder head bolt holes, then clean the holes with compressed air - make sure that nothing remains in the holes.

❋❋ WARNING:

Wear eye protection when using compressed air!

15 Once the cylinder head's gasket surface is clean, check the cylinder head for warpage (see illustration). Check the cylinder head gasket, intake and exhaust manifold surfaces.

16 Install any components that were removed from the cylinder head.

17 Position the new cylinder head gasket over the dowel pins in the block and carefully set the cylinder head on the block without disturbing the gasket.

18 Before installing the new cylinder head bolts, apply a small amount of clean engine oil to the threads and hardened washers. The chamfered side of the washers must face the bolt heads, and the flat side of the washers must face the cylinder head.

19 Install the new cylinder head bolts and tighten them, following the recommended sequence (see illustration), to the torque listed in this Chapter's Specifications.

20 Install the lifters and camshafts (see Section 9).

21 Install the timing chain (see Section 8), then check the valve clearances (see Chapter 1).

22 The remaining installation steps are the reverse of removal.

23 Refill the cooling system, install a new oil filter and add oil to the engine (see Chapter 1).

24 Reconnect the battery and perform the necessary re-learn procedures (see Chapter 5).

12 Oil pan - removal and installation

➡**Note: The following procedure describes removing the lower (steel) oil pan and the upper (aluminum) oil pan. if you're just removing the lower oil pan, many of the following steps are not necessary, as the pan is readily accessible.**

REMOVAL

▶ **Refer to illustration 12.16**

1 Disconnect the cable from the negative terminal of the battery (see Chapter 5).

2 Loosen the right front wheel lug nuts, raise the front of the vehicle and support it securely on jackstands, then remove the wheel.

3 Drain the engine oil (see Chapter 1).

4 Remove the front section of exhaust pipe.

5 Remove the air conditioning compressor drivebelt (see Chapter 1).

6 Disconnect the power steering lines from the steering gear. Tape the ends to prevent contamination.

7 Remove the power steering cooler hose bracket from the subframe.

8 Remove the subframe (see Chapter 10).

9 Disconnect the electrical connector from the air conditioning compressor, then unbolt the compressor and move it out of the way.

❋❋ CAUTION:

Don't disconnect the refrigerant lines.

10 Remove the rear engine mount torque rod bracket.

11 Remove the intermediate shaft support bearing bracket from the oil pan if required.

12 The oil pan is a two-piece design. A steel pan is attached to an aluminum section which is bolted to the engine block. Remove the oil pan bolts following the reverse of the recommended tightening

12.16 After cutting the pan seal with a putty knife, pry at the rear corners near the transmission - do not pry in the gasket area

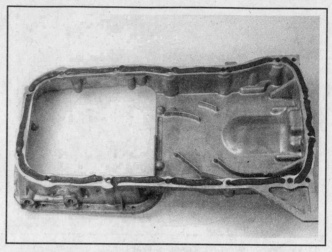

12.20 Apply a bead of RTV sealant around the perimeter of the aluminum section of the pan

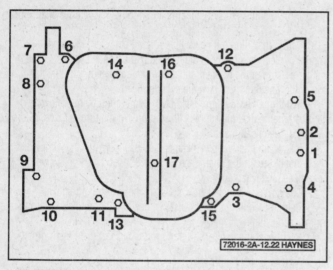

12.22 Bolt tightening sequence for the aluminum upper oil pan

sequence (see illustration 12.23). Separate the steel pan by inserting a thin putty knife between the steel and aluminum sections.

➡ **Note: Be sure to mark each bolt to insure they are positioned in their original locations on reassembly.**

⁎⁎ CAUTION:

Do not pry with a screwdriver between the steel pan and the aluminum flange or damage to the sealing surface may result.

13 Remove the oil pump screen.

14 Remove the transmission torque converter/flywheel cover and remove the bolts that mount the upper oil pan to the transmission.

15 Remove the bolts attaching the aluminum section (upper oil pan) to the engine block following the reverse of the tightening sequence (see illustration 12.22).

16 The sealant used to seal the aluminum section to the engine block can be very difficult to separate without damaging the aluminum section. Using a thin putty knife, work around the perimeter cutting the pan free before prying the pan down at the transmission end (see illustration).

INSTALLATION

➤ **Refer to illustrations 12.20, 12.22 and 12.23**

17 Use a scraper to remove all traces of old gasket material and sealant from the block and oil pan. Clean the mating surfaces with brake system cleaner.

⁎⁎ CAUTION:

Be careful not to scratch or gouge the gasket surface of the block or oil pan. A leak could develop after the repairs have been completed.

18 Make sure the threaded bolt holes in the block are clean.

19 Check the steel pan flange for distortion, particularly around the bolt holes. If necessary, place the pan on a wood block and use a hammer to flatten and restore the gasket surface.

20 Apply a 3/16-inch wide bead of RTV sealant around the perimeter of the aluminum section (upper oil pan) (see illustration).

➡ **Note: The oil pan must be installed within 15 minutes once the sealant has been applied.**

21 Install new O-rings into the upper oil pan, if equipped.

22 Carefully position the aluminum section on the engine block and install the bolts, tightening them hand-tight. Tighten the pan-to-transmission bolts a little tighter than hand-tight, then tighten the oil pan-to-block fasteners in three or four steps, and in the recommended sequence, to the torque listed in this Chapter's Specifications (see illustration). Finally, tighten the pan-to-transmission bolts (transmission mounting bolts) to the torque listed in the Chapter 7 Specifications.

23 Apply a bead of RTV sealant around the perimeter of the steel

pan and install it within 15 minutes of application. Tighten the bolts to the torque listed in this Chapter's Specifications in the recommended sequence (see illustration).

24 The remainder of installation is the reverse of removal. Be sure to install a new oil filter and wait at least thirty minutes for the RTV to set-up before adding oil.

25 Reconnect the battery and perform the necessary re-learn procedures (sec Chapter 5).

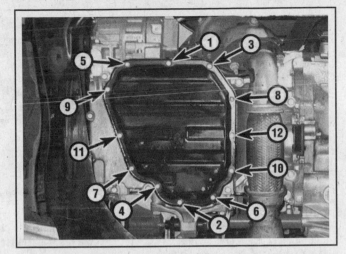

12.23 Bolt tightening sequence for the steel lower oil pan

13 Oil pump - removal, inspection and installation

REMOVAL

▶ **Refer to illustration 13.3**

1 The oil pump is located inside the timing chain cover and is driven by the crankshaft.

2 The timing chain cover must be removed for access to the oil pump. Remove the timing chain cover (see Section 8).

3 Remove the bolts/screws retaining the oil pump cover to the oil pump body (see illustration), disassemble the inner and outer rotors.

❋❋ CAUTION:

Be very careful with these components; the close tolerances are critical in creating the correct oil pressure. Any nicks or damage will require replacement of the complete pump/timing chain cover assembly.

13.3 The oil pump is located inside the timing chain cover - remove the fasteners, then remove the oil pump cover

INSPECTION

Refer to illustrations 13.5, 13.6a, 13.6b, 13.6c and 13.6d

4 Clean all the components, including the timing chain cover and engine block gasket surfaces, with solvent, then inspect all surfaces for excessive wear and/or damage.

5 Disassemble the relief valve by removing the cap, washer, spring and regulator valve (see illustration). Check the oil pressure regulator valve sliding surface and valve spring. The regulator, when clean and oiled, should slide easily in the valve bore. If either the spring or the valve is damaged, they must be replaced as a set. If no damage is found, reassemble the relief valve parts, coating the parts with clean engine oil, and reinstall it in the oil pump cover.

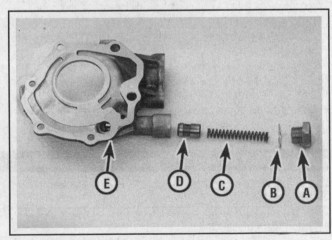

13.5 Remove the oil pump pressure regulator valve assembly for cleaning and inspection

A	Cap	D	Relief valve
B	Washer	E	Oil pump cover
C	Spring		

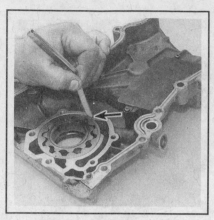

13.6a Check the outer rotor-to-body clearance with a feeler gauge as shown

13.6b Check the clearance between the inner and outer rotor tips

13.6c With a precision straightedge placed over the pump body and rotors, check the clearance between the inner and outer rotors and the pump body cover

6   Check the oil pump component clearance with a feeler gauge (see illustrations) and compare the results to this Chapter's Specifications. If any of the Specifications are exceeded, replace both the timing chain cover and the oil pump components.

INSTALLATION

7   Assemble the oil pump components. There is a punch mark on each rotor; these marks must face away from the timing chain cover and toward the engine. Pour a generous amount of clean engine oil into the pump cavity and around the rotors. Install the cover to the pump body and tighten the fasteners to the torque listed in this Chapter's Specifications.

8   Install the timing chain cover, using a bead of RTV sealant on the cover-to-block surface (see Section 8).

➡Note: Align the flats on the inner oil pump rotor with the crankshaft when installing the timing chain cover.

Refer to Sections 9 and 11 and install the cylinder head and other components.

9   Install the oil pan (see Section 12). Install a new oil filter and add engine oil to the crankcase.

10 Start the engine and check for oil pressure and leaks.

11 Perform the necessary re-learn procedures (see Chapter 5, Section 3).

12 Recheck the engine oil level.

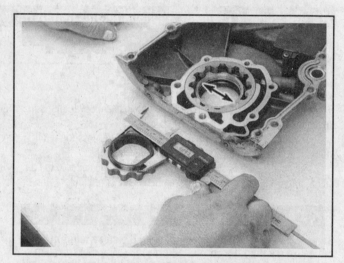

13.6d Measure the outer flanged surface of the inner rotor with a micrometer or precision calipers, then measure its bearing surface in the pump body - the difference is the inner rotor bearing clearance

14 Flywheel/driveplate - removal and installation

REMOVAL

Refer to illustration 14.3

1   Remove the engine/transaxle assembly (see Chapter 2C).

2   If equipped with a manual transmission, remove the pressure plate and clutch disc (see Chapter 8).

3   Use a center-punch or paint to make alignment marks on the flywheel/driveplate and crankshaft to ensure correct alignment during installation (see illustration).

4   Remove the bolts that secure the flywheel/driveplate to the crankshaft.

5   Remove the flywheel/driveplate from the crankshaft.

✳✳ WARNING:

Since the flywheel is fairly heavy, be sure to support it while removing the last bolt. Flywheel teeth can be sharp; wear gloves or use rags to hold the flywheel.

INSTALLATION

6   If equipped with a manual transaxle, clean the flywheel to remove grease and oil. Inspect the surface for cracks, rivet grooves, burned areas and score marks. Light scoring can be removed with emery cloth. Check for cracked and broken ring-gear teeth. Lay the flywheel on a flat surface and use a straightedge to check for warpage.

7   Clean and inspect the mating surfaces of the flywheel/driveplate and the crankshaft. If the crankshaft rear seal is leaking, replace it before reinstalling the flywheel/driveplate.

8   Position the flywheel/driveplate against the crankshaft. Be sure to install the spacer (if equipped) and align the marks made during removal. Some engines have an alignment dowel or staggered bolt holes to ensure correct installation. Before installing the bolts, apply thread-locking compound to the threads.

9   Wedge a screwdriver in the ring gear teeth to keep the flywheel/driveplate from turning as you tighten the bolts to the torque listed in this Chapter's Specifications. Follow a criss-cross pattern and work up to the final torque in three or four steps.

10   The remainder of installation is the reverse of removal.

11   Reconnect the battery and perform the necessary re-learn procedures (see Chapter 5).

14.3 Mark the flywheel/driveplate and the crankshaft so they can be reassembled in the same relative positions

15   Rear main oil seal - replacement

1   Remove the transaxle (see Chapter 7).

2   Remove the flywheel/driveplate (see Section 14).

3   Use a screwdriver wrapped with tape to pry the seal out, being careful not to gouge or nick the housing.

4   Lubricate the crankshaft seal journal and the lip of the new seal with multi-purpose grease.

5   Install the seal with the seal lip toward the engine and the dust seal toward the transmission.

6   Tap the seal into place using a seal driver to make sure that it doesn't become tilted.

7   Install the seal so that its rear edge is flush with the face of the engine block or up to 0.020 inch recessed.

8   The remaining steps are the reverse of removal.

9   Reconnect the battery and perform the necessary re-learn procedures (see Chapter 5).

16   Engine mounts - check and replacement

1   Engine mounts seldom require attention, but broken or deteriorated mounts should be replaced immediately or the added strain placed on the driveline components may cause damage or wear.

CHECK

‣ **Refer to illustration 16.6**

2   During the check, the engine must be raised slightly to remove the weight from the mounts.

3   Raise the vehicle and support it securely on jackstands and remove the splash shields.

4   Position a jack under the engine oil pan. Place a large wood block between the jack head and the oil pan, then carefully raise the engine just enough to take the weight off the mounts. Do not place the wood block under the oil pan drain plug.

✳✳ WARNING:

DO NOT place any part of your body under the engine when it's supported only by a jack!

5   Check the mounts to see if the rubber is cracked, hardened or separated from the metal plates. Sometimes the rubber will split right down the center.

16.6 A long prybar can be used to check for relative movement in the engine mounts

6 Check for relative movement between the mount plates and the engine or frame using a large screwdriver or prybar to attempt to move the mounts (see illustration). If movement is noted, lower the engine and tighten the mount fasteners.

7 Rubber preservative should be applied to the mounts to slow deterioration.

REPLACEMENT

→Note: Some models have active engine mounts to help reduce vibration. Be sure to disconnect the vacuum line from the engine mount before removing it.

8 Disconnect the cable from the negative terminal of the battery (see Chapter 5). Raise the vehicle and support it securely on jackstands. Support the engine as described in Step 4.

9 To remove the front engine mount, refer to Section 4.

10 To remove either of the two lower engine mounts, remove the through-bolts and the bolts retaining the mount to the subframe.

11 Remove the engine block-to-mount bolts and remove the mount.

12 Installation is the reverse of removal. Use thread-locking compound on the mount bolts/nuts and be sure to tighten them securely.

Specifications

General

Displacement	2.5L (152 cu. in.)
Designation	QR25DE
Cylinder numbers (timing chain end-to-transmission end)	1-2-3-4
Firing order	1-3-4-2

Cylinder locations

Valve clearance (cold)

Intake	0.009 to 0.013 inch
Exhaust	0.010 to 0.013 inch

Warpage limits

Cylinder head-to-block surface	0.004 inch

Camshaft

Endplay	0.0045 to 0.0074 inch
Camshaft journal diameter	
No. 1	1.0998 to 1.1006 inches
No. 2 through 5	0.9226 to 0.9234 inch
Camshaft bearing inside diameter	
No. 1	1.1024 to 1.1032 inches
No. 2 through 5	0.9252 to 0.9260 inch
Bearing oil clearance	
Standard	0.0018 to 0.0034 inch
Service limit	0.0047 inch
Runout limit (all)	0.0016 inch maximum
Intake lobe height	1.7646 to 1.7718 inches
Exhaust lobe height	1.7313 to 1.7388 inches

Oil pump

Body-to-outer rotor clearance	0.0045 to 0.0070 inch
Inner rotor-to-outer rotor tip clearance	0.0067 to 0.0087 inch
Inner rotor-to-cover clearance	0.0014 to 0.0028 inch
Outer rotor-to-cover clearance	0.0024 to 0.0043 inch
Inner rotor-to-body clearance	0.0012 to 0.0028 inch

Torque specifications   Ft-lbs (unless otherwise indicated)

➡ Note: One foot-pound (ft-lb) of torque is equivalent to 12 inch-pounds (in-lbs) of torque. Torque values below approximately 15 ft-lbs are expressed in inch-pounds, since most foot-pound torque wrenches are not accurate at these smaller values.

Intake manifold bolts/nuts	168 in-lbs
Exhaust manifold-to-block bolts/nuts	35
Crankshaft pulley-to-crankshaft bolt (2)*	
Step 1	31
Step 2	Tighten an additional 60 degrees
Flywheel/driveplate bolts	80
Balance shaft sprocket bolt (2)*	48
Balance shaft assembly bolts (1)* (2)* (3)*	
Step 1	
Bolts 1 through 5	31
Bolt 6	27
Step 2	
Bolts 1 through 5	Tighten an additional 120 degrees
Bolt 6	Tighten an additional 90 degrees
Step 3	Completely loosen all bolts in reverse sequence
Step 4	
Bolts 1 through 5	31
Bolt 6	27
Step 5	
Bolts 1 through 5	Tighten an additional 120 degrees
Bolt 6	Tighten an additional 90 degrees
Cylinder head bolts (1)* (2)* (3)*	
Step 1	72
Step 2	Loosen all bolts completely in reverse sequence
Step 3	29
Step 4	Tighten an additional 75 degrees
Step 5	Tighten an additional 75 degrees
Camshaft bearing cap bolts (3)*	
Step 1 (bolts 9 through 11)	17 in-lbs
Step 2 (bolts 1 through 8)	17 in-lbs
Step 3 (bolts 1 through 11)	52 in-lbs
Step 4 (bolts 1 through 11)	80 to 104 in-lbs
Camshaft sprocket bolt (2)*	
Intake sprocket assembly	76
Exhaust sprocket	105

Torque specifications (continued)   Ft-lbs (unless otherwise indicated)

Engine mount bolts/nuts	
Left (transmission) and right engine mounts	
Through-bolts	32 to 40
Engine mount bolts/nuts	
Nuts	37 to 43
Bolts	54 to 66
Front and rear engine mounts	
Through-bolts	56 to 72
Engine mount bolts/nuts	61 to 72
Timing chain cover bolts (3)*	
Bolts A	36
Bolts B	108 in-lbs
Bolts C	108 in-lbs
Bolts D	36
IVT cover bolts	108 in-lbs
Engine mounting bracket bolts	32 to 40
IVT solenoid mounting bolts	48 to 64 in-lbs
Timing chain components	
Timing chain slack guide bolts	144 in-lbs
Timing chain guide bolts	144 in-lbs
Timing chain tensioner bolts	61 in-lbs
Balance shaft chain tensioner bolts	61 in-lbs
Oil pump pressure relief valve bolt	29 to 50
Oil pump-to-timing chain cover bolts	52 to 70 in-lbs
Oil pick-up to block bolts	58 to 65 in-lbs
Oil pan	
Aluminum section-to-block (3)*	16
Steel pan-to-aluminum section (3)*	61 in-lbs
Drain plug	25
Valve cover bolts (3)*	
Step 1	17 in-lbs
Step 2	74 in-lbs

(1)* Bolt(s) must be replaced with NEW ones

(2)* Lubricate fastener threads and heads with clean engine oil prior to installation

(3)* Tighten the fasteners in the correct sequence. See text for diagrams

Section

1 General information
2 Repair operations possible with the engine in the vehicle
3 Top Dead Center (TDC) for number one piston - locating
4 Valve covers - removal and installation
5 Valve springs, retainers and seals - replacement
6 Timing chain and sprockets - removal, inspection and installation
7 Camshafts and lifters - removal and installation
8 Intake manifold - removal and installation
9 Exhaust manifold - removal, inspection and installation
10 Cylinder head - removal and installation
11 Crankshaft pulley - removal and installation
12 Crankshaft front oil seal - replacement
13 Oil pan - removal and installation
14 Oil pump - removal, inspection and installation
15 Engine oil cooler and oil filter adapter - general information and replacement
16 Flywheel/driveplate - removal and installation
17 Rear main oil seal - replacement
18 Engine mounts - check and replacement

Reference to other Chapters

Cylinder compression check - See Chapter 2C
Drivebelt check, adjustment and replacement - See Chapter 1
Engine - removal and installation - See Chapter 2C
Engine oil and filter change - See Chapter 1
Engine overhaul - general information - See Chapter 2C
Spark plug replacement - See Chapter 1
Valve clearance - check and adjustment - See Chapter 1
Valves - servicing - See Chapter 2C
Water pump - removal and installation - See Chapter 3

2B

V6 ENGINE

1 General information

This Part of Chapter 2 is devoted to in-vehicle repair procedures for the VQ35DE 3.5L Dual Overhead Camshaft (DOHC) V6 engine. Information concerning engine removal and installation and engine overhaul can be found in Part C of this Chapter.

The following repair procedures are based on the assumption that the engine is installed in the vehicle. If the engine has been removed from the vehicle and mounted on a stand, many of the steps outlined in this Part of Chapter 2 will not apply.

2 Repair operations possible with the engine in the vehicle

Many major repair operations can be accomplished without removing the engine from the vehicle.

Clean the engine compartment and the exterior of the engine with some type of degreaser before any work is done. It will make the job easier and help keep dirt out of the internal areas of the engine.

Depending on the components involved, it may be helpful to remove the hood to improve access to the engine as repairs are performed (refer to Chapter 11 if necessary). Cover the fenders to prevent damage to the paint. Special pads are available, but an old bedspread or blanket will also work.

If vacuum, exhaust, oil or coolant leaks develop, indicating a need for gasket or seal replacement, the repairs can generally be made with the engine in the vehicle. The intake and exhaust manifold gaskets and crankshaft oil seals are accessible with the engine in place.

Some exterior engine components, such as the intake and exhaust manifolds, the lower oil pan, the water pump (see Chapter 3), the starter motor, the alternator and the fuel system components (see Chapter 4) can be removed for replacement with the engine in place.

The upper oil pan can't be removed with the engine in place on automatic transmission models. Because of this, the cylinder heads and timing chains can't be removed without first removing the engine on these vehicles.

3 Top Dead Center (TDC) for number one piston - locating

▶ **Refer to illustration 3.8**

1   Top Dead Center (TDC) is the highest point in the cylinder that each piston reaches as it travels up-and-down when the crankshaft turns. Each piston reaches TDC on the compression stroke and again on the exhaust stroke, but TDC generally refers to piston position on the compression stroke.

2   Positioning the number one piston at TDC is an essential part of many procedures, such as camshaft and timing chain removal.

3   Before beginning this procedure, be sure to place the transmission in Neutral and apply the parking brake or block the rear wheels. If method b) or c) in the next Step will be used to rotate the engine, disable the fuel system by removing the fuel pump fuse (see Chapter 4, Section 2). Remove the spark plugs (see Chapter 1).

4   In order to bring any piston to TDC, the crankshaft must be turned using one of the methods outlined below. When looking at the front of the engine (timing chain end), normal crankshaft rotation is clockwise.

   a) *The preferred method is to turn the crankshaft with a socket and ratchet attached to the bolt threaded into the front of the crankshaft.*

   b) *A remote starter switch, which may save some time, can also be used. Follow the instructions included with the switch. Once the piston is close to TDC, use a socket and ratchet as described in the previous paragraph.*

   c) *If an assistant is available to turn the ignition switch to the Start position in short bursts, you can get the piston close to TDC without a remote starter switch. Make sure your assistant is out of the vehicle, away from the ignition switch, then use a socket and ratchet as described in Paragraph a) to complete the procedure.*

5   Install a compression pressure gauge in the number one spark plug hole (see Chapter 2C). It should be a gauge with a screw-in fitting and a hose at least six inches long.

6   Loosen the right front wheel lug nuts. Raise the front of the vehicle and support it securely on jackstands. Remove the wheel and the inner fender splash shield (see illustration 3.6 in Chapter 2A). Rotate the crankshaft using one of the methods described above while observing for pressure on the compression gauge. The moment the gauge shows pressure indicates that the number one cylinder has begun the compression stroke.

7   Once the compression stroke has begun, TDC for the compression stroke is reached by bringing the piston to the top of the cylinder.

8   Continue turning the crankshaft until the TDC notch in the crankshaft damper is aligned with the pointer on the timing chain cover (see illustration). At this point, the number one cylinder is at TDC on the compression stroke. If the marks are aligned but there was no compression, the piston was on the exhaust stroke. Continue rotating the crankshaft 360-degrees (1-turn).

➡**Note: If a compression gauge is not available, you can simply place a blunt object (such as the end of a screwdriver handle) over the spark plug hole and listen for compression as the engine is rotated. Once compression at the No. 1 spark plug hole is noted, the remainder of the Step is the same.**

9   After the number one piston has been positioned at TDC on the compression stroke, TDC for any of the remaining cylinders can be located by turning the crankshaft 120-degrees and following the firing order (refer to the Specifications). For example, rotating the engine 120-degrees past TDC #1 will put the engine at TDC compression for cylinder #2.

3.8 Align the TDC notch on the crankshaft pulley with the pointer on the timing chain cover - the TDC notch is the one farthest to the left when facing the front of the engine

1	*TDC mark*	3	*15-degrees BTDC*
2	*10-degrees BTDC*		

4   Valve covers - removal and installation

REMOVAL

1   Disconnect the cable from the negative terminal of the battery (see Chapter 5).
2   Remove the engine cover.
3   Remove the camshaft position sensor(s) (see Chapter 6).

Left (front) valve cover

4   Remove the front air inlet duct.
5   Remove the blow-by hose from the valve cover.

Right (rear) valve cover

6   Remove the intake manifold collector (see Section 8).

All valve covers

7   Remove the ignition coils from the cover to be removed (see Chapter 5).
8   Detach the PCV hose and any wiring which would interfere with valve cover removal.
9   Remove the valve cover bolts and washers in the reverse order of the tightening sequence (see illustration 4.16).
10   Detach the valve cover.

➡**Note: If the cover is stuck to the cylinder head, bump one end with a block of wood and a hammer to jar it loose. If that doesn't work, try to slip a flexible putty knife between the cylinder head and cover to break the gasket seal. Don't pry at the cover-to-cylinder head joint or damage to the sealing surfaces may occur (leading to oil leaks in the future).**

INSTALLATION

▸ **Refer to illustrations 4.13 and 4.16**

11   The mating surfaces of each cylinder head and valve cover must be perfectly clean when the covers are installed. Use a gasket scraper to remove all traces of sealant and old gasket material, then clean the mating surfaces with brake system cleaner.

12   If necessary, clean the bolt threads with a wire wheel to remove any corrosion. Make sure the threaded holes in the cylinder head are clean - run a tap into them to remove corrosion and restore damaged threads.

13   Replace the spark plug tube seals (see illustration).

14   Apply a thin coat of RTV sealant to the cover groove and to the corners on the front camshaft journal cap, then position the gasket inside the cover and allow the sealant to set up so the gasket adheres to the cover. If the sealant isn't allowed to set, the gasket may fall out of the cover as it's installed on the engine.

15   Carefully position the cover on the cylinder head and install the bolts.

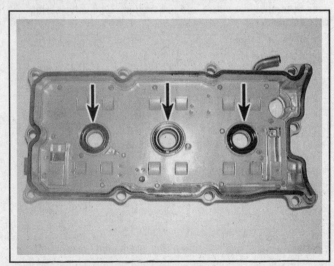

4.13 Be sure to install new spark plug tube seals into the valve cover

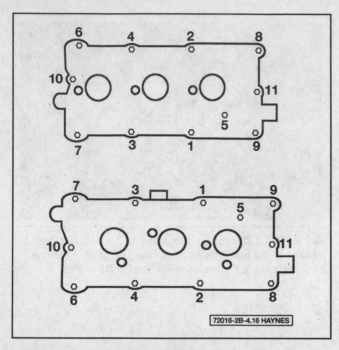

4.16 Valve cover bolt TIGHTENING sequence

16 Following the recommended tightening sequence, tighten the bolts, in two steps, to the torque listed in this Chapter's Specifications (see illustration).

17 The remaining installation steps are the reverse of removal.

18 Reconnect the battery and perform the necessary re-learn procedures (see Chapter 5).

5 Valve springs, retainers and seals - replacement

▶ Refer to illustrations 5.5, 5.7a, 5.7b, 5.13 and 5.15

➡Note: Broken valve springs and defective valve stem seals can be replaced without removing the cylinder heads. Two special tools and a compressed air source are normally required to perform this operation, so read through this Section carefully. If you want to leave the head on, obtain a special on-vehicle valve spring compressor (see illustration 10.1 in Chapter 2A). Verify the availability of the correct spring compressor before beginning the job. If you can't get the special tools, then you'll have to remove the heads and use a clamp type valve spring compressor

1 Remove the intake manifold collector (see Section 8) and the valve cover(s) (see Section 4).

2 Remove the timing chain (see Section 6) and the camshafts and lifters from both cylinder heads (see Section 7).

3 Remove the spark plugs.

4 Turn the crankshaft until the piston in the affected cylinder is at Top Dead Center (see Section 3). If you're replacing all of the valve stem seals, begin with cylinder number one and work on the valves for one cylinder at a time. Move from cylinder-to-cylinder following the firing order sequence, turning the crankshaft 120-degrees to bring the next cylinder to TDC (see this Chapter's Specifications).

5 Thread a long adapter into the spark plug hole and connect an air hose from a compressed air source to it (see illustration). Most auto parts stores can supply the air hose adapter.

➡Note: Because of the length of the spark plug tubes, it will be necessary to use a long spark plug adapter with a length of hose attached (as used on many cylinder compression gauges) utilizing a quick-disconnect fitting to hook to your air source.

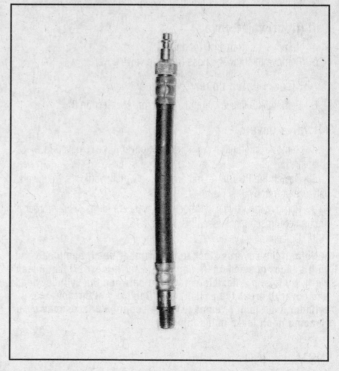

5.5 Thread the air hose adapter into the spark plug hole - adapters are commonly available from auto parts stores

5.7a Compress the valve spring enough to release the valve stem locks . . .

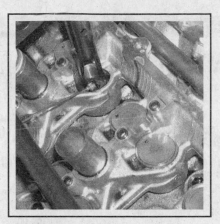

5.7b . . . and lift them out with a magnet or needle-nose pliers

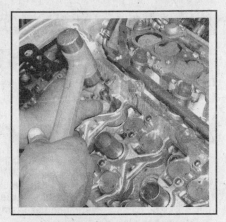

5.13 Using a deep socket and hammer, gently tap the new seals onto the valve guide only until seated

6   Apply compressed air to the cylinder.

☀☀ WARNING:

The piston may be forced down by the compressed air, causing the crankshaft to turn suddenly. If the wrench used when positioning the number one piston at TDC is still attached to the bolt in the crankshaft nose, it could cause damage or injury when the crankshaft moves.

7   Stuff shop rags into the cylinder head holes around the valves to prevent parts and tools from falling into the engine, then use a valve spring compressor to compress the spring (see illustrations). Remove the valve stem locks with small needle-nose pliers or a magnet.

➡**Note: The valves should be held in place by the air pressure. If the valve faces or seats are in poor condition, leaks may prevent air pressure from retaining the valves. If the valves cannot hold air, the cylinder head should be removed for a valve job at a machine shop.**

8   Remove the spring retainer and valve spring, then remove the valve stem seal.

9   Wrap a rubber band or tape around the top of the valve stem so the valve won't fall into the combustion chamber, then release the air pressure.

10   Inspect the valve stem for damage. Rotate the valve in the guide and check the end for eccentric movement, which would indicate that the valve is bent.

11   Move the valve up-and-down in the guide and make sure it doesn't bind. If the valve stem binds, either the valve is bent or the guide is damaged. In either case, the cylinder head will have to be removed for repair.

12   Reapply air pressure to the cylinder to retain the valve in the closed position, then remove the tape or rubber band from the valve stem.

13   Lubricate the valve stems with engine oil and install the new valve stem seals. Valve stem seals can be installed with a special tool, or a deep socket and hammer - tap the seal only until seated (see illustration).

14   Install the valve spring in position over the valve, with the more closely-wound spring coils and the paint mark toward the cylinder head.

15   Install the valve spring retainer. Compress the valve springs and carefully position the valve stem locks in the groove. Apply a small dab of grease to the inside of each valve stem lock to hold it in place (see illustration).

16   Remove the force from the spring tool and make sure the valve stem locks are seated.

17   Disconnect the air hose and remove the adapter from the spark plug hole.

18   When all of the seals to be replaced have been replaced, position the crankshaft at TDC (see illustration 3.8).

19   Install the camshafts and lifters (see Section 7), then install the timing chain (see Section 6).

20   Install the valve covers (see Section 4).

21   Install the spark plugs, ignition coils and the intake manifold collector, referring to the appropriate Sections as necessary.

22   Start and run the engine, then check for oil leaks and unusual sounds coming from the valve cover area.

5.15 Apply a small dab of grease to each valve stem lock as shown here before installation - it will hold them in place on the valve stem as the spring is released

6 Timing chain and sprockets - removal, inspection and installation

❋❋ WARNING:

The engine must be completely cool before beginning this procedure.

❋❋ CAUTION:

The timing system is complex. Severe engine damage will occur if you make any mistakes. Do not attempt this procedure unless you are highly experienced with this type of repair. If you are at all unsure of your abilities, consult an expert. Double-check all your work and be sure everything is correct before you attempt to start the engine.

REMOVAL

◆ Refer to illustrations 6.20, 6.22, 6.23, 6.24, 6.25a, 6.25b, 6.26, 6.28 and 6.29

1   Have a qualified air conditioning shop recover the refrigerant from the air conditioning system.

2   Relieve the fuel system pressure (see Chapter 4), then disconnect the cable from the negative terminal of the battery (see Chapter 5).

3   Block the rear wheels and set the parking brake. Raise the front of the vehicle and support it securely on jackstands.

4   Drain the cooling system, the power steering fluid and the engine oil (see Chapter 1). Remove the power steering fluid reservoir.

5   Remove the top and bottom engine covers and the right inner fender splash shield. Remove the front air inlet duct.

6   Remove the intake manifold collector (see Section 8).

7   Remove the valve covers (see Section 4) and the dipstick.

8   Position the number one piston at TDC on the compression stroke (see Section 3).

9   Remove the drivebelt (see Chapter 1).

10 Remove the upper radiator hose and disconnect the lower radiator hose from the engine. Remove the coolant reservoir and the cooling fan assembly (see Chapter 3).

11 Remove the starter (see Chapter 5).

12 Remove the power steering pump (see Chapter 10).

13 Remove the air conditioning compressor (see Chapter 3).

14 Remove the alternator and its bracket (see Chapter 5).

15 Remove the crankshaft pulley (see Section 11).

➡Note: Don't allow the crankshaft to rotate during removal of the pulley. If the crankshaft moves, the number one piston will no longer be at TDC.

16 Remove the bolts from the engine oil cooler tube and remove its bracket.

17 Disconnect the wiring from the oil pressure switch and the valve timing control wiring harness. Label and disconnect any other interfering wiring and hoses.

18 Remove the bolts from the IVT covers in the reverse of the tightening sequence (see illustration 6.43c). Pull the covers straight off so they disengage from the intake camshaft sprocket actuator assemblies.

19 Remove the drivebelt tensioner. Remove the air conditioning idler pulley and its bracket.

20 Remove the bolts of the front timing chain cover in the reverse of the tightening sequence (see illustration 6.42b). Pry the cover off using the slots at the top of the cover (see illustration). Note that various types and sizes of bolts are used. They must be reinstalled in their original locations. Mark each bolt or make a sketch to help remember where they go.

21 Remove the O-ring below each intake camshaft sprocket.

22 Confirm that the number one piston is still at TDC on the compression stroke by verifying that the intake and exhaust camshaft lobes on the number one cylinder are pointing upward (see illustration).

23 Relieve tension on the primary timing chain. Depress the primary tensioner inward and lock it into place by inserting a suitable stopper pin into the hole on the front of the tensioner (see illustration).

➡Note: This engine utilizes three timing chains. The primary timing chain runs around the crankshaft sprocket, the water pump and around two intake camshaft sprockets. This chain synchronizes the valve timing with the crankshaft and pistons, while two secondary timing chains run around the rear of the intake sprockets and separate exhaust camshaft sprockets to synchronize the intake and exhaust camshafts.

24 Remove the primary timing chain tensioner, the tensioner pivot arm/chain guide and the upper timing chain guides from the primary timing chain (see illustration).

6.20 Insert a screwdriver into the notch at the top of the timing cover and pry the front timing cover off the engine

6.22 Verify that cylinder no. 1 is at TDC on the compression stroke by confirming that the intake and exhaust camshaft lobes on cylinder no. 1 are pointing upward

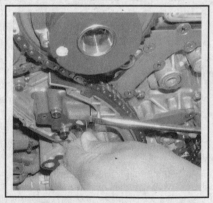

6.23 An ordinary paper clip can be straightened and used to lock the timing chain tensioner(s) in place

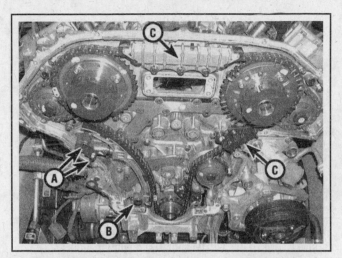

6.24 Remove the primary timing chain tensioner mounting bolts (A), the tensioner arm/chain guide pivot bolt (B) and the upper chain guides (C)

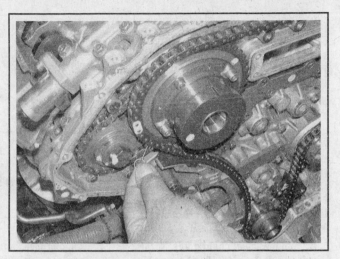

6.25a Bend two paper clips so that they're long enough to protrude out past the camshaft sprocket once they're installed . . .

6.25b . . . then depress the secondary tensioners with a screwdriver and lock them in place by inserting a paper clip into the hole on the side of each tensioner - note that the secondary tensioner on the right bank points downward, while the secondary tensioner on the left bank points upward

6.26 Hold the lug on the camshaft with a wrench to keep it from rotating as the sprocket bolts are loosened

25 Depress the secondary timing chain tensioners and lock the tensioners in place by inserting a suitable stopper pin into the hole on the front of each tensioner (see illustrations).

26 Remove the camshaft sprocket bolts (see illustration).

27 Disengage the primary timing chain from the teeth on the chain sprockets and remove it from the engine.

28 Mark the camshaft sprockets with either an R or L to indicate the right or left side, then remove the camshaft sprockets and the secondary timing chains from the engine. Don't mix the sprockets up. They must be installed on the same camshaft from which they were removed (see illustration).

❋❋ CAUTION:

The intake camshaft sprockets are identified by the variable valve timing actuator and sensor ring which is fastened to the front of the sprocket. Be extremely careful not to damage or place a magnetic object of any kind near the sensor ring or a no start condition may occur after installation. Do Not disassemble the variable valve timing actuator assembly from the intake camshaft sprocket for any reason.

6.28 Note that the left intake camshaft sprocket has a sensor ring which is fastened to the front of the sprocket - be extremely careful not to damage or place a magnetic object of any kind near the sensor ring or a no start condition may occur

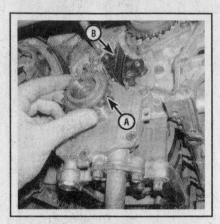

6.29 Remove the crankshaft sprocket (A) and the lower chain guide; make a note that the mark (B) on the chain guide must face up when reinstalling

6.30a Examine the chain guides for deep grooves and excessive wear - replace them if necessary

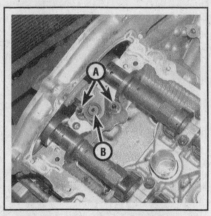

6.30b Secondary timing chain tensioner(s) mounting bolts (A) - make sure to replace the O-ring (B) before reinstalling the front camshaft bearing cap

29 Remove the crankshaft sprocket and the lower timing chain guide (see illustration).

INSPECTION

▸ **Refer to illustrations 6.30a and 6.30b**

30 Inspect the camshaft, water pump and crankshaft sprockets for wear on the teeth and keyways. Inspect the chains for cracks or excessive wear of the rollers. Inspect the facing of the chain guides and the secondary timing chain tensioners for excessive wear (see illustration).

➡**Note: If the secondary timing chain tensioners need to be replaced, the front camshaft bearing cap will have to be removed from the affected cylinder head to allow access to the secondary tensioner bolts (see illustration).**

INSTALLATION

▸ **Refer to illustrations 6.34, 6.36a, 6.36b, 6.41, 6.42a, 6.42b, 6.43a, 6.43b and 6.43c**

※※ CAUTION:

Before starting the engine, carefully rotate the crankshaft by hand through at least two full revolutions using a socket and breaker bar on the crankshaft pulley bolt. If you feel any resistance, STOP! There is something wrong - most likely, valves are hitting the pistons. You must find the problem before proceeding.

31 Install the crankshaft sprocket and the lower timing chain guide with the mark facing up (see illustration 6.29).

32 Verify that you have the correct timing chains for your vehicle by counting the number of links each chain has and comparing the new chains with the old chains. Also compare the position of the colored links in the new chains with the position of the colored links in the old chains.

33 If the secondary tensioners were removed, reinstall them and make sure the tensioner spring is locked in place.

34 Make sure the camshafts are positioned with the dowels on the exhaust camshafts in the 12 o'clock position in relation to the top of the cylinder head mating surface; the intake camshafts must be positioned with the small diameter dowel pin hole in the 12 o'clock position in relation to the top of the cylinder head mating surface. Install the secondary timing chains and sprocket assemblies on the camshafts with the timing marks aligned as shown (see illustration). Install the camshaft sprocket bolts hand tight.

35 Reconfirm that the secondary camshaft sprocket timing marks are aligned correctly with the colored links on the secondary timing chains, and remove the stopper pins from the secondary chain tensioners.

36 Install the primary timing chain onto the engine by looping the chain around the crankshaft sprocket and aligning the orange colored chain link with the mark on the crankshaft sprocket. Place the chain around the water pump sprocket and finally around the primary camshaft sprockets, making sure the pink colored links align with their respective marks on the sprockets (see illustrations).

➡**Note: It may be necessary to rotate the camshafts slightly in order to align the pink colored chain links with the marks on the intake camshaft sprockets.**

37 Install the upper timing chain guides.

38 Install the primary tensioner arm/chain guide and the timing chain tensioner assembly (see illustration 6.24). Reconfirm that the number one piston is still at TDC on the compression stroke and that the timing marks on the camshaft and crankshaft sprockets are aligned with the colored links on the chain, then remove the stopper pin from the primary timing chain tensioner.

39 Tighten the camshaft sprocket bolts to the torque listed in this Chapter's Specifications.

40 Remove all traces of old sealant from the timing chain cover, the cover bolts and the rear cover bolt holes.

41 Install new O-rings in the variable valve timing oil control orifice of the rear timing cover (see illustration).

42 Apply a 1/8-inch bead of RTV sealant to the timing chain cover sealing surfaces (see illustration). Place the timing chain cover in position on the engine and install the bolts in their original locations.

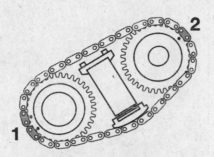
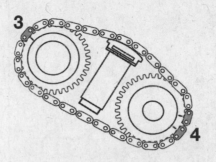

Rear cylinder bank　　**Front cylinder bank**

72016-2B-6.34 HAYNES

6.34 Secondary timing chain alignment details

1　Rear cylinder bank exhaust camshaft sprocket: Align the two colored links with the two round marks

2　Rear cylinder bank intake camshaft sprocket: Align the single colored link with the single round mark (mark is on the backside of sprocket)

3　Front cylinder bank intake camshaft sprocket: Align the single colored link with the single oval mark (mark is on the backside of sprocket)

4　Front cylinder bank exhaust camshaft sprocket: Align the two colored links with the two oval marks

6.36a The orange colored link on the timing chain aligns with the mark on the crankshaft sprocket

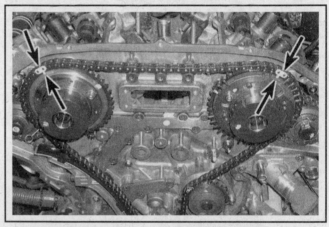

6.36b Make sure the pink colored links (upper arrows) on the primary timing chain align with the marks (lower arrows) on the intake camshaft sprockets

6.41 Install new O-rings at the indicated area on the right and left side of the rear timing chain case

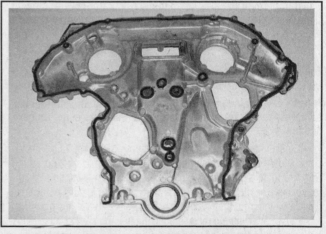

6.42a Apply RTV sealant to the timing chain cover at the areas shown - be sure to wipe off any excess sealant

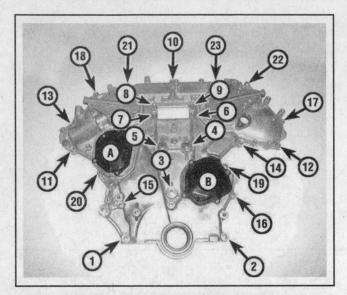

6.42b Front timing chain cover TIGHTENING sequence - (A) is the primary timing chain cover and (B) is the water pump cover, neither of these covers need be removed during this procedure unless they are leaking

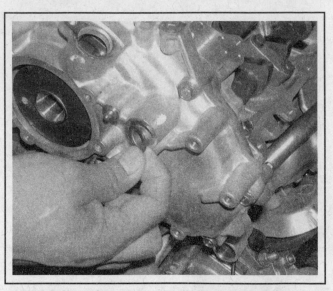

6.43a Install new O-rings in both of the IVT orifices on the front timing chain cover

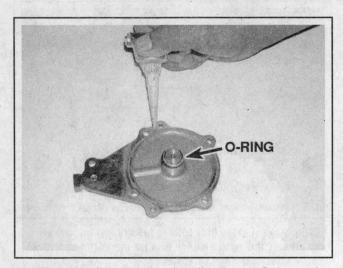

6.43b Apply a light film of engine oil to the new O-rings and install them in the groove on the IVT actuator covers, then apply a 1/8-inch bead of RTV sealant to the indicated areas

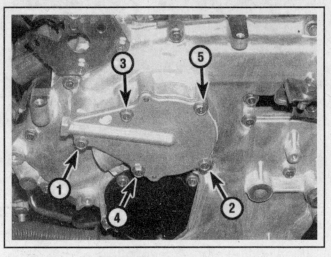

6.43c IVT cover TIGHTENING sequence

Following the recommended tightening sequence, tighten the bolts to the torque listed in this Chapter's Specifications (see illustration).

➡**Note: It will also be necessary to install the air conditioning compressor bracket in order to tighten the bolts in the proper sequence.**

43 Install new O-rings in the IVT orifices of the front timing chain cover and on the IVT actuator covers. Then apply a 1/8-inch bead of RTV sealant to the sealing surface of the variable valve timing actuator covers (see illustrations). Place the IVT covers in position over the dowels on the front timing cover and install the bolts in their original locations. Following the recommended tightening sequence (see illustration), tighten the bolts to the torque listed in this Chapter's Specifications.

44 The remainder of the installation is the reverse of removal. Be sure to follow the sealant manufacturer's recommendations for assembly and sealant curing times. Allow all sealant to fully cure before starting the engine.

45 Fill the crankcase with oil and install a new filter (see Chapter 1). Refill the cooling system (see Chapter 1)

46 Reconnect the battery and perform the necessary re-learn procedures (see Chapter 5).

➡**Note: Timing chain noise may be apparent after performing this procedure. This noise is normal and should only last until the air has bled out of the high pressure chamber of the primary timing chain tensioner. If after several minutes the noise is still apparent, run the engine at 3,000 rpm with the transmission in Neutral or Park until the noise subsides.**

7   Camshafts and lifters - removal and installation

→Note: The camshafts and lifters should always be thoroughly inspected before installation, and camshaft endplay should always be checked prior to camshaft removal. Refer to Chapter 2A for the camshaft and lifter inspection procedures.

REMOVAL

▶ **Refer to illustrations 7.4, 7.5 and 7.6**

1   Remove the timing chains and the camshaft sprockets (see Section 6).
2   Remove the camshaft position sensor brackets from the driver's ends of the cylinder heads.
3   Mark each camshaft so it can be installed in the same position.
4   Mark the camshaft bearing caps from 1 to 4, and with an "I" or an "E," to indicate intake or exhaust. Also mark arrows indicating the front of the engine (see illustration). All the components must also be marked to indicate which cylinder head they came from. Loosen the camshaft bearing caps in two or three steps, in the reverse order of the tightening sequence (see illustration 7.15a).

✳ CAUTION:

Keep the caps in order. They must go back in the same location they were removed from.

5   Remove the bearing caps and the camshafts. Make a note of the camshaft markings to ensure correct installation (see illustration).
→Note: The intake camshaft has a drill spot on the side of the sprocket mounting flange.
6   Remove the lifters from the cylinder head (see illustration).

✳ CAUTION:

Keep the lifters in order. They must go back in the same locations from which they were removed.

7   Inspect the camshaft and lifters as described in Chapter 2A (but refer to the values listed in this Chapter's Specifications).

INSTALLATION

▶ **Refer to illustrations 7.13a, 7.13b, 7.15a and 7.15b**

8   Remove all old RTV sealant from the bolts and the front bearing caps.
9   Set the number one piston at TDC if it has been moved.
10   Lubricate the lifters with clean engine oil, then install the lifters into their original locations.
11   Apply moly-based engine assembly lubricant to the camshaft lobes and journals.
12   Install the exhaust camshafts in their original positions with the dowel pins facing up (12 o'clock in relation to the cylinder head mating surface) and inline with the cylinder bank. The small dowel hole in the end of each intake camshaft should also be facing up.

7.4 The camshaft bearing caps should be marked with a number and letter stamp or a marker to ensure correct reinstallation

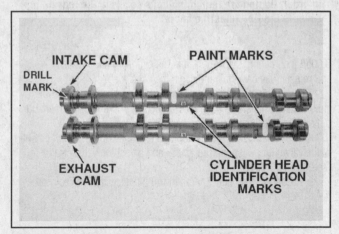

7.5 The ID mark in the center of each camshaft identifies which cylinder head the camshaft belongs to; L for left (front) and R for right (rear) - paint marks between the number 1 and number 2 journals indicate that it is an intake camshaft, while paint marks between the number 3 and number 4 journals indicate that it is an exhaust camshaft

7.6 The lifters and shims can be stored in individually marked plastic bags or a divided box as shown

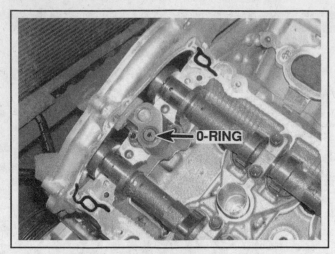

7.13a Apply RTV sealant to the cylinder head at the areas shown and install the secondary tensioner O-ring(s) - be sure to wipe off any excess sealant

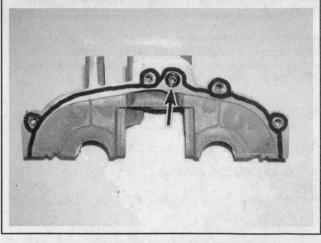

7.13b Apply a small dab of grease to the IVT oil control orifice O-ring to hold it in place on the No. 1 bearing cap, then apply RTV sealant to the areas shown

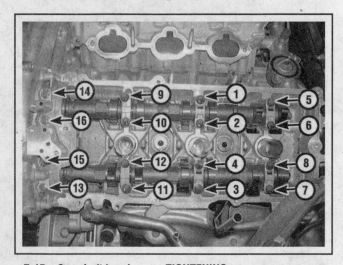

7.15a Camshaft bearing cap TIGHTENING sequence

7.15b After the camshaft bearing caps have been tightened in order, tighten the remaining bolts securing the rear timing cover to the No. 1 bearing cap(s)

13 Apply a bead of RTV sealant to the sealing surfaces of the No. 1 bearing cap(s) and the cylinder head. Install new O-rings on the secondary timing chain tensioner(s) and the IVT oil control orifice on the No. 1 bearing cap(s) (see illustrations).

14 Install the bearing caps and bolts and tighten them hand tight. The stamp marks on the bearing caps should be in order.

15 Tighten the bearing cap bolts in three steps, to the torque listed in this Chapter's Specifications, using the proper tightening sequence (see illustrations).

16 Check the protrusion of the front bearing caps in front of the cylinder head front surface. The front bearing cap should be close to

0.0055 inch behind the front face of the cylinder head. If it isn't, remove and reinstall the camshaft and caps, then check again.

17 Install the camshaft sprockets and timing chain (see Section 6). Hold the camshafts with a suitable wrench as you tighten the sprocket bolts to the specified torque.

18 The remainder of installation is the reverse of removal. If any part of the valve train was replaced, check and adjust the valve clearance (see Chapter 1).

19 Reconnect the battery and perform the necessary re-learn procedures (see Chapter 5).

8 Intake manifold - removal and installation

✳✳ WARNING:

The engine must be completely cool before beginning this procedure.

INTAKE MANIFOLD COLLECTOR

▶ **Refer to illustration 8.10**

➡ **Note: Intake manifold collector refers to the upper intake manifold.**

1 Remove the engine cover.

2 Remove the cowl cover (see Chapter 11).

3 Disconnect the cable from the negative terminal of the battery (see Chapter 5).

4 Remove the front air intake duct and hose.

5 Clamp-off the hoses leading to the throttle body, then disconnect them from the throttle body.

6 Label and disconnect the hoses and electrical connectors attached to the intake manifold collector and the throttle body. These include the brake booster vacuum hose, the EVAP purge hose, the PCV hose, the wiring for the throttle body and the fuel injector wiring connectors. Disconnect the vacuum hoses from the VIAS system.

7 Move the EVAP purge valve aside after removing its mounting bolt.

8 Loosen the intake manifold collector bolts in the reverse of the tightening sequence (see illustration 8.10). Remove it with the throttle body attached.

9 Clean the mounting surfaces of the collector and the upper intake manifold, removing all traces of the old gasket material or sealant.

10 Install the new gaskets, then install the intake manifold collector onto the upper intake manifold and tighten the bolts to the torque listed in this Chapter's Specifications. The bolts must be tightened in the proper sequence (see illustration).

11 The remainder of installation is the reverse of removal.

12 Reconnect the battery and perform the necessary re-learn procedures (see Chapter 5).

LOWER INTAKE MANIFOLD

▶ **Refer to illustration 8.22**

13 Relieve the fuel pressure (see Chapter 4). Drain the engine coolant (see Chapter 1).

14 Remove the intake manifold collector (see Steps 1 through 8).

15 Remove the fuel rail and injectors (see Chapter 4).

16 Label and detach any remaining hoses which would interfere with the removal of the lower intake manifold.

17 Loosen the manifold bolts in the reverse of the tightening sequence (see illustration 8.22).

18 Remove the manifold. The manifold will probably be stuck to the cylinder heads and force may be required to break the gasket seal.

✳✳ CAUTION:

Don't pry between the manifold and the heads or damage to the gasket sealing surfaces may occur, leading to vacuum leaks.

19 Carefully use a scraper to remove all traces of old gasket material and sealant from the manifold and cylinder heads, then clean the mating surfaces with brake system cleaner.

20 Use a precision straightedge and a feeler gauge to check the flatness of the top surface of the manifold. Compare your measurement to that listed in the Specifications in this Chapter. If it's excessive, replace the manifold.

21 Install new gaskets, then position the lower manifold on the engine. Make sure the gaskets and manifolds are aligned over the studs in the cylinder heads and install the bolts.

22 Following the correct tightening sequence, tighten the nuts/bolts, in several steps, to the torque listed in this Chapter's Specifications (see illustration).

23 The remainder of the installation is the reverse of the removal procedure. Refer to Steps 9 through 12 to install the intake manifold collector.

24 Reconnect the battery and perform the necessary re-learn procedures (see Chapter 5).

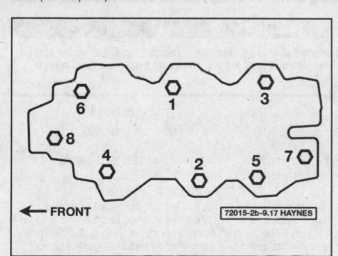

8.10 Upper intake manifold bolts/nuts tightening sequence

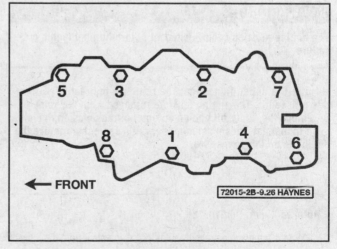

8.22 Lower intake manifold bolt tightening sequence

9 Exhaust manifold - removal, inspection and installation

✳✳ WARNING:

The engine must be completely cool before beginning this procedure.

➡Note: This procedure is only for vehicles with manual transmissions. The engine must be removed for removal of the exhaust manifolds on automatic transmission models.

REMOVAL

1 Drain the power steering fluid.
2 Remove the front air inlet duct and hose. Remove the air filter housing (see Chapter 4).
3 Remove the front subframe (see Chapter 11).

Left (front) side

4 Drain some of the engine coolant (see Chapter 1).
5 Disconnect the cable from the negative terminal of the battery (see Chapter 5). Perform the idle air volume learning procedure when connecting the battery (see Chapter 5). Remove the battery tray.
6 Remove the engine cooling fan assembly (see Chapter 3).
7 Disconnect the heater hose from the engine.
8 Remove the front engine mount support bracket.

Right (rear) side

9 Remove the cowl (see Chapter 11).
10 Disconnect the brake booster vacuum hose and the EVAP hose.
11 Support the engine with an appropriate fixture and remove the rear engine mount (see Section 18).

Both sides

12 Remove the support brackets from the catalytic converter.
13 Disconnect or remove the oxygen sensors (see Chapter 6).
14 Remove the exhaust manifold heat shields.
15 Remove the catalytic converter from the exhaust manifold.
16 Loosen the manifold nuts and bolts a little at a time, then remove them.
17 Remove the manifold-to-head nuts/bolts and detach the manifold and gaskets.

INSPECTION

18 Use a precision straightedge and a feeler gauge to check the flatness of the exhaust manifold sealing surface. Compare the measurement to the maximum allowable listed in this Chapter's Specifications. Replace the manifold or have it surfaced if the warpage is excessive.

INSTALLATION

19 Use a scraper to remove all traces of old gasket material and carbon deposits from the manifold and cylinder head mating surfaces.
20 Position the new exhaust manifold gaskets over the studs on the cylinder head.
21 Install the manifold and thread the mounting nuts/bolts into place.
22 Tighten the nuts/bolts a little at a time, working from the center out, to the torque listed in this Chapter's Specifications.
23 Reinstall the remaining parts in the reverse order of removal.
24 Reconnect the battery and perform the necessary re-learn procedures (see Chapter 5).

10 Cylinder head - removal and installation

✳✳ WARNING:

The engine must be completely cool before beginning this procedure

➡Note: The upper oil pan must be removed in order to perform this procedure. The engine must be removed from the vehicle to remove the upper oil pan on automatic transmission models. Even in manual transmission models, it's easiest to remove the engine to do this procedure.

REMOVAL

▸ Refer to illustration 10.12

1 Remove the engine (see Chapter 2C). Separate it from the transmission.
2 Remove the timing chains and sprockets (see Section 6).

✳✳ CAUTION:

Be careful not to disturb the crankshaft from TDC on the compression stroke of the No. 1 cylinder during the remainder of this procedure.

3 Remove the camshafts (see Section 7).
4 Remove the lower intake manifold (see Section 8).
5 Remove the coolant outlet.
6 Remove the rear timing chain cover bolts in the reverse order of the tightening sequence (see illustration 10.26d).
7 Detach the rear timing cover from the engine.

➡Note: If the cover is stuck to the cylinder head or engine block, bump one end with a block of wood and a hammer to jar it loose. If that doesn't work, try to slip a flexible putty knife between the cover and the engine to break the gasket seal. Don't pry at the cover-to-cylinder head joint or damage to the sealing surfaces may occur (leading to oil leaks in the future).

10.12 Pry on a casting protrusion to break the head loose

10.15 Carefully remove all traces of old gasket material from the sealing surfaces

8   Remove the O-rings from the front of the cylinder heads and the engine block.

9   Remove the IVT (Intake Variable Valve Timing Control) valves.

10   Label and remove any remaining items attached to the cylinder head, such as coolant fittings, tubes, cables, hoses, wires or brackets.

11   Using a breaker bar and the appropriate sized Allen-head socket, loosen the cylinder head bolts in 1/4-turn increments until they can be removed by hand. Loosen the bolts in the reverse order of the tightening sequence (see illustration 10.24) to avoid warping or cracking the head. Obtain new head bolts for installation.

12   Lift the cylinder head off the engine block. If it's stuck, very carefully pry up at a casting protrusion, beyond the gasket surface (see illustration).

13   Remove all external components from the head to allow for thorough cleaning and inspection.

INSTALLATION

♦ **Refer to illustrations 10.15, 10.24, 10.26a, 10.26b, 10.26c and 10.26d**

14   The mating surfaces of the cylinder head and block must be perfectly clean when the head is installed.

15   Use a gasket scraper to remove all traces of carbon and old gasket material from the cylinder head and engine block, then clean the mating surfaces with brake system cleaner (see illustration). If there's oil on the mating surfaces when the head is installed, the gasket may not seal correctly and leaks could develop.

16   When working on the block, stuff the cylinders with clean shop rags to keep out debris. Use a vacuum cleaner to remove material that falls into the cylinders.

17   Check the block and head mating surfaces for nicks, deep scratches and other damage. If damage is slight, it can be removed with a file; if it's excessive, machining may be the only alternative.

18   Use a tap of the correct size to chase the threads in the head bolt holes, then clean the holes with compressed air - make sure that nothing remains in the holes.

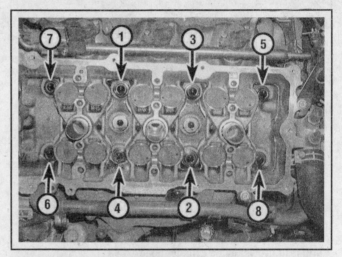

10.24 Cylinder head bolt TIGHTENING sequence

❋❋ WARNING:

Wear eye protection when using compressed air!

19   Check the cylinder head for warpage (see Chapter 2C). Check the head gasket, intake and exhaust manifold surfaces.

20   Install the components that were removed from the head.

21   Position the new cylinder head gasket over the dowel pins on the block, noting which direction on the gasket faces up.

22   Carefully set the head on the block without disturbing the gasket.

23   Before installing the head bolts, apply a small amount of clean engine oil to the threads and hardened washers (if equipped). The chamfered side of the washers must face the bolt heads.

24   Install the NEW bolts in their original locations and tighten them finger tight. Then tighten all the bolts in several steps, following the proper sequence (see illustration), to the torque listed in this Chapter's Specifications.

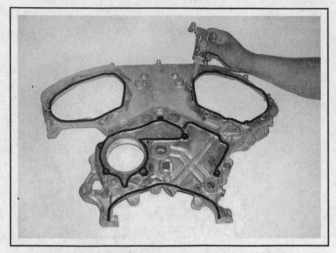

10.26a Apply RTV sealant to the rear timing chain cover at the areas shown - be sure to wipe off any excess sealant

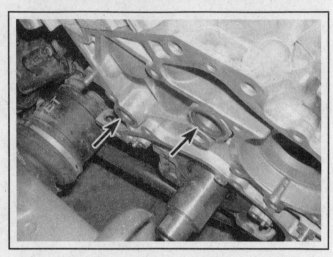

10.26b Install new O-rings in the front of the engine block . . .

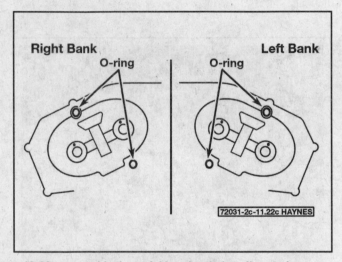

10.26c . . . and in the variable valve timing oil control orifices (arrows) in the cylinder head

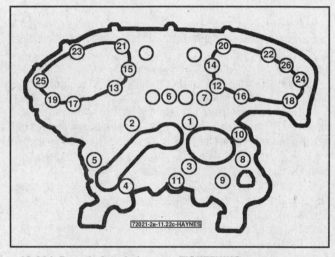

10.26d Rear timing chain cover TIGHTENING sequence

25 Remove all traces of old sealant from the rear timing chain cover and the cover bolts.

26 Apply a bead of RTV sealant to the rear timing cover sealing surfaces (see illustration). Install new O-rings in the front of the engine block and in the variable valve timing oil control orifices in the cylinder head (see illustrations). Place the rear timing chain cover in position over the dowels on the engine and install the bolts in their original locations. Following the recommended tightening sequence, tighten the bolts to the torque listed in this Chapter's Specifications (see illustration).

27 Install the camshafts (see Section 7), then install the timing chains and sprockets (see Section 6). The remaining installation steps are the reverse of removal. If any part of the valve train was replaced, check and adjust the valve clearance (see Chapter 1).

28 Install the engine in the vehicle.

29 Refill the cooling system and engine oil, and install a new oil filter (see Chapter 1).

30 Reconnect the battery and perform the necessary re-learn procedures (see Chapter 5).

31 Start the engine and check for oil and coolant leaks.

11 Crankshaft pulley - removal and installation

1 Disconnect the cable from the negative terminal of the battery (see Chapter 5).

2 Block the rear wheels and set the parking brake.

3 Loosen the lug nuts of the right front wheel.

4 Raise the front of the vehicle and support it securely on jackstands. Remove the right front wheel.

5 Remove the engine splash shield.

6 Remove the drivebelt (see Chapter 1).

7 Remove the starter (see Chapter 5) and lock the flywheel using a large screwdriver.

8   Loosen the crankshaft pulley bolt.

9   Use a puller to remove the pulley from the crankshaft (see illustration).

※※ **CAUTION:**

Be sure to use the proper adapter on the end of the crankshaft to prevent damage to the threads or end of the crankshaft. Also, the jaws of the puller must bolt to the hub of the pulley or grasp the hub of the pulley, not the outer diameter.

10   To install the crankshaft pulley, align the pulley groove with the key on the crankshaft and slide the pulley onto the crankshaft.

11   Install the crankshaft pulley retaining bolt and tighten it to the torque listed in this Chapter's Specifications.

12   The remainder of installation is the reverse of removal.

13   Reconnect the battery and perform the necessary re-learn procedures (see Chapter 5).

12   Crankshaft front oil seal - replacement

▶ **Refer to illustrations 12.2 and 12.4**

1   Remove the crankshaft pulley (see Section 11).

2   Carefully pry the seal out of the cover with a seal removal tool or a large screwdriver (see illustration).

※※ **CAUTION:**

Be careful not to scratch, gouge or distort the area that the seal fits into or an oil leak will develop.

3   Clean the bore to remove any old seal material and corrosion. Position the new seal in the bore with the seal lip (usually the side with the spring) facing IN (toward the engine). A small amount of oil applied to the outer edge of the new seal will make installation easier.

4   Drive the seal into the bore with a large socket and hammer (see illustration). Select a socket that's the same outside diameter as the seal and make sure the new seal is pressed into place until it's flush with the face of the case.

5   Check the surface of the damper that the oil seal rides on. If the surface has been grooved from long-time contact with the seal, the new seal will leak. Replace the crankshaft pulley.

6   Lubricate the seal lips with engine oil and reinstall the crankshaft pulley. Install the crankshaft pulley retaining bolt and tighten it to the torque listed in this Chapter's Specifications.

7   The remainder of installation is the reverse of the removal. Run the engine and check for oil leaks.

12.2 Pry the seal out very carefully with a seal removal tool or screwdriver, being careful not to nick or gouge the seal bore or the crankshaft

12.4 Use a large socket, seal driver or large-diameter pipe to drive the new seal into the cover

13   Oil pan - removal and installation

LOWER OIL PAN

▶ **Refer to illustration 13.9**

1   Raise the vehicle and support it securely on jackstands.

2   Remove the under-vehicle splash shield.

3   Refer to Chapter 1 and drain the engine oil.

4   Loosen the lower oil pan bolts in the reverse order of the tightening sequence (see illustration 13.9). Remove the bolts.

5   Use a plastic-face hammer to bump the side of the oil pan to break it loose. If that doesn't work, tap a putty knife or other thin tool between the upper and lower oil pans. Remove the lower oil pan.

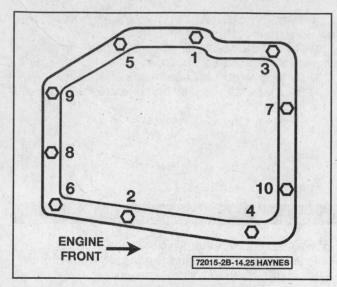

13.9 Lower (steel) oil pan TIGHTENING sequence

13.31 Insert a flathead screwdriver or small pry bar into the notch on the side of the oil pan to break it loose - be careful not to damage the sealing surfaces!

6   Clean all remnants of silicone sealer from the sealing surfaces. Wipe the surfaces with lacquer thinner to remove all traces of oil.

7   Check the lower steel oil pan flange for distortion, particularly around the bolt holes. If necessary, place the pan on a wood block and use a hammer to flatten and restore the gasket surface.

8   Apply a bead of RTV sealant around the steel oil pan flange and install the steel oil pan.

➡Note: The oil pan must be installed within 15 minutes once the sealant has been applied.

9   Following the recommended sequence, tighten the oil pan fasteners in several steps to the torque listed in this Chapter's Specifications (see illustration).

10   The remainder of installation is the reverse of removal.

UPPER OIL PAN

Removal

▶ Refer to illustration 13.31

➡Note: This procedure is for manual transmission models only. The engine must be removed from the vehicle to do this procedure on automatic transmission vehicles. If the engine has been removed, begin with Step 28.

11   Disconnect the cable from the negative terminal of the battery (see Chapter 5). Perform the idle air volume learning procedure when connecting the battery (see Chapter 5).

12   Set the parking brake and block the rear wheels. Drain the oil and remove the oil filter (see Chapter 1).

13   Raise the front of the vehicle and support it securely on jackstands.

14   Remove the lower oil pan (see Steps 1 through 5).

15   Remove the engine splash shield and the inner fender splash shields.

16   Drain the engine oil and remove the oil filter (see Chapter 1).

17   Remove the dipstick and dipstick tube.

18   Drain the coolant (see Chapter 1).

19   Remove the intake manifold collector (see Section 8).

20   Remove the engine cooling fan (see Chapter 3).

21   Remove the drivebelt (see Chapter 1).

22   Remove the front subframe (see Chapter 11).

23   Unbolt the air conditioning compressor. Move the assembly aside without disconnecting the lines.

24   Disconnect the engine coolant tubes from the oil cooler. Tape the ends to prevent contamination.

25   Remove the Crankshaft Position (CKP) sensor (see Chapter 6) and the oil pressure switch.

26   Remove the right driveaxle and its center bearing support (see Chapter 8).

27   Remove the oxygen sensors from the catalytic converters (see Chapter 6).

28   Remove the rear cover from the upper oil pan.

29   Remove the four bolts that attach the upper oil pan to the transmission.

30   Remove the upper oil pan bolts in the reverse of the tightening sequence (see illustration 13.38).

31   Put a prying tool into the notch in the oil pan top rail and use it to break the oil pan loose (see illustration). Remove the upper oil pan.

32   Remove the two O-rings from the block and the housing of the oil pump.

33   Remove the gaskets from the front timing cover and the rear seal retainer.

Installation

▶ Refer to illustrations 13.37 and 13.38

34   Use a scraper to remove all traces of old gasket material and sealant from the upper aluminum section of the oil pan, the lower steel pan and the engine block. Clean the mating surfaces with brake system cleaner.

❋❋ CAUTION:

Be careful not to scratch or gouge the gasket surface of the block or oil pan. A leak could develop after the repairs have been completed.

35   Make sure the threaded bolt holes in the block and aluminum section of the oil pan are clean.

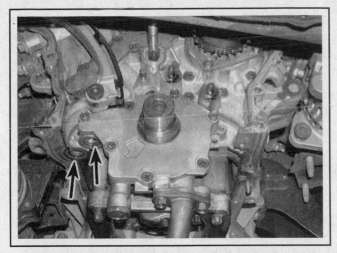

13.37 Install new O-rings in the block and the oil pump housing

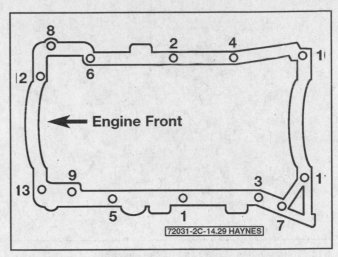

13.38 Upper (aluminum) oil pan TIGHTENING sequence

36 Apply a bead of RTV sealant to the ends of the timing chain cover gasket and the rear oil seal retainer gasket, then place the gaskets in position on the oil pan. Apply a bead of RTV sealant around the upper aluminum oil pan flange.

➡**Note: The oil pan must be installed within 15 minutes once the sealant has been applied.**

37 Install new O-rings in the engine block and the oil pump body (see illustration).

38 Carefully position the upper aluminum section of the oil pan on the engine block and install the bolts. Following the recommended sequence, tighten the fasteners in three or four steps to the torque listed in this Chapter's Specifications (see illustration).

39 Install the transmission mounting bolts.

40 The remainder of installation is the reverse of removal. Be sure to install a new oil filter (see Chapter 1) and wait at least 30 minutes after applying the silicone sealer before adding oil.

14 Oil pump - removal, inspection and installation

REMOVAL

◆ **Refer to illustration 14.3**

1 Remove the primary timing chain and the crankshaft sprocket (see Section 6).

➡**Note: It is not necessary to remove the camshaft sprockets, the camshaft sprocket bolts, the secondary timing chains or the primary timing chain tensioner pivot arm/chain guide during this procedure. Simply pivot the tensioner arm/chain guide over to the left side to allow removal of the oil pump housing.**

2 Remove the oil pans (see Section 13).

3 Remove the oil strainer-to-oil pump bolts from the lower section of the oil pump. Remove the oil pump-to-engine block bolts (see illustration).

4 Gently pry the oil pump housing outward enough to clear the dowel pins on the engine block and remove it from the engine.

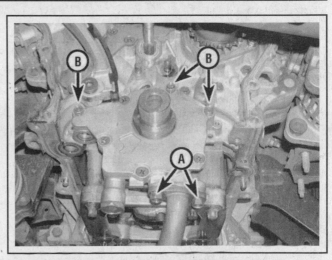

14.3 Remove the mounting bolts (A) and detach the oil strainer from the oil pump, then remove the oil pump housing retaining bolts (B)

14.5 Remove the screws and lift the cover off

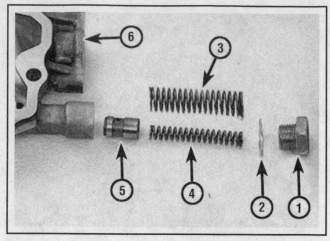

14.7 Oil pressure relief valve components

1 Plug	4 Inner spring (if equipped)
2 Washer	5 Relief valve
3 Outer spring	6 Oil pump housing

14.8a Use feeler gauges to measure the rotor tooth tip clearance . . .

14.8b . . . and the outer rotor-to-body clearance

14.8c Measure the cover-to-rotor end clearance with a straightedge and feeler gauge - measure (A) above the inner rotor and (B) above the outer rotor

INSPECTION

♦ **Refer to illustrations 14.5, 14.7, 14.8a, 14.8b, 14.8c, 14.8d and 14.8e**

5   Use a large Phillips screwdriver to remove the screws holding the front cover on the oil pump housing (see illustration).

6   Clean all components with solvent, then inspect them for wear and damage.

7   Remove the oil pressure regulator cap, washer, spring(s) and valve (see illustration). Check the oil pressure regulator valve sliding surface and valve spring. If either the spring or the valve is damaged, they must be replaced as a set.

8   Check the clearance of the following oil pump components with a feeler gauge (see illustrations) and compare the measurements to the clearance listed in this Chapter's Specifications:

  a) Rotor tooth tip clearance
  b) Outer rotor-to-body clearance
  c) Cover-to-inner rotor clearance

  d) Cover-to-outer rotor clearance
  e) Inner rotor ridge clearance

If any clearance is excessive, replace the entire oil pump assembly.

9   Assemble the oil pump and tighten the screws securely.

➥**Note: Pack the pump with grease to prime it. Install the oil pressure regulator valve, spring and washer, then tighten the oil pressure regulator valve cap.**

INSTALLATION

♦ **Refer to illustration 14.10**

10 Installation is the reverse of removal. Use new gaskets (where applicable) on all disassembled parts. Align the flats on the crankshaft (see illustration) with the flats on the oil pump gear. Tighten all fasteners to the torque listed in this Chapter's Specifications.

➥**Note: Before installing the oil pan, be sure to replace the O-rings on the oil pump housing and engine block (see illustration 13.37).**

14.8d Use calipers to measure the diameter of the inner rotor ridge (the part of the inner rotor that rides in the pump body) . . .

14.8e . . . and subtract the inner rotor ridge diameter from the opening in the pump body where the inner rotor rides to obtain the inner rotor ridge-to-body clearance

14.10 There is a flat surface on each side of the crankshaft - align them with the flats on the inner gear

15 Engine oil cooler and oil filter adapter - general information and replacement

GENERAL INFORMATION

1   These engines are equipped with a combination oil cooler/oil filter adapter that is mounted to the right end of the oil pan. The oil cooler/oil filter adapter also incorporates an oil pressure relief valve, which redirects oil flow to bypass the oil cooler when pressures are too high. The oil cooler has two hoses connecting the cooler to the engine.

REPLACEMENT

◆ Refer to illustrations 15.5, 15.6 and 15.7

✻✻ WARNING:

The engine must be completely cool before performing this procedure.

2   Loosen the lug nuts of the right front wheel. Raise the vehicle and support it securely on jackstands. Remove the right front wheel.
3   Remove the right front inner fender splash shield (see Chapter 11).
4   Drain the cooling system (see Chapter 1).
5   Place rags under the cooler to catch oil and coolant spillage. Detach the hose clamps and disconnect the inlet and outlet hoses from the oil cooler (see illustration).
6   Remove the oil filter, then remove the oil cooler connector bolt and remove the oil cooler and O-ring from the oil pan (see illustration).
7   Lubricate the new oil cooler O-ring with engine oil. Install the O-ring in the groove on the oil cooler (see illustration).
8   Position the oil cooler onto the oil pan and install the connector bolt.
9   Tighten the oil cooler connector bolt to the torque listed in this Chapter's Specifications. Do not overtighten.
10   Connect the coolant hoses to the cooler and install the clamps. Install a new oil filter, change the engine oil and refill the cooling system (see Chapter 1).

15.5 Detach the coolant hoses from the oil cooler

15.6 Remove the oil cooler connector bolt

15.7 Install a new O-ring into the groove in the oil cooler

16 Flywheel/driveplate - removal and installation

▶ **Refer to illustration 16.4**

1   Raise the vehicle and support it securely on jackstands, then refer to Chapter 7 and remove the transmission.

❋❋ WARNING:

The engine must be supported from above with an engine hoist or three-bar support fixture before working underneath the vehicle with the transmission removed.

2   If the vehicle is equipped with a manual transmission, remove the pressure plate and clutch disc (see Chapter 8). Now is a good time to check/replace the clutch components and pilot bearing if necessary. If the vehicle is equipped with an automatic transmission, now would be a good time to check and replace the front pump seal/O-ring.

3   Use paint or a center-punch to make alignment marks on the flywheel/driveplate and crankshaft to ensure correct alignment during reinstallation.

4   Remove the bolts that secure the flywheel/driveplate to the crankshaft (see illustration). If the crankshaft turns, hold the flywheel with a pry bar or wedge a screwdriver into the ring gear teeth to jam the flywheel.

5   Remove the flywheel/driveplate from the crankshaft. Since the flywheel is fairly heavy, be sure to support it while removing the last bolt.

6   Clean the flywheel to remove grease and oil. Inspect the surface for cracks, rivet grooves, burned areas and score marks. Light scoring can be removed with emery cloth. Check for cracked and broken ring gear teeth or a loose ring gear. Lay the flywheel on a flat surface and use a straightedge to check for warpage.

7   Clean and inspect the mating surfaces of the flywheel/driveplate and the crankshaft. If the crankshaft rear seal is leaking, replace it before reinstalling the flywheel/driveplate.

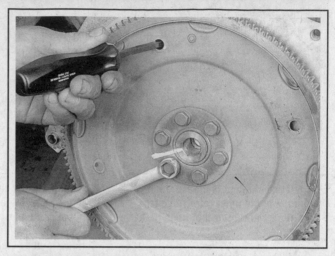

16.4 Hold a lever against a casting protrusion on the engine block or place a screwdriver through a hole in the driveplate to hold the driveplate while the mounting bolts are removed - note the painted marks made at the crank and driveplate for alignment

8   Position the flywheel/driveplate against the crankshaft. Be sure to align the marks made during removal. Note that some engines have an alignment dowel or staggered bolt holes to ensure correct installation. Before installing the bolts, apply thread locking compound to the threads.

9   Wedge a screwdriver into the ring gear teeth to keep the flywheel/driveplate from turning as you tighten the bolts to the torque listed in this Chapter's Specifications.

10   The remainder of installation is the reverse of the removal.

17 Rear main oil seal - replacement

1   The engine/transaxle assembly must be removed from the vehicle for this procedure (see Chapter 2C). Separate the transaxle from the engine (see Chapter 7).

2   Remove the flywheel or driveplate (see Section 16).

3   Remove the bolts from the rear seal retainer. Tap the retainer sideways with a plastic hammer to break the seal and remove it. Discard the seal/retainer assembly - it must be replaced with a new assembly.

4   Remove all old RTV sealant from the rear of the engine and the oil pan. Clean the surfaces with brake system cleaner.

5   Obtain special seal installation tool J-47128. It is available from automotive tool suppliers and Nissan dealerships.

6   Loosen the tool's wingnut.

7   Install the tool onto the rear of the crankshaft so it covers the sealing surface. Tighten the wingnut.

8   Apply a bead of RTV sealant to the sealing surface of the new retainer.

9   Lightly lubricate the oil seal lip with clean engine oil, then slide it over the tool and into position.

10   Loosen the wingnut and remove the tool.

11   Tighten the retainer bolts to the torque listed in this Chapter's Specifications.

12   The remaining steps are the reverse of removal.

18 Engine mounts - check and replacement

1 There are three engine mounts and one transaxle mount. The engine mounts are located on the passenger's side of the vehicle and on the front and rear side of the engine block. The transaxle mount is bolted to the left side of the transaxle.

CHECK

2 During the check, the engine must be raised slightly to remove the weight from the mounts.

3 Raise the vehicle and support it securely on jackstands. Support the engine/transmission from above using a hoist or three bar support fixture.

4 Check the mounts to see if the rubber is cracked, hardened or separated from the bushing in the center of the mount.

5 Check for relative movement between the mounts and the engine or frame (use a large screwdriver or prybar to attempt to move the mounts). If movement is noted, lower the engine and tighten the mount fasteners.

REPLACEMENT

6 If you're replacing a front or rear engine mount, raise the front of the vehicle and support it securely on jackstands. Remove the splash shields from under the vehicle.

7 Attach an engine hoist to the top of the engine for lifting.

❄❄ CAUTION:

Do not use a jack under the oil pan to support the entire weight of the engine or the oil pump pick-up could be damaged.

8 Remove the engine mount-to-chassis fasteners.

9 Remove the engine mount-to-engine mount bracket nut.

10 Raise the engine slightly until the engine mount can be removed from the vehicle.

11 Installation is the reverse of removal.

Specifications

General

Displacement	3.5L (213 cubic inches)	
Designation	VQ35DE	
Bore	3.760 inches	
Stroke	3.205 inches	
Cylinder numbers (front to rear)		
Right (rear) side	1-3-5	
Left (front) side	2-4-6	
Firing order	1-2-3-4-5-6	

3.5L engine

72015-1-specs HAYNES

Cylinder location diagram

Camshaft

Camshaft endplay	
Standard	0.0045 to 0.0074 inch
Limit	0.0094 inch
Camshaft journal diameter	
No. 1	1.0211 to 1.0218 inches
No. 2 through 4	0.9230 to 0.9238 inch
Camshaft bearing inside diameter	
No. 1	1.0236 to 1.0244 inches
No. 2 through 4	0.9252 to 0.9260 inch
Bearing oil clearance	
No. 1	0.0018 to 0.0034 inch
No. 2 through 4	0.0014 to 0.0030 inch
Service limit	0.0047 inch
Runout limit	0.0020 inch maximum
Lobe height	
Intake	1.7904 to 1.7978 inches
Exhaust	1.7907 to 1.7982 inches

Exhaust manifold

Maximum allowable warpage	0.012 inch

Intake manifold, lower

Maximum allowable warpage, upper surface	0.004 inch

Valve clearance (cold)

Intake	0.010 to 0.013 inch
Exhaust	0.011 to 0.015 inch

Oil pump

Outer gear-to-body clearance	0.0045 to 0.0102 inch
Inner gear-to-outer gear tip clearance	0.0071 inch maximum
Inner gear-to-housing side clearance	0.0012 to 0.0028 inch
Outer gear-to-housing side clearance	0.0020 to 0.0043 inch
Inner rotor hub-to-housing clearance	0.0018 to 0.0036 inch

Torque specifications　　　　　Ft-lbs (unless otherwise indicated)

➡ **Note: One foot-pound (ft-lb) of torque is equivalent to 12 inch-pounds (in-lbs) of torque. Torque values below approximately 15 ft-lbs are expressed in inch-pounds, since most foot-pound torque wrenches are not accurate at these smaller values.**

Camshaft sprocket bolts (1)*	76
Camshaft bearing cap bolts (see illustration 7.15a or 7.15b)	
Step 1 (bolts 7 through 10)	17 in-lbs
Step 2 (bolts 1 through 6)	17 in-lbs
Step 3 (all bolts)	52 in-lbs
Step 4 (bolts 1 through 6)	96 in-lbs
Crankshaft pulley bolt (1)*	
Step 1	32
Step 2	Tighten an additional 90-degrees
Cylinder head bolts (in sequence; see illustration 10.24) (1)* (2)* (3)*	
2007 and 2008 models	
Step 1	72
Step 2	Loosen completely (in reverse of tightening sequence)
Step 3	29
Step 4	Tighten an additional 90-degrees
Step 5	Tighten an additional 90-degrees
2009 and later models	
Step 1	72
Step 2	Loosen completely (in reverse of tightening sequence)
Step 3	29
Step 4	Tighten an additional 103-degrees
Step 5	Tighten an additional 103-degrees
Valve cover bolts (2)*	
Step 1	17 in-lbs
Step 2	74 in-lbs
Flywheel/driveplate bolts (1)*	80
Exhaust manifold nuts (2)*	23

Torque specifications   **Ft-lbs** (unless otherwise indicated)

Exhaust manifold heat shield bolts	52 in-lbs
Intake manifold collector (upper intake manifold)**	96 in-lbs
Intake manifold (lower intake manifold) (2)*	
Step 1	65 in-lbs
Step 2	19
Oil cooler connector bolt	36
Oil pan bolts	
Upper (aluminum) oil pan (2)*	16
Lower (steel) oil pan (2)*	78 in-lbs
Oil pan-to-transmission	37
Oil pan drain plug	26
Oil pan rear cover mounting plate	61 in-lbs
Oil pick-up tube mounting bolts	15
Oil pressure switch	132 in-lbs
Oil pump cover screws	61 in-lbs
Oil pressure relief plug	40
Front timing chain cover bolts (2)*	
6 mm	108 in-lbs
8 mm	21
Rear timing chain cover bolts (2)*	108 in-lbs
Variable valve timing cover bolts	96 in-lbs
Upper timing chain guide(s) bolts	75 in-lbs
Main timing chain tensioner bolts	75 in-lbs
Main timing chain guide pivot bolt	144 in-lbs
Secondary timing chain tensioner bolts	75 in-lbs
Rear main oil seal retainer bolts	78 in-lbs
Engine mount bolts/nuts	
Left (transmission) and right engine mounts	
Through-bolts	32 to 40
Engine mount bolts/nuts	
Mount-to-transmission bolts	32 to 40
Mount-to-frame bolts	54 to 62
Front and rear engine mounts	
Through-bolts	56 to 72
Engine mount nuts	32 to 40

*(1)*Lubricate fastener threads and heads with clean engine oil prior to installation*
*(2)*Tighten fasteners in the proper sequence. See text for diagrams*
*(3)*Bolts must be replaced with NEW ones*

Notes

Section

Reference to other Chapters

CHECK ENGINE/MIL light on - See Chapter 6

2C

GENERAL
ENGINE
OVERHAUL
PROCEDURES

1 General information - engine overhaul

◆ **Refer to illustrations 1.1, 1.2, 1.3, 1.4, 1.5 and 1.6**

Included in this portion of Chapter 2 are general information and diagnostic testing procedures for determining the overall mechanical condition of your engine.

The information ranges from advice concerning preparation for an overhaul and the purchase of replacement parts and/or components to detailed, step-by-step procedures covering removal and installation.

The following Sections have been written to help you determine whether your engine needs to be overhauled and how to remove and install it once you've determined it needs to be rebuilt. For information concerning in-vehicle engine repair, see Chapter 2A or 2B.

The Specifications included in this Part are general in nature and include only those necessary for testing the oil pressure and engine compression, and bottom-end torque specifications. Refer to Chapter 2A or 2B for additional engine Specifications.

It's not always easy to determine when, or if, an engine should be completely overhauled, because a number of factors must be considered.

High mileage is not necessarily an indication that an overhaul is needed, while low mileage doesn't preclude the need for an overhaul. Frequency of servicing is probably the most important consideration. An engine that's had regular and frequent oil and filter changes, as well as other required maintenance, will most likely give many thousands of miles of reliable service. Conversely, a neglected engine may require an overhaul very early in its service life.

Excessive oil consumption is an indication that piston rings, valve seals and/or valve guides are in need of attention. Make sure that oil leaks aren't responsible before deciding that the rings and/or guides are bad. Perform a cylinder compression check to determine the extent of the work required (see Section 3). Also, check the vacuum readings under various conditions (see Section 4).

Check the oil pressure with a gauge installed in place of the oil pressure sending unit and compare it to this Chapter's Specifications (see Section 2). If it's extremely low, the bearings and/or oil pump are probably worn out.

Loss of power, rough running, knocking or metallic engine noises, excessive valve train noise and high fuel consumption rates may also point to the need for an overhaul, especially if they're all present at the same time. If a complete tune-up doesn't remedy the situation, major mechanical work is the only solution.

An engine overhaul involves restoring the internal parts to the specifications of a new engine. During an overhaul, the piston rings are replaced and the cylinder walls are reconditioned (rebored and/or honed) (see illustrations 1.1 and 1.2). If a rebore is done by an automotive machine shop, new oversize pistons will also be installed. The main bearings, connecting rod bearings and camshaft bearings are generally replaced with new ones and, if necessary, the crankshaft may be reground to restore the journals (see illustration 1.3). Generally, the valves are serviced as well, since they're usually in less-than-perfect condition at this point. While the engine is being overhauled, other components, such as the distributor, starter and alternator, can be rebuilt as well. The end result should be similar to a new engine that will give many trouble free miles.

➡**Note: Critical cooling system components such as the hoses, drivebelts, thermostat and water pump should be replaced with new parts when an engine is overhauled. The radiator should be checked carefully to ensure that it isn't clogged or leaking (see Chapter 3). If you purchase a rebuilt engine or short block, some rebuilders will not warranty their engines unless the radiator has been professionally flushed. Also, we don't recommend overhauling the oil pump - always install a new one when an engine is rebuilt.**

Overhauling the internal components on today's engines is a difficult and time-consuming task which requires a significant amount of specialty tools and is best left to a professional engine rebuilder (see illustrations 1.4, 1.5 and 1.6). A competent engine rebuilder will handle the inspection of your old parts and offer advice concerning the reconditioning or replacement of the original engine, never purchase parts or have machine work done on other components until the block has been thoroughly inspected by a professional machine shop. As a general rule, time is the primary cost of an overhaul, especially since the vehicle may be tied up for a minimum of two weeks or more. Be aware that some engine builders only have the capability to rebuild the engine you bring them while other rebuilders have a large inventory of rebuilt exchange engines in stock. Also be aware that many machine shops could take as much as two weeks time to completely rebuild your engine depending on shop workload. Sometimes it makes more sense to simply exchange your engine for another engine that's already rebuilt to save time.

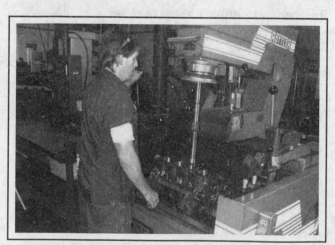

1.1 An engine block being bored. An engine rebuilder will use special machinery to recondition the cylinder bores

1.2 If the cylinders are bored, the machine shop will normally hone the engine on a machine like this

1.3 A crankshaft having a main bearing journal ground

1.4 A machinist checks for a bent connecting rod, using specialized equipment

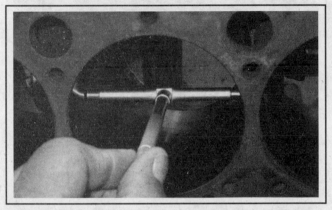

1.5 A bore gauge being used to check the main bearing bore

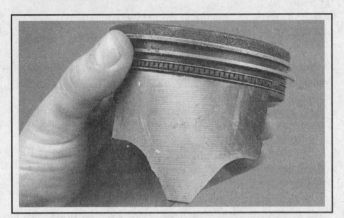

1.6 Uneven piston wear like this indicates a bent connecting rod

2 Oil pressure check

▶ **Refer to illustrations 2.2a and 2.2b**

1   Low engine oil pressure can be a sign of an engine in need of rebuilding. A "low oil pressure" indicator (often called an "idiot light") is not a test of the oiling system. Such indicators only come on when the oil pressure is dangerously low. Even a factory oil pressure gauge in the instrument panel is only a relative indication, although much better for driver information than a warning light. A better test is with a mechanical (not electrical) oil pressure gauge.

2   Locate the oil pressure indicator sending unit - on four-cylinder engines, it's located on the firewall side of the engine, near the front (passenger) end (see illustration); on V6 engines, it's located below the crankshaft pulley (see illustration).

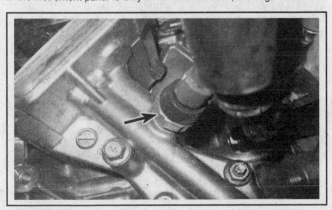

2.2a The oil pressure sending unit on the four-cylinder engine is located on the firewall side of the engine (seen from below in this photo)

2.2b The oil pressure sending unit on the V6 engine is located at the right end of the engine, below the crankshaft pulley

3   Unscrew and remove the oil pressure sending unit and then screw in the hose for your oil pressure gauge. If necessary, install an adapter fitting. Use Teflon tape or thread sealant on the threads of the adapter and/or the fitting on the end of your gauge's hose.

4   Connect an accurate tachometer to the engine, according to the tachometer manufacturer's instructions.

5   Check the oil pressure with the engine running (normal operating temperature) at the specified engine speed, and compare it to this Chapter's Specifications. If it's extremely low, the bearings and/or oil pump are probably worn out.

3   Cylinder compression check

♦ Refer to illustration 3.6

1   A compression check will tell you what mechanical condition the upper end of your engine (pistons, rings, valves, head gaskets) is in. Specifically, it can tell you if the compression is down due to leakage caused by worn piston rings, defective valves and seats or a blown head gasket.

➡Note: The engine must be at normal operating temperature and the battery must be fully charged for this check.

2   Begin by cleaning the area around the spark plugs before you remove them (compressed air should be used, if available). The idea is to prevent dirt from getting into the cylinders as the compression check is being done.

3   Remove the ignition coil assemblies (see Chapter 5). Also disable the fuel pump by removing the fuel pump fuse (see Chapter 4, Section 2).

4   Remove all of the spark plugs (see Chapter 1).

5   Block the throttle wide open.

6   Install a compression gauge in the spark plug hole (see illustration).

7   Crank the engine over at least seven compression strokes and watch the gauge. The compression should build up quickly in a healthy engine. Low compression on the first stroke, followed by gradually increasing pressure on successive strokes, indicates worn piston rings. A low compression reading on the first stroke, which doesn't build up during successive strokes, indicates leaking valves or a blown head gasket (a cracked head could also be the cause). Deposits on the undersides of the valve heads can also cause low compression. Record the highest gauge reading obtained.

8   Repeat the procedure for the remaining cylinders and compare the results to this Chapter's Specifications.

9   Add some engine oil (about three squirts from a plunger-type oil can) to each cylinder, through the spark plug hole, and repeat the test.

10 If the compression increases after the oil is added, the piston rings are definitely worn. If the compression doesn't increase significantly, the leakage is occurring at the valves or head gasket. Leakage past the valves may be caused by burned valve seats and/or faces or

3.6 Use a compression gauge with a threaded fitting for the spark plug hole, not the type that requires hand pressure to maintain the seal

warped, cracked or bent valves.

11 If two adjacent cylinders have equally low compression, there's a strong possibility that the head gasket between them is blown. The appearance of coolant in the combustion chambers or the crankcase would verify this condition.

12 If one cylinder is slightly lower than the others, and the engine has a slightly rough idle, a worn lobe on the camshaft could be the cause.

13 If the compression is unusually high, the combustion chambers are probably coated with carbon deposits. If that's the case, the cylinder head(s) should be removed and decarbonized.

14 If compression is way down or varies greatly between cylinders, it would be a good idea to have a leak-down test performed by an automotive repair shop. This test will pinpoint exactly where the leakage is occurring and how severe it is.

4   Vacuum gauge diagnostic checks

♦ Refer to illustrations 4.4 and 4.6

1   A vacuum gauge provides inexpensive but valuable information about what is going on in the engine. You can check for worn rings or cylinder walls, leaking head or intake manifold gaskets, incorrect carburetor adjustments, restricted exhaust, stuck or burned valves, weak valve springs, improper ignition or valve timing and ignition problems.

2   Unfortunately, vacuum gauge readings are easy to misinterpret, so they should be used in conjunction with other tests to confirm the diagnosis.

3   Both the absolute readings and the rate of needle movement are important for accurate interpretation. Most gauges measure vacuum in inches of mercury (in-Hg). The following references to vacuum assume the diagnosis is being performed at sea level. As elevation increases (or atmospheric pressure decreases), the reading will decrease. For every 1,000 foot increase in elevation above approximately 2,000 feet, the

gauge readings will decrease about one inch of mercury.

4   Connect the vacuum gauge directly to the intake manifold vacuum, not to ported (throttle body) vacuum (see illustration). Some models are equipped with a vacuum fitting built into the brake booster vacuum hose grommet at the brake booster. Other models are equipped with a vacuum hose fitting on the intake manifold. Use a T-fitting to access the vacuum signal. Be sure no hoses are left disconnected during the test or false readings will result.

5   Before you begin the test, allow the engine to warm up completely. Block the wheels and set the parking brake. With the transaxle in Park, start the engine and allow it to run at normal idle speed.

✳✳ WARNING:

Keep your hands and the vacuum gauge clear of the fans.

6   Read the vacuum gauge; an average, healthy engine should normally produce about 17 to 22 in-Hg with a fairly steady needle (see illustration). Refer to the following vacuum gauge readings and what they indicate about the engine's condition:

7   A low, steady reading usually indicates a leaking gasket between the intake manifold and cylinder head(s) or throttle body, a leaky vacuum hose, late ignition timing or incorrect camshaft timing. Check ignition timing with a timing light and eliminate all other possible causes,

4.4 A simple vacuum gauge can be handy in diagnosing engine condition and performance - be sure to connect it to intake manifold vacuum (not "ported" vacuum)

utilizing the tests provided in this Chapter before you remove the timing chain cover to check the timing marks.

8   If the reading is three to eight inches below normal and it fluctuates at that low reading, suspect an intake manifold gasket leak at an intake port or a faulty fuel injector.

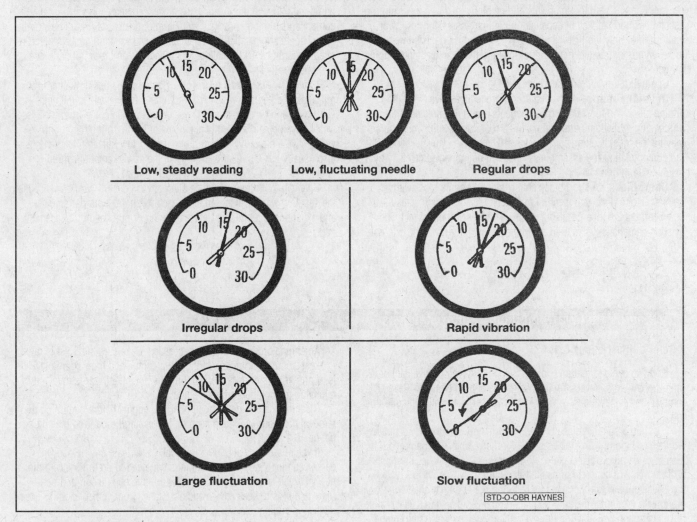

4.6 Typical vacuum gauge readings

9   If the needle has regular drops of about two-to-four inches at a steady rate, the valves are probably leaking. Perform a compression check or leak-down test to confirm this.

10   An irregular drop or down-flick of the needle can be caused by a sticking valve or an ignition misfire. Perform a compression check or leak-down test and read the spark plugs.

11   A rapid vibration of about four in-Hg vibration at idle combined with exhaust smoke indicates worn valve guides. Perform a leak-down test to confirm this. If the rapid vibration occurs with an increase in engine speed, check for a leaking intake manifold gasket or head gasket, weak valve springs, burned valves or ignition misfire.

12   A slight fluctuation, say one inch up and down, may mean ignition problems. Check all the usual tune-up items and, if necessary, run the engine on an ignition analyzer.

13   If there is a large fluctuation, perform a compression or leak-down test to look for a weak or dead cylinder or a blown head gasket.

14   If the needle moves slowly through a wide range, check for a clogged PCV system, incorrect idle fuel mixture, throttle body or intake manifold gasket leaks.

15   Check for a slow return after revving the engine by quickly snapping the throttle open until the engine reaches about 2,500 rpm and let it shut. Normally the reading should drop to near zero, rise above normal idle reading (about 5 in-Hg over) and then return to the previous idle reading. If the vacuum returns slowly and doesn't peak when the throttle is snapped shut, the rings may be worn. If there is a long delay, look for a restricted exhaust system (often the muffler or catalytic converter). An easy way to check this is to temporarily disconnect the exhaust ahead of the suspected part and redo the test.

5   Engine rebuilding alternatives

The do-it-yourselfer is faced with a number of options when purchasing a rebuilt engine. The major considerations are cost, warranty, parts availability and the time required for the rebuilder to complete the project. The decision to replace the engine block, piston/connecting rod assemblies and crankshaft depends on the final inspection results of your engine. Only then can you make a cost effective decision whether to have your engine overhauled or simply purchase an exchange engine for your vehicle.

Some of the rebuilding alternatives include:

Individual parts - If the inspection procedures reveal that the engine block and most engine components are in reusable condition, purchasing individual parts and having a rebuilder rebuild your engine may be the most economical alternative. The block, crankshaft and piston/connecting rod assemblies should all be inspected carefully by a machine shop first.

Short block - A short block consists of an engine block with a crankshaft and piston/connecting rod assemblies already installed. All new bearings are incorporated and all clearances will be correct. The existing camshafts, valve train components, cylinder head and external parts can be bolted to the short block with little or no machine shop work necessary.

Long block - A long block consists of a short block plus an oil pump, oil pan, cylinder head, valve cover, camshaft and valve train components, timing sprockets and chain or gears and timing cover. All components are installed with new bearings, seals and gaskets incorporated throughout. The installation of manifolds and external parts is all that's necessary.

Low mileage used engines - Some companies now offer low mileage used engines which is a very cost effective way to get your vehicle up and running again. These engines often come from vehicles which have been in totaled in accidents or come from other countries which have a higher vehicle turn over rate. A low mileage used engine also usually has a similar warranty like the newly remanufactured engines.

Give careful thought to which alternative is best for you and discuss the situation with local automotive machine shops, auto parts dealers and experienced rebuilders before ordering or purchasing replacement parts.

6   Engine removal - methods and precautions

▶ **Refer to illustrations 6.1, 6.2, and 6.3**

If you've decided that an engine must be removed for overhaul or major repair work, several preliminary steps should be taken. Read all removal and installation procedures carefully prior to committing to this job.

Locating a suitable place to work is extremely important. Adequate work space, along with storage space for the vehicle, will be needed. If a shop or garage isn't available, at the very least a flat, level, clean work surface made of concrete or asphalt is required.

These engines are removed by lowering the engine to the floor, along with the transaxle, and then raising the vehicle sufficiently to slide the assembly out; this will require a vehicle hoist as well as an engine hoist.

An engine hoist will also be necessary. Make sure the hoist is rated in excess of the combined weight of the engine and transaxle. Safety is of primary importance, considering the potential hazards involved in removing the engine from the vehicle.

Cleaning the engine compartment and engine before beginning the removal procedure will help keep tools clean and organized (see illustrations 6.1 and 6.2).

If you're a novice at engine removal, get at least one helper. One person cannot easily do all the things you need to do to remove a big heavy engine and transaxle assembly from the engine compartment. Also helpful is to seek advice and assistance from someone who's experienced in engine removal.

Plan the operation ahead of time. Arrange for or obtain all of the

6.1 After tightly wrapping water-vulnerable components, use a spray cleaner on everything, with particular concentration on the greasiest areas, usually around the valve cover and lower edges of the block. If one section dries out, apply more cleaner

6.2 Depending on how dirty the engine is, let the cleaner soak in according to the directions and then hose off the grime and cleaner. Get the rinse water down into every area you can get at; then dry important components with a hair dryer or paper towels

tools and equipment you'll need prior to beginning the job (see illustration 6.3). Some of the equipment necessary to perform engine removal and installation safely and with relative ease are (in addition to a vehicle hoist and an engine hoist) a heavy duty floor jack (preferably fitted with a transmission jack head adapter), complete sets of wrenches and sockets as described in the front of this manual, wooden blocks, plenty of rags and cleaning solvent for mopping up spilled oil, coolant and gasoline.

Plan for the vehicle to be out of use for quite a while. A machine shop can do the work that is beyond the scope of the home mechanic. Machine shops often have a busy schedule, so before removing the engine, consult the shop for an estimate of how long it will take to rebuild or repair the components that may need work.

6.3 Get an engine stand sturdy enough to firmly support the engine while you're working on it. Stay away from three-wheeled models; they have a tendency to tip over more easily, so get a four-wheeled unit

7 Engine - removal and installation

***** WARNING:**

Gasoline is extremely flammable, so take extra precautions when you work on any part of the fuel system. Don't smoke or allow open flames or bare light bulbs near the work area, and don't work in a garage where a gas-type appliance (such as a water heater or clothes dryer) is present. Since gasoline is carcinogenic, wear fuel-resistant gloves when there's a possibility of being exposed to fuel, and, if you spill any fuel on your skin, rinse it off immediately with soap and water. Mop up any spills immediately and do not store fuel-soaked rags where they could ignite. The fuel system is under constant pressure, so, if any fuel lines are to be disconnected, the fuel pressure in the system must be relieved first (see Chapter 4 for more information). When you perform any kind of work on the fuel system, wear safety glasses and have a Class B type fire extinguisher on hand.

***** WARNING:**

The air conditioning system is under high pressure. Do not loosen any hose fittings or remove any components until after the system has been discharged. Air conditioning refrigerant must be properly discharged into an EPA-approved recovery/recycling unit at a dealer service department or an automotive air conditioning repair facility. Always wear eye protection when disconnecting air conditioning system fittings.

***** WARNING:**

The engine must be completely cool before beginning this procedure.

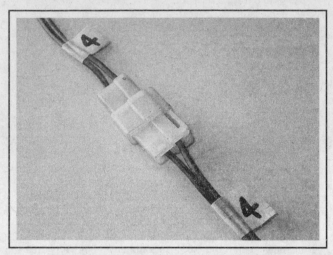

7.17 Label both ends of each wire or vacuum connection before disconnecting them

→Note: Engine removal on these vehicles is a difficult job, especially for do-it-yourselfer working at home. The manufacturer states that the engine and transaxle have to be removed as a unit from the bottom of the vehicle, not the top. With a floor jack and jackstands, it can't be raised high enough or supported safely enough for the engine/transaxle to slide out from underneath. The manufacturer recommends that removal of the engine/transaxle only be performed with a frame-contact type hoist.

→Note: During this procedure you'll have to adjust the height of the vehicle with the vehicle hoist to perform certain operations.

REMOVAL

▶ Refer to illustration 7.17

1 On V6 models, have the air conditioning system evacuated by a shop with the proper equipment.

2 Park the car on a vehicle hoist, then raise the hoist arms to contact the jacking points on each side of the vehicle, but don't raise the vehicle yet.

3 Relieve the fuel system pressure (see Chapter 4), then remove the battery and battery tray (see Chapter 4).

4 Drain the engine coolant (see Chapter 1) and the power steering fluid.

5 Drain the transaxle fluid (see Chapter 1). On manual transaxle models, disconnect the hydraulic line from the release cylinder fitting at the transaxle.

6 Remove the air inlet duct and the air filter housing (see Chapter 4).

7 Removing the hood (see Chapter 11) will make it easier to work on the vehicle but isn't necessary.

8 Loosen the lug nuts of the front wheels. Raise the vehicle on the hoist. Remove the front wheels and the under-vehicle splash shields.

9 Remove the cowl panel (see Chapter 11) and the front strut support bar.

10 Remove the inner fender splash shields (see Chapter 11).

11 Remove the driveaxles (see Chapter 8).

12 Remove the radiator hoses (see Chapter 3).

13 On manual transaxle vehicles, disconnect the shift cables, and all wiring from the transaxle.

14 On automatic transaxle vehicles, disconnect the shift cable, the fluid cooler lines and the wiring from the transaxle.

15 Disconnect all vacuum hoses between the engine and chassis, and also disconnect the heater hoses.

16 Disconnect the transaxle cooler lines from the radiator on automatic transaxle vehicles.

17 Remove the cover from the IPDM E/R fuse/relay box and power distribution module. Disconnect the wiring, then remove it along with its bracket. Label and disconnect all interfering wiring (see illustration). Make sure that nothing will prevent the engine from being lowered.

18 Remove the power steering reservoir and hoses.

19 Disconnect the power steering feed and return lines from the steering gear (see Chapter 10) and seal the ends to prevent contamination.

20 Remove the front portion of the exhaust system.

21 Separate the steering shaft from the steering gear (see Chapter 10).

Four-cylinder models

22 Disconnect the wiring from the PCM (see Chapter 6). Remove the PCM bracket.

23 Remove the drivebelt (see Chapter 1).

24 Unbolt the air conditioning compressor and secure it out of the way without disconnecting the refrigerant lines.

V6 models

25 Remove the cooling fan assembly (see Chapter 3).

26 Remove the air conditioning compressor.

27 Remove the transmission control module from automatic transaxle vehicles.

All models

28 Remove the engine rear cover plate.

29 Remove the torque converter bolts from automatic transaxle models, rotating the driveplate as you go.

30 Support the engine/transaxle assembly from above with an engine hoist. Attach the hoist chain to lift brackets bolted to opposite corners of the cylinder head(s). Make certain that the chains are connected to components that are solid enough to support the weight of the entire assembly. Use washers under bolt heads to prevent pull-through. The chains must be attached so they don't apply force to components that could be damaged.

✳✳ WARNING:

Don't put any part of your body under the engine or transaxle when it's supported only by a hoist or other lifting device.

31 Take up the slack in the chain until there is slight tension on the hoist. Make sure it's connected so that the engine/transaxle is balanced.

→Note: The chain must be long enough to allow the hoist to lower the engine/transaxle assembly to the ground without letting the hoist arm contact the vehicle.

32 On four-cylinder models and V6 models with manual transaxles, refer to Chapter 10 and remove the front subframe.

→Note: The engine and transaxle must be removed while connected to the front subframe on V6 automatic transaxle models.

On V6 automatic transaxle models, perform all of the subframe removal Steps but don't disconnect the engine or transaxle from the subframe.

33 Check to be sure that there is nothing connecting the engine/transaxle to the vehicle. Label and disconnect anything remaining.

34 Lower the engine/transaxle assembly slowly to the floor. On V6 automatic transaxle models, you'll be lowering the entire subframe that's attached to the engine/transaxle assembly.

35 Disconnect the engine hoist after blocking the engine so it can't tip.

36 Raise the vehicle on the hoist.

37 Reconnect the chain of the engine hoist to the engine/transaxle to support it. The assembly can now be moved from under the vehicle to another work area.

38 Remove the starter, the crankshaft position sensor and the transaxle wiring harness. Remove the subframe if necessary.

39 Separate the transaxle from the engine. Be careful to support the engine and the transaxle securely so they can't fall.

40 Mount the engine on an engine stand using the hoist.

INSTALLATION

41 Installation is the reverse of removal noting these points:
  a) *Check the engine and transaxle mounts. If they're worn or damaged, replace them.*
  b) *Attach the transaxle to the engine following the procedure in Chapter 7.*
  c) *Tighten the subframe mounting bolts to the torque listed in Chapter 11.*
  d) *Tighten the wheel lug nuts to the torque listed in Chapter 1. Tighten the driveaxle/hub nuts to the torque listed in Chapter 8. Tighten the steering and suspension fasteners to the torque values listed in Chapter 10.*
  e) *Refill the engine coolant, oil, power steering fluid, clutch fluid and transaxle fluid (see Chapter 1).*
  f) *Reconnect the battery and perform the necessary re-learn procedures (see Chapter 5). Recheck all fluid levels.*

8 Engine overhaul - disassembly sequence

1 It's much easier to remove the external components if it's mounted on a portable engine stand. A stand can often be rented quite cheaply from an equipment rental yard. Before the engine is mounted on a stand, the flywheel/driveplate should be removed from the engine.

2 If a stand isn't available, it's possible to remove the external engine components with it blocked up on the floor. Be extra careful not to tip or drop the engine when working without a stand.

3 If you're going to obtain a rebuilt engine, all external components must come off first, to be transferred to the replacement engine. These components include:

  Flywheel/driveplate
  Ignition coils and wiring harnesses
  Emissions-related components
  Engine mounts and mount brackets
  Intake/exhaust manifolds
  Fuel injection components

  Oil filter and oil cooler
  Spark plugs
  Thermostat and housing assembly
  Water pump

➡**Note: When removing the external components from the engine, pay close attention to details that may be helpful or important during installation. Note the installed position of gaskets, seals, spacers, pins, brackets, washers, bolts and other small items.**

4 If you're going to obtain a short block (assembled engine block, crankshaft, pistons and connecting rods), then remove the timing chain, cylinder head, oil pan, oil pump pick-up tube, oil pump and water pump from your engine so that you can turn in your old short block to the rebuilder as a core. See *Engine rebuilding alternatives* for additional information regarding the different possibilities to be considered.

9 Pistons and connecting rods - removal and installation

REMOVAL

◗ **Refer to illustrations 9.1, 9.3 and 9.4**

➡**Note: Prior to removing the piston/connecting rod assemblies, remove the cylinder head and oil pan (see Chapter 2A or 2B).**

1 Use your fingernail to feel if a ridge has formed at the upper limit of ring travel (about 1/4-inch down from the top of each cylinder). If carbon deposits or cylinder wear have produced ridges, they must be completely removed with a special tool (see illustration). Follow the manufacturer's instructions provided with the tool. Failure to remove the ridges before attempting to remove the piston/connecting rod assemblies may result in piston breakage.

2 After the cylinder ridges have been removed, turn the engine so the crankshaft is facing up.

9.1 Before you try to remove the pistons, use a ridge reamer to remove the raised material (ridge) from the top of the cylinders

9.3 Checking the connecting rod endplay (side clearance)

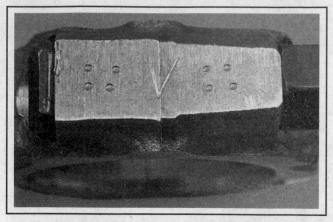

9.4 If the connecting rods or caps are not marked, use permanent ink or paint to mark the caps to the rods by cylinder number (for example, this would be number 4 cylinder connecting rod)

3 Before the main bearing cap assembly and connecting rods are removed, check the connecting rod endplay with feeler gauges. Slide them between the first connecting rod and the crankshaft throw until the play is removed (see illustration). Repeat this procedure for each connecting rod. The endplay is equal to the thickness of the feeler gauge(s). Check with an automotive machine shop for the endplay service limit (a typical endplay should measure between 0.005 to 0.015 inch [0.127 to 0.381 mm]). If the play exceeds the service limit, new connecting rods will be required. If new rods (or a new crankshaft) are installed, the endplay may fall under the minimum allowable. If it does, the rods will have to be machined to restore it. If necessary, consult an automotive machine shop for advice.

4 Check the connecting rods and caps for identification marks. If they aren't plainly marked, use paint or marker (see illustration) to clearly identify each rod and cap (1, 2, 3, etc., depending on the cylinder they're associated with). Do not interchange the rod caps. Install the exact same rod cap onto the same connecting rod.

✳✳ CAUTION:

Do not use a punch and hammer to mark the connecting rods or they may be damaged.

5 Loosen each of the connecting rod cap bolts or nuts 1/2-turn at a time until they can be removed by hand.

6 Remove the number one connecting rod cap and bearing insert. Don't drop the bearing insert out of the cap.

7 Remove the bearing insert and push the connecting rod/piston assembly out through the top of the engine. Use a wooden or plastic hammer handle to push on the upper bearing surface in the connecting rod. If resistance is felt, double-check to make sure that all of the ridge was removed from the cylinder.

8 Repeat the procedure for the remaining cylinders.

9 After removal, reassemble the connecting rod caps and bearing inserts in their respective connecting rods and install the cap bolts finger tight. Leaving the old bearing inserts in place until reassembly will help prevent the connecting rod bearing surfaces from being accidentally nicked or gouged.

10 The pistons and connecting rods are now ready for inspection and overhaul at an automotive machine shop.

PISTON RING INSTALLATION

▶ **Refer to illustrations 9.13, 9.14, 9.15, 9.19a, 9.19b and 9.22**

11 Before installing the new piston rings, the ring end gaps must be checked. It's assumed that the piston ring side clearance has been checked and verified correct.

12 Lay out the piston/connecting rod assemblies and the new ring sets so the ring sets will be matched with the same piston and cylinder during the end gap measurement and engine assembly.

13 Insert the top (number one) ring into the first cylinder and square it up with the cylinder walls by pushing it in with the top of the piston (see illustration). The ring should be near the bottom of the cylinder, at the lower limit of ring travel.

14 To measure the end gap, slip feeler gauges between the ends of the ring until a gauge equal to the gap width is found (see illustration). The feeler gauge should slide between the ring ends with a slight amount of drag. A typical ring gap should fall between 0.010 and 0.020 inch (0.25 to 0.50 mm) for compression rings and up to 0.030 inch (0.76 mm) for the oil ring steel rails. If the gap is larger or smaller than specified, double-check to make sure you have the correct rings before proceeding.

15 If the gap is too small, it must be enlarged or the ring ends may come in contact with each other during engine operation, which can cause serious damage to the engine. If necessary, increase the end gaps by filing the ring ends very carefully with a fine file. Mount the file in a vise equipped with soft jaws, slip the ring over the file with the ends contacting the file face and slowly move the ring to remove material from the ends. When performing this operation, file only by pushing the ring from the outside end of the file towards the vise (see illustration).

16 Excess end gap isn't critical unless it's greater than 0.040 inch (1.01 mm). Again, double-check to make sure you have the correct ring type.

17 Repeat the procedure for each ring that will be installed in the first cylinder and for each ring in the remaining cylinders. Remember to keep rings, pistons and cylinders matched up.

18 Once the ring end gaps have been checked/corrected, the rings can be installed on the pistons.

19 The oil control ring (lowest one on the piston) is usually installed first. It's composed of three separate components. Slip the spacer/expander into the groove (see illustration). If an anti-rotation tang is

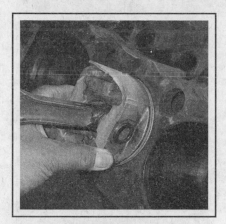

9.13 Install the piston ring into the cylinder then push it down into position using a piston so the ring will be square in the cylinder

9.14 With the ring square in the cylinder, measure the ring end gap with a feeler gauge

9.15 If the ring end gap is too small, clamp a file in a vise as shown and file the piston ring ends - be sure to remove all raised material

9.19a Installing the spacer/expander in the oil ring groove

9.19b DO NOT use a piston ring installation tool when installing the oil control side rails

9.22 Use a piston ring installation tool to install the compression rings - on some engines the number two compression ring has a directional mark that must face toward the top of the piston

used, make sure it's inserted into the drilled hole in the ring groove. Next, install the lower side rail in the same manner (see illustration). Don't use a piston ring installation tool on the oil ring side rails, as they may be damaged. Instead, place one end of the side rail into the groove between the spacer/expander and the ring land, hold it firmly in place and slide a finger around the piston while pushing the rail into the groove. Finally, install the upper side rail.

20 After the three oil ring components have been installed, check to make sure that both the upper and lower side rails can be rotated smoothly inside the ring grooves.

21 The number two (middle) ring is installed next. It's usually stamped with a mark which must face up, toward the top of the piston. Do not mix up the top and middle rings, as they have different cross-sections.

➡Note: Always follow the instructions printed on the ring package or box - different manufacturers may require different approaches.

22 Use a piston ring installation tool and make sure the identification mark is facing the top of the piston, then slip the ring into the middle groove on the piston (see illustration). Don't expand the ring any more than necessary to slide it over the piston.

➡Note: Be careful not to confuse the number one and number two rings.

23 Install the number one (top) ring in the same manner.

24 Repeat the procedure for the remaining pistons and rings.

INSTALLATION

25 Before installing the piston/connecting rod assemblies, the cylinder walls must be perfectly clean, the top edge of each cylinder bore must be chamfered, and the crankshaft must be in place.

26 Remove the cap from the end of the number one connecting rod (refer to the marks made during removal). Remove the original bearing inserts and wipe the bearing surfaces of the connecting rod and cap with a clean, lint-free cloth. They must be kept spotlessly clean.

ENGINE BEARING ANALYSIS

Debris

Babbitt bearing embedded with debris from machinings

Microscopic detail of debris

Microscopic detail of gouges

Overplated copper alloy bearing gouged by cast iron debris

Aluminum bearing embedded with glass beads

Microscopic detail of glass beads

Damaged lining caused by dirt left on the bearing back

Misassembly

Result of a lower half assembled as an upper - blocking the oil flow

Excessive oil clearance is indicated by a short contact arc

Polished and oil-stained backs are a result of a poor fit in the housing bore

Result of a wrong, reversed, or shifted cap

Overloading

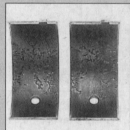

Damage from excessive idling which resulted in an oil film unable to support the load imposed

Damaged upper connecting rod bearings caused by engine lugging; the lower main bearings (not shown) were similarly affected

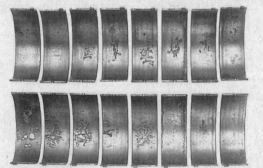

The damage shown in these upper and lower connecting rod bearings was caused by engine operation at a higher-than-rated speed under load

Misalignment

A warped crankshaft caused this pattern of severe wear in the center, diminishing toward the ends

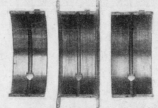

A poorly finished crankshaft caused the equally spaced scoring shown

A tapered housing bore caused the damage along one edge of this pair

A bent connecting rod led to the damage in the "V" pattern

Lubrication

Result of dry start: The bearings on the left, farthest from the oil pump, show more damage

Result of a low oil supply or oil starvation

Severe wear as a result of inadequate oil clearance

Corrosion

Microscopic detail of corrosion

Corrosion is an acid attack on the bearing lining generally caused by inadequate maintenance, extremely hot or cold operation, or inferior oils or fuels

Microscopic detail of cavitation

Example of cavitation - a surface erosion caused by pressure changes in the oil film

Damage from excessive thrust or insufficient axial clearance

Bearing affected by oil dilution caused by excessive blow-by or a rich mixture

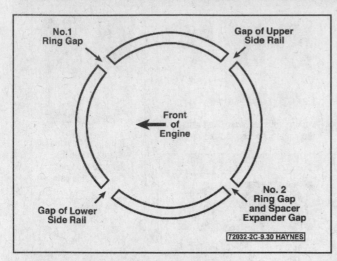

9.30 Position the piston ring end gaps as shown

9.35 Use a plastic or wooden hammer handle to push the piston into the cylinder

Connecting rod bearing oil clearance check

▶ Refer to illustrations 9.30, 9.35, 9.37 and 9.41

27 Clean the back side of the new upper bearing insert, then lay it in place in the connecting rod.

28 Make sure the tab on the bearing fits into the recess in the rod. Don't hammer the bearing insert into place and be very careful not to nick or gouge the bearing face. Don't lubricate the bearing at this time.

29 Clean the back side of the other bearing insert and install it in the rod cap. Again, make sure the tab on the bearing fits into the recess in the cap, and don't apply any lubricant. It's critically important that the mating surfaces of the bearing and connecting rod are perfectly clean and oil free when they're assembled.

30 Position the piston ring gaps at the intervals around the piston as shown (see illustration).

31 Lubricate the piston and rings with clean engine oil and attach a piston ring compressor to the piston. Leave the skirt protruding about 1/4-inch to guide the piston into the cylinder. The rings must be compressed until they're flush with the piston.

32 Rotate the crankshaft until the number one connecting rod journal is at BDC (bottom dead center) and apply a liberal coat of engine oil to

9.37 Place Plastigage on each connecting rod bearing journal parallel to the crankshaft centerline

the cylinder walls. Refer to the TDC locating procedure in Chapter 2A or 2B for additional information.

33 With the "front" mark (letter F or arrow) on the piston facing the front (timing chain end) of the engine, gently insert the piston/connecting rod assembly into the number one cylinder bore and rest the bottom edge of the ring compressor on the engine block.

➡ Note: Some engines have a letter "F" marking on the side of the piston near the wrist pin, others have an arrow, or a dimple or groove on the top of the piston. All of these are marks that indicate the front of the piston.

34 Tap the top edge of the ring compressor to make sure it's contacting the block around its entire circumference.

35 Gently tap on the top of the piston with the end of a wooden or plastic hammer handle (see illustration) while guiding the end of the connecting rod into place on the crankshaft journal. The piston rings may try to pop out of the ring compressor just before entering the cylinder bore, so keep some downward pressure on the ring compressor. Work slowly, and if any resistance is felt as the piston enters the cylinder, stop immediately. Find out what's hanging up and fix it before proceeding. Do not, for any reason, force the piston into the cylinder - you might break a ring and/or the piston.

36 Once the piston/connecting rod assembly is installed, the connecting rod bearing oil clearance must be checked before the rod cap is permanently installed.

37 Cut a piece of the appropriate size Plastigage slightly shorter than the width of the connecting rod bearing and lay it in place on the number one connecting rod journal, parallel with the journal axis (see illustration).

38 Clean the connecting rod cap bearing face and install the rod cap. Make sure the mating mark on the cap is on the same side as the mark on the connecting rod (see illustration 9.4).

39 Install the rod bolts and tighten them to the torque listed in this Chapter's Specifications.

➡ Note: Use a thin-wall socket to avoid erroneous torque readings that can result if the socket is wedged between the rod cap and the bolt or nut. If the socket tends to wedge itself between the fastener and the cap, lift up on it slightly until it no longer contacts the cap. DO NOT rotate the crankshaft at any time during this operation.

40 Remove the fasteners and detach the rod cap, being very careful

not to disturb the Plastigage. Discard the cap bolts at this time from V6 engines as they cannot be reused.

→Note: You MUST use new connecting rod bolts on V6 engines, and it is recommended that new bolts be used on four-cylinder engines.

41 Compare the width of the crushed Plastigage to the scale printed on the Plastigage envelope to obtain the oil clearance (see illustration). The connecting rod bearing oil clearance is usually about 0.001 to 0.002 inch. Consult an automotive machine shop for the clearance specified for the rod bearings on your engine.

42 If the clearance is not as specified, the bearing inserts may be the wrong size (which means different ones will be required). Before deciding that different inserts are needed, make sure that no dirt or oil was between the bearing inserts and the connecting rod or cap when the clearance was measured. Also, recheck the journal diameter. If the Plastigage was wider at one end than the other, the journal may be tapered. If the clearance still exceeds the limit specified, the bearing will have to be replaced with an undersize bearing.

❊❊ CAUTION:

When installing a new crankshaft always use a standard size bearing.

Final installation

43 Carefully scrape all traces of the Plastigage material off the rod journal and/or bearing face. Be very careful not to scratch the bearing - use your fingernail or the edge of a plastic card.

44 Make sure the bearing faces are perfectly clean, then apply a uniform layer of clean moly-base grease or engine assembly lube to both of them. You'll have to push the piston into the cylinder to expose the face of the bearing insert in the connecting rod.

45 Slide the connecting rod back into place on the journal, install the rod cap, install the nuts or bolts and tighten them to the torque listed in this Chapter's Specifications.

→Note: You MUST install new connecting rod bolts on V6 engines.

46 Repeat the entire procedure for the remaining pistons/connecting rods.

9.41 Use the scale on the Plastigage package to determine the bearing oil clearance - be sure to measure the widest part of the Plastigage and use the correct scale; it comes with both standard and metric scales

47 The important points to remember are:
a) Keep the back sides of the bearing inserts and the insides of the connecting rods and caps perfectly clean when assembling them.
b) Make sure you have the correct piston/rod assembly for each cylinder.
c) The mark on the piston must face the front (timing chain end) of the engine.
d) Lubricate the cylinder walls liberally with clean oil.
e) Lubricate the bearing faces when installing the rod caps after the oil clearance has been checked.

48 After all the piston/connecting rod assemblies have been correctly installed, rotate the crankshaft a number of times by hand to check for any obvious binding.

49 As a final step, check the connecting rod endplay again. If it was correct before disassembly and the original crankshaft and rods were reinstalled, it should still be correct. If new rods or a new crankshaft were installed, the endplay may be inadequate. If so, the rods will have to be removed and taken to an automotive machine shop for machining.

10 Crankshaft - removal and installation

REMOVAL

▶ Refer to illustrations 10.1 and 10.3

→Note: The crankshaft can be removed only after the engine has been removed from the vehicle. It's assumed that the flywheel or driveplate, crankshaft pulley, timing chain, oil pan, oil pump, oil filter and piston/connecting rod assemblies have already been removed. The rear main oil seal retainer must be unbolted and separated from the block before proceeding with crankshaft removal on V6 engines.

1 Before the crankshaft is removed, measure the endplay. Mount a dial indicator with the indicator in line with the crankshaft and touching the end of the crankshaft (see illustration).

2 Pry the crankshaft all the way to the rear and zero the dial indicator. Next, pry the crankshaft to the front as far as possible and check

10.1 Checking crankshaft endplay with a dial indicator

10.3 Checking crankshaft endplay with feeler gauges at the thrust bearing journal

the reading on the dial indicator. The distance traveled is the endplay. A typical crankshaft endplay will fall between 0.003 to 0.010 inch (0.076 to 0.254 mm). If it is greater than that, check the crankshaft thrust washer/bearing assembly surfaces for wear after it's removed. If no wear is evident, new main bearings should correct the endplay. Refer to Step 14 for the location of the thrust washer/bearing assembly on each engine.

3 If a dial indicator isn't available, feeler gauges can be used. Gently pry the crankshaft all the way to the front of the engine. Slip feeler gauges between the crankshaft and the front face of the thrust bearing or washer to determine the clearance (see illustration).

4 Loosen the main bearing cap/bedplate bolts 1/4-turn at a time each, until they can be removed by hand.

5 Gently tap the main bearing caps or bedplate assembly with a soft-face hammer around the perimeter of the assembly. Pull the main bearing cap/bedplate assembly straight up and off the cylinder block. Try not to drop the bearing inserts if they come out with the assembly.

➡Note: The bedplate has built in pry points; don't pry anywhere else or damage to the bedplate will occur.

6 Carefully lift the crankshaft out of the engine. It may be a good idea to have an assistant available, since the crankshaft is quite heavy and awkward to handle. With the bearing inserts in place inside the engine block and main bearing caps, reinstall the main bearing cap assembly onto the engine block and tighten the bolts finger tight. Make

10.14 Insert the thrust washer into the machined surface between the crankshaft and the upper bearing saddle, then rotate it down into the block until it's flush with the parting line on the main bearing saddle - make sure the oil grooves on the thrust washer face the crankshaft

sure you install the main bearing cap assembly with the arrow facing the front of the engine.

INSTALLATION

7 Crankshaft installation is the first step in engine reassembly. It's assumed at this point that the engine block and crankshaft have been cleaned, inspected and repaired or reconditioned.

8 Position the engine block with the bottom facing up.

9 Remove the mounting bolts and lift off the main bearing cap assembly.

10 If they're still in place, remove the original bearing inserts from the block and from the main bearing cap assembly. Wipe the bearing surfaces of the block and main bearing cap assembly with a clean, lint-free cloth. They must be kept spotlessly clean. This is critical for determining the correct bearing oil clearance.

MAIN BEARING OIL CLEARANCE CHECK

▶ **Refer to illustrations 10.14, 10.17, 10.18a, 10.18b, 10.19a, 19.19b and 10.21**

11 Without mixing them up, clean the back sides of the new upper main bearing inserts (with grooves and oil holes) and lay one in each main bearing saddle in the block. Each upper bearing has an oil groove and oil hole in it.

❋❋ CAUTION:

The oil holes in the block must line up with the oil holes in the upper bearing inserts.

Clean the back sides of the lower main bearing inserts and lay them in the corresponding location in the main bearing cap. Make sure the tab on the bearing insert fits into the recess in the block or main bearing cap. The upper bearings with the oil holes are installed into the engine block while the lower bearings without the oil holes are installed in the caps or bedplate.

❋❋ CAUTION:

Do not hammer the bearing insert into place and don't nick or gouge the bearing faces. DO NOT apply any lubrication at this time.

12 Clean the faces of the bearing inserts in the block and the crankshaft main bearing journals with a clean, lint-free cloth.

➡Note: The backs of all bearings and the surfaces in which they are installed must be kept clean and free of oil at all times.

13 Check or clean the oil holes in the crankshaft, as any dirt here can go only one way - straight through the new bearings.

14 Once you're certain the crankshaft is clean, carefully lay it in position in the block, which should be oriented on the engine stand to have the bottom side Up. Lube and insert the thrust washers on either side of journal #3 on both four-cylinder and V6 engines. The thrust washers must be installed in the correct journal.

➡Note: Install the thrust washers with the groove in the thrust washer facing the crankshaft with the smooth sides facing the main bearing saddle (see illustration). On V6 engines, thrust washers are also installed along with the #3 main bearing cap.

10.17 Place the Plastigage onto the crankshaft bearing journal as shown

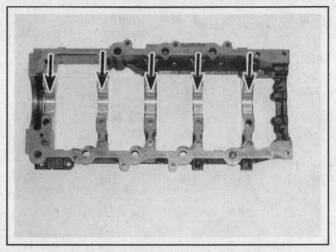

10.18a The bearings are installed into the corresponding saddles in the bedplate (typical four-cylinder engine) . . .

10.18b . . . then the bedplate is set over the crankshaft onto the dowels on the engine block

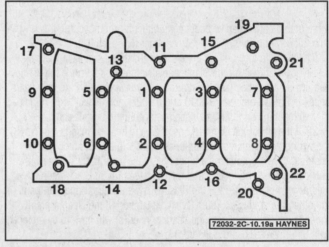

10.19a Main bearing cap/bedplate bolt tightening sequence on the 2.5L four-cylinder engine

15 Before the crankshaft can be permanently installed, the main bearing oil clearance must be checked.

16 Cut several strips of the appropriate size of Plastigage. They must be slightly shorter than the width of the main bearing journal.

17 Place one piece on each crankshaft main bearing journal, parallel with the journal axis as shown (see illustration).

18 Clean the faces of the bearing inserts in the main bearing caps or bedplate assembly (see illustrations). Hold the bearing inserts in place and install the assembly onto the crankshaft and cylinder block. DO NOT disturb the Plastigage. Make sure you install the main bearing cap assembly with the arrow facing the front (timing chain end) of the engine.

19 Apply clean engine oil to all bolt threads prior to installation, then install all bolts finger-tight. Tighten the main bearing caps/bedplate assembly bolts in the sequence shown (see illustrations) progressing in steps, to the torque listed in this Chapter's Specifications. DO NOT rotate the crankshaft at any time during this operation.

20 Remove the bolts in the reverse order of the tightening sequence and carefully lift the main bearing cap or bedplate assembly straight up and off the block. Do not disturb the Plastigage or rotate the crankshaft.

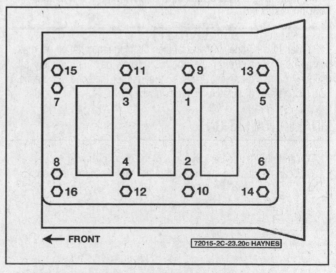

10.19b Main bearing cap/support beam bolt tightening sequence on the 3.5L V6 engine

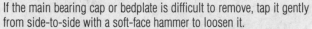

10.21 Use the scale on the Plastigage package to determine the bearing oil clearance - be sure to measure the widest part of the Plastigage and use the correct scale; it comes with both standard and metric scales

10.28 Apply a 3/16-inch bead of RTV sealant to the engine block-to-bedplate sealing surface as shown (typical)

If the main bearing cap or bedplate is difficult to remove, tap it gently from side-to-side with a soft-face hammer to loosen it.

21 Compare the width of the crushed Plastigage on each journal to the scale printed on the Plastigage envelope to determine the main bearing oil clearance (see illustration). A typical main bearing oil clearance should fall between 0.0015 and 0.0023-inch. Check with an automotive machine shop for the clearance specified for your engine.

22 If the clearance is not as specified, the bearing inserts may be the wrong size (which means different ones will be required). Before deciding if different inserts are needed, make sure that no dirt or oil was between the bearing inserts and the cap assembly or block when the clearance was measured. If the Plastigage was wider at one end than the other, the crankshaft journal may be tapered. If the clearance still exceeds the limit specified, the bearing insert(s) will have to be replaced with an undersize bearing insert(s).

❊❊ CAUTION:

When installing a new crankshaft, always install a standard bearing insert set.

23 Carefully scrape all traces of the Plastigage material off the main bearing journals and/or the bearing insert faces. Be sure to remove all residue from the oil holes. Use your fingernail or the edge of a plastic card - don't nick or scratch the bearing faces.

FINAL INSTALLATION

24 Carefully lift the crankshaft out of the cylinder block.
25 Clean the bearing insert faces in the cylinder block, then apply

a thin, uniform layer of moly-base grease or engine assembly lube to each of the bearing surfaces that contact the crankshaft. Be sure to coat the thrust faces as well as the journal face of the thrust washers.

26 Make sure the crankshaft journals are clean, then lay the crankshaft back in place in the cylinder block.

27 Clean the bearing insert faces and then apply the same lubricant to them. Clean the engine block thoroughly. The surfaces must be free of oil residue. Install the thrust washers. The grooves on the thrust washers face outward, away from the bearing.

28 On four-cylinder engines, apply a 5/32-inch (4 mm) bead of RTV sealant to the bedplate sealing area on the cylinder block (see illustration).

29 Install the bedplate (four-cylinder engines) or each main bearing cap (with the support beam on V6 engines) onto the crankshaft and cylinder block.

30 Prior to installation, apply clean engine oil to all bolt threads, wiping off any excess, then install all bolts finger-tight.

➥**Note: The main bearing cap bolts MUST be replaced with new ones on V6 engines, and it's recommended that they be replaced on four-cylinder engines.**

31 Tighten the main bearing cap bolts or bedplate assembly bolts to the torque listed in this Chapter's Specifications (in the proper sequence) (see illustrations 10.19a and 10.19b).

32 Recheck crankshaft endplay with a feeler gauge or a dial indicator. The endplay should be correct if the crankshaft thrust faces aren't worn or damaged and if new bearings have been installed.

33 Rotate the crankshaft a number of times by hand to check for any obvious binding. It should rotate with a running torque of 50 in-lbs or less. If the running torque is too high, identify and correct the problem at this time.

34 Install the new rear main oil seal (see Chapter 2A and 2B).

11 Engine overhaul - reassembly sequence

1   Before beginning engine reassembly, make sure you have all the necessary new parts, gaskets and seals as well as the following items on hand:

    Common hand tools
    A 1/2-inch drive torque wrench
    New engine oil
    Oil filter
    Gasket sealant
    Thread locking compound

2   If you obtained a short block it will be necessary to install the cylinder head, the oil pump and pick-up tube, the oil pan, the water pump, the timing chain and timing cover, and the valve cover (see Chapter 2A or 2B). In order to save time and avoid problems, the external components must be installed in the following general order:

    Thermostat and housing cover
    Water pump
    Intake and exhaust manifolds
    Fuel injection components
    Emission control components
    Spark plugs
    Ignition coils
    Oil filter and oil cooler
    Engine mounts and mount brackets
    Flywheel/driveplate

12 Initial start-up and break-in after overhaul

❋❋ WARNING:

Have a fire extinguisher handy when starting the engine for the first time.

1   Once the engine has been installed in the vehicle, double-check the engine oil and coolant levels.

2   With the spark plugs out of the engine and the and the fuel pump disabled (see Chapter 4, Section 2), crank the engine until oil pressure registers on the gauge or the light goes out.

3   Install the spark plugs and ignition coils, and reinstall the fuel pump fuse.

4   Start the engine. It may take a few moments for the fuel system to build up pressure, but the engine should start without a great deal of effort.

5   After the engine starts, it should be allowed to warm up to normal operating temperature. While the engine is warming up, make a thorough check for fuel, oil and coolant leaks.

6   Shut the engine off and recheck the engine oil and coolant levels.

7   Drive the vehicle to an area with minimum traffic, accelerate from 30 to 50 mph, then allow the vehicle to slow to 30 mph with the throttle closed. Repeat the procedure 10 or 12 times. This will load the piston rings and cause them to seat properly against the cylinder walls. Check again for oil and coolant leaks.

8   Drive the vehicle gently for the first 500 miles (no sustained high speeds) and keep a constant check on the oil level. It is not unusual for an engine to use oil during the break-in period.

9   At approximately 500 to 600 miles, change the oil and filter.

10 For the next few hundred miles, drive the vehicle normally. Do not pamper it or abuse it.

11 After 2000 miles, change the oil and filter again and consider the engine broken in.

GLOSSARY

B

Backlash - The amount of play between two parts. Usually refers to how much one gear can be moved back and forth without moving the gear with which it's meshed.

Bearing Caps - The caps held in place by nuts or bolts which, in turn, hold the bearing surface. This space is for lubricating oil to enter.

Bearing clearance - The amount of space left between shaft and bearing surface. This space is for lubricating oil to enter.

Bearing crush - The additional height which is purposely manufactured into each bearing half to ensure complete contact of the bearing back with the housing bore when the engine is assembled.

Bearing knock - The noise created by movement of a part in a loose or worn bearing.

Blueprinting - Dismantling an engine and reassembling it to EXACT specifications.

Bore - An engine cylinder, or any cylindrical hole; also used to describe the process of enlarging or accurately refinishing a hole with a cutting tool, as to bore an engine cylinder. The bore size is the diameter of the hole.

Boring - Renewing the cylinders by cutting them out to a specified size. A boring bar is used to make the cut.

Bottom end - A term which refers collectively to the engine block, crankshaft, main bearings and the big ends of the connecting rods.

Break-in - The period of operation between installation of new or rebuilt parts and time in which parts are worn to the correct fit. Driving at reduced and varying speed for a specified mileage to permit parts to wear to the correct fit.

Bushing - A one-piece sleeve placed in a bore to serve as a bearing surface for shaft, piston pin, etc. Usually replaceable.

C

Camshaft - The shaft in the engine, on which a series of lobes are located for operating the valve mechanisms. The camshaft is driven by gears or sprockets and a timing chain. Usually referred to simply as the cam.

Carbon - Hard, or soft, black deposits found in combustion chamber, on plugs, under rings, on and under valve heads.

Cast iron - An alloy of iron and more than two percent carbon, used for engine blocks and heads because it's relatively inexpensive and easy to mold into complex shapes.

Chamfer - To bevel across (or a bevel on) the sharp edge of an object.

Chase - To repair damaged threads with a tap or die.

Combustion chamber - The space between the piston and the cylinder head, with the piston at top dead center, in which air-fuel mixture is burned.

Compression ratio - The relationship between cylinder volume (clearance volume) when the piston is at top dead center and cylinder volume when the piston is at bottom dead center.

Connecting rod - The rod that connects the crank on the crankshaft with the piston. Sometimes called a con rod.

Connecting rod cap - The part of the connecting rod assembly that attaches the rod to the crankpin.

Core plug - Soft metal plug used to plug the casting holes for the coolant passages in the block.

Crankcase - The lower part of the engine in which the crankshaft rotates; includes the lower section of the cylinder block and the oil pan.

Crank kit - A reground or reconditioned crankshaft and new main and connecting rod bearings.

Crankpin - The part of a crankshaft to which a connecting rod is attached.

Crankshaft - The main rotating member, or shaft, running the length of the crankcase, with offset throws to which the connecting rods are attached; changes the reciprocating motion of the pistons into rotating motion.

Cylinder sleeve - A replaceable sleeve, or liner, pressed into the cylinder block to form the cylinder bore.

D

Deburring - Removing the burrs (rough edges or areas) from a bearing.

Deglazer - A tool, rotated by an electric motor, used to remove glaze from cylinder walls so a new set of rings will seat.

E

Endplay - The amount of lengthwise movement between two parts. As applied to a crankshaft, the distance that the crankshaft can move forward and back in the cylinder block.

F

Face - A machinist's term that refers to removing metal from the end of a shaft or the face of a larger part, such as a flywheel.

Fatigue - A breakdown of material through a large number of loading and unloading cycles. The first signs are cracks followed shortly by breaks.

Feeler gauge - A thin strip of hardened steel, ground to an exact thickness, used to check clearances between parts.

Free height - The unloaded length or height of a spring.

Freeplay - The looseness in a linkage, or an assembly of parts, between the initial application of force and actual movement. Usually perceived as slop or slight delay.

Freeze plug - See Core plug.

G

Gallery - A large passage in the block that forms a reservoir for engine oil pressure.

Glaze - The very smooth, glassy finish that develops on cylinder walls while an engine is in service.

H

Heli-Coil - A rethreading device used when threads are worn or damaged. The device is installed in a retapped hole to reduce the thread size to the original size.

I

Installed height - The spring's measured length or height, as installed on the cylinder head. Installed height is measured from the spring seat to the underside of the spring retainer.

J

Journal - The surface of a rotating shaft which turns in a bearing.

K

Keeper - The split lock that holds the valve spring retainer in position on the valve stem.

Key - A small piece of metal inserted into matching grooves machined into two parts fitted together - such as a gear pressed onto a shaft - which prevents slippage between the two parts.

Knock - The heavy metallic engine sound, produced in the combustion chamber as a result of abnormal combustion - usually detonation. Knock is usually caused by a loose or worn bearing. Also referred to as detonation, pinging and spark knock. Connecting rod or main bearing knocks are created by too much oil clearance or insufficient lubrication.

L

Lands - The portions of metal between the piston ring grooves.

Lapping the valves - Grinding a valve face and its seat together with lapping compound.

Lash - The amount of free motion in a gear train, between gears, or in a mechanical assembly, that occurs before movement can begin. Usually refers to the lash in a valve train.

Lifter - The part that rides against the cam to transfer motion to the rest of the valve train.

M

Machining - The process of using a machine to remove metal from a metal part.

Main bearings - The plain, or babbitt, bearings that support the crankshaft.

Main bearing caps - The cast iron caps, bolted to the bottom of the block, that support the main bearings.

O

O.D. - Outside diameter.

Oil gallery - A pipe or drilled passageway in the engine used to carry engine oil from one area to another.

Oil ring - The lower ring, or rings, of a piston; designed to prevent excessive amounts of oil from working up the cylinder walls and into the combustion chamber. Also called an oil-control ring.

Oil seal - A seal which keeps oil from leaking out of a compartment. Usually refers to a dynamic seal around a rotating shaft or other moving part.

O-ring - A type of sealing ring made of a special rubberlike material; in use, the O-ring is compressed into a groove to provide the sealing action.

Overhaul - To completely disassemble a unit, clean and inspect all parts, reassemble it with the original or new parts and make all adjustments necessary for proper operation.

P

Pilot bearing - A small bearing installed in the center of the flywheel (or the rear end of the crankshaft) to support the front end of the input shaft of the transmission.

Pip mark - A little dot or indentation which indicates the top side of a compression ring.

Piston - The cylindrical part, attached to the connecting rod, that moves up and down in the cylinder as the crankshaft rotates. When the fuel charge is fired, the piston transfers the force of the explosion to the connecting rod, then to the crankshaft.

Piston pin (or wrist pin) - The cylindrical and usually hollow steel pin that passes through the piston. The piston pin fastens the piston to the upper end of the connecting rod.

Piston ring - The split ring fitted to the groove in a piston. The ring contacts the sides of the ring groove and also rubs against the cylinder wall, thus sealing space between piston and wall. There are two types of rings: Compression rings seal the compression pressure in the combustion chamber; oil rings scrape excessive oil off the cylinder wall.

Piston ring groove - The slots or grooves cut in piston heads to hold piston rings in position.

Piston skirt - The portion of the piston below the rings and the piston pin hole.

Plastigage - A thin strip of plastic thread, available in different sizes, used for measuring clearances. For example, a strip of plastigage is laid across a bearing journal and mashed as parts are assembled. Then parts are disassembled and the width of the strip is measured to determine clearance between journal and bearing. Commonly used to measure crankshaft main-bearing and connecting rod bearing clearances.

Press-fit - A tight fit between two parts that requires pressure to force the parts together. Also referred to as drive, or force, fit.

Prussian blue - A blue pigment; in solution, useful in determining the area of contact between two surfaces. Prussian blue is commonly used to determine the width and location of the contact area between the valve face and the valve seat.

R

Race (bearing) - The inner or outer ring that provides a contact surface for balls or rollers in bearing.

Ream - To size, enlarge or smooth a hole by using a round cutting tool with fluted edges.

Ring job - The process of reconditioning the cylinders and installing new rings.

Runout - Wobble. The amount a shaft rotates out-of-true.

S

Saddle - The upper main bearing seat.

Scored - Scratched or grooved, as a cylinder wall may be scored by abrasive particles moved up and down by the piston rings.

Scuffing - A type of wear in which there's a transfer of material between parts moving against each other; shows up as pits or grooves in the mating surfaces.

Seat - The surface upon which another part rests or seats. For example, the valve seat is the matched surface upon which the valve face rests. Also used to refer to wearing into a good fit; for example, piston rings seat after a few miles of driving.

Short block - An engine block complete with crankshaft and piston and, usually, camshaft assemblies.

Static balance - The balance of an object while it's stationary.

Step - The wear on the lower portion of a ring land caused by excessive side and back-clearance. The height of the step indicates the ring's extra side clearance and the length of the step projecting from the back wall of the groove represents the ring's back clearance.

Stroke - The distance the piston moves when traveling from top dead center to bottom dead center, or from bottom dead center to top dead center.

Stud - A metal rod with threads on both ends.

T

Tang - A lip on the end of a plain bearing used to align the bearing during assembly.

Tap - To cut threads in a hole. Also refers to the fluted tool used to cut threads.

Taper - A gradual reduction in the width of a shaft or hole; in an engine cylinder, taper usually takes the form of uneven wear, more pronounced at the top than at the bottom.

Throws - The offset portions of the crankshaft to which the connecting rods are affixed.

Thrust bearing - The main bearing that has thrust faces to prevent excessive endplay, or forward and backward movement of the crankshaft.

Thrust washer - A bronze or hardened steel washer placed between two moving parts. The washer prevents longitudinal movement and provides a bearing surface for thrust surfaces of parts.

Tolerance - The amount of variation permitted from an exact size of measurement. Actual amount from smallest acceptable dimension to largest acceptable dimension.

U

Umbrella - An oil deflector placed near the valve tip to throw oil from the valve stem area.

Undercut - A machined groove below the normal surface.

Undersize bearings - Smaller diameter bearings used with re-ground crankshaft journals.

V

Valve grinding - Refacing a valve in a valve-refacing machine.

Valve train - The valve-operating mechanism of an engine; includes all components from the camshaft to the valve.

Vibration damper - A cylindrical weight attached to the front of the crankshaft to minimize torsional vibration (the twist-untwist actions of the crankshaft caused by the cylinder firing impulses). Also called a harmonic balancer.

W

Water jacket - The spaces around the cylinders, between the inner and outer shells of the cylinder block or head, through which coolant circulates.

Web - A supporting structure across a cavity.

Woodruff key - A key with a radiused backside (viewed from the side).

Specifications

General

Engine designation	
Four-cylinder engine	QR25DE
V6 engine	VQ35DE
Displacement	
Four-cylinder engine	2.5 liters (152 cubic inches)
V6 engine	3.5 liters (213 cubic inches)
Compression ratio	
Four-cylinder engine	9.5:1
V6 engine	10.3:1
Cylinder compression pressure	
Four-cylinder engine	
Standard	181 psi
Minimum	154 psi
V6 engine	
Standard	185 psi
Minimum	142 psi
Maximum variation between cylinders	14 psi
Oil pressure (minimum, warm engine)	
Idle	14 psi
2000 rpm	43 psi

Torque specifications*   Ft-lbs (unless otherwise indicated)

➡ **Note: One foot-pound (ft-lb) of torque is equivalent to 12 inch-pounds (in-lbs) of torque. Torque values below approximately 15 ft-lbs are expressed in inch-pounds, since most foot-pound torque wrenches are not accurate at these smaller values.**

Connecting rod cap bolts	
Four-cylinder engine	
Step 1	22
Step 2	Loosen completely
Step 3	168 in-lbs
Step 4	Tighten an additional 90-degrees
V6 engine**	
Step 1	14 to 15
Step 2	Tighten an additional 90 to 95-degrees
Main bearing cap bolts (lower crankcase-to-block)	
Four-cylinder engine	
Step 1, bolts 11 through 22	19
Step 2, bolts 1 through 10	29
Step 3, bolts 1 through 10	Tighten an additional 60-degrees
V6 engine**	
Step 1	24 to 28
Step 2	Tighten an additional 90 to 95-degrees

*Refer to Part A or B of this Chapter for additional torque specifications.
**Replace with NEW bolts.

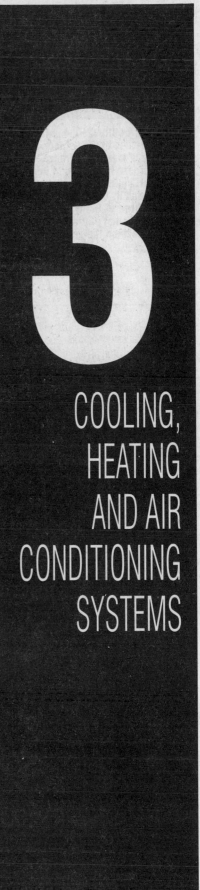

3

COOLING, HEATING AND AIR CONDITIONING SYSTEMS

1 General information

❄❄ WARNING:

Do not allow antifreeze to come in contact with your skin or painted surfaces of the vehicle. Rinse off spills immediately with plenty of water. Antifreeze is highly toxic if ingested. Never leave antifreeze lying around in an open container or in puddles on the floor; children and pets are attracted by it's sweet smell and may drink it. Check with local authorities about disposing of used antifreeze. Many communities have collection centers which will see that antifreeze is disposed of safely. Never dump used antifreeze on the ground or pour it into drains.

ENGINE COOLING SYSTEM

All modern vehicles employ a pressurized engine cooling system with thermostatically controlled coolant circulation. The cooling system consists of a radiator, an expansion tank or coolant reservoir, a pressure cap (located on the expansion tank or radiator), a thermostat, a cooling fan, and a water pump.

The water pump circulates coolant through the engine. The coolant flows around each cylinder and around the intake and exhaust ports, near the spark plug areas and in close proximity to the exhaust valve guides.

A thermostat controls engine coolant temperature. During warm up, the closed thermostat prevents coolant from circulating through the radiator. As the engine nears normal operating temperature, the thermo-stat opens and allows hot coolant to travel through the radiator, where it's cooled before returning to the engine.

HEATING SYSTEM

The heating system consists of a blower fan and heater core located in a housing under the dash, the hoses connecting the heater core to the engine cooling system and the heater/air conditioning control head on the dashboard. Hot engine coolant is circulated through the heater core. When the heater mode is activated, a flap door in the housing opens to expose the heater core to the passenger compartment through air ducts. A fan switch on the control head activates the blower motor, which forces air through the core, heating the air.

AIR CONDITIONING SYSTEM

The air conditioning system consists of a condenser mounted in front of the radiator, an evaporator mounted adjacent to the heater core, a compressor mounted on the engine, a receiver-drier or accumulator and the plumbing connecting all of the above components.

A blower fan forces the warmer air of the passenger compartment through the evaporator core (sort of a radiator-in-reverse), transferring the heat from the air to the refrigerant. The liquid refrigerant boils off into low pressure vapor, taking the heat with it when it leaves the evaporator.

2 Troubleshooting

COOLANT LEAKS

▶ **Refer to illustration 2.2**

1   A coolant leak can develop anywhere in the cooling system, but the most common causes are:
   a) *A loose or weak hose clamp*
   b) *A defective hose*
   c) *A faulty pressure cap*
   d) *A damaged radiator*
   e) *A bad heater core*
   f) *A faulty water pump*
   g) *A leaking gasket at any joint that carries coolant*

2   Coolant leaks aren't always easy to find. Sometimes they can only be detected when the cooling system is under pressure. Here's where a cooling system pressure tester comes in handy. After the engine has cooled completely, the tester is attached in place of the pressure cap, then pumped up to the pressure value equal to that of the pressure cap rating (see illustration). Now, leaks that only exist when the engine is fully warmed up will become apparent. The tester can be left connected to locate a nagging slow leak.

COOLANT LEVEL DROPS, BUT NO EXTERNAL LEAKS

▶ **Refer to illustrations 2.5a and 2.5b**

3   If you find it necessary to keep adding coolant, but there are no

2.2 The cooling system pressure tester is connected in place of the pressure cap, then pumped up to pressurize the system

external leaks, the probable causes include:
   a) *A blown head gasket*
   b) *A leaking intake manifold gasket (only on engines that have coolant passages in the manifold)*
   c) *A cracked cylinder head or cylinder block*

4   Any of the above problems will also usually result in contamina-

2.5a The combustion leak detector consists of a bulb, syringe and test fluid

2.5b Place the tester over the cooling system filler neck and use the bulb to draw a sample into the tester

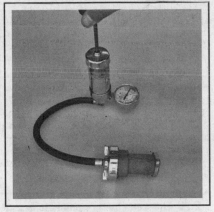

2.8 Checking the cooling system pressure cap with a cooling system pressure tester

tion of the engine oil, which will cause it to take on a milkshake-like appearance. A bad head gasket or cracked head or block can also result in engine oil contaminating the cooling system.

5   Combustion leak detectors (also known as block testers) are available at most auto parts stores. These work by detecting exhaust gases in the cooling system, which indicates a compression leak from a cylinder into the coolant. The tester consists of a large bulb-type syringe and bottle of test fluid (see illustration). A measured amount of the fluid is added to the syringe. The syringe is placed over the cooling system filler neck and, with the engine running, the bulb is squeezed and a sample of the gases present in the cooling system are drawn up through the test fluid (see illustration). If any combustion gases are present in the sample taken, the test fluid will change color.

6   If the test indicates combustion gas is present in the cooling system, you can be sure that the engine has a blown head gasket or a crack in the cylinder head or block, and will require disassembly to repair.

PRESSURE CAP

♦ **Refer to illustration 2.8**

✳✳ WARNING:

Wait until the engine is completely cool before beginning this check.

7   The cooling system is sealed by a spring-loaded cap, which raises the boiling point of the coolant. If the cap's seal or spring are worn out, the coolant can boil and escape past the cap. With the engine completely cool, remove the cap and check the seal; if it's cracked, hardened or deteriorated in any way, replace it with a new one.

8   Even if the seal is good, the spring might not be; this can be checked with a cooling system pressure tester (see illustration). If the cap can't hold a pressure within approximately 1-1/2 lbs of its rated pressure (which is marked on the cap), replace it with a new one.

9   The cap is also equipped with a vacuum relief spring. When the engine cools off, a vacuum is created in the cooling system. The vacuum relief spring allows air back into the system, which will equalize the pressure and prevent damage to the radiator (the radiator tanks could collapse if the vacuum is great enough). If, after turning the

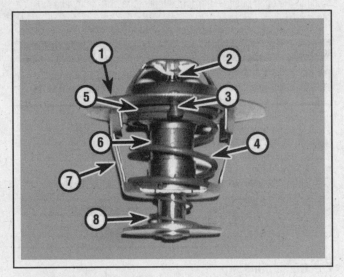

2.10 Typical thermostat:

1	Flange	5	Valve seat
2	Piston	6	Valve
3	Jiggle valve	7	Frame
4	Main coil spring	8	Secondary coil spring

engine off and allowing it to cool down you notice any of the cooling system hoses collapsing, replace the pressure cap with a new one.

THERMOSTAT

♦ **Refer to illustration 2.10**

10   Before assuming the thermostat or water control valve (see illustration) is responsible for a cooling system problem, check the coolant level (see Chapter 1), drivebelt tension (see Chapter 1) and temperature gauge (or light) operation.

11   If the engine takes a long time to warm up (as indicated by the temperature gauge or heater operation), the thermostat is probably stuck open. Replace the thermostat or water control valve with a new one.

12   If the engine runs hot or overheats, a thorough test of the thermostat should be performed.

2.28 The water pump weep hole is generally located on the underside of the pump

13 Definitive testing of the thermostat or water control valve can only be made when it is removed from the vehicle. If the thermostat is stuck in the open position at room temperature, it is faulty and must be replaced.

> ⁜ **CAUTION:**
>
> **Do not drive the vehicle without a thermostat. The computer may stay in open loop and emissions and fuel economy will suffer.**

14 To test a thermostat, suspend the (closed) thermostat on a length of string or wire in a pot of cold water.

15 Heat the water on a stove while observing thermostat. The thermostat should fully open before the water boils.

16 If the thermostat doesn't open and close as specified, or sticks in any position, replace it.

COOLING FAN

Electric cooling fan

17 If the engine is overheating and the cooling fan is not coming on when the engine temperature rises to an excessive level, unplug the fan motor electrical connector(s) and connect the motor directly to the battery with fused jumper wires. If the fan motor doesn't come on, replace the motor.

18 If the radiator fan motor is okay, but it isn't coming on when the engine gets hot, the fan relay might be defective. A relay is used to control a circuit by turning it on and off in response to a control decision by the Powertrain Control Module (PCM). These control circuits are fairly complex, and checking them should be left to a qualified automotive technician. Sometimes, the control system can be fixed by simply identifying and replacing a bad relay.

19 Locate the fan relays in the engine compartment fuse/relay box.

20 Test the relay (see Chapter 12).

21 If the relay is okay, check all wiring and connections to the fan motor. Refer to the wiring diagrams at the end of Chapter 12. If no obvious problems are found, the problem could be the Engine Coolant Temperature (ECT) sensor or the Powertrain Control Module (PCM). Have the cooling fan system and circuit diagnosed by a dealer service department or repair shop with the proper diagnostic equipment.

➥Note: **These models are equipped with a cooling fan motor resistor. Have the resistor checked if the fan motor does not respond to the speed variations signaled by the PCM.**

Belt-driven cooling fan

22 Disconnect the cable from the negative terminal of the battery and rock the fan back and forth by hand to check for excessive bearing play.

23 With the engine cold (and not running), turn the fan blades by hand. The fan should turn freely.

24 Visually inspect for substantial fluid leakage from the clutch assembly. If problems are noted, replace the clutch assembly.

25 With the engine completely warmed up, turn off the ignition switch and disconnect the negative battery cable from the battery. Turn the fan by hand. Some drag should be evident. If the fan turns easily, replace the fan clutch.

WATER PUMP

26 A failure in the water pump can cause serious engine damage due to overheating.

Drivebelt-driven water pump

▶ **Refer to illustration 2.28**

27 There are two ways to check the operation of the water pump while it's installed on the engine. If the pump is found to be defective, it should be replaced with a new or rebuilt unit.

28 Water pumps are equipped with weep (or vent) holes (see illustration). If a failure occurs in the pump seal, coolant will leak from the hole.

29 If the water pump shaft bearings fail, there may be a howling sound at the pump while it's running. Shaft wear can be felt with the drivebelt removed if the water pump pulley is rocked up and down (with the engine off). Don't mistake drivebelt slippage, which causes a squealing sound, for water pump bearing failure.

Timing chain or timing belt-driven water pump

30 Water pumps driven by the timing chain or timing belt are located underneath the timing chain or timing belt cover.

31 Checking the water pump is limited because of where it is located. However, some basic checks can be made before deciding to remove the water pump. If the pump is found to be defective, it should be replaced with a new or rebuilt unit.

32 One sign that the water pump may be failing is that the heater (climate control) may not work well. Warm the engine to normal operating temperature, confirm that the coolant level is correct, then run the heater and check for hot air coming from the ducts.

33 Check for noises coming from the water pump area. If the water pump impeller shaft or bearings are failing, there may be a howling sound at the pump while the engine is running.

➥Note: **Be careful not to mistake drivebelt noise (squealing) for water pump bearing or shaft failure.**

34 It you suspect water pump failure due to noise, wear can be confirmed by feeling for play at the pump shaft. This can be done by rocking the drive sprocket on the pump shaft up and down. To do this you will need to remove the tension on the timing chain or belt as well as access the water pump.

All water pumps

35 In rare cases or on high-mileage vehicles, another sign of water pump failure may be the presence of coolant in the engine oil. This condition will adversely affect the engine in varying degrees.

➥Note: **Finding coolant in the engine oil could indicate other serious issues besides a failed water pump, such as a blown head gasket or a cracked cylinder head or block.**

36 Even a pump that exhibits no outward signs of a problem, such as noise or leakage, can still be due for replacement. Removal for close examination is the only sure way to tell. Sometimes the fins on the back of the impeller can corrode to the point that cooling efficiency is diminished significantly.

HEATER SYSTEM

37 Little can go wrong with a heater. If the fan motor will run at all speeds, the electrical part of the system is okay. The three basic heater problems fall into the following general categories:

a) *Not enough heat*
b) *Heat all the time*
c) *No heat*

38 If there's not enough heat, the control valve or door is stuck in a partially open position, the coolant coming from the engine isn't hot enough, or the heater core is restricted. If the coolant isn't hot enough, the thermostat in the engine cooling system is stuck open, allowing coolant to pass through the engine so rapidly that it doesn't heat up quickly enough. If the vehicle is equipped with a temperature gauge instead of a warning light, watch to see if the engine temperature rises to the normal operating range after driving for a reasonable distance.

39 If there's heat all the time, the control valve or the door is stuck wide open.

40 If there's no heat, coolant is probably not reaching the heater core, or the heater core is plugged. The likely cause is a collapsed or plugged hose, core, or a frozen heater control valve. If the heater is the type that flows coolant all the time, the cause is a stuck door or a broken or kinked control cable.

AIR CONDITIONING SYSTEM

41 If the cool air output is inadequate:

a) *Inspect the condenser coils and fins to make sure they're clear*
b) *Check the compressor clutch for slippage.*
c) *Check the blower motor for proper operation.*
d) *Inspect the blower discharge passage for obstructions.*
e) *Check the system air intake filter for clogging.*

42 If the system provides intermittent cooling air:

a) *Check the circuit breaker, blower switch and blower motor for a malfunction.*

b) *Make sure the compressor clutch isn't slipping.*
c) *Inspect the plenum door to make sure it's operating properly.*
d) *Inspect the evaporator to make sure it isn't clogged.*
e) *If the unit is icing up, it may be caused by excessive moisture in the system, incorrect super heat switch adjustment or low thermostat adjustment.*

43 If the system provides no cooling air:

a) *Inspect the compressor drivebelt. Make sure it's not loose or broken.*
b) *Make sure the compressor clutch engages. If it doesn't, check for a blown fuse.*
c) *Inspect the wire harness for broken or disconnected wires.*
d) *If the compressor clutch doesn't engage, bridge the terminals of the A/C pressure switch(es) with a jumper wire; if the clutch now engages, and the system is properly charged, the pressure switch is bad.*
e) *Make sure the blower motor is not disconnected or burned out.*
f) *Make sure the compressor isn't partially or completely seized.*
g) *Inspect the refrigerant lines for leaks.*
h) *Check the components for leaks.*
i) *Inspect the receiver-drier/accumulator or expansion valve/tube for clogged screens.*

44 If the system is noisy:

a) *Look for loose panels in the passenger compartment.*
b) *Inspect the compressor drivebelt. It may be loose or worn.*
c) *Check the compressor mounting bolts. They should be tight.*
d) *Listen carefully to the compressor. It may be worn out.*
e) *Listen to the idler pulley and bearing and the clutch. Either may be defective.*
f) *The winding in the compressor clutch coil or solenoid may be defective.*
g) *The compressor oil level may be low.*
h) *The blower motor fan bushing or the motor itself may be worn out.*
i) *If there is an excessive charge in the system, you'll hear a rumbling noise in the high pressure line, a thumping noise in the compressor, or see bubbles or cloudiness in the sight glass.*
j) *If there's a low charge in the system, you might hear hissing in the evaporator case at the expansion valve, or see bubbles or cloudiness in the sight glass.*

3　Air conditioning and heating system - check and maintenance

AIR CONDITIONING SYSTEM

▶ **Refer to illustration 3.1**

❋❋ WARNING:

The air conditioning system is under high pressure. Do not loosen any hose fittings or remove any components until after the system has been discharged. Air conditioning refrigerant should be properly discharged into an EPA-approved recovery/recycling unit at a dealer service department or an automotive air conditioning repair facility. Always wear eye protection when disconnecting air conditioning system fittings.

❋❋ CAUTION 1:

All models covered by this manual use environmentally friendly R-134a. This refrigerant (and its appropriate refrigerant oils) are not compatible with R-12 refrigerant system components and must never be mixed or the components will be damaged.

❋❋ CAUTION 2:

When replacing entire components, additional refrigerant oil should be added equal to the amount that is removed with the component being replaced. Be sure to read the can before adding any oil to the system, to make sure it is compatible with the R-134a system.

3.1 The evaporator drain hose extends through the floor to allow collected water to run out

3.9 Insert a thermometer in the center vent, turn on the air conditioning system and wait for it to cool down; depending on the humidity, the output air should be 30 to 40 degrees cooler than the ambient air temperature

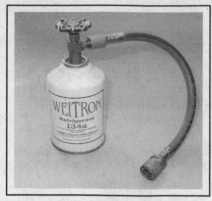

3.11 R-134a automotive air conditioning charging kit

1   The following maintenance checks should be performed on a regular basis to ensure that the air conditioning continues to operate at peak efficiency.

    a) *Inspect the condition of the compressor drivebelt. If it is worn or deteriorated, replace it (see Chapter 1).*

    b) *Check the drivebelt tension (see Chapter 1).*

    c) *Inspect the system hoses. Look for cracks, bubbles, hardening and deterioration. Inspect the hoses and all fittings for oil bubbles or seepage. If there is any evidence of wear, damage or leakage, replace the hose(s).*

    d) *Inspect the condenser fins for leaves, bugs and any other foreign material that may have embedded itself in the fins. Use a fin comb or compressed air to remove debris from the condenser.*

    e) *Make sure the system has the correct refrigerant charge.*

    f) *If you hear water sloshing around in the dash area or have water dripping on the carpet, check the evaporator housing drain tube (see illustration) and insert a piece of wire into the opening to check for blockage.*

2   It's a good idea to operate the system for about ten minutes at least once a month. This is particularly important during the winter months because long term non-use can cause hardening, and subsequent failure, of the seals. Note that using the Defrost function operates the compressor.

3   If the air conditioning system is not working properly, proceed to Step 6 and perform the general checks outlined below.

4   Because of the complexity of the air conditioning system and the special equipment necessary to service it, in-depth troubleshooting and repairs beyond checking the refrigerant charge and the compressor clutch operation are not included in this manual. However, simple checks and component replacement procedures are provided in this Chapter.

5   The most common cause of poor cooling is simply a low system refrigerant charge. If a noticeable drop in system cooling ability occurs, one of the following quick checks will help you determine if the refrigerant level is low.

Checking the refrigerant charge

▶ **Refer to illustration 3.9**

6   Warm the engine up to normal operating temperature.

7   Place the air conditioning temperature selector at the coldest setting and put the blower at the highest setting.

8   After the system reaches operating temperature, feel the larger pipe exiting the evaporator at the firewall. The outlet pipe should be cold (the tubing that leads back to the compressor). If the evaporator outlet pipe is warm, the system probably needs a charge.

9   Insert a thermometer in the center air distribution duct (see illustration) while operating the air conditioning system at its maximum setting - the temperature of the output air should be 35 to 40 degrees F below the ambient air temperature (down to approximately 40 degrees F). If the ambient (outside) air temperature is very high, say 110 degrees F, the duct air temperature may be as high as 60 degrees F, but generally the air conditioning is 30 to 40 degrees F cooler than the ambient air.

10 Further inspection or testing of the system requires special tools and techniques and is beyond the scope of the home mechanic.

Adding refrigerant

▶ **Refer to illustrations 3.11 and 3.13**

✳✳ CAUTION:

Make sure any refrigerant, refrigerant oil or replacement component you purchase is designated as compatible with R-134a systems.

11 Purchase an R-134a automotive charging kit at an auto parts store (see illustration). A charging kit includes a can of refrigerant, a tap valve and a short section of hose that can be attached between the tap valve and the system low side service valve.

✳✳ CAUTION:

Never add more than one can of refrigerant to the system. If more refrigerant than that is required, the system should be evacuated and leak tested.

12 Back off the valve handle on the charging kit and screw the kit onto the refrigerant can, making sure first that the O-ring or rubber seal

inside the threaded portion of the kit is in place.

13 Remove the dust cap from the low-side charging port and attach the hose's quick-connect fitting to the port (see illustration).

14 Warm up the engine and turn On the air conditioning. Keep the charging kit hose away from the fan and other moving parts.

➡**Note: The charging process requires the compressor to be running. If the clutch cycles off, you can put the air conditioning switch on High and leave the car doors open to keep the clutch on and compressor working. The compressor can be kept on during the charging by removing the connector from the pressure switch and bridging it with a paper clip or jumper wire during the procedure.**

15 Turn the valve handle on the kit until the stem pierces the can, then back the handle out to release the refrigerant. You should be able to hear the rush of gas. Keep the can upright at all times, but shake it occasionally. Allow stabilization time between each addition.

➡**Note: The charging process will go faster if you wrap the can with a hot-water-soaked rag to keep the can from freezing up.**

16 If you have an accurate thermometer, you can place it in the center air conditioning duct inside the vehicle and keep track of the output air temperature. A charged system that is working properly should cool down to approximately 40 degrees F. If the ambient (outside) air temperature is very high, say 110 degrees F, the duct air temperature may be as high as 60 degrees F, but generally the air conditioning is 35 to 40 degrees F cooler than the ambient air.

17 When the can is empty, turn the valve handle to the closed position and release the connection from the low-side port. Reinstall the dust cap.

18 Remove the charging kit from the can and store the kit for future use with the piercing valve in the UP position, to prevent inadvertently piercing the can on the next use.

HEATING SYSTEMS

19 If the carpet under the heater core is damp, or if antifreeze vapor or steam is coming through the vents, the heater core is leaking. Remove it (see Section 10) and install a new unit (most radiator shops will not repair a leaking heater core).

20 If the air coming out of the heater vents isn't hot, the problem could stem from any of the following causes:

a) *The thermostat is stuck open, preventing the engine coolant from warming up enough to carry heat to the heater core. Replace the thermostat (see Section 4).*

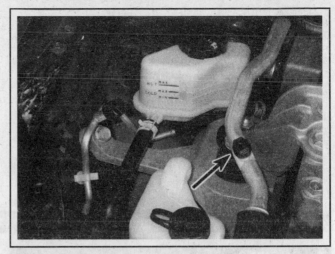

3.13 Location of the low-side charging port

b) *There is a blockage in the system, preventing the flow of coolant through the heater core. Feel both heater hoses at the firewall. They should be hot. If one of them is cold, there is an obstruction in one of the hoses or in the heater core, or the heater control valve is shut. Detach the hoses and back flush the heater core with a water hose. If the heater core is clear but circulation is impeded, remove the two hoses and flush them out with a water hose.*

c) *If flushing fails to remove the blockage from the heater core, the core must be replaced (see Section 10).*

ELIMINATING AIR CONDITIONING ODORS

21 Unpleasant odors that often develop in air conditioning systems are caused by the growth of a fungus, usually on the surface of the evaporator core. The warm, humid environment there is a perfect breeding ground for mildew to develop.

22 The evaporator core on most vehicles is difficult to access, and factory dealerships have a lengthy, expensive process for eliminating the fungus by opening up the evaporator case and using a powerful disinfectant and rinse on the core until the fungus is gone. You can service your own system at home, but it takes something much stronger than basic household germ-killers or deodorizers.

23 Aerosol disinfectants for automotive air conditioning systems are available in most auto parts stores, but remember when shopping for them that the most effective treatments are also the most expensive. The basic procedure for using these sprays is to start by running the system in the RECIRC mode for ten minutes with the blower on its highest speed. Use the highest heat mode to dry out the system and keep the compressor from engaging by disconnecting the wiring connector at the compressor.

24 The disinfectant can usually comes with a long spray hose. Insert the nozzle into an intake port inside the cabin, and spray according to the manufacturer's recommendations. Follow the manufacturer's recommendations for the length of spray and waiting time between applications.

25 Once the evaporator has been cleaned, the best way to prevent the mildew from coming back again is to make sure your evaporator housing drain tube is clear (see illustration 3.1).

AUTOMATIC HEATING AND AIR CONDITIONING SYSTEMS

26 Some vehicles are equipped with an optional automatic climate control system. This system has its own computer that receives inputs from various sensors in the heating and air conditioning system. This computer, like the PCM, has self-diagnostic capabilities to help pinpoint problems or faults within the system. Vehicles equipped with automatic heating and air conditioning systems are very complex and considered beyond the scope of the home mechanic. Vehicles equipped with automatic heating and air conditioning systems should be taken to dealer service department or other qualified facility for repair.

4 Thermostat - replacement

✳✳ WARNING:

Wait until the engine is completely cool before beginning this procedure.

1 Drain the cooling system (see Chapter 1). If the coolant is relatively new, or is in good condition (see Section 2), save it and re-use it.

✳✳ WARNING:

See Warning in Section 1.

FOUR-CYLINDER ENGINES

➡**Note: This engine uses a thermostat on the coolant inlet (located below the exhaust manifold) and a water control valve on the coolant outlet (at the driver's end of the cylinder head). Although they have different names, these devices perform similar functions and are very similar in appearance.**

Thermostat

2 Remove the fresh air intake duct.

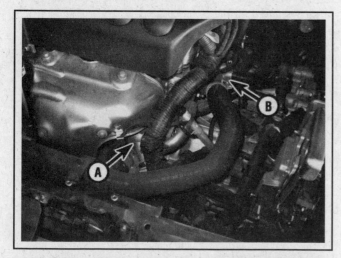

4.5a The four-cylinder engine uses a thermostat (A) and a water control valve (B) to regulate the flow of coolant

3 Remove the lower radiator hose from the housing cover. If the hose is stuck, grasp it near the end with a pair of large adjustable pliers and twist it to break the seal, then pull it off. If the hose is old or deteriorated, cut it off and install a new one.

Water control valve

▸ **Refer to illustrations 4.5a and 4.5b**

4 Remove the air filter housing (see Chapter 4).
5 Disconnect the hoses from the coolant outlet (see illustrations). If a hose is stuck, grasp it near the end with a pair of large adjustable pliers and twist it to break the seal, then pull it off. If the hose is old or deteriorated, cut it off and install a new one.
6 Detach the hoses from the heater pipe, then unscrew the fastener and remove the heater pipe from the engine. Install a new O-ring on the end of the heater pipe where it mates with the engine.

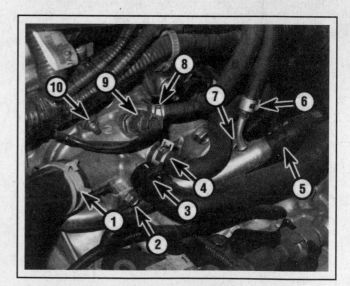

4.5b Water control valve details (four-cylinder engine)

1	Radiator hose	9	Engine Coolant Temperature
2	Heater pipe bolt		(ECT) sensor
3	Heater hose	10	Water control valve
4	Oil cooler hose		mounting fastener (others not
5	Heater hose		visible in this photo)
6	Throttle body hose		
7	Oil cooler hose		
8	Throttle body hose		

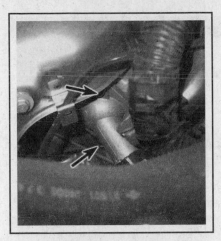

4.7 Thermostat cover bolts (four-cylinder engine)

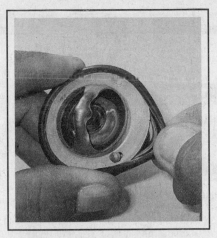

4.9a The thermostat and water control valve sealing ring fits around the edge of the flange

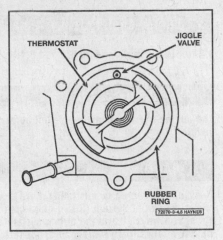

4.9b The thermostat's or water control valve's jiggle valve or air bleed must be at the 12 o'clock position when installed

Both thermostat and water control valve

▶ **Refer to illustrations 4.7, 4.9a and 4.9b**

7   Remove the fasteners and detach the housing cover (see illustration). If the cover is stuck, tap it with a soft-face hammer to jar it loose. Be prepared for some coolant to spill as the gasket seal is broken. Clean the mating surfaces of all gasket or sealant.

8   Remove the thermostat or water control valve.

9   Install a new sealing ring onto the thermostat or water control valve (see illustration), then insert the valve into the housing. Make sure the air bleed faces up (see illustration) and the spring end of the valve is directed toward the engine.

10 If you're installing the thermostat, apply a bead of RTV sealant to the thermostat cover. If you're installing the water control valve, be sure to use a new gasket when installing the housing.

11 Install the cover and bolts. Tighten the bolts evenly to the torque listed in this Chapter's Specifications.

12 The remainder of installation is the reverse of removal.

13 Refill the cooling system (see Chapter 1).

14 Start the engine and allow it to reach normal operating temperature, then check for leaks and proper thermostat/water valve operation.

V6 ENGINES

▶ **Refer to illustration 4.19**

15 Remove the water pump drain plug and allow the remaining coolant to drain (see illustration 7.18).

16 Remove the coolant reservoir.

17 Disconnect the electrical connector from the IVT valve.

18 Disconnect the lower radiator hose. If the hose is stuck, grasp it

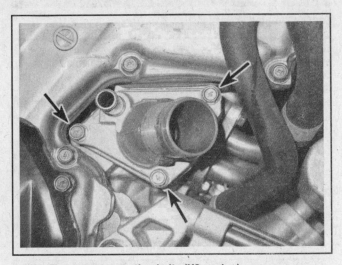

4.19 Thermostat mounting bolts (V6 engine)

near the end with a pair of large adjustable pliers and twist it to break the seal, then pull it off. If the hose is old or deteriorated, cut it off and install a new one.

19 Remove the thermostat housing/thermostat assembly (see illustration).

➡ **Note: If the thermostat is defective, replace the entire cover/thermostat assembly.**

20 Installation is the reverse of removal. Be sure to position the jiggle valve at the upper part of the unit.

21 Refill the cooling system (see Chapter 1).

22 Start the engine and allow it to reach normal operating temperature, then check for leaks and proper thermostat operation.

5 Engine cooling fans - replacement

♦ Refer to illustrations 5.7, 5.9 and 5.10

✳✳ **WARNING:**

The engine must be completely cool before beginning this procedure.

✳✳ **WARNING:**

The models covered by this manual are equipped with a Supplemental Restraint System (SRS), more commonly known as airbags. Always disarm the airbag system before working in the vicinity of any airbag system component to avoid the possibility of accidental deployment of the airbag, which could cause personal injury (see Chapter 12). Do not use a memory saving device to preserve the PCM's memory when working on or near airbag system components.

✳✳ **WARNING:**

See the Warning in Section 1.

➡Note: The two engine cooling fans have two speeds and are controlled by the PCM (computer). The PCM receives input from the coolant temperature sensor, as well as sensors for air conditioning, vehicle speed and engine rpm. The PCM determines when the electric fan(s) should turn on, and at which speed, High or Low.

1 Disconnect the cable from the negative terminal of the battery (see Chapter 5).

2 Drain some coolant from the radiator (to a level that's lower than the upper radiator hose) (see Chapter 1).

3 On four-cylinder models, remove the front air inlet duct.

4 On V6 models with an automatic transaxle, remove the Transmission Control Module.

5 On V6 models, remove the battery and battery tray.

6 Disconnect the upper radiator hose from the radiator.

7 Disconnect the electrical connectors from the fans (see illustration).

8 Remove the bolts at the upper corners of the fan support, then pull it upward to detach it at the bottom. Remove the fan assembly.

9 If necessary, remove the nut and detach the fan blade assembly from the motor shaft (see illustration).

10 Remove the screws retaining the fan motor to the fan shroud, then detach the motor (see illustration).

11 Installation is the reverse of removal. Refill the cooling system (see Chapter 1)

12 Reconnect the battery and perform the necessary re-learn procedures (see Chapter 5).

5.7 Engine cooling fan electrical connector locations

5.9 To replace the fan motor, unbolt the fan blade nut and remove the fan blade

5.10 Remove the mounting screws that hold the motor to the fan shroud and remove the motor

6 Radiator and coolant reservoir - removal and installation

RADIATOR

▶ **Refer to illustrations 6.8 and 6.10**

1 Have the air conditioning system discharged by an automotive air conditioning technician.

2 Disconnect the cable from the negative terminal of the battery (see Chapter 5). Drain the cooling system (see Chapter 1).

3 On sedan models, refer to Chapter 11 and remove the grille. On coupe models, remove the front bumper.

4 Raise the vehicle and support it securely on jackstands. Remove the under-vehicle splash shield. On V6 models, remove the front wheels and the inner fender side covers.

5 Remove the front air inlet duct.

6 Remove the battery tray on automatic transaxle-equipped vehicles.

7 Remove the air conditioning condenser (see Section 12).

8 Disconnect the coolant overflow hose from the fitting below the radiator cap (see illustration).

9 Disconnect the upper and lower radiator hoses.

10 On automatic transaxle-equipped vehicles, disconnect the fluid cooler lines from the radiator (see illustration). Seal the ends with tape to prevent contamination.

11 Lift the radiator to separate the pins at the bottom from the frame and remove it.

12 With the radiator removed, it can be inspected for leaks and damage. If it needs repair, have a radiator shop or dealer service department perform the work as special techniques are required.

13 Bugs and dirt can be removed from the radiator with a soft brush, followed by forcing water from a garden hose through the core from the engine side. Don't bend the cooling fins as this is done.

14 Installation is the reverse of the removal procedure. Be sure the radiator mounting pads are seated properly at the base of the radiator.

15 After installation, fill the cooling system with the proper mixture of antifreeze and water (see Chapter 1).

16 Reconnect the battery and perform the necessary re-learn procedures (see Chapter 5). Allow the engine to reach normal operating temperature, indicated by the upper radiator hose becoming hot. Recheck the coolant level and add more if required.

17 If you're working on an automatic transaxle-equipped vehicle, check and add transmission fluid as needed (see Chapter 1). Have the air conditioning system recharged by the shop that discharged it.

COOLANT RESERVOIR

▶ **Refer to illustration 6.19**

18 Disconnect the overflow hose from the fitting by the radiator cap.

19 Unbolt the coolant reservoir and remove it from the vehicle (see illustration).

20 Pour the coolant into a container. Wash out the reservoir, using soapy water and a long brush to make the coolant level easier to read. Inspect the reservoir for cracks and chafing. Replace it if any damage is found.

21 Installation is the reverse of removal.

6.8 Disconnect the coolant overflow hose

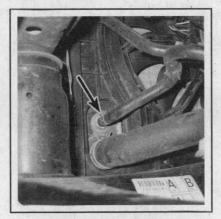

6.10 There are two automatic transaxle cooler hoses connected to the radiator (lower hose shown)

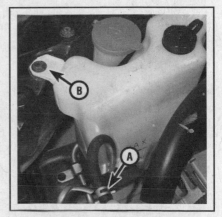

6.19 Detach the hose near the radiator cap (A), then remove the coolant reservoir mounting bolt (B)

7 Water pump - replacement

✳✳ WARNING:

Wait until the engine is completely cool before beginning this procedure.

✳✳ WARNING:

See the Warning in Section 1.

1   Disconnect the cable from the negative terminal of the battery (see Chapter 5).

2   Drain the cooling system (see Chapter 1). If the coolant is relatively new, or is in good condition, save it and re-use it.

3   Loosen the right-front wheel lug nuts. Raise the vehicle and support it securely on jackstands.

4   Remove the right front wheel and the inner fender splash shield (see Chapter 11).

FOUR-CYLINDER ENGINE

▶ **Refer to illustrations 7.5, 7.8a and 7.8b**

5   Remove the drivebelt (see Chapter 1) and the water pump pulley (see illustration).

6   Remove the front air inlet duct and the engine ground cable.

7   Remove the alternator and its bracket (see Chapter 5).

8   Remove the water pump bolts and separate the pump from the pump housing (see illustrations). If the pump is stuck, gently tap it with a soft faced hammer to break the gasket seal.

9   If necessary, remove the complete water pump housing and pump assembly from the block and the water pipe. Remove the housing-to-block bolts and the two bolts connecting the rear of the water pump to the water pipe.

10 If the housing was removed, clean the mating surfaces.

11 If removed, install the pump/housing assembly to the block and connect the water pipe.

12 Place a new gasket on the water pump and install the pump to the housing. Tighten the pump-to-housing bolts to the torque listed in this Chapter's Specifications.

13 Reinstall the alternator and any other components removed for

access to the water pump.

14 Refill the cooling system (see Chapter 1). Reconnect the battery and perform the necessary re-learn procedures (see Chapter 5).

V6 ENGINE

▶ **Refer to illustrations 7.18, 7.23, 7.24 and 7.26**

15 Set the engine to TDC on the compression stroke (see Chapter 2B). Make sure that the pointer is aligned with the TDC mark on the crankshaft pulley and that the engine is on the compression stroke.

16 Remove the drivebelt (see Chapter 1).

17 Remove the belt idler pulley and the air conditioning idler pulley.

18 Remove the coolant drain plug from the water pump side of the engine block (see illustration).

19 Support the engine from below using a floor jack and a block of wood or from above using an engine support fixture.

20 Remove the front engine mount and its bracket.

21 Disconnect the wiring from the right IVT control valve. Remove the right IVT control valve cover.

22 Remove the water pump cover.

23 Remove the chain tensioner cover and the water pump cover from the engine front cover (see illustration).

24 Pull the timing chain tensioner lever down to release the plunger stopper tab. Insert a stopper pin into the tensioner body hole to retain the lever in the released (no chain tension) position (see illustration). Move the plunger into the tensioner by pressing the chain guide and pushing with a screwdriver. Remove the tensioner.

✳✳ CAUTION:

Don't allow the bolts to drop into the timing chain cover.

25 Carefully rotate the crankshaft pulley counterclockwise about 20-degrees until the timing chain becomes somewhat loose on the water pump sprocket.

26 Install two 8 mm bolts about 2 inches long and of the proper thread pitch (1.25 mm) into the water pump bolt holes and tighten them equally until they bottom against the timing chain cover (see illustration). It will be necessary to rotate the water pump slightly to allow the

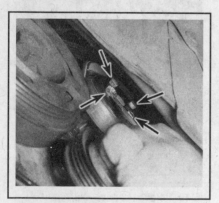

7.5 Loosen the water pump pulley bolts with tension on the drivebelt, then remove the belt and the pulley

7.8a Remove these three water pump bolts from underneath . . .

7.8b . . . and these water pump bolts from above

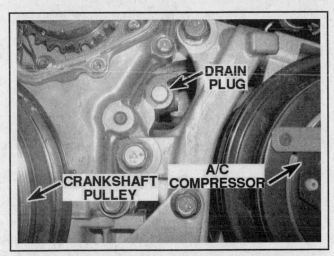

7.18 Location of the water pump drain plug on the V6 engine

7.23 Remove the timing chain tensioner cover (A) and the water pump cover (B) from the timing chain cover

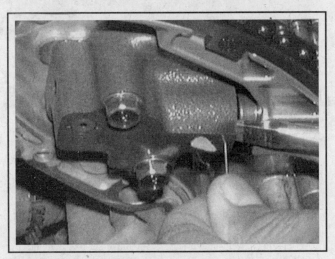

7.24 Depress the timing chain tensioner and lock it into place using a paper clip into the hole on the front of the tensioner

7.26 After the water pump mounting bolts have been removed, install the two M8 x 1.25 bolts into the holes designated by the letter A and tighten them evenly until the water pump is forced out of the engine block

bolts to drive against the rear timing chain case cover instead of the bolt holes. Remove the three water pump mounting bolts.

27 Remove the water pump.

28 Clean the sealant from the mating surface and replace the O-rings.

29 Install the O-ring with the white paint mark into the groove clos-

est to the pump flange and the second O-ring into its groove. Apply a light amount of oil to the O-rings. Tighten the pump bolts to the torque listed in this Chapter's Specifications.

30 Installation is the reverse of removal.

31 Refill the cooling system (see Chapter 1). Reconnect the battery and perform the necessary re-learn procedures (see Chapter 5).

8   Blower motor - removal and installation

◆ Refer to illustration 8.4

❊❊ WARNING:

The models covered by this manual are equipped with a Supplemental Restraint System (SRS), more commonly known as airbags. Always disarm the airbag system before working in the vicinity of any airbag system component to avoid the possibility of accidental deployment of the airbag, which could cause

personal injury (see Chapter 12). Do not use a memory saving device to preserve the PCM's memory when working on or near airbag system components.

1 Disconnect the cable from the negative terminal of the battery (see Chapter 5).

2 Remove the glove box (see Chapter 11).

3 Remove the right-side console finish panel (see Chapter 11).

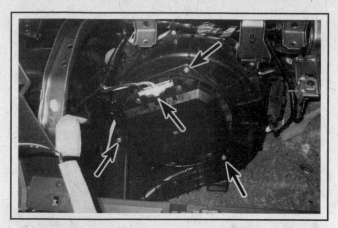

8.4 Blower motor mounting screws and electrical connector

4 Disconnect the electrical connector from the blower motor (see illustration).

5 Remove the three screws and lower the blower motor out.

6 Installation is the reverse of removal.

7 Reconnect the battery and perform the necessary re-learn procedures (see Chapter 5).

9 Heater and air conditioning control assembly - removal and installation

♦ Refer to illustrations 9.3, 9.4a, 9.4b, 9.5 and 9.6

❋❋ WARNING:

The models covered by this manual are equipped with a Supplemental Restraint System (SRS), more commonly known as airbags. Always disarm the airbag system before working in the vicinity of any airbag system component to avoid the possibility of accidental deployment of the airbag, which could cause personal injury (see Chapter 12). Do not use a memory saving device to preserve the PCM's memory when working on or near airbag system components.

1 Disconnect the cable from the negative terminal of the battery (see Chapter 5).

2 Use a plastic trim tool or a screwdriver wrapped with tape to carefully pry up the grille from the center instrument panel vent.

3 Pry off the trim panel below the control unit (see illustration).

4 Remove the control unit mounting screws (see illustrations).

5 Pull the control unit out far enough to disconnect the wiring from the rear (see illustration).

6 Remove the two side brackets, then remove the control unit (see illustration).

7 Installation is the reverse of removal.

8 Reconnect the battery and perform the necessary re-learn procedures (see Chapter 5).

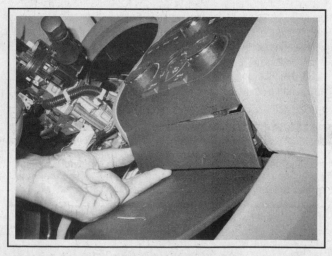

9.3 Remove the panel below the control unit . . .

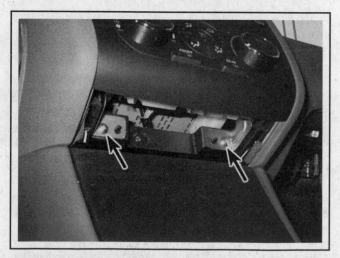

9.4a . . . then remove the lower . . .

9.4b ... and upper control unit mounting screws

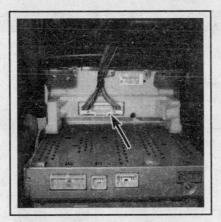

9.5 Pull the control unit out and disconnect the electrical connectors

9.6 These brackets must be removed in order to pull out the heater control unit

10 Heater core - removal and installation

✳✳ WARNING:

Wait until the engine is completely cool before beginning this procedure.

✳✳ WARNING:

The models covered by this manual are equipped with a Supplemental Restraint System (SRS), more commonly known as airbags. Always disarm the airbag system before working in the vicinity of any airbag system component to avoid the possibility of accidental deployment of the airbag, which could cause personal injury (see Chapter 12). Do not use a memory saving device to preserve the PCM's memory when working on or near airbag system components.

➡Note: Replacement of the heater core is a difficult procedure for the home mechanic, involving removal of the entire dashboard, console, and many wiring connectors. If you attempt it at home, keep track of the assemblies by taking notes and keeping screws and other hardware in small, marked plastic bags for reassembly.

REMOVAL

1   Have the air conditioning system evacuated by a properly-equipped shop.

2   Disconnect the cable from the negative terminal of the battery (see Chapter 5).

3   Drain the cooling system (see Chapter 1).

4   Remove the wiper motor and linkage (see Chapter 12).

5   Remove the strut tower reinforcement bar, if equipped.

6   Remove the lower right side cowl panel (see Chapter 11).

7   Disconnect the heater hoses from the pipes that protrude through the firewall.

8   Disconnect the air conditioning lines from the expansion valve block at the firewall. Seal all open ends to prevent contamination.

9   Remove the entire instrument panel assembly (see Chapter 11).

10 Remove the steering column (see Chapter 10).

11 Disconnect the condensate drain hose from the heater unit.

12 Unbolt and remove the heating/cooling and steering units from the vehicle as one complete assembly.

13 Remove the heater tubing grommet, support and cover from the heater tubes.

14 Remove the left foot air duct.

15 Slide the heater core from the case.

16 Reinstall the heater core into the heater unit and replace the assembly in the reverse order of removal.

17 Refill the cooling system (see Chapter 1). Reconnect the battery and perform the necessary re-learn procedures (see Chapter 5). Check for leaks and proper system operation. Check the operation of all electrical components of the steering column and dash.

18 Have the air conditioning system recharged by the shop that discharged it.

11 Air conditioning compressor - removal and installation

▶ Refer to illustration 11.11

> **✳✳ WARNING:**
>
> The air conditioning system is under high pressure. Do not loosen any fittings or remove any components until after the system has been discharged. Air conditioning refrigerant should be properly discharged into an EPA-approved container at a dealer service department or an automotive air conditioning repair facility. Always wear eye protection when disconnecting air conditioning system fittings.

1   Have the refrigerant discharged at a dealer service department or an automotive air conditioning repair facility.
2   Disconnect the cable from the negative terminal of the battery (see Chapter 5).
3   On four-cylinder models, remove the front air inlet duct.
4   On V6 models, remove the engine cooling fan unit (see Section 5).
5   Loosen the lug nuts of the right front wheel. Raise the vehicle and support it securely on jackstands. Remove the right front wheel.
6   Remove the right-side engine lower splash shields.
7   Remove the access cover from the right wheel well.
8   Remove the drivebelt (see Chapter 1).
9   Move the power steering fluid tube aside.
10 Disconnect the electrical connector from the compressor.
11 Disconnect both refrigerant lines from the compressor and seal all openings with tape to prevent contamination (see illustration).
12 Remove the compressor mounting bolts and remove the compressor from the engine compartment.

➡ **Note: Keep the compressor level during handling and storage.**

13 Prior to installation, turn the center of the clutch six times to evenly disperse any oil that has collected in the head.
14 Install the compressor in the reverse order of removal.
15 If you are installing a new compressor, the cycling clutch assembly may have to be transferred to the new compressor.

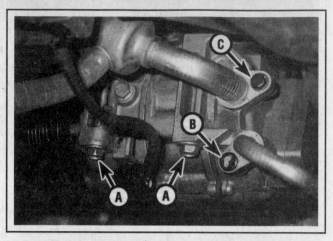

11.11 Compressor mounting bolts (A, lower two bolts not visible), high pressure line bolt (B) and suction line bolt (C)

➡ **Note: The removal of the clutch assembly will require the use of several special tools. You may want to have the clutch assembly transferred to the new compressor by an air conditioning shop or dealer service department.**

Refer to the compressor manufacturer's instructions for adding refrigerant oil to the system.

> **✳✳ CAUTION:**
>
> Use only refrigerant oil compatible with the R-134a system in your vehicle.

16 Reconnect the battery and perform the necessary re-learn procedures (see Chapter 5).
17 Have the system evacuated, charged and leak tested by the shop that discharged it.

12 Air conditioning condenser - removal and installation

▶ Refer to illustrations 12.3 and 12.5

> **✳✳ WARNING:**
>
> The models covered by this manual are equipped with a Supplemental Restraint System (SRS), more commonly known as airbags. Always disarm the airbag system before working in the vicinity of any airbag system component to avoid the possibility of accidental deployment of the airbag, which could cause personal injury (see Chapter 12). Do not use a memory saving device to preserve the PCM's memory when working on or near airbag system components.

> **✳✳ WARNING:**
>
> The air conditioning system is under high pressure. Do not loosen any fittings or remove any components until after the system has been discharged. Air conditioning refrigerant should be properly discharged into an EPA-approved container at a dealer service department or an automotive air conditioning repair facility. Always wear eye protection when disconnecting air conditioning system fittings.

➡ **Note: This air conditioning system doesn't have a separate receiver-drier. The condenser has an attached liquid tank that isn't serviced separately.**

12.3 Air conditioning condenser refrigerant line connection (A) and typical retaining clip (B)

12.5 The air conditioning system pressure sensor is mounted on the receiver-drier; the receiver-drier is a part of the condenser

1   Have the refrigerant discharged at a dealer service department or an automotive air conditioning repair facility.

2   On sedan models, remove the grille (see Chapter 11). On coupes, remove the front bumper (see Chapter 11).

3   Disconnect the refrigerant lines from the condenser (see illustration).

4   Immediately cap the open fittings to prevent the entry of dirt and moisture.

5   Disconnect the wiring from the pressure sensor on top of the liquid tank (see illustration).

6   Release the two upper mounting clips, then pull the condenser up and lift it out of the vehicle. Store it upright to prevent oil loss.

7   Installation is the reverse of removal.

8   If a new condenser is installed, add 2.5 ounces (75 cc) of refrigerant oil to the system.

❋❋ CAUTION:

Use only refrigerant oil compatible with the R-134a system in your vehicle.

9   Have the system evacuated, charged and leak tested by the shop that discharged it.

Specifications

General

Radiator cap pressure rating	Refer to pressure specification on cap
Cooling system capacity	See Chapter 1
Refrigerant type	R-134a
Refrigerant capacity	1.2 lbs

Torque specifications   Ft-lbs (unless otherwise indicated)

➡ Note: One foot-pound (ft-lb) of torque is equivalent to 12 inch-pounds (in-lbs) of torque. Torque values below approximately 15 foot-pounds are expressed in inch-pounds, because most foot-pound torque wrenches are not accurate at these smaller values.

Thermostat housing and water control valve housing bolts	
Four-cylinder engine	16
V6 engine	87 in-lbs
Water pump bolts	
Four-cylinder engine	16
V6 engine	85 in-lbs

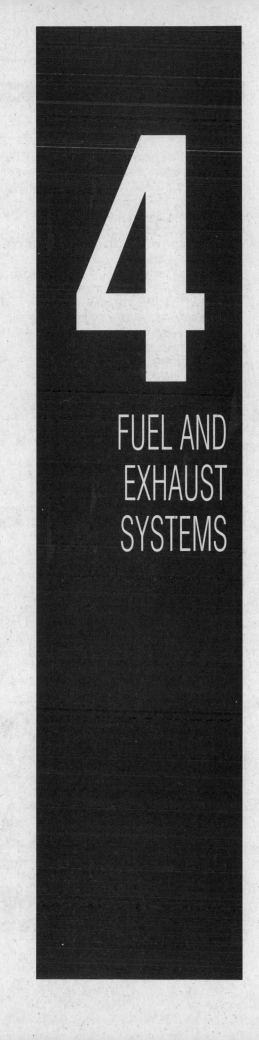

4

FUEL AND
EXHAUST
SYSTEMS

Section

1 General information

FUEL SYSTEM WARNINGS

Gasoline is extremely flammable and repairing fuel system components can be dangerous. Consider your automotive repair knowledge and experience before attempting repairs which may be better suited for a professional mechanic.

- Don't smoke or allow open flames or bare light bulbs near the work area
- Don't work in a garage with a gas-type appliance (water heater, clothes dryer)
- Use fuel-resistant gloves. If any fuel spills on your skin, wash it off immediately with soap and water
- Clean up spills immediately
- Do not store fuel-soaked rags where they could ignite
- Prior to disconnecting any fuel line, you must relieve the fuel pressure (see Section 3)
- Wear safety glasses
- Have a proper fire extinguisher on hand

FUEL SYSTEM

The fuel system consists of the fuel tank, electric fuel pump/fuel level sending unit (located in the fuel tank), fuel rail and fuel injectors. The fuel injection system is a multi-port system; multi-port fuel injection uses timed impulses to inject the fuel directly into the intake port of each cylinder. The Powertrain Control Module (PCM) controls the injectors. The PCM monitors various engine parameters and delivers the exact amount of fuel required into the intake ports.

Fuel is circulated from the fuel pump to the fuel rail through fuel lines running along the underside of the vehicle. Various sections of the fuel line are either rigid metal or nylon, or flexible fuel hose. The various sections of the fuel hose are connected either by quick-connect fittings or threaded metal fittings.

EXHAUST SYSTEM

The exhaust system consists of the exhaust manifold(s), catalytic converter(s), muffler(s), tailpipe and all connecting pipes, flanges and clamps. The catalytic converters are an emission control device added to the exhaust system to reduce pollutants.

2 Troubleshooting

FUEL PUMP

▶ **Refer to illustration 2.2**

1 The fuel pump is located inside the fuel tank. Sit inside the vehicle with the windows closed, turn the ignition key to ON (not START) and listen for the sound of the fuel pump as it's briefly activated. You will only hear the sound for a second or two, but that sound tells you that the pump is working. Alternatively, have an assistant listen at the fuel filler cap.

2.2 The fuel pump fuse is located in the engine compartment fuse box

2 If the pump does not come on, check the fuel pump fuse (see illustration). If the fuse is okay, check the wiring back to the fuel pump. If the fuse and wiring are okay, the pump might be defective. Other possibilities include a faulty fuel pump relay, which is part of the Intelligent Power Distribution Module (which is part of the underhood fuse/relay box), or a faulty Powertrain Control Module (PCM). If the pump runs continuously with the ignition key in the ON position, the Powertrain Control Module (PCM) is probably defective. Have the PCM checked by a professional mechanic.

FUEL INJECTION SYSTEM

▶ **Refer to illustration 2.9**

➡**Note: The following procedure is based on the assumption that the fuel pump is working and the fuel pressure is adequate (see Section 4).**

3 Check all electrical connectors that are related to the system. Check the ground wire connections for tightness.

4 Verify that the battery is fully charged (see Chapter 5).

5 Inspect the air filter element (see Chapter 1).

6 Check all fuses related to the fuel system (see Chapter 12).

7 Check the air induction system between the throttle body and the intake manifold for air leaks. Also inspect the condition of all vacuum hoses connected to the intake manifold and to the throttle body.

8 Remove the air intake duct from the throttle body and look for dirt, carbon, varnish, or other residue in the throttle body, particularly around the throttle plate. If it's dirty, clean it with carb cleaner, a toothbrush and a clean shop towel.

9   With the engine running, place an automotive stethoscope against each injector, one at a time, and listen for a clicking sound that indicates operation (see illustration).

✳✳ WARNING:

Stay clear of the drivebelt and any rotating or hot components.

10 If you can hear the injectors operating, but the engine is misfiring, the electrical circuits are functioning correctly, but the injectors might be dirty or clogged. Try a commercial injector cleaning product (available at auto parts stores). If cleaning the injectors doesn't help, replace the injectors.

11 If an injector is not operating (it makes no sound), disconnect the injector electrical connector and measure the resistance across the injector terminals with an ohmmeter. Compare this measurement to the other injectors. If the resistance of the non-operational injector is quite different from the other injectors, replace it.

12 If the injector is not operating, but the resistance reading is within the range of resistance of the other injectors, the PCM or the circuit between the PCM and the injector might be faulty.

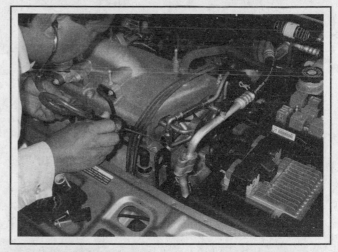

2.9 An automotive stethoscope is used to listen to the fuel injectors in operation

3   Fuel pressure relief procedure

✳✳ WARNING:

Gasoline is extremely flammable. See *Fuel system warnings* in Section 1.

➡Note: After the fuel pressure has been relieved, it's a good idea to lay a shop towel over any fuel connection to be disassembled, to absorb the residual fuel that may leak out when servicing the fuel system.

1   Remove the fuel pump fuse from the underhood fuse/relay box (see illustration 2.2).

2   Start the engine and allow it to run until it stops. This should take only a few seconds. Disconnect the cable from the negative terminal of the battery before working on the fuel system (see Chapter 5).

3   The fuel system pressure is now relieved. It is a good idea to surround any fuel line that will be disconnected using a shop rag to catch fuel that might spill out.

4   When you're finished working on the fuel system, install the fuel pump fuse back into the fuse panel, connect the negative cable to the battery and perform the necessary re-learn procedures (see Chapter 5).

4   Fuel pressure - check

▶ **Refer to illustrations 4.1a, 4.1b and 4.1c**

✳✳ WARNING:

Gasoline is extremely flammable. See *Fuel system warnings* in Section 1.

➡Note: To perform the fuel pressure test, you will need to obtain a special fuel pressure gauge and adapter set (fuel line fittings).

1   Relieve the fuel pressure (see Section 3). Disconnect the quick-connect fuel supply line fitting at the fuel rail (see illustrations). You must connect a special tee adapter in the line that incorporates a fuel pressure gauge. This special tee can be purchased or you can fabricate your own out of various fittings, hose and hose clamps (see illustration).

4.1a Fuel line quick-connect fitting at the fuel rail (below the throttle body) - four-cylinder engine

4.1b Fuel supply line fitting at the fuel rail - V6 engine

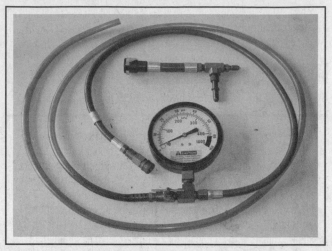

4.1c A typical fuel pressure gauge, with hoses and fittings suitable for tee-ing into the fuel delivery system

2   With the gauge connected and leak-tested, start the engine and allow it to idle. Note the gauge reading as soon as it stabilizes and compare it with the pressure listed in this Chapter's Specifications.

3   If the fuel pressure is far out of specification, check the following:

a) *Check for a restriction in the fuel system (kinked fuel line, plugged fuel pump inlet strainer or clogged fuel filter). If no restrictions are found, replace the fuel pump module (see Section 7).*

b) *If the fuel pressure is higher than specified, replace the fuel pump module (see Section 7).*

4   Turn off the engine. Fuel pressure should not fall more than 8 psi over five minutes. If it does, the problem could be a leaky fuel injector, fuel line leak, or faulty fuel pump module.

5   Disconnect the fuel pressure gauge. Wipe up any spilled gasoline.

5   Fuel lines and fittings - general information and disconnection

✳✳ WARNING:

Gasoline is extremely flammable. See *Fuel system warnings* in Section 1.

1   Relieve the fuel pressure before servicing fuel lines or fittings (see Section 3), then disconnect the cable from the negative battery terminal (see Chapter 5) before proceeding.

2   The fuel supply line connects the fuel pump in the fuel tank to the fuel rail on the engine. The Evaporative Emission (EVAP) system lines connect the fuel tank to the EVAP canister and connect the canister to the intake manifold.

3   Whenever you're working under the vehicle, be sure to inspect all fuel and evaporative emission lines for leaks, kinks, dents and other damage. Always replace a damaged fuel or EVAP line immediately.

4   If you find signs of dirt in the lines during disassembly, disconnect all lines and blow them out with compressed air. Inspect the fuel strainer on the fuel pump pick-up unit for damage and deterioration.

STEEL TUBING

5   It is critical that the fuel lines be replaced with lines of equivalent type and specification.

6   Some steel fuel lines have threaded fittings. When loosening these fittings, hold the stationary fitting with a wrench while turning the tube nut.

PLASTIC TUBING

7   When replacing fuel system plastic tubing, use only original equipment replacement plastic tubing.

✳✳ CAUTION:

When removing or installing plastic fuel line tubing, be careful not to bend or twist it too much, which can damage it. Also, plastic fuel tubing is NOT heat resistant, so keep it away from excessive heat.

FLEXIBLE HOSES

8   When replacing fuel system flexible hoses, use only original equipment replacements.

9   Don't route fuel hoses (or metal lines) within four inches of the exhaust system or within ten inches of the catalytic converter. Make sure that no rubber hoses are installed directly against the vehicle, particularly in places where there is any vibration. If allowed to touch some vibrating part of the vehicle, a hose can easily become chafed and it might start leaking. A good rule of thumb is to maintain a minimum of 1/4-inch clearance around a hose (or metal line) to prevent contact with the vehicle underbody.

Disconnecting Fuel Line Fittings

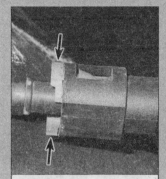

Two-tab type fitting; depress both tabs with your fingers, then pull the fuel line and the fitting apart

On this type of fitting, depress the two buttons on opposite sides of the fitting, then pull it off the fuel line

Threaded fuel line fitting; hold the stationary portion of the line or component (A) while loosening the tube nut (B) with a flare-nut wrench

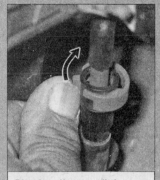

Plastic collar-type fitting; rotate the outer part of the fitting

Metal collar quick-connect fitting; pull the end of the retainer off the fuel line, and disengage the other end from the female side of the fitting . . .

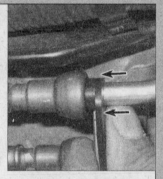

. . . insert a fuel line separator tool into the female side of the fitting, push it into the fitting until it releases the locking tabs inside the fitting, and pull the two halves of the fitting apart

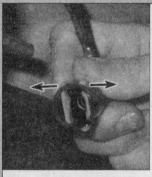

Hairpin-type clip; spread the two legs of the clip apart . . .

. . . pull the clip out and detach the coupling from the component (fitting detached for clarity)

Spring-lock coupling; remove the safety cover . . .

. . . install a coupling release tool and close the clamshell halves of the tool around the coupling . . .

. . . push the tool into the fitting, then pull the two lines apart

6 Exhaust system servicing - general information

▶ Refer to illustration 6.1

✳✳ WARNING:

Allow exhaust system components to cool before inspection or repair. Also, when working under the vehicle, make sure it is securely supported on jackstands.

1   The exhaust system consists of the exhaust manifolds, catalytic converter, muffler, tailpipe and all connecting pipes, flanges and clamps. The exhaust system is isolated from the vehicle body and from chassis components by a series of rubber hangers (see illustration). Periodically inspect these hangers for cracks or other signs of deterioration, replacing them as necessary.

2   Conduct regular inspections of the exhaust system to keep it safe and quiet. Look for any damaged or bent parts, open seams, holes, loose connections, excessive corrosion or other defects which could allow exhaust fumes to enter the vehicle. Do not repair deteriorated exhaust system components; replace them with new parts.

3   If the exhaust system components are extremely corroded, or rusted together, a cutting torch is the most convenient tool for removal. Consult a properly-equipped repair shop. If a cutting torch is not available, you can use a hacksaw, or if you have compressed air, there are special pneumatic cutting chisels that can also be used. Wear safety goggles to protect your eyes from metal chips and wear work gloves to protect your hands.

4   Here are some simple guidelines to follow when repairing the exhaust system:

a) Work from the back to the front when removing exhaust system components.

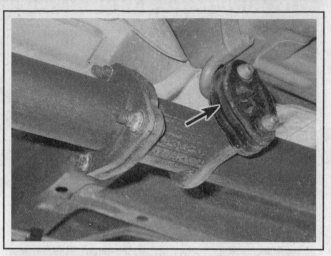

6.1 A typical exhaust system hanger. Inspect regularly and replace at the first sign of damage or deterioration

b) Apply penetrating oil to the exhaust system component fasteners to make them easier to remove.
c) Use new gaskets, hangers and clamps.
d) Apply anti-seize compound to the threads of all exhaust system fasteners during reassembly.
e) Be sure to allow sufficient clearance between newly installed parts and all points on the underbody to avoid overheating the floor pan and possibly damaging the interior carpet and insulation. Pay particularly close attention to the catalytic converter and heat shield.

7 Fuel pump/fuel level sensor module - removal and installation

✳✳ WARNING:

Gasoline is extremely flammable. See *Fuel system warnings* in Section 1.

➡Note: The components of the module (with the exception of the fuel level sender) are not replaceable individually. The entire module must be replaced if any part of it is defective.

REMOVAL

▶ Refer to illustrations 7.4, 7.5, 7.7 and 7.8

1   Relieve the fuel pressure (see Section 3).

2   Disconnect the cable from the negative terminal of the battery (see Chapter 5). Perform the idle air volume learning procedure when connecting the battery (see Chapter 5).

3   Remove the rear seat cushion from the vehicle (see Chapter 11).

4   Remove the access cover for the fuel pump/fuel level sending unit assembly (see illustration).

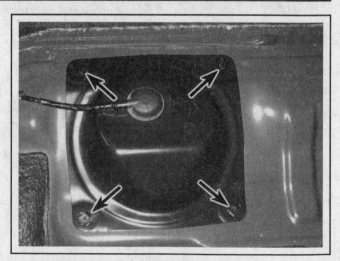

7.4 Fuel pump/fuel level sensor inspection hole cover. Turn the retainers clockwise to release them

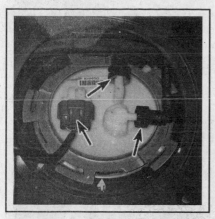

7.5 Depress the tang and disconnect the electrical connector, then detach the fuel and EVAP lines

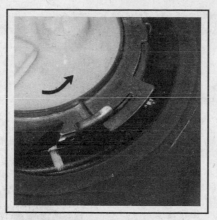

7.7 Use a brass drift and a hammer to rotate the locking ring

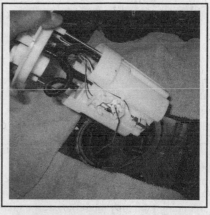

7.8 The fuel level float arm is easily bent, so proceed carefully when lifting the fuel pump module out

7.9 The fuel level sensor is secured with a clip; depress it, then slide the sensor downward

7.12 Install a new O-ring seal

7.14 The alignment mark on the fuel pump module must face the front of the vehicle

5   Disconnect the electrical connectors from the fuel pump/fuel level sending unit (see illustration).

6   Disconnect the hoses and lines from the fuel level sending unit/fuel pump assembly.

7   Using a brass drift and hammer, tap the lock ring on the assembly counterclockwise (see illustration). Remove the lock ring from assembly.

❈❈ CAUTION:

The manufacturer recommends that the lock ring and the O-ring be replaced with new ones.

8   Lift the fuel pump module from the fuel tank. Manipulate it as you lift so you don't bend the float arm (see illustration).

FUEL LEVEL SENSOR REPLACEMENT

▶ **Refer to illustration 7.9**

9   Depress the tang and slide the sensor down to detach it from the module (see illustration).

10 Disconnect the sensor wires from the module.

11 Reverse the procedure to install the replacement sensor.

INSTALLATION

▶ **Refer to illustrations 7.12 and 7.14**

12 Replace the O-ring seal (see illustration).

13 Carefully lower the fuel pump module into the fuel tank.

14 Rotate the assembly until the alignment mark is positioned facing the front of the vehicle (see illustration).

15 Reconnect the hoses and electrical connector, the reinstall the access cover.

16 Reinstall the rear seat cushion.

17 Reconnect the battery and perform the necessary re-learn procedures (see Chapter 5).

8 Fuel tank - removal and installation

▶ **Refer to illustration 8.6**

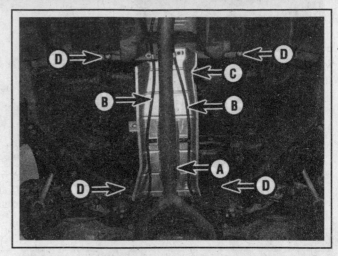

⁂ WARNING:

Gasoline is extremely flammable. See *Fuel system warnings* in Section 1.

➡**Note:** The following procedure is much easier to perform if the fuel tank is empty. Drain the fuel into an approved fuel container using a commercially available siphoning kit (NEVER start the siphoning action by mouth) or wait until the fuel tank is nearly empty, if possible.

1 Remove the fuel tank filler cap to relieve fuel tank pressure.
2 Relieve the fuel system pressure (see Section 3).
3 Disconnect the cable from the negative terminal of the battery (see Chapter 5).
4 Raise the vehicle and place it securely on jackstands.
5 If there is still fuel in the tank, siphon it out from the fuel feed line. Remember - NEVER start the siphoning action by mouth! Use a siphoning kit, which can be purchased at most auto parts stores.
6 Remove the exhaust pipe (see illustration).
7 Disconnect the hoses and electrical connector from the fuel tank (see illustration 7.5).
8 Disconnect the parking brake cables from their brackets. Move the cables aside and secure them in place with wire.
9 Remove the fuel tank shield.
10 Disconnect the lines and wiring from the fuel pump module at the top of the fuel tank (see Section 4). If desired, the fuel pump module

8.6 Remove the rear section of the exhaust system (A), detach the parking brake cables (B), then remove the heat shield (C) before removing the fuel tank support strap bolts (D)

can be removed at this time.
11 Support the fuel tank with a floor jack. Position a wood block between the jack head and the fuel tank to protect the tank.
12 Remove the fuel tank strap bolts.
13 Remove the tank from the vehicle.
14 Installation is the reverse of removal.
15 Reconnect the battery and perform the necessary re-learn procedures (see Chapter 5).

9 Air filter housing - removal and installation

▶ **Refer to illustration 9.5**

1 Separate the air filter housing halves and remove the air filter element (see Chapter 1).
2 Detach the front half of the housing from the air inlet duct.
3 Disconnect the air duct that connects to the throttle body.
4 On four-cylinder models, disconnect the transmission breather hose.
5 Disconnect the Mass Air Flow (MAF) sensor electrical connector and dislodge the harness retainer from the housing (see illustration).
6 Remove the air filter housing mounting bolts, then remove the housing.
7 Installation is the reverse of removal.

9.5 The mass airflow sensor wiring is secured to the air filter housing (A); typical housing mounting bolt (B)

10 Throttle body - removal and installation

▶ **Refer to illustration 10.4**

✳ WARNING:

The engine must be completely cool before beginning this procedure.

1   Disconnect the cable from the negative terminal of the battery (see Chapter 5).

2   Remove the engine cover.

3   Remove the air duct that connects the throttle body to the air filter housing.

4   Clamp-off the coolant hoses to the throttle body, then disconnect them (see illustration).

5   Disconnect the electrical connector from the throttle body.

6   Loosen the throttle body mounting bolts a little at a time in a criss-cross pattern to prevent distortion.

7   Remove the throttle body.

8   Installation is the reverse of removal; use a new throttle body O-ring if the old one is not in perfect condition. Tighten the bolts a little at a time in a criss-cross pattern to the torque listed in this Chapter's Specifications.

9   Reconnect the battery and perform the necessary re-learn procedures (see Chapter 5).

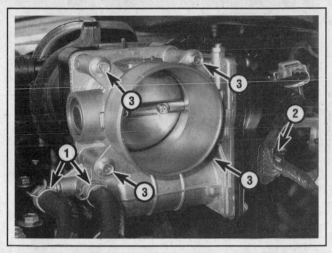

10.4 Throttle body details

1   Coolant hoses
2   Electrical connector
3   Mounting bolt

11 Fuel rail and injectors - removal and installation

▶ **Refer to illustrations 11.6, 11.8a, 11.8b, 11.9 and 11.10**

1   Relieve the fuel system pressure (see Section 3).

2   Disconnect the cable from the negative terminal of the battery (see Chapter 5).

3   On four-cylinder engines, remove the intake manifold (see Chapter 2A). On V6 engines, remove the intake manifold collector (upper intake manifold) (see Chapter 2B).

4   Disconnect the fuel supply line from the fuel rail (see Section 5).

5   Disconnect the electrical connector from each fuel injector.

6   Remove the fuel rail mounting bolts (see illustrations).

11.6 Fuel rail mounting bolts - four-cylinder engine

11.8a To free each injector from the fuel rail, pull off the retainer with a pair of pliers . . .

11.8b . . . then pull the injector straight out of its bore in the fuel rail

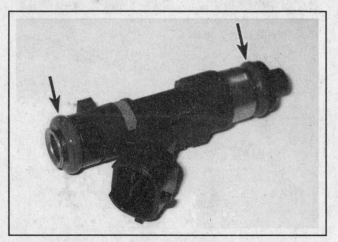

11.9 Whether you're installing new injectors or reusing the old ones, always remove the old O-rings and replace them with new ones

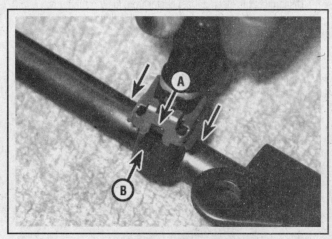

11.10 To install an injector, align the slot in the clip (A) with the tab (B) on the fuel rail, then push the injector firmly into place until the clip snaps onto the ridge of the injector bore

7   Carefully lift the fuel rail from the engine with the injectors attached.

8   Remove the injectors from the fuel rail, then remove and discard the O-rings (see illustrations).

9   Replace both O-rings of each fuel injector and lubricate them with clean engine oil prior to installation (see illustration).

10 Install the injector retaining clips and insert each injector into its bore in the fuel rail until the retaining clip snaps into place (see illustration).

11 The remainder of installation is the reverse of removal.

12 Reconnect the battery and perform the necessary re-learn procedures (see Chapter 5).

Specifications

Fuel system pressure, at idle (approximate)	51 psi

Torque specifications

➡ **Note: One foot-pound (ft-lb) of torque is equivalent to 12 inch-pounds (in-lbs) of torque. Torque values below approximately 15 ft-lbs are expressed in inch-pounds, since most foot-pound torque wrenches are not accurate at these smaller values.**

Throttle body mounting fasteners	84 in-lbs

Section

5

ENGINE ELECTRICAL SYSTEMS

1 General information and precautions

GENERAL INFORMATION

Ignition system

The electronic ignition system consists of the Crankshaft Position (CKP) sensor, the Camshaft Position (CMP) sensor, the Knock Sensor (KS), the Powertrain Control Module (PCM), the ignition switch, the battery, the individual ignition coils or a coil pack, and the spark plugs. For more information on the CKP, CMP and KS sensors, as well as the PCM, refer to Chapter 6.

Charging system

The charging system includes the alternator (with an integral voltage regulator), the Powertrain Control Module (PCM), the Body Control Module (BCM), a charge indicator light on the dash, the battery, a fuse or fusible link and the wiring connecting all of these components. The charging system supplies electrical power for the ignition system, the lights, the radio, etc. The alternator is driven by a drivebelt.

Starting system

The starting system consists of the battery, the ignition switch, the starter relay, the Powertrain Control Module (PCM), the Body Control Module (BCM), the Transmission Range (TR) switch, the starter motor and solenoid assembly, and the wiring connecting all of the components.

PRECAUTIONS

Always observe the following precautions when working on the electrical system:

a) *Be extremely careful when servicing engine electrical components. They are easily damaged if checked, connected or handled improperly.*

b) *Never leave the ignition switched on for long periods of time when the engine is not running.*

c) *Never disconnect the battery cables while the engine is running.*

d) *Maintain correct polarity when connecting battery cables from another vehicle during jump starting - see the "Booster battery (jump) starting" Section at the front of this manual.*

e) *Always disconnect the cable from the negative battery terminal before working on the electrical system, but read the battery disconnection procedure first (see Section 3).*

It's also a good idea to review the safety-related information regarding the engine electrical systems located in the *Safety first!* Section at the front of this manual before beginning any operation included in this Chapter.

Electrical system components - four-cylinder model (engine cover removed)

1 Battery
2 Alternator

3 Ignition coil
4 Starter (under fresh air intake duct)

2 Troubleshooting

IGNITION SYSTEM

1   If a malfunction occurs in the ignition system, do not immediately assume that any particular part is causing the problem. First, check the following items:

a) *Make sure that the cable clamps at the battery terminals are clean and tight.*
b) *Test the condition of the battery (see Steps 21 through 24). If it doesn't pass all the tests, replace it.*
c) *Check the ignition coil or coil pack connections.*
d) *Check any relevant fuses in the engine compartment fuse and relay box (see Chapter 12). If they're burned, determine the cause and repair the circuit.*

Check
♦ **Refer to illustration 2.3**

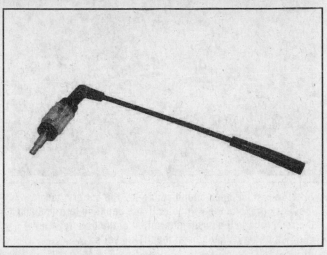

2.3 Spark tester

✳✳ WARNING:

Because of the high voltage generated by the ignition system, use extreme care when performing a procedure involving ignition components.

➡**Note 1: The ignition system components on these vehicles are difficult to diagnose. In the event of ignition system failure that you can't diagnose, have the vehicle tested at a dealer service department or other qualified auto repair facility.**

➡**Note 2: You'll need a spark tester for the following test. Spark testers are available at most auto supply stores.**

2   If the engine turns over but won't start, verify that there is sufficient ignition voltage to fire the spark plugs as follows.

3   On models with a coil-over-plug type ignition system, remove a coil and install the tester between the boot at the lower end of the coil and the spark plug (see illustration). On models with spark plug wires, disconnect a spark plug wire from a spark plug and install the tester between the spark plug wire boot and the spark plug.

4   Crank the engine and note whether or not the tester flashes.

✳✳ CAUTION:

Do NOT crank the engine or allow it to run for more than five seconds; running the engine for more than five seconds may set a Diagnostic Trouble Code (DTC) for a cylinder misfire.

Models with a coil-over-plug type ignition system

5   If the tester flashes during cranking, the coil is delivering sufficient voltage to the spark plug to fire it. Repeat this test for each cylinder to verify that the other coils are OK.

6   If the tester doesn't flash, remove a coil from another cylinder and swap it for the one being tested. If the tester now flashes, you know that the original coil is bad. If the tester still doesn't flash, the PCM or wiring harness is probably defective. Have the PCM checked out by a dealer service department or other qualified repair shop (testing the PCM is beyond the scope of the do-it-yourselfer because it requires expensive special tools).

7   If the tester flashes during cranking but a misfire code (related

to the cylinder being tested) has been stored, the spark plug could be fouled or defective.

Models with spark plug wires

8   If the tester flashes during cranking, sufficient voltage is reaching the spark plug to fire it.

9   Repeat this test on the remaining cylinders.

10   Proceed on this basis until you have verified that there's a good spark from each spark plug wire. If there is, then you have verified that the coils in the coil pack are functioning correctly and that the spark plug wires are OK.

11   If there is no spark from a spark plug wire, then either the coil is bad, the plug wire is bad or a connection at one end of the plug wire is loose. Assuming that you're using new plug wires or known good wires, then the coil is probably defective. Also inspect the coil pack electrical connector. Make sure that it's clean, tight and in good condition.

12   If all the coils are firing correctly, but the engine misfires, then one or more of the plugs might be fouled. Remove and check the spark plugs or install new ones (see Chapter 1).

13   No further testing of the ignition system is possible without special tools. If the problem persists, have the ignition system tested by a dealer service department or other qualified repair shop.

CHARGING SYSTEM

14   If a malfunction occurs in the charging system, do not automatically assume the alternator is causing the problem. First check the following items:

a) *Check the drivebelt tension and condition, as described in Chapter 1. Replace it if it's worn or deteriorated.*
b) *Make sure the alternator mounting bolts are tight.*
c) *Inspect the alternator wiring harness and the connectors at the alternator and voltage regulator. They must be in good condition, tight and have no corrosion.*
d) *Check the fusible link (if equipped) or main fuse in the underhood fuse/relay box. If it is burned, determine the cause, repair the circuit and replace the link or fuse (the vehicle will not start and/or the accessories will not work if the fusible link or main fuse is blown).*

2.21 To test the open circuit voltage of the battery, touch the black probe of the voltmeter to the negative terminal and the red probe to the positive terminal of the battery; a fully charged battery should be at least 12.6 volts

2.23 Connect a battery load tester to the battery and check the battery condition under load following the tool manufacturer's instructions

e) *Start the engine and check the alternator for abnormal noises (a shrieking or squealing sound indicates a bad bearing).*
f) *Check the battery. Make sure it's fully charged and in good condition (one bad cell in a battery can cause overcharging by the alternator).*
g) *Disconnect the battery cables (negative first, then positive). Inspect the battery posts and the cable clamps for corrosion. Clean them thoroughly if necessary (see Chapter 1). Reconnect the cables (positive first, negative last).*

Alternator - check

15 Use a voltmeter to check the battery voltage with the engine off. It should be at least 12.6 volts (see illustration 2.21).

16 Start the engine and check the battery voltage again. It should now be approximately 13.5 to 15 volts.

17 If the voltage reading is more or less than the specified charging voltage, the voltage regulator is probably defective, which will require replacement of the alternator (the voltage regulator is not replaceable separately). Remove the alternator and have it bench tested (most auto parts stores will do this for you).

18 The charging system (battery) light on the instrument cluster lights up when the ignition key is turned to ON, but it should go out when the engine starts.

19 If the charging system light stays on after the engine has been started, there is a problem with the charging system. Before replacing the alternator, check the battery condition, alternator belt tension and electrical cable connections.

20 If replacing the alternator doesn't restore voltage to the specified range, have the charging system tested by a dealer service department or other qualified repair shop.

Battery - check

▶ **Refer to illustrations 2.21 and 2.23**

21 Check the battery state of charge. Visually inspect the indicator eye on the top of the battery (if equipped with one); if the indicator eye is black in color, charge the battery as described in Chapter 1. Next perform an open circuit voltage test using a digital voltmeter.

➡**Note: The battery's surface charge must be removed before accurate voltage measurements can be made. Turn on the high beams for ten seconds, then turn them off and let the vehicle stand for two minutes.**

With the engine and all accessories Off, touch the negative probe of the voltmeter to the negative terminal of the battery and the positive probe to the positive terminal of the battery (see illustration). The battery voltage should be 12.6 volts or slightly above. If the battery is less than the specified voltage, charge the battery before proceeding to the next test. Do not proceed with the battery load test unless the battery charge is correct.

22 Disconnect the negative battery cable, then the positive cable from the battery.

23 Perform a battery load test. An accurate check of the battery condition can only be performed with a load tester (see illustration). This test evaluates the ability of the battery to operate the starter and other accessories during periods of high current draw. Connect the load tester to the battery terminals. Load test the battery according to the tool manufacturer's instructions. This tool increases the load demand (current draw) on the battery.

24 Maintain the load on the battery for 15 seconds and observe that the battery voltage does not drop below 9.6 volts. If the battery condition is weak or defective, the tool will indicate this condition immediately.

➡**Note: Cold temperatures will cause the minimum voltage reading to drop slightly. Follow the chart given in the manufacturer's instructions to compensate for cold climates. Minimum load voltage for freezing temperatures (32 degrees F) should be approximately 9.1 volts.**

STARTING SYSTEM

The starter rotates, but the engine doesn't

25 Remove the starter (see Section 8). Check the overrunning clutch and bench test the starter to make sure the drive mechanism extends fully for proper engagement with the flywheel ring gear. If it doesn't, replace the starter.

26 Check the flywheel ring gear for missing teeth and other damage. With the ignition turned off, rotate the flywheel so you can check the entire ring gear.

The starter is noisy

27 If the solenoid is making a chattering noise, first check the battery (see Steps 21 through 24). If the battery is okay, check the cables and connections.

28 If you hear a grinding, crashing metallic sound when you turn the key to Start, check for loose starter mounting bolts. If they're tight, remove the starter and inspect the teeth on the starter pinion gear and flywheel ring gear. Look for missing or damaged teeth.

29 If the starter sounds fine when you first turn the key to Start, but then stops rotating the engine and emits a zinging sound, the problem is probably a defective starter drive that's not staying engaged with the ring gear. Replace the starter.

The starter rotates slowly

30 Check the battery (see Steps 21 through 24).

31 If the battery is okay, verify all connections (at the battery, the starter solenoid and motor) are clean, corrosion-free and tight. Make sure the cables aren't frayed or damaged.

32 Check that the starter mounting bolts are tight so it grounds properly. Also check the pinion gear and flywheel ring gear for evidence of a mechanical bind (galling, deformed gear teeth or other damage).

The starter does not rotate at all

33 Check the battery (see Steps 21 through 24).

34 If the battery is okay, verify all connections (at the battery, the starter solenoid and motor) are clean, corrosion-free and tight. Make sure the cables aren't frayed or damaged.

35 Check all of the fuses in the underhood fuse/relay box.

36 Check that the starter mounting bolts are tight so it grounds properly.

37 Check for voltage at the starter solenoid "S" terminal when the ignition key is turned to the start position. If voltage is present, replace the starter/solenoid assembly. If no voltage is present, the problem could be the starter relay, the Transmission Range (TR) switch (see Chapter 6) or clutch start switch (see Chapter 8), or with an electrical connector somewhere in the circuit (see the wiring diagrams at the end of Chapter 12). Also, on many modern vehicles, the Powertrain Control Module (PCM) and the Body Control Module (BCM) control the voltage signal to the starter solenoid; on such vehicles a special scan tool is required for diagnosis.

3 Battery - disconnection and reconnection

※※ CAUTION:

Always disconnect the cable from the negative battery terminal FIRST and hook it up LAST or the battery may be shorted by the tool being used to loosen the cable clamps.

Some systems on the vehicle require battery power to be available at all times, either to maintain continuous operation (alarm system, power door locks, etc.), or to maintain control unit memory (radio station presets, Powertrain Control Module and other control units). When the battery is disconnected, the power that maintains these systems is cut. So, before you disconnect the battery, please note that on a vehicle with power door locks, it's a wise precaution to remove the key or keyless entry fob, so that it does not get locked inside if the power door locks should engage accidentally when the battery is reconnected!

Devices known as "memory-savers" can be used to avoid some of these problems. Precise details vary according to the device used. The typical memory saver is plugged into the cigarette lighter and is connected to a spare battery. Then the vehicle battery can be disconnected from the electrical system. The memory saver will provide sufficient current to maintain audio unit security codes, PCM memory, etc. and will provide power to always hot circuits such as the clock and radio memory circuits.

※※ WARNING 1:

Some memory savers deliver a considerable amount of current in order to keep vehicle systems operational after the main battery is disconnected. If you're using a memory saver, make sure that the circuit concerned is actually open before servicing it.

※※ WARNING 2:

If you're going to work near any of the airbag system components, the battery MUST be disconnected and a memory saver must NOT be used. If a memory saver is used, power will be supplied to the airbag, which means that It could accidentally deploy and cause serious personal injury.

DISCONNECTION

1 Install a memory saver device to avoid having to reprogram several of the vehicle's systems (see above).

※※ WARNING:

If you're working near any airbag system component, DO NOT use a memory saver.

2 To disconnect the battery for service procedures requiring power to be cut from the vehicle, loosen the cable end bolt and disconnect the cable from the negative battery terminal. Isolate the cable end to prevent it from coming into accidental contact with the battery terminal.

RECONNECTION

3 Connect the positive battery cable first (if it was disconnected), followed by the negative cable.

4 After reconnecting the battery, several re-learn procedures must be performed. These include:

Accelerator pedal released position learning
Throttle valve closed position learning
Idle air volume learning
*Power window initialization and anti-pinch feature**
*Sunroof memory and anti-pinch feature**
*Radio presets**
*Navigation system adjustment**

If a memory saver was used when the battery was disconnected, these functions won't have to be performed.

5 Refer to your owner's manual for information on resetting the radio presets and navigation system adjustment.

Accelerator pedal released position learning

6 With the accelerator pedal at rest (fully released), turn the ignition to On and wait at least two seconds.

7 Turn the ignition Off and wait at least ten seconds.

8 Turn the ignition back On again and wait at least two seconds.

9 Turn the ignition Off and wait at least ten seconds.

Throttle valve closed position learning

10 Open the hood.

11 With the accelerator pedal at rest (fully released), turn the ignition to On, then Off. Within a ten-second period, listen for the sound of the throttle body motor actuating, indicating that it has moved and found the closed position of the throttle plate.

Idle air volume learning

12 The engine and transmission must be at operating temperature for this procedure. Also make sure that the transmission is in Park or Neutral (neutral with a manual transmission).

13 The air conditioner, headlights and defogger must be off. Point the wheels straight ahead and make sure the vehicle isn't moving. If the vehicle has daytime running lights, set the parking brake before starting the engine to turn them off.

14 Perform the accelerator pedal released position learning procedure (Steps 6 through 9) and the throttle valve closed learning procedure (Steps 10 and 11).

15 Start the engine and make sure it's warm and all the above conditions are satisfied.

16 Turn the engine Off and wait ten seconds or longer.

17 Ensure that the accelerator pedal is not touched. Turn the ignition On and wait three seconds.

18 Press the accelerator pedal to the floor and release it completely five times within a five second period.

19 Wait for seven seconds with the pedal fully released.

20 Press the pedal to the floor and hold it there for 20 seconds. The CHECK ENGINE light will blink during this period. When it stops blinking and stays on, release the pedal within three seconds.

21 Start the engine and let it idle for 20 seconds.

Power window initialization and anti-pinch feature check

22 Turn the ignition to the On position.

23 Open the window completely (if it already isn't open completely).

24 Pull the power window switch up to close the window, holding the switch in the Up position for at least four seconds after the glass has closed completely.

25 Open the window completely, then place a piece of wood or other object near the top of the window frame.

✳✳ WARNING:

Do not use any part of your body for this check.

26 Using the AUTO-UP feature, close the window; confirm that the window automatically reverses direction as soon as it contacts the object.

Sunroof initialization and anti-pinch feature check

27 Turn the ignition to the On position.

28 Operate the sunroof switch in the tilt up position; hold it there until the sunroof has tilted up completely.

29 Hold the switch in the tilt up position again. The sunroof should back up after a pause; release the switch.

30 Within five seconds, push the switch to the tilt up position again and hold it there; the sunroof should move from the tilt up position to the fully open position, then back to the fully closed position. Release the switch.

31 Open the sunroof completely, then place a piece of wood or other object near the front of the sunroof opening.

✳✳ WARNING:

Do not use any part of your body for this check.

32 Operate the sunroof switch with the auto-close function and verify that the sunroof does not pinch the object.

---

4   Battery - removal and installation

▶ **Refer to illustration 4.2**

1 Install a memory saver device to avoid having to reprogram several of the vehicle's systems (see Section 3).

✳✳ WARNING:

If you're working near any airbag system component, DO NOT use a memory saver.

2 Disconnect the negative battery cable, then the positive battery cable, from the battery (see illustration).

✳✳ WARNING:

Always disconnect the negative cable first and hook it up last or the battery may be shorted by the tool being used to loosen the cable clamps.

4.2 Battery details:

1	Negative battery cable	3	Battery hold-down clamp
2	Positive battery cable		

3   Locate the battery hold-down clamp straddling the top of the battery. Remove the nuts and the hold-down clamp.

4   Lift out the battery. Special battery lifting straps that attach to the battery posts are available at auto parts stores; lifting and moving the battery is much easier if you use one.

5   Installation is the reverse of removal. Connect the positive cable first, then the negative cable. Refer to Section 3 and perform the necessary re-learn procedures.

5   Battery cables - replacement

1   When removing the cables, always disconnect the cable from the negative battery terminal first and hook it up last, or you might accidentally short out the battery with the tool you're using to loosen the cable clamps. Even if you're only replacing the cable for the positive terminal, be sure to disconnect the negative cable from the battery first.

2   Disconnect the old cables from the battery, then trace each of them to their opposite ends and disconnect them. Be sure to note the routing of each cable before disconnecting it to ensure correct installation.

3   If you are replacing any of the old cables, take them with you when buying new cables. It is vitally important that you replace the cables with identical parts.

4   Clean the threads of the solenoid or ground connection with a wire brush to remove rust and corrosion. Apply a light coat of battery terminal corrosion inhibitor or petroleum jelly to the threads to prevent future corrosion.

5   Attach the cable to the solenoid or ground connection and tighten the mounting nut/bolt securely.

6   Before connecting a new cable to the battery, make sure that it reaches the battery post without having to be stretched.

7   Connect the cable to the positive battery terminal first, then connect the ground cable to the negative battery terminal.

6   Ignition coil(s) - replacement

▶ **Refer to illustrations 6.3 and 6.4**

1   Remove the engine cover.

2   If you're removing the coils from the right (rear) cylinder bank on a V6 engine, refer to Chapter 2B and remove the intake manifold collector (upper intake manifold).

3   Disconnect the electrical connector from the coil(s) (see illustration).

4   Remove the coil mounting bolt, then pull the coil straight out (see illustration).

5   Installation is the reverse of the removal procedure. Before installing the ignition coils, coat the interior of the boots with silicone dielectric compound.

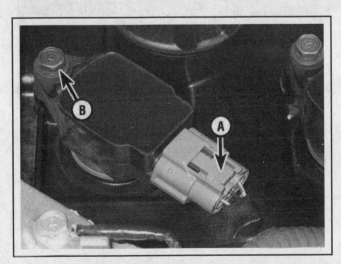

6.3 Press the tab (A) and disconnect the electrical connector, then remove the coil mounting bolt (B)

6.4 Twist the coil, then lift it straight out

7 Alternator - removal and installation

1 Disconnect the cable from the negative terminal of the battery (see Section 3).

2 Remove the engine cover.

3 Remove the drivebelt (see Chapter 1).

FOUR-CYLINDER ENGINE

♦ **Refer to illustrations 7.4 and 7.5**

4 Disconnect the electrical connectors from the alternator (see illustration).

5 Remove the mounting bolts and separate the alternator from the engine (see illustration).

6 Installation is the reverse of removal.

7 Refer to Section 3 and perform the necessary re-learn procedures.

V6 ENGINE

☀ WARNING:

The engine must be completely cool before beginning this procedure.

8 Have the air conditioning system evacuated by a shop with the proper equipment.

9 Remove the engine lower splash shield.

10 Drain some of the engine coolant (enough to bring the level below the upper radiator hose) (see Chapter 1).

11 Remove the air filter housing and ducts (see Chapter 4).

12 Connect a memory-saver device, then remove the battery (see Section 4).

13 Remove the PCM (see Chapter 6).

14 Disconnect the automatic transmission control module, if so equipped.

15 Remove the PCM mounting bracket.

16 Remove the current sensor from the battery tray, then remove the battery tray.

17 Remove the engine cooling fan (see Chapter 3).

18 Release the power steering line clip and position the line out of the way.

19 Remove the air conditioning compressor (see Chapter 3).

20 Remove the air conditioning idler pulley.

21 Disconnect the wiring from the oil pressure switch and the alternator.

22 Remove the alternator mounting fasteners, then slide the alternator out and remove it.

23 Installation is the reverse of removal. Add coolant (see Chapter 1), then refer to Section 3 and perform the necessary re-learn procedures.

24 Have the air conditioning system recharged by the shop that discharged it.

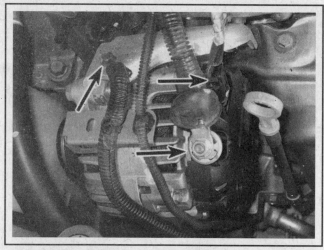

7.4 Alternator wiring connections and ground cable - four-cylinder engine

7.5 Alternator mounting bolts - four-cylinder engine

8   Starter motor - removal and installation

▶ **Refer to illustrations 8.3 and 8.4**

1   Disconnect the cable from the negative terminal of the battery (see Section 3). Remove the fresh air intake duct.

2   On models with an automatic transaxle, remove the air filter housing (see Chapter 4), then remove the battery (see Section 4) and the battery tray.

3   Disconnect the wiring from the starter (see illustration).

➡**Note: The wiring and mounting bolts are accessible from above on some models, but on other models they are more easily accessed from below.**

4   Remove the two mounting bolts and remove the starter (see illustration).

5   Installation is the reverse of removal.

6   Reconnect the battery and perform the necessary re-learn procedures (see Section 3).

8.3 Starter motor B+ terminal (A), S terminal (B) and lower mounting bolt (C) (four-cylinder engine)

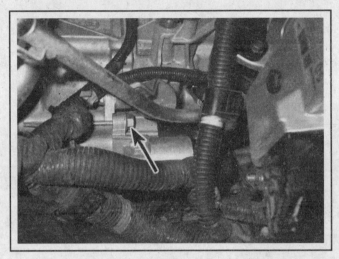

8.4 Starter motor upper mounting bolt (four-cylinder engine)

Notes

6

EMISSIONS
AND ENGINE
CONTROL
SYSTEMS

Section

To prevent pollution of the atmosphere from incompletely burned and evaporating gases, and to maintain good driveability and fuel economy, a number of emission control systems are incorporated. They include the:

CATALYTIC CONVERTER

A catalytic converter is an emission control device in the exhaust system that reduces certain pollutants in the exhaust gas stream. There are two types of converters: oxidation converters and reduction converters.

Oxidation converters contain a monolithic substrate (a ceramic honeycomb) coated with the semi-precious metals platinum and palladium. An oxidation catalyst reduces unburned hydrocarbons (HC) and carbon monoxide (CO) by adding oxygen to the exhaust stream as it passes through the substrate, which, in the presence of high temperature and the catalyst materials, converts the HC and CO to water vapor (H_2O) and carbon dioxide (CO_2).

Reduction converters contain a monolithic substrate coated with platinum and rhodium. A reduction catalyst reduces oxides of nitrogen (NOx) by removing oxygen, which in the presence of high temperature and the catalyst material produces nitrogen (N) and carbon dioxide (CO_2).

Catalytic converters that combine both types of catalysts in one assembly are known as "three-way catalysts" or TWCs. A TWC can reduce all three pollutants.

EVAPORATIVE EMISSIONS CONTROL (EVAP) SYSTEM

The Evaporative Emissions Control (EVAP) system prevents fuel system vapors (which contain unburned hydrocarbons) from escaping into the atmosphere. On warm days, vapors trapped inside the fuel tank expand until the pressure reaches a certain threshold. Then the fuel vapors are routed from the fuel tank through the fuel vapor vent valve and the fuel vapor control valve to the EVAP canister, where they're stored temporarily until the next time the vehicle is operated. When the conditions are right (engine warmed up, vehicle up to speed, moderate or heavy load on the engine, etc.) the PCM opens the canister purge valve, which allows fuel vapors to be drawn from the canister into the intake manifold. Once in the intake manifold, the fuel vapors mix with incoming air before being drawn through the intake ports into the combustion chambers where they're burned up with the rest of the air/ fuel mixture. The EVAP system is complex and virtually impossible to troubleshoot without the right tools and training.

EXHAUST GAS RECIRCULATION (EGR) SYSTEM

The EGR system reduces oxides of nitrogen by recirculating exhaust gases from the exhaust manifold, through the EGR valve and intake manifold, then back to the combustion chambers, where it mixes with the incoming air/fuel mixture before being consumed. These recirculated exhaust gases dilute the incoming air/fuel mixture, which cools the combustion chambers, thereby reducing NOx emissions.

The EGR system consists of the Powertrain Control Module

(PCM), the EGR valve, the EGR valve position sensor and various other information sensors that the PCM uses to determine when to open the EGR valve. The degree to which the EGR valve is opened is referred to as "EGR valve lift." The PCM is programmed to produce the ideal EGR valve lift for varying operating conditions. The EGR valve position sensor, which is an integral part of the EGR valve, detects the amount of EGR valve lift and sends this information to the PCM. The PCM then compares it with the appropriate EGR valve lift for the operating conditions. The PCM increases current flow to the EGR valve to increase valve lift and reduces the current to reduce the amount of lift. If EGR flow is inappropriate to the operating conditions (idle, cold engine, etc.) the PCM simply cuts the current to the EGR valve and the valve closes.

SECONDARY AIR INJECTION (AIR) SYSTEM

Some models are equipped with a secondary air injection (AIR) system. The secondary air injection system is used to reduce tailpipe emissions on initial engine start-up. The system uses an electric motor/pump assembly, relay, vacuum valve/solenoid, air shut-off valve, check valves and tubing to inject fresh air directly into the exhaust manifolds. The fresh air (oxygen) reacts with the exhaust gas in the catalytic converter to reduce HC and CO levels. The air pump and solenoid are controlled by the PCM through the AIR relay. During initial start-up, the PCM energizes the AIR relay, the relay supplies battery voltage to the air pump and the vacuum valve/solenoid, engine vacuum is applied to the air shut-off valve which opens and allows air to flow through the tubing into the exhaust manifolds. The PCM will operate the air pump until closed loop operation is reached (approximately four minutes). During normal operation, the check valves prevent exhaust backflow into the system.

POWERTRAIN CONTROL MODULE (PCM)

The Powertrain Control Module (PCM) is the brain of the engine management system. It also controls a wide variety of other vehicle systems. In order to program the new PCM, the dealer needs the vehicle as well as the new PCM. If you're planning to replace the PCM with a new one, there is no point in trying to do so at home because you won't be able to program it yourself.

POSITIVE CRANKCASE VENTILATION (PCV) SYSTEM

The Positive Crankcase Ventilation (PCV) system reduces hydrocarbon emissions by scavenging crankcase vapors, which are rich in unburned hydrocarbons. A PCV valve or orifice regulates the flow of gases into the intake manifold in proportion to the amount of intake vacuum available.

The PCV system generally consists of the fresh air inlet hose, the PCV valve or orifice and the crankcase ventilation hose (or PCV hose). The fresh air inlet hose connects the air intake duct to a pipe on the valve cover. The crankcase ventilation hose (or PCV hose) connects the PCV valve or orifice in the valve cover to the intake manifold.

Emissions and engine control system components - four cylinder engine

1 Accelerator Pedal Position (APP) sensor (at the top of the accelerator pedal)
2 Camshaft Position (CMP) sensor
3 Upstream oxygen (HO2) sensor (in exhaust manifold under heat shield)
4 EVAP purge control valve
5 Mass Air Flow/Intake Air Temperature (MAF/IAT) sensor

6 Engine Coolant Temperature (ECT) sensor (mounted on coolant outlet
7 Throttle Position (TPS) sensor (part of throttle body assembly)
8 Crankshaft Position (CKP) sensor (mounted on engine block near transaxle bellhousing)
9 Intake Valve Timing (IVT) solenoid (mounted on timing chain cover)
10 Knock (KS) sensor (on firewall-side of engine block)

Information Sensors

Accelerator Pedal Position (APP) sensor - as you press the accelerator pedal, the APP sensor alters its voltage signal to the PCM in proportion to the angle of the pedal, and the PCM commands a motor inside the throttle body to open or close the throttle plate accordingly

Camshaft Position (CMP) sensor - produces a signal that the PCM uses to identify the number 1 cylinder and to time the firing sequence of the fuel injectors

Crankshaft Position (CKP) sensor - produces a signal that the PCM uses to calculate engine speed and crankshaft position, which enables it to synchronize ignition timing with fuel injector timing, and to detect misfires

Engine Coolant Temperature (ECT) sensor - a thermistor (temperature-sensitive variable resistor) that sends a voltage signal to the PCM, which uses this data to determine the temperature of the engine coolant

Fuel tank pressure sensor - measures the fuel tank pressure and controls fuel tank pressure by signaling the EVAP system to purge the fuel tank vapors when the pressure becomes excessive

Intake Air Temperature (IAT) sensor - monitors the temperature of the air entering the engine and sends a signal to the PCM to determine injector pulse-width (the duration of each injector's on-time) and to adjust spark timing (to prevent spark knock)

Knock sensor - a piezoelectric crystal that oscillates in proportion to engine vibration which produces a voltage output that is monitored by the PCM. This retards the ignition timing when the oscillation exceeds a certain threshold

Manifold Absolute Pressure (MAP) sensor - monitors the pressure or vacuum inside the intake manifold. The PCM uses this data to determine engine load so that it can alter the ignition advance and fuel enrichment

Mass Air Flow (MAF) sensor - measures the amount of intake air drawn into the engine. It uses a hot-wire sensing element to measure the amount of air entering the engine

Oxygen sensors - generates a small variable voltage signal in proportion to the difference between the oxygen content in the exhaust stream and the oxygen content in the ambient air. The PCM uses this information to maintain the proper air/fuel ratio. A second oxygen sensor monitors the efficiency of the catalytic converter

Throttle Position (TP) sensor - a potentiometer that generates a voltage signal that varies in relation to the opening angle of the throttle plate inside the throttle body. Works with the PCM and other sensors to calculate injector pulse width (the duration of each injector's on-time)

Photos courtesy of Wells Manufacturing, except APP and MAF sensors.

2 On Board Diagnosis (OBD) system

GENERAL DESCRIPTION

1 All models are equipped with the second generation OBD-II system. This system consists of an on-board computer known as the Powertrain Control Module (PCM), and information sensors, which monitor various functions of the engine and send data to the PCM. This system incorporates a series of diagnostic monitors that detect and identify fuel injection and emissions control system faults and store the information in the computer memory. This system also tests sensors and output actuators, diagnoses drive cycles, freezes data and clears codes.

2 The PCM is the brain of the electronically controlled fuel and emissions system. It receives data from a number of sensors and other electronic components (switches, relays, etc.). Based on the information it receives, the PCM generates output signals to control various relays, solenoids (fuel injectors) and other actuators. The PCM is specifically calibrated to optimize the emissions, fuel economy and driveability of the vehicle.

3 It isn't a good idea to attempt diagnosis or replacement of the PCM or emission control components at home while the vehicle is under warranty. Because of a federally-mandated warranty which covers the emissions system components and because any owner-induced damage to the PCM, the sensors and/or the control devices may void this warranty, take the vehicle to a dealer service department if the PCM or a system component malfunctions.

SCAN TOOL INFORMATION

▶ **Refer to illustrations 2.4a and 2.4b**

4 Because extracting the Diagnostic Trouble Codes (DTCs) from an engine management system is now the first step in troubleshooting many computer-controlled systems and components, a code reader, at the very least, will be required (see illustration). More powerful scan tools can also perform many of the diagnostics once associated with expensive factory scan tools (see illustration). If you're planning to obtain a generic scan tool for your vehicle, make sure that it's compatible with OBD-II systems. If you don't plan to purchase a code reader or scan tool and don't have access to one, you can have the codes extracted by a dealer service department or an independent repair shop.

➡ **Note: Some auto parts stores even provide this service.**

2.4a Simple code readers are an economical way to extract trouble codes when the CHECK ENGINE light comes on

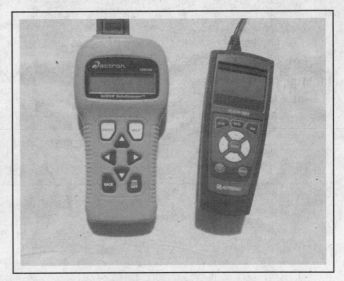

2.4b Hand-held scan tools like these can extract computer codes and also perform diagnostics

3 Obtaining and clearing Diagnostic Trouble Codes (DTCs)

All models covered by this manual are equipped with on-board diagnostics. When the PCM recognizes a malfunction in a monitored emission or engine control system, component or circuit, it turns on the Malfunction Indicator Light (MIL) on the dash. The PCM will continue to display the MIL until the problem is fixed and the Diagnostic Trouble Code (DTC) is cleared from the PCM's memory. You'll need a scan tool to access any DTCs stored in the PCM.

Before outputting any DTCs stored in the PCM, thoroughly inspect ALL electrical connectors and hoses. Make sure that all electrical connections are tight, clean and free of corrosion. And make sure that all hoses are correctly connected, fit tightly and are in good condition (no cracks or tears).

ACCESSING THE DTCS

▶ **Refer to illustration 3.1**

1 The Diagnostic Trouble Codes (DTCs) can only be accessed with a code reader or scan tool. Professional scan tools are expensive, but relatively inexpensive generic code readers or scan tools (see illustrations 2.4a and 2.4b) are available at most auto parts stores. Simply plug the connector of the scan tool into the diagnostic connector (see illustration). Then follow the instructions included with the scan tool to extract the DTCs.

2 Once you have outputted all of the stored DTCs, look them up on the accompanying DTC chart.

3 After troubleshooting the source of each DTC, make any necessary repairs or replace the defective component(s).

Clearing the DTCs

4 Clear the DTCs with the code reader or scan tool in accordance with the instructions provided by the tool's manufacturer.

DIAGNOSTIC TROUBLE CODES

5 The accompanying tables are a list of the Diagnostic Trouble Codes (DTCs) that can be accessed by a do-it-yourselfer working at home (there are many, many more DTCs available to professional mechanics with proprietary scan tools and software, but those codes cannot be accessed by a generic scan tool). If, after you have checked and repaired the connectors, wire harness and vacuum hoses (if applicable) for an emission-related system, component or circuit, the problem persists, have the vehicle checked by a dealer service department or other qualified repair shop.

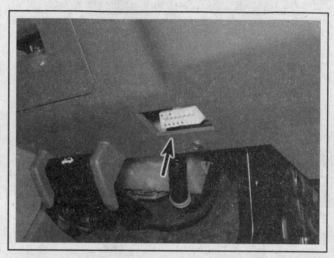

3.1 The Data Link Connector (DLC) is located under the lower edge of the dash, to the left of the steering column

TROUBLE CODES

Code	Code identification
P0011	Intake valve timing control solenoid performance
P0031	Upstream oxygen sensor heater control circuit low voltage signal (Bank 1)
P0032	Upstream oxygen sensor heater control circuit high voltage signal (Bank 1)
P0037	Downstream oxygen sensor heater control circuit low voltage signal (Bank 1)
P0038	Downstream oxygen sensor heater control circuit high voltage signal (Bank 1)
P0043	HO2S heater control circuit low (sensor 3)
P0044	HO2S heater control circuit high (sensor 3)
P0051	Upstream oxygen sensor heater control circuit low voltage signal (Bank 2)
P0052	Upstream oxygen sensor heater control circuit high voltage signal (Bank 2)

Code	Code identification
P0057	Downstream oxygen sensor heater control circuit low voltage signal (Bank 2)
P0058	Downstream oxygen sensor heater control circuit high voltage signal (Bank 2)
P0075	Intake valve timing control solenoid circuit (Bank 1)
P0081	Intake valve timing control solenoid circuit (Bank 2)
P0101	Mass Air Flow sensor circuit range or performance fault
P0102	Mass Air Flow sensor circuit low input
P0103	Mass Air Flow sensor circuit high input
P0112	Intake Air Temperature sensor circuit low input
P0113	Intake Air Temperature sensor circuit high input
P0117	Engine Coolant Temperature sensor circuit low input
P0116	Engine coolant temperature circuit range/performance problem
P0117	Engine coolant temperature circuit, low input
P0118	Engine Coolant Temperature sensor circuit high input
P0122	Throttle Position Sensor circuit low input
P0123	Throttle Position Sensor circuit high input
P0125	Engine Coolant Temperature sensor or circuit fault
P0127	Intake Air Temperature too high
P0128	Thermostat function - engine coolant does not reach correct temperature after warm-up
P0130	Upstream oxygen sensor or circuit fault (Bank 1)
P0131	Upstream oxygen sensor lean shift monitor fault (Bank 1)
P0132	Upstream oxygen sensor rich shift monitor fault (Bank 1)
P0137	Downstream oxygen sensor minimum voltage monitor fault
P0138	Downstream oxygen sensor maximum voltage monitor fault
P0139	Downstream oxygen sensor circuit slow response fault
P014C	Oxygen sensor 1 problem
P014D	Oxygen sensor 1 problem
P0143	O2 sensor circuit, low voltage (bank 1, sensor 3)
P0144	O2 sensor circuit, high voltage (bank 1, sensor 3)
P0145	O2 sensor circuit, slow response (bank 1, sensor 3)
P0146	O2 sensor circuit - no activity detected (bank 1, sensor 3)

TROUBLE CODES (CONTINUED)

Code	Code identification
P0150	Upstream oxygen sensor or circuit fault (Bank 2)
P0151	Upstream oxygen sensor lean shift monitor fault (Bank 2)
P0152	Upstream oxygen sensor rich shift monitor fault (Bank 2)
P0153	Upstream oxygen sensor circuit slow response fault (Bank 2)
P0154	Upstream oxygen sensor circuit high voltage fault (Bank 2)
P0157	Downstream oxygen sensor minimum voltage monitor fault
P0158	Downstream oxygen sensor maximum voltage monitor fault
P0159	Downstream oxygen sensor circuit slow response fault
P0171	Fuel injection system lean (Bank 1)
P0172	Fuel injection system rich (Bank 1)
P0174	System too lean (bank 2)
P0175	System too rich (bank 2)
P0181	Fuel Tank Temperature sensor circuit range or performance
P0182	Fuel Tank Temperature sensor circuit low input
P0183	Fuel Tank Temperature sensor circuit high input
P0196	Fuel rail pressure sensor circuit, range or performance problem
P0197	Fuel rail pressure sensor circuit, low input
P0198	Fuel rail pressure sensor circuit, high input
P0222	Throttle Position Sensor circuit low input
P0223	Throttle Position Sensor circuit high input
P0300	Multiple cylinder misfire detected
P0301	Cylinder no. 1 misfire detected
P0302	Cylinder no. 2 misfire detected
P0303	Cylinder no. 3 misfire detected
P0304	Cylinder no. 4 misfire detected
P0305	Cylinder no. 5 misfire detected
P0306	Cylinder no. 6 misfire detected
P0327	Knock Sensor circuit low input

Code	Code identification
P0328	Knock Sensor circuit high input
P0322	Crankshaft Position (CKP) sensor/engine speed (RPM) sensor - no signal
P0323	Crankshaft Position (CKP) sensor/engine speed (RPM) sensor - circuit intermittent
P0335	Crankshaft Position sensor (CKP) or circuit fault
P0340	Camshaft Position sensor or circuit fault (Bank 1)
P0345	Camshaft Position sensor or circuit fault (Bank 2)
P0420	Catalyst system defective (Bank 1)
P0430	Catalyst system defective (Bank 2)
P0441	EVAP control system incorrect purge flow
P0442	EVAP system small leak (negative pressure check)
P0443	EVAP canister purge control valve circuit fault
P0444	EVAP canister purge control valve circuit open
P0445	EVAP canister purge control valve circuit shorted
P0447	EVAP canister vent control valve circuit open
P0448	EVAP canister vent control valve remains closed under certain driving conditions
P0451	EVAP system pressure sensor or circuit fault
P0452	EVAP system pressure sensor low input voltage signal
P0453	EVAP system pressure sensor high input
P0455	EVAP system gross leak
P0456	EVAP system very small leak (negative pressure check)
P0460	Fuel level sensor or circuit fault
P0461	Fuel level sensor or circuit fault
P0462	Fuel level sensor circuit low input
P0463	Fuel level sensor circuit high input
P0500	Vehicle Speed Sensor or circuit fault
P0506	Idle Air Control system signal low
P0507	Idle Air Control system signal high
P0550	Power steering pressure sensor range
P050A	Cold start control problem
P050B	Cold start control problem

TROUBLE CODES (CONTINUED)

Code	Code identification
P050E	Cold start control problem
P0603	PCM back-up RAM does not function properly
P0605	PCM or EEPROM fault
P0607	Control module performance
P0643	PCM detects sensor power supply low or high voltage
P0850	Park/Neutral position switch circuit fault in Drive and Park
P1148	Closed loop control fault
P1168	Oxygen sensors or circuit, bank 2, closed-loop function not available
P1211	Traction Control System (TCS), problem with ABS control unit
P1212	Traction control system communication line fault
P1217	Engine overheating
P1225	Closed throttle position learning value low
P1226	Closed throttle position learning performance fault
P1550	Battery current sensor problem
P1551	Battery current sensor problem
P1552	Battery current sensor problem
P1553	Battery current sensor problem
P1554	Battery current sensor problem
P1564	ACSD steering switch problem
P1572	ASCD brake switch or circuit fault
P1574	ASCD speed sensor signal performance fault
P1700	Automatic transmission control system problem
P1715	Input speed sensor problem
P1720	Vehicle speed sensor problem
P1800	VIAS control solenoid valve circuit performance fault
P1805	Brake switch or circuit fault
P2A00	Oxygen sensor 1
P2A03	Oxygen sensor 1

Code	Code identification
P2004	Tumble control valve problem
P2014	Tumble control valve position sensor problem
P2100	Throttle Control motor voltage signal is open or low voltage
P2103	Throttle Control motor relay voltage signal is shorted (ON)
P2101	Electric throttle control function problem
P2118	Throttle Control motor performance fault in circuit and/or throttle control motor
P2119	Throttle Control motor defective or stuck in position
P2122	Accelerator Pedal Position sensor 1 circuit low
P2123	Accelerator Pedal Position sensor 1 circuit high
P2127	Accelerator Pedal Position sensor 2 circuit low
P2128	Accelerator Pedal Position sensor 2 circuit high
P2135	Throttle Position Sensor circuit range or performance
P2138	Accelerator Pedal Position sensor or circuit range or performance
P2423	HC absorption catalyst function

4 Accelerator Pedal Position (APP) sensor - replacement

▶ **Refer to illustration 4.2**

1 Disconnect the cable from the negative terminal of the battery (see Chapter 5).

2 Disconnect the wiring from the sensor/pedal assembly (see illustration).

3 Remove the pedal fasteners and remove the pedal.

4 Installation is the reverse of removal.

5 Reconnect the battery and perform the necessary re-learn procedures (see Chapter 5).

4.2 The Accelerator Pedal Position (APP) sensor is part of the pedal assembly

5 Camshaft Position (CMP) sensor - replacement

◆ **Refer to illustrations 5.1a and 5.1b**

1   The CMP sensor is mounted on the top of the engine at the driver's side on four-cylinder engines (see illustration). On V6 engines, there are two CMP sensors, located at the driver's end of each valve cover (see illustration). If you're removing the sensor from the rear cyl-inder bank on a V6 engine, remove the intake manifold collector (upper intake manifold) (see Chapter 2B).

2   Disconnect the electrical connector from the sensor.

3   Remove the mounting bolt and pull the sensor out.

4   Installation is the reverse of removal.

5.1a The Camshaft Position (CMP) sensor is located at the driver's side of the engine on four-cylinder models

5.1b On V6 engines, the Camshaft Position (CMP) sensors are located at the left end of each valve cover

6 Intake Valve Timing (IVT) control solenoid(s) - replacement

◆ **Refer to illustration 6.1**

1   The IVT solenoid on all engines is installed in the IVT cover, which is on the upper part of the timing chain cover (see illustration). The V6 engine has two IVT solenoid valves. This solenoid valve directs oil to the intake camshaft actuator in order to vary the timing of the intake camshaft. It receives commands from the PCM.

2   On four-cylinder models, support the engine from below using a floor jack with a block of wood on it, then remove the right upper engine mount assembly (see Chapter 2A).

➡ **Note: It is possible to work around the engine mount on some models.**

3   Remove the mounting bolt from the IVT solenoid valve, then remove it.

4   Installation is the reverse of removal. Replace the O-ring (if used) with a new one.

6.1 The intake valve timing control solenoid is installed in the rear of the IVT housing, at the top of the timing chain cover

7 Crankshaft Position (CKP) sensor - replacement

♦ **Refer to illustrations 7.1a and 7.1b**

1 The CKP sensor is mounted on the lower front side of the engine (see illustrations).

2 Raise the vehicle and support it securely on jackstands.
3 Remove the under-vehicle splash shield(s).
4 Remove the sensor mounting bolt, then remove the sensor.
5 Installation is the reverse of removal.

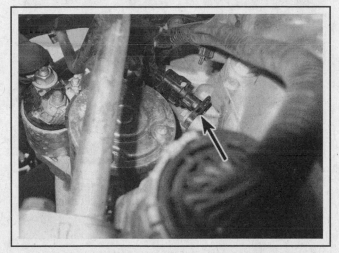

7.1a The Crankshaft Position (CKP) sensor on four-cylinder models is mounted near the starter

7.1b Location of the Crankshaft Position (CKP) sensor on V6 models

8 Engine Coolant Temperature (ECT) sensor - replacement

♦ **Refer to illustrations 8.1a and 8.1b**

❉ WARNING:

Wait until the engine has completely cooled before beginning this procedure.

1 The ECT sensor is mounted in the water outlet at the left (driver's)

side of the engine (see illustrations).
2 Remove the engine cover and the air intake duct (see Chapter 4).
3 Drain some engine coolant (see Chapter 1) to minimize coolant spillage.
4 Disconnect the electrical connector from the ECT sensor.
5 Unscrew the sensor from the engine and discard the sealing washer (a new one should be used).
6 Installation is the reverse of removal. Refill the cooling system (see Chapter 1).

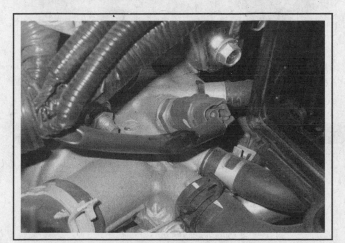

8.1a The Engine Coolant Temperature (ECT) sensor is located in the water outlet at the left (driver's side) end of the engine - four-cylinder model shown

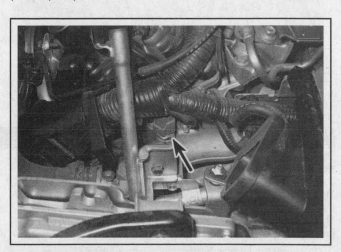

8.1b Location of the Engine Coolant Temperature (ECT) sensor on V6 models

9   Mass Air Flow/Intake Air Temperature (MAF/IAT) sensor - replacement

▶ **Refer to illustration 9.1**

   1   The MAF/IAT sensor is mounted on the air filter housing (see illustration).
   2   Disconnect the electrical connector from the MAF/IAT sensor.
   3   Remove the screws and remove the sensor from the air filter housing.
   4   Installation is the reverse of removal.

9.1 The Mass Air Flow/Intake Air Temperature (MAF/IAT) sensor is installed in the air filter housing and is retained by two screws

10   Knock sensor - replacement

▶ **Refer to illustration 10.1**

   1   The knock sensor is mounted to the side of the engine block on four-cylinder engines (see illustration). On V6 engines, the knock sensor(s) is/are mounted in the engine valley between the cylinder heads (2007 and 2008 models have one sensor, 2009 and later models have two).
   2   If you're working on a V6 model, remove the intake manifold (see Chapter 2B).
   3   Disconnect the electrical connector from the knock sensor.
   4   Remove the sensor mounting bolt, then remove the sensor.
   5   Installation is the reverse of removal. Tighten the mounting bolt to 16 ft-lbs.

10.1 The knock sensor on four-cylinder engines is located on the firewall-side of the engine block, below the intake manifold

11   Oxygen sensors - replacement

➡ **Note: Because it is installed in the exhaust system, which contracts when cool, an oxygen sensor can be very difficult to loosen when the engine is cold. Rather than risking damage to the sensor or its mounting threads, run the engine for a minute or two, then shut it off. Be careful to avoid burns during this procedure.**

   1   Be very careful when servicing an oxygen sensor:
     a) *The oxygen sensor has a permanently attached pigtail and electrical connector which should not be removed from the sensor.*

Damage or removal of the pigtail or electrical connector can adversely affect operation of the sensor.
     b) *Grease, dirt and other contaminants should be kept away from the electrical connector and the louvered end of the sensor.*
     c) *Do not use cleaning solvents of any kind on the oxygen sensor.*
     d) *Do not drop or roughly handle the sensor.*
     e) *The silicone boot must be installed in the correct position to prevent the boot from being melted and to allow the sensor to operate properly.*

REPLACEMENT

Upstream oxygen sensors

▶ Refer to illustration 11.2

2 Locate the upstream oxygen sensor electrical connector and disconnect it (see illustration). Detach the sensor wiring harness from any clips.

3 Unscrew the sensor with an oxygen sensor socket if one is available. You may have to raise the vehicle and support it securely on jackstands to reach it.

4 If you're going to install the old sensor, apply anti-seize compound to the threads to ease future removal. If you're installing a new sensor, the threads will already have anti-seize on them.

5 Installation is the reverse of removal. Tighten the sensor securely.

Downstream oxygen sensors

▶ Refer to illustration 11.7

6 Raise the vehicle and support it securely on jackstands.

7 Disconnect the wiring harness from the pigtail of the sensor (see illustration).

8 Unscrew the sensor, using an oxygen sensor socket if one is available.

9 If you're going to install the old sensor, apply anti-seize compound to the threads to ease future removal. If you're installing a new sensor, the threads will already have anti-seize on them.

10 Installation is the reverse of removal. Tighten the sensor securely.

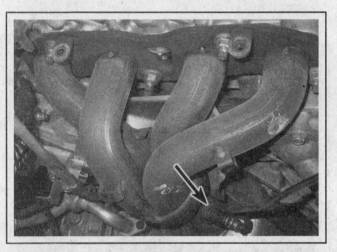

11.2 Typical upstream oxygen sensor (manifold heat shield removed). Follow the wiring harness to the electrical connector, then unplug it

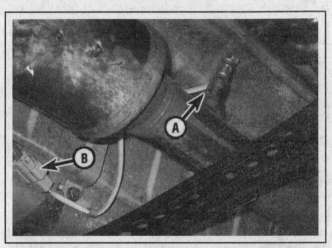

11.7 Typical downstream oxygen sensor (A), installed in the exhaust pipe after the catalytic converter, and its electrical connector (B)

12 Transmission range switch - replacement and adjustment

REPLACEMENT

▶ Refer to illustration 12.1

1 The transmission range switch is mounted on top of the automatic transaxle (see illustration).

2 Remove the nut, then remove the manual lever from the range switch assembly.

3 Disconnect the electrical connector from the switch.

4 Remove the mounting bolts and remove the range switch.

5 Installation is the reverse of removal. Align the range switch to its original position.

6 Verify that the engine will start only in Park or Neutral. Verify that the back-up lights come on only in Reverse. Adjust the range switch as necessary to ensure that these conditions are met.

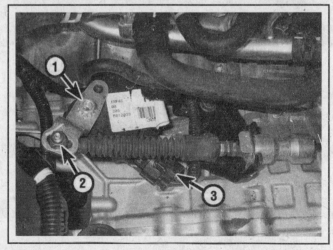

12.1 The Transmission Range (TR) switch details

1	*Manual lever nut*	*3* *Electrical connector*
2	*Shift cable nut*	

ADJUSTMENT

7　Set the parking brake.

8　Loosen the nut on the end of the shift cable.

9　Make sure the shift lever inside the vehicle and the manual lever on the transaxle are in Park.

10　Tighten the nut while making sure the transmission manual lever stays in Park.

11　Refer to Step 6 and check for proper operation.

13　Transmission speed sensors - replacement

♦ **Refer to illustrations 13.1a and 13.1b**

➡**Note: This procedure applies to automatic transaxles only.**

1　The transmission speed sensors are mounted on top of the transmission (see illustrations). The primary speed sensor senses the speed of the primary pulley and the secondary speed sensor senses the speed of the output shaft.

2　Disconnect the electrical connector from the sensor.

3　Remove the mounting bolt and remove the sensor. Discard the O-ring.

4　Apply some transmission fluid to the new O-ring and install it on the sensor.

5　Installation is the reverse of removal.

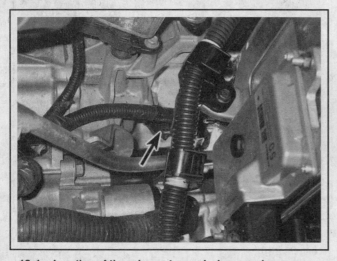

13.1a Location of the primary transmission speed sensor

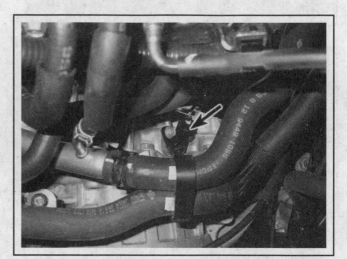

13.1b Location of the secondary transmission speed sensor

14　Powertrain Control Module (PCM) - replacement

The Powertrain Control Module (PCM) cannot be replaced at home because the new unit must be programmed with the Vehicle Identification Number (VIN) and other data. Doing so is impossible without a factory scan tool. Do not disconnect or remove the PCM.

15　Catalytic converter - replacement

Because the catalytic converters are part of the exhaust system, converter replacement requires replacement of the exhaust manifold (see Chapter 2) or front exhaust pipe assembly (an expensive part), or cutting out and welding in a new converter (take the vehicle to a dealer service department or a muffler shop if you lack the necessary skill and equipment to do this).

16 Evaporative Emissions Control (EVAP) system - component replacement

EVAP PURGE CONTROL SOLENOID VALVE

Four-cylinder models

♦ **Refer to illustrations 16.1a and 16.1b**

1 Working between the firewall and the engine, disconnect the hoses from the solenoid valve (see illustrations).

2 Disconnect the electrical connector from the solenoid valve.

3 Remove the mounting bolts, then remove the solenoid valve.

4 Installation is the reverse of removal.

V6 models

♦ **Refer to illustration 16.5**

5 The solenoid valve is mounted at the top of the front valve cover toward the driver's side (see illustration). Detach the two hoses from the solenoid valve.

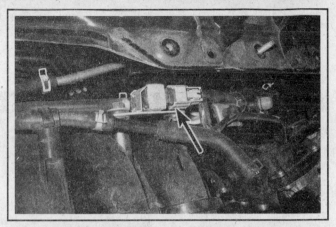

16.1a Location of the EVAP purge control solenoid valve (four-cylinder models)

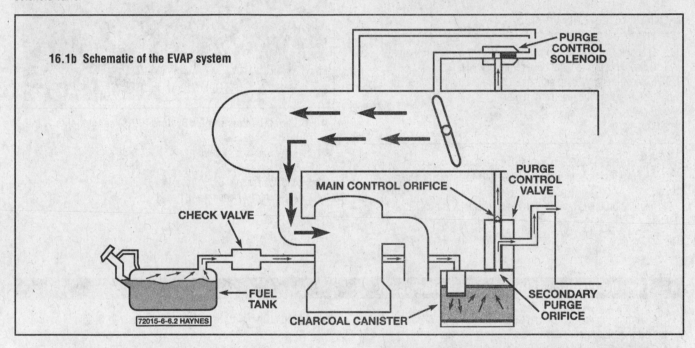

16.1b Schematic of the EVAP system

PURGE CONTROL SOLENOID

PURGE CONTROL VALVE

MAIN CONTROL ORIFICE

CHECK VALVE

SECONDARY PURGE ORIFICE

FUEL TANK

CHARCOAL CANISTER

72015-6-6.2 HAYNES

6 Disconnect the electrical connector from the solenoid valve.

7 Remove the mounting bolts, then remove the valve.

8 Installation is the reverse of removal.

EVAP CANISTER

9 Raise the vehicle and support it securely on jackstands.

10 Remove the mounting bolt, then detach the canister.

11 Disconnect the hoses from the canister.

12 Remove the EVAP control system pressure sensor from the canister by pulling it out. Replace the O-ring before replacing the sensor.

13 Remove the EVAP canister vent control valve by twisting it counterclockwise. Replace the O-ring before replacing the valve.

14 Installation is the reverse of removal.

16.5 Location of the EVAP purge control solenoid valve (V6 models)

17 Positive Crankcase Ventilation (PCV) valve - replacement

Refer to Chapter 1, Section 28 for information on the PCV system.

18 Variable Induction Air System (VIAS) solenoid valves and actuators (V6 engine) - replacement

▶ **Refer to illustration 18.1**

1   This system consists of two solenoid valves which control vacuum to the power valve actuators (see illustration). The actuators move internal components of the intake manifold to change the lengths of the inlet passages for improved performance. The control solenoids are controlled electrically by the PCM.

2   The control solenoids are mounted at the front of the intake manifold. There is one actuator at each end of the intake manifold collector.

VACUUM SOLENOID VALVES

3   Disconnect the electrical connector from the solenoid valve.
4   Disconnect the vacuum hoses from the valve.
5   Remove the mounting bolt and remove the control solenoid valve.
6   Installation is the reverse of removal.

ACTUATORS

7   Disconnect the vacuum hose from the actuator.
8   Remove the mounting bolts and remove the actuator. Discard the gasket.
9   Installation is the reverse of removal. Replace the gasket with a new one.

18.1 Variable Induction Air System (VIAS) components

1   *Power valve actuator no. 1*
2   *Power valve actuator no. 2*
3   *VIAS control solenoid valve no. 1*
4   *VIAS control solenoid valve no. 2*

19 Throttle Position (TP) sensor - replacement

The Throttle Position sensor on these vehicles is an integral part of the throttle body and is not serviceable separately. Refer to Chapter 4 for the throttle body replacement procedure.

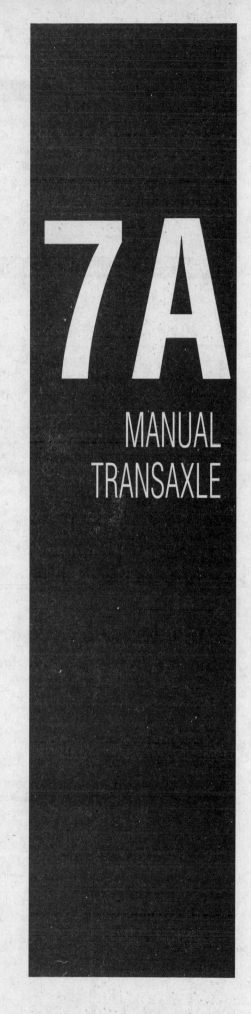

7A

MANUAL TRANSAXLE

Section

Reference to other Chapters

1 General information

The vehicles covered by this manual are equipped with a 6-speed manual transaxle or an automatic transaxle. Information on the manual transaxle is included in this Part of Chapter 7. Service procedures for the automatic transaxle are contained in Chapter 7, Part B.

The manual transaxle is a compact, two-piece, lightweight aluminum alloy housing containing both the transmission and differential assemblies.

Because of the complexity of the transaxle and the special tools needed to work on it, internal repair procedures for the manual transaxle are beyond the scope of this manual. The information in this Chapter is devoted to removal and installation procedures.

2 Shift cables - removal, installation and adjustment

1 Raise the vehicle and support it securely on jackstands.

REMOVAL AND INSTALLATION

2 Remove the center console (see Chapter 11).
3 Place the shifter in Neutral.
4 Remove the air filter housing and ducts (see Chapter 4) for access to the top of the transaxle.
5 Detach the cables from the shift levers and brackets.
6 Detach the cables from the shift assembly.
7 Remove the bracket that covers the grommet in the floor of the vehicle.
8 Remove the grommet/retainer.
9 Pull the cables from the vehicle.
10 The shifter can be removed now if required.
11 Installation is the reverse of removal. Be sure to adjust the select cable before installing the center console (see Steps 12 through 21).

ADJUSTMENT

▶ **Refer to illustration 2.15**

12 Remove the bezel from around the shift lever if not already done.
13 Place the transaxle in Neutral.
14 Pry the select cable from the shifter with a screwdriver.
15 Slide the lock to the released position (away from the end of the cable) (see illustration).
16 Push out the adjustment button to release it.

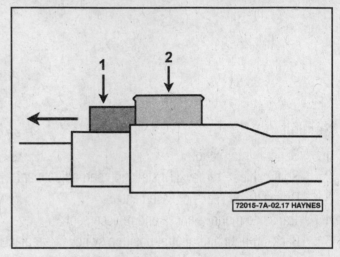

2.15 Shift cable adjuster details

| 1 | Lock | 2 | Adjustment button |

17 Snap the cable back onto the shifter.
18 Hold the shift lever so the space between the shifter base and the reverse gate stopper is 1/4-inch.
19 Push the adjustment button back in.
20 Slide the lock to the locked position.
21 Make sure the shifting action is smooth. If not, repeat the adjustment procedure.

3 Driveaxle oil seal - replacement

▶ **Refer to illustrations 3.4 and 3.5**

1 Oil leaks can occur as a result of worn seals or O-rings. Replacement of these seals or O-rings is relatively easy, since the repairs can usually be performed without removing the transaxle from the vehicle.

2 The driveaxle oil seals are located on the sides of the transaxle, where the inner ends of the driveaxles are splined into the differential side gears. If you suspect that a driveaxle oil seal is leaking, raise the vehicle and support it securely on jackstands. If the seal is leaking, you'll see lubricant on the side of the transaxle, below the seal.

3 Remove the driveaxle (left side) or driveaxle and intermediate shaft (right side) (see Chapter 8).

4 Using a screwdriver or seal removal tool, carefully pry the seal out of the transaxle bore (see illustration).

5 Using a seal driver or a large deep socket as a drift, install the new oil seal. Drive it into the bore squarely and make sure it's fully seated (see illustration). Lubricate the lip of the new seal with multi-purpose grease.

6 Install the driveaxle (or driveaxle and extension shaft). Be careful not to damage the lip(s) of the new seal(s). Check the transaxle lubricant level and add some, if necessary, to bring it up to the required level (see Chapter 1).

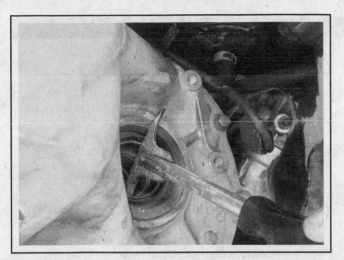

3.4 Carefully pry out the driveaxle oil seal with a seal removal tool or a large screwdriver; make sure you don't damage the seal bore or the new seal may leak

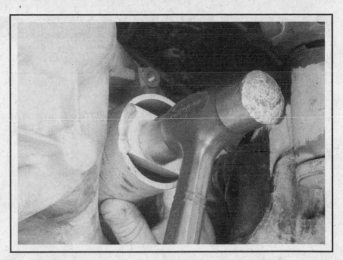

3.5 Use a seal installer or a large socket to install the new seal

4 Transaxle mount - check and replacement

▶ Refer to illustration 4.2

1 Raise the vehicle and place it securely on jackstands.

2 Insert a large screwdriver or prybar between the mount and the bracket and pry against it (see illustration).

3 Check to make sure the rubber within the mount is not cracked or separated from the bushing in the center. If it is, replace the mount.

4 To replace a mount, support the transaxle with a jack, remove the nuts and bolts and remove the mount. It may be necessary to raise the transaxle slightly to provide enough clearance to remove the mount.

5 Installation is the reverse of removal.

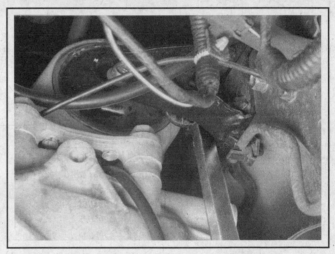

4.2 To check a transaxle mount, place a large screwdriver or prybar between the mount and the bracket and try to lever the transaxle up and down; if it moves excessively, replace the mount

5 Back-up light and neutral position switches - replacement

➡Note: The back-up light switch should have continuity only in Reverse; the neutral position switch should have continuity only in Neutral.

1 Raise the vehicle and support it securely on jackstands. Disconnect the electrical connector from the switch.

2 Remove the hold-down bolt and pull the switch straight out of the transaxle.

3 Apply a light coat of clean oil to a new O-ring, install the new switch and O-ring, and tighten the hold-down bolt securely.

4 Plug in the electrical connector.

5 Check the switch to ensure it's working properly.

6 Remove the jackstands and lower the vehicle.

6   Manual transaxle - removal and installation

REMOVAL

▶ **Refer to illustrations 6.4a and 6.4b**

1   Remove the engine and transaxle as an assembly (see Chapter 2C).
2   Disconnect the wiring from the transaxle connections and remove the wiring harness.
3   Remove the starter (see Chapter 5).
4   Remove the transaxle-to-engine mounting bolts. Organize the bolts so they can be installed in their original positions - there are several different lengths used (see illustrations).
5   Separate the transaxle from the engine.

INSTALLATION

6   If removed, install the clutch components (see Chapter 8). Always replace the clutch release assembly that's contained in the bellhousing any time you remove the transaxle.
7   Slide the transaxle forward, engaging the two dowel pins on the transaxle with the corresponding holes in the block and the input shaft with the clutch plate hub splines. Do not use excessive force to install the transaxle - if the input shaft does not slide into place, readjust the angle of the transaxle so it is level and/or turn the input shaft so the splines engage properly with the clutch plate hub.
8   Install the transaxle housing-to-engine bolts and tighten them to the torque listed in this Chapter's Specifications. Be sure the bolts are installed in the correct holes (see illustrations 6.4a or 6.4b).
9   The remainder of installation is the reverse of removal.

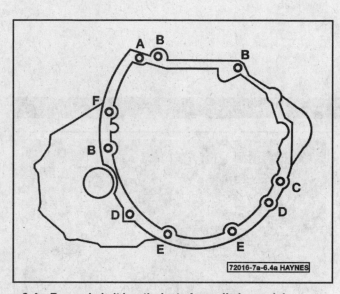

6.4a Transaxle bolt length chart - four cylinder models

A	1.77 inches		D	1.77 inches
B	1.77 inches		E	1.38 inches
C	3.15 inches		F	1.77 inches

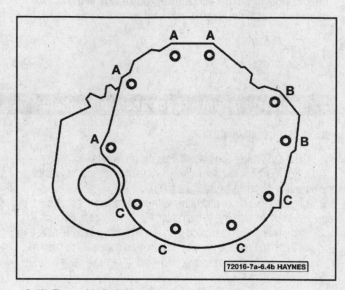

6.4b Transaxle bolt length chart - V6 models

A	2.17 inches		C	1.77 inches
B	4.59 inches			

7   Manual transaxle overhaul - general information

1   Overhauling a manual transaxle is a difficult job for the do-it-yourselfer. It involves the disassembly and reassembly of many small parts. Numerous clearances must be precisely measured and, if necessary, changed with select fit spacers and snap-rings. As a result, if transaxle problems arise, it can be removed and installed by a competent do-it-yourselfer, but overhaul should be left to a transmission repair shop. Rebuilt transaxles may be available - check with your dealer parts department and auto parts stores. At any rate, the time and money involved in an overhaul is almost sure to exceed the cost of a rebuilt unit.

2   Nevertheless, it's not impossible for an inexperienced mechanic to rebuild a transaxle if the special tools are available and the job is done in a deliberate step-by-step manner so nothing is overlooked.

3   The tools necessary for an overhaul include internal and external snap-ring pliers, a bearing puller, a slide hammer, a set of pin punches, a dial indicator and possibly a hydraulic press. In addition, a large, sturdy workbench and a vise or transmission stand will be required.

4   During disassembly of the transaxle, make careful notes of how each piece comes off, where it fits in relation to other pieces and what holds it in place. Your notes plus the manufacturer's shop manual, which contains exploded views, will make it easier to get the transaxle back together.

5   Before taking the transaxle apart for repair, it will help if you have some idea what area of the transaxle is malfunctioning. Certain problems can be closely tied to specific areas in the transaxle, which can make component examination and replacement easier. Refer to the "Troubleshooting" Section at the front of this manual for information regarding possible sources of trouble.

Torque specifications	Ft-lbs
Transaxle mounting bolts	
Four-cylinder models	
Bolt A	26
Bolts B	55
Bolt C (long)	55
Bolt D	31
Bolt E (short)	31
Bolt F	35
V6 models	
Bolts A	55
Bolts B (long)	55
Bolts C (short)	37

Notes

Notes

7B

AUTOMATIC TRANSAXLE

1 General information

The vehicles covered by this manual are equipped with either a 6-speed manual transaxle or an automatic transaxle. Information on the automatic transaxle is included in this Part of Chapter 7. Information for the manual transaxle can be found in Part A of this Chapter.

Because of the complexity of the automatic transaxle and the specialized equipment needed to service it, this Chapter contains only those procedures related to general diagnosis, routine maintenance, adjustment, and removal and installation.

If the transaxle requires major repair work, it should be taken to a dealer service department or an automotive or transmission repair shop. You can, however, save money by removing and installing the transaxle yourself, even if the repair work is done by a shop.

2 Diagnosis - general

➡Note: Automatic transaxle malfunctions may be caused by five general conditions: poor engine performance, improper adjustments, hydraulic malfunctions, mechanical malfunctions or malfunctions in the computer or its signal network. Diagnosis of these problems should always begin with a check of the easily repaired items: fluid level and condition (see Chapter 1), shift cable adjustment and throttle linkage adjustment. Next, perform a road test to determine if the problem has been corrected or if more diagnosis is necessary. If the problem persists after the preliminary tests and corrections are completed, additional diagnosis should be done by a dealer service department or transmission repair shop. Refer to the "Troubleshooting" Section at the front of this manual for information on symptoms of transaxle problems.

PRELIMINARY CHECKS

1   Drive the vehicle to warm the transaxle to normal operating temperature.

2   Check the fluid level as described in Chapter 1:

a) *If the fluid level is unusually low, add enough fluid to bring the level within the designated area of the dipstick, then check for external leaks (see below).*

b) *If the fluid level is abnormally high, drain off the excess, then check the drained fluid for contamination by coolant. The presence of engine coolant in the automatic transmission fluid indicates that a failure has occurred in the internal radiator walls that separate the coolant from the transmission fluid (see Chapter 3).*

c) *If the fluid is foaming, drain it and refill the transaxle, then check for coolant in the fluid, or a high fluid level.*

3   Check for the presence of any stored diagnostic trouble codes (see Chapter 6). There are many potential transaxle-specific trouble codes that could be set, but certain engine-related problems can also affect transaxle operation.

4   Inspect the shift cable (see Section 4). Make sure that it's properly adjusted and operates smoothly.

FLUID LEAK DIAGNOSIS

5   Most fluid leaks are easy to locate visually. Repair usually consists of replacing a seal or gasket. If a leak is difficult to find, the following procedure may help.

6   Identify the fluid. Make sure it's transmission fluid and not engine oil or brake fluid (automatic transmission fluid is a deep red color).

7   Try to pinpoint the source of the leak. Drive the vehicle several miles, then park it over a large sheet of cardboard. After a minute or two, you should be able to locate the leak by determining the source of the fluid dripping onto the cardboard.

8   Make a careful visual inspection of the suspected component and the area immediately around it. Pay particular attention to gasket mating surfaces. A mirror is often helpful for finding leaks in areas that are hard to see.

9   If the leak still cannot be found, clean the suspected area thoroughly with a degreaser or solvent, then dry it.

10 Drive the vehicle for several miles at normal operating temperature and varying speeds. After driving the vehicle, visually inspect the suspected component again.

11 Once the leak has been located, the cause must be determined before it can be properly repaired. If a gasket is replaced but the sealing flange is bent, the new gasket will not stop the leak. The bent flange must be straightened.

12 Before attempting to repair a leak, check to make sure that the following conditions are corrected or they may cause another leak.

➡Note: Some of the following conditions cannot be fixed without highly specialized tools and expertise. Such problems must be referred to a transmission shop or a dealer service department.

Gasket leaks

13 Check the pan periodically. Make sure the bolts are tight, no bolts are missing, the gasket is in good condition and the pan is flat (dents in the pan may indicate damage to the valve body inside).

14 If the pan gasket is leaking, the fluid level or the fluid pressure may be too high, the vent may be plugged, the pan bolts may be too tight, the pan sealing flange may be warped, the sealing surface of the transaxle housing may be damaged, the gasket may be damaged or the transaxle casting may be cracked or porous. If sealant instead of gasket material has been used to form a seal between the pan and the transaxle housing, it may be the wrong sealant.

Seal leaks

15 If a transaxle seal is leaking, the fluid level or pressure may be too high, the vent may be plugged, the seal bore may be damaged, the seal itself may be damaged or improperly installed, the surface of the shaft protruding through the seal may be damaged or a loose bearing may be causing excessive shaft movement.

16 Make sure the dipstick tube seal is in good condition and the tube is properly seated. Periodically check the area around the speedometer gear or sensor for leakage. If transmission fluid is evident, check the O-ring for damage.

Case leaks

17 If the case itself appears to be leaking, the casting is porous and will have to be repaired or replaced.

18 Make sure the oil cooler hose fittings are tight and in good condition.

Fluid comes out vent pipe or fill tube

19 If this condition occurs, the transaxle is overfilled, there is coolant in the fluid, the case is porous, the dipstick is incorrect, the vent is plugged or the drain-back holes are plugged.

3   Shifter assembly - removal and installation

▸ **Refer to illustrations 3.2a, 3.2b and 3.4**

✳ WARNING:

The models covered by this manual are equipped with Supplemental Restraint Systems (SRS), more commonly known as airbags. Always disable the airbag system before working in the vicinity of any airbag system components to avoid the possibility of accidental deployment of the airbags, which could cause personal injury (see Chapter 12).

1 Remove the center console (see Chapter 11).
2 Detach the shift cable from the shifter (see illustrations).
3 Disconnect the wiring harness from the shifter.
4 Remove the shifter assembly mounting bolts, then remove the shifter (see illustration).
5 Installation is the reverse of removal. Adjust the shift cable (see Section 4).

3.2a Pry the cable end off of the shifter . . .

3.2b . . . then detach the cable from the shifter bracket

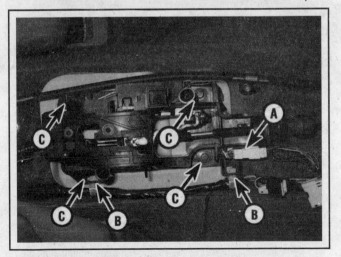

3.4 Shifter mounting details

A	Electrical connector	C	Shifter assembly
B	Wiring harness		mounting bolts
	retainer clips		

4 Shift cable - adjustment and replacement

ADJUSTMENT

▶ **Refer to illustration 4.3**

1 Remove the air filter housing (see Chapter 4).
2 Place the shift lever in the "P" position.
3 Loosen the shift cable-to-manual lever locknut (see illustration) and place the transaxle manual shift lever fully in the Park position.
4 Holding the manual lever in position, tighten the locknut.
5 Move the shift lever from "P" to "1." Make sure that it moves smoothly.

REPLACEMENT

❋❋ WARNING:

The models covered by this manual are equipped with Supplemental Restraint Systems (SRS), more commonly known as airbags. Always disable the airbag system before working in the vicinity of any airbag system components to avoid the possibility of accidental deployment of the airbags, which could cause personal injury (see Chapter 12).

6 Place the shifter in Park.
7 Remove the air filter housing (see Chapter 4).
8 Remove the cable-to-manual lever locknut (see illustration 4.3).
9 Remove the cable retaining clip and detach the cable from the transaxle bracket.

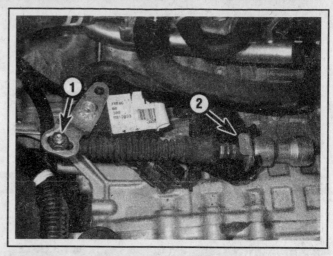

4.3 Shift cable details at the transaxle

1 *Cable-to-manual lever locknut*
2 *Cable-to-bracket retaining clip*

10 Remove the center console (see Chapter 11).
11 Remove the bracket from over the cable grommet in the body of the car, then remove the grommet bolts.
12 Detach the cable end from the shifter.
13 Remove the cable.
14 Installation is the reverse of removal. Be sure to adjust the cable.

5 Automatic transaxle - removal and installation

REMOVAL

▶ **Refer to illustration 5.2**

1 Remove the engine and transaxle assembly from the vehicle (see Chapter 2C).
2 Paint match marks on the torque converter and driveplate so they can be assembled in the same position (see illustration). Remove the torque converter bolts.
3 Disconnect the wiring from the transaxle components and remove the wiring harness.
4 Remove the dipstick tube. Detach the transaxle mounts from the subframe.
5 Remove the engine-to-transaxle bolts. Keep them organized so they can be installed in the same positions.
6 Separate the transaxle from the engine and slide it away. Remove the torque converter and seal the open end to prevent contamination.

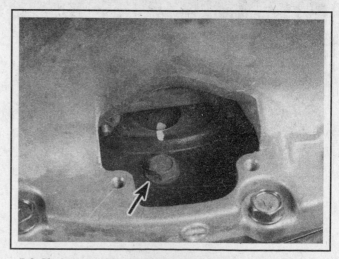

5.2 Mark the position of the torque converter to the driveplate, then remove the torque converter bolts by turning the crankshaft to bring each bolt into the opening

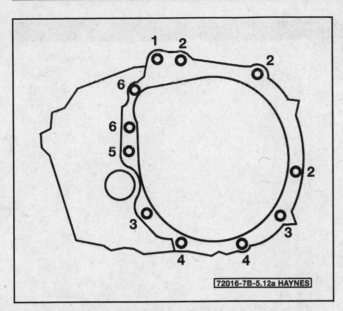

5.12a Transaxle mounting bolt length chart - four-cylinder models

1	1.77 inches	4	1.38 inches
2	1.77 inches	5	1.77 inches
3	1.77 inches	6	1.77 inches

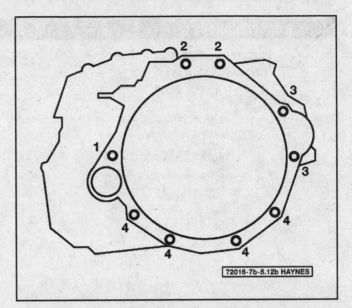

5.12b Transaxle mounting bolt length chart - V6 models

1	2.17 inches	3	4.25 inches
2	1.54 inches	4	1.77 inches

INSTALLATION

▶ **Refer to illustrations 5.12a and 5.12b**

7 Flush the transaxle cooler and the cooler hoses and lines with solvent whenever the transaxle is removed from the vehicle. Flush the lines and fluid cooler thoroughly and make sure no solvent remains in the lines or cooler after flushing. It's a good idea to repeat the flushing procedure with clean automatic transmission fluid to ensure that no solvent remains in the lines or cooler.

8 Prior to installation, make sure that the torque converter hub is securely engaged in the pump. The front face of the torque converter must be at least 1/2-inch behind the front edge of the transaxle housing to be fully seated.

9 Maneuver the transaxle to the rear of the engine.

10 Turn the torque converter to line it up with the driveplate. The marks you made on the torque converter and the driveplate must line up.

11 Move the transaxle forward carefully until the dowel pins and the torque converter are engaged.

12 Install the transaxle mounting bolts. Make sure the bolts are installed in the proper locations (see illustrations).

✳✳ CAUTION:

Don't use the bolts to force the transaxle and engine together. If the transaxle doesn't slide easily up against the engine, find out why before you tighten the bolts.

13 Tighten the bolts to the torque values listed in this Chapter's Specifications.

14 Install the torque converter bolts and tighten them to the Specifications listed in this Chapter.

15 The remainder of installation is the reverse of removal.

16 Refill the transaxle with fluid to the specified level (see Chapter 1). Note that the transaxle may require more fluid than in a normal fluid and filter change, since the torque converter may be empty (the converter is not drained during a fluid change).

17 Start the engine, set the parking brake and shift the transaxle through all gears three times. Make sure the shift cable is working properly (see Section 4).

18 Allow the engine to reach its proper operating temperature with the transaxle in Park or Neutral, then turn it off and check the fluid level.

19 Road test the vehicle and check for fluid leaks.

Torque specifications	Ft-lbs
Driveplate-to-torque converter bolts	40
Transaxle mounting bolts	
Four-cylinder engines	
Bolt 1	26
Bolts 2	55
Bolts 3	32
Bolts 4 (shorter bolts)	32
Bolt 5	35
Bolts 6	35
V6 engines	
Bolts 1 through 3	55
Bolts 4	32

8

CLUTCH AND DRIVELINE

Section

Reference to other Chapters

1 General information

The information in this Chapter deals with the components from the rear of the engine to the front wheels, except for the transaxle, which is dealt with in Chapters 7A and 7B. For the purposes of this Chapter, these components are grouped into two categories: clutch and driveaxles. Separate Sections within this Chapter offer general descriptions and checking procedures for both groups.

Since nearly all the procedures covered in this Chapter involve working under the vehicle, make sure it's securely supported on sturdy jackstands or a hoist where the vehicle can be easily raised and lowered.

2 Clutch - description

1 All vehicles with a manual transaxle use a single dry plate, diaphragm spring type clutch. The clutch disc has a splined hub which allows it to slide along the splines of the transaxle input shaft. The clutch and pressure plate are held in contact by spring pressure exerted by the diaphragm in the pressure plate.

2 The clutch release system is hydraulically operated. The release system consists of the clutch pedal, the clutch master cylinder, the clutch release cylinder and bearing and the hydraulic line between the master cylinder and release cylinder.

3 When force is applied to the clutch pedal to release the clutch, the clutch master cylinder transmits this movement to the clutch release cylinder and bearing. As the bearing moves, it pushes against the fingers of the diaphragm spring of the pressure plate assembly, which in turn releases the clutch plate.

4 Terminology can be a problem regarding the clutch components because common names have in some cases changed from that used by the manufacturer. For example, the clutch release cylinder is sometimes referred to as a concentric slave cylinder, the driven plate is also called the clutch plate or disc and the pressure plate assembly is also known as the clutch cover.

3 Clutch master cylinder - removal and installation

1 Remove the cowl panel (see Chapter 11).
2 Remove the air filter housing and the air duct (see Chapter 4).
3 Place rags under the master cylinder to catch spillage. Disconnect the hose from the clutch master cylinder. Immediately plug or seal the open ends to prevent fluid from dripping on painted parts.

✳✳ CAUTION:

Brake fluid will damage paint.

4 Working under the instrument panel, disconnect the clutch master cylinder pushrod from the pedal.
5 Make sure that rags are under the master cylinder. Remove the lock from the end of the clutch fluid pressure hose and disconnect the hose from the master cylinder.
6 Turn the master cylinder 45 degrees and remove it.
7 Installation is the reverse of removal.
8 Fill the clutch master cylinder reservoir with brake fluid conforming to DOT 3 specifications and bleed the clutch system (see Section 5).

4 Clutch release cylinder - removal and installation

➡ **Note: This vehicle uses a concentric release cylinder that fits around the input shaft of the transaxle. It can only be removed after the transaxle has been separated from the engine.**

1 Remove the transaxle (see Chapter 7A).
2 Unbolt the release cylinder from the transaxle bellhousing and remove it.
3 Installation is the reverse of removal.
4 Fill the clutch master cylinder with brake fluid (conforming to DOT 3 specifications) and bleed the clutch hydraulic system (see Section 5).

5   Clutch hydraulic system - bleeding

1   The hydraulic system should be bled of all air whenever any part of the system has been removed or if the fluid level has been allowed to fall so low that air has been drawn into the master cylinder. The procedure is similar to bleeding a brake system.

2   Fill the master cylinder with new brake fluid conforming to DOT 3 specifications.

✳✳ CAUTION:

Do not re-use any of the fluid coming from the system during the bleeding operation or use fluid which has been inside an open container for an extended period of time.

3   Raise the vehicle and place it securely on jackstands to gain access to the release cylinder bleeder valve.

4   Locate the bleeder valve of the clutch release cylinder. Remove the dust cap that fits over the bleeder valve and push a length of plastic hose over the valve. Place the other end of the hose into a clear container with about two inches of brake fluid in it. The hose end must be submerged in the fluid.

5   Have an assistant slowly push the clutch pedal in and then release it over about a three second period. Repeat this 15 times.

6   Push in the lock pin of the bleed connector. Hold it in to avoid having it pop off when the pedal is pumped.

7   Slide the bleed connector back about 0.4 inch.

8   Have the assistant push in the pedal and hold it down. Check for the presence of air bubbles in the clutch fluid.

9   Put the bleed connector back in place and release the lock pin.

10   Wait 5 seconds.

11   Repeat Steps 5 through 10 until there are no more air bubbles visible in the fluid. Disconnect the plastic tube and lower the vehicle.

12   Attach the plastic tube to the air bleed connector at the master cylinder.

13   Push in the clutch pedal a few times, then hold it down.

14   Open the air bleed valve, then close it.

15   Release the clutch pedal, then wait at least 5 seconds.

16   Repeat Steps 13 through 15 until there are no more air bubbles visible in the fluid.

17   Add fluid to the reservoir as necessary (see Chapter 1).

6   Clutch components - removal, inspection and installation

✳✳ WARNING:

Dust produced by clutch wear and deposited on clutch components is hazardous to your health. DO NOT blow it out with compressed air and DO NOT inhale it. DO NOT use gasoline or petroleum-based solvents to remove the dust. Brake system cleaner should be used to flush the dust into a drain pan. After the clutch components are wiped clean with a rag, dispose of the contaminated rags and cleaner in a labeled, covered container.

REMOVAL

▶ **Refer to illustration 6.4**

1   Access to the clutch components is normally accomplished by removing the transaxle. If the engine is being removed for major overhaul, then the opportunity should always be taken to check the clutch for wear and replace worn components as necessary. However, the relatively low cost of the clutch components compared to the time and labor involved in gaining access to them warrants their replacement any time the engine or transaxle is removed, unless they are new or in near-perfect condition.

2   Remove the transaxle (see Chapter 7A).

3   To support the clutch disc during removal, install a clutch alignment tool through the clutch disc hub (see illustration 6.12).

4   Carefully inspect the flywheel and pressure plate for indexing marks. The marks are usually an X, an O or a white letter. If they cannot be found, scribe marks yourself so the pressure plate and the flywheel will be in the same alignment during installation (see illustration).

5   Slowly loosen the pressure plate-to-flywheel bolts. Work in a diagonal pattern and loosen each bolt a little at a time until all spring

6.4 Mark the relationship of the pressure plate to the flywheel (if you're going to re-use the same pressure plate)

pressure is relieved.

6   Hold the pressure plate securely and completely remove the bolts, followed by the pressure plate and clutch disc.

INSPECTION

▶ **Refer to illustrations 6.9, 6.11a and 6.11b**

7   Ordinarily, when a problem occurs in the clutch, it can be attributed to wear of the clutch driven plate assembly (clutch disc). However, all components should be inspected at this time.

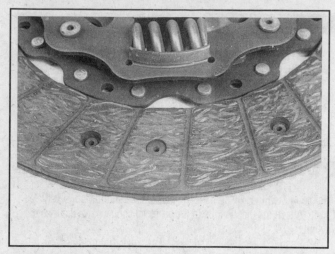

6.9 Examine the clutch disc for evidence of excessive wear, such as burned friction material, loose rivets, worn hub splines and distorted damper cushions or springs

6.11a Examine the pressure plate friction surface for score marks, cracks and evidence of overheating (blue spots)

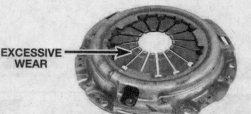

NORMAL FINGER WEAR   EXCESSIVE WEAR   **EXCESSIVE FINGER WEAR**   **BROKEN OR BENT FINGERS**

6.11b Replace the pressure plate if any of these conditions are noted

8 Inspect the flywheel for cracks, heat checking, score marks and other damage. If the imperfections are slight, a machine shop can resurface it to make it flat and smooth. Refer to Chapter 2 for the flywheel removal procedure.

9 Inspect the lining on the clutch disc. There should be at least 1/16-inch of lining above the rivet heads. Check for loose rivets, distortion, cracks, broken springs and other obvious damage (see illustra-

tion). As mentioned above, ordinarily the clutch disc is replaced as a matter of course, so if in doubt about the condition, replace it with a new one.

10 The slave cylinder/release bearing should be replaced along with the clutch disc (see Section 4).

11 Check the machined surface and the diaphragm spring fingers of the pressure plate (see illustrations). If the surface is grooved or otherwise damaged, replace the pressure plate assembly. Also check for obvious damage, distortion, cracking, etc. Light glazing can be removed with emery cloth or sandpaper. If a new pressure plate is indicated, new or factory rebuilt units are available.

INSTALLATION

▶ **Refer to illustration 6.12**

12 Carefully wipe the flywheel and pressure plate machined surfaces clean. It's important that no oil or grease is on these surfaces or the lining of the clutch disc. Handle these parts only with clean hands. Position the clutch disc and pressure plate with the clutch held in place with an alignment tool (see illustration). Make sure it's installed properly (most replacement clutch plates will be marked "flywheel side" or something similar - if not marked, install the clutch disc with the damper springs or cushion toward the transaxle).

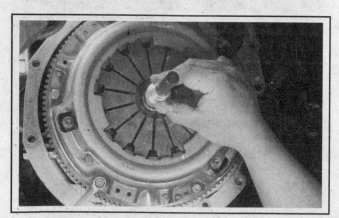

6.12 Center the clutch disc in the pressure plate with a clutch alignment tool, then tighten the pressure plate-to-flywheel bolts

13 Tighten the pressure plate-to-flywheel bolts only finger tight, working around the pressure plate.

14 Center the clutch disc by ensuring the alignment tool is through the splined hub and into the recess in the crankshaft. Wiggle the tool up, down or side-to-side as needed to bottom the tool. Tighten the pressure plate-to-flywheel bolts a little at a time, working in a criss-cross pattern to prevent distortion of the cover. After all of the bolts are snug, tighten them to the torque listed in this Chapter's Specifications. Remove the alignment tool.

15 Install the transaxle and all components removed previously, tightening all fasteners to the proper torque specifications.

7   Clutch interlock and ASCD switches - replacement and adjustment

➡**Note: The interlock switch allows the engine to start only when the clutch pedal is depressed. The ASCD (Automatic Speed Control Device) switch turns off the cruise control when the clutch pedal is depressed.**

➡**Note: Refer to Chapter 9 for more information about these switches - they are also used on the brake pedal.**

ADJUSTMENT

1   Both switches are located at the top of the clutch pedal.

2   With the pedal RELEASED, check the clearance between the clutch pedal and the threaded part of the ASCD switch and compare it to the Specifications in this Chapter.

3   Disconnect the electrical connector, then turn the switch to adjust it.

4   With the pedal fully DEPRESSED, check the clearance between the clutch pedal and the threaded part of the interlock switch and compare it to the Specifications in this Chapter.

5   Disconnect the wiring, then loosen the locknut and turn the switch to adjust it.

REPLACEMENT

6   Disconnect the wiring from the switch.

7   Remove the locknut and remove the switch.

8   Installation is the reverse of removal. Adjust the switch (see Steps 2 through 5).

8   Driveaxles - general information

1   Power is transmitted from the transaxle to the wheels through a pair of driveaxles. The inner end of each driveaxle is splined into the differential side gears. The outer ends of the driveaxles are splined to the axle hubs and locked in place by a large nut.

2   The inner ends of the driveaxle are equipped with tripod-type constant velocity joints which are capable of both angular and axial motion.

3   The outer CV joints are the ball and cage type. They can also be disassembled, cleaned and inspected, but they must be replaced as a single unit if they are defective

4   The boots should be inspected periodically for damage and leaking lubricant. Torn CV joint boots must be replaced as soon as possible or the joints can be damaged. Boot replacement involves removal of the driveaxle (see Section 10). The most common symptom of worn or damaged CV joints, besides lubricant leaks, is a clicking noise in turns, a clunk when accelerating after coasting and vibration at highway speeds. To check for wear in the CV joints and driveaxle shafts, grasp each axle (one at a time) and rotate it in both directions while holding the CV joint housings, feeling for play indicating worn splines or sloppy CV joints.

9   Driveaxles - removal and installation

REMOVAL

▶ **Refer to illustrations 9.2, 9.10a and 9.10b**

1   Loosen the front wheel lug nuts, raise the vehicle and support it securely on jackstands. Remove the wheel.

2   Remove the cotter pin and unscrew the driveaxle/hub nut (see illustration).

3   Remove the lock nut and washer from the end of the driveaxle (see illustration).

4   Remove the wheel speed sensor from the steering knuckle.

5   Disconnect the brake hose from the suspension strut.

6   Remove the brake caliper (see Chapter 9). Hang it out of the way on a length of wire; don't let it hang by the hose.

7   Remove the lower strut mounting bolts and disconnect the strut from the steering knuckle.

9.2 Place a prybar between two wheel studs while you loosen the driveaxle nut

9.10a If you're removing the left driveaxle, carefully pry the inner CV joint out of the transaxle

9.10b Remove these bolts to take off the inner bearing retainer of the right driveaxle

8   Push the driveaxle out of the hub. If the driveaxle splines are frozen, free them by tapping the end of the driveaxle with a soft-faced hammer or a hammer and a brass punch, or use a puller to push the driveaxle from the hub.

9   Remove the under-vehicle splash shield. Place a drain pan underneath the transaxle to catch the lubricant that may spill out when the driveaxles are removed.

10   If you're removing the left driveaxle, carefully pry the inner CV joint out of the transaxle (see illustration). The inner CV joint housing on the right (passenger's side) driveaxle terminates at a support bracket. To detach the right driveaxle assembly from the bracket, remove the retainer-to-bracket bolts, mark the relationship of the bearing to the support bracket and pull out the driveaxle assembly (see illustration). Do not try to separate the bearing from the inner CV joint until you have the entire assembly on the bench (see Section 10).

11   Install a new driveaxle oil seal (see Chapter 7A).

INSTALLATION

12   Installation is the reverse of the removal procedure, but with the following additional points:

a)   *When installing the left driveaxle, push the driveaxle in sharply to seat the retaining ring on the inner CV joint in its groove in the differential side gear. To ease insertion and seating of the retaining ring, position the gap in the ring at the bottom.*

b)   *When installing the right driveaxle, tighten the retainer bolts to the torque listed in this Chapter's Specifications.*

c)   *Tighten the strut-to-steering knuckle fasteners to the torque listed in the Chapter 10 Specifications.*

d)   *Tighten the driveaxle/hub nut to the torque listed in this Chapter's Specifications, then install a new cotter pin.*

e)   *Tighten the brake caliper mounting bolts to the torque listed in the Chapter 9 Specifications.*

f)   *Install the wheel and lug nuts, lower the vehicle and tighten the lug nuts to the torque listed in the Chapter 1 Specifications.*

g)   *Check the transaxle lubricant and add, if necessary, to bring it to the proper level (see Chapter 1).*

10   Driveaxle boot - replacement

➡**Note: If the CV joints must be overhauled (usually due to torn boots), explore all options before beginning the job. Complete rebuilt driveaxles are available on an exchange basis, which eliminates much time and work. Whichever route you choose to take, check on the cost and availability of parts before disassembling the vehicle.**

INNER CV JOINT

Disassembly

▸ **Refer to illustrations 10.2a, 10.2b, 10.3, 10.4, 10.5 and 10.6**

1   Remove the driveaxle (see Section 9).

2   Remove the boot clamps (see illustrations).

3   Pull the boot back from the inner CV joint, remove the retaining ring, then slide the joint housing off (see illustration).

4   Use a center punch to mark the tripod and axleshaft to ensure that they are reassembled properly (see illustration).

5   Remove the snap-ring from the end of the axleshaft with a pair of snap-ring pliers (see illustration).

6   Use a hammer and a brass punch to drive the tripod joint from the driveaxle (see illustration). Some driveaxles are equipped with a rubber dynamic balancer that is retained by clamps. If it is necessary to remove the balancer, be sure to first mark the location of the balancer and clamps so they can be reinstalled in the same location.

10.2a Pry up the retaining tabs on the boot clamps . . .

10.2b . . . then open the clamps and remove them from the boot

10.3 Pull the boot back, then pry the retaining ring from its groove

10.4 Use a center punch to place marks (arrows) on the tripod and the driveaxle to ensure that they're properly reassembled

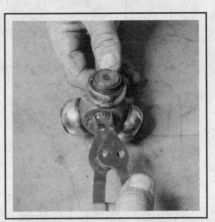

10.5 Remove the snap-ring from the groove in the end of the axleshaft

10.6 Drive the tripod joint from the axleshaft with a brass punch and hammer - make sure you don't damage the bearing surfaces or the splines on the shaft

Check

7   Clean all components with solvent to remove the grease, and check for cracks, pitting, scoring and other signs of wear.

Reassembly

♦ Refer to illustrations 10.8a, 10.8b, 10.11a, 10.11b, 10.11c and 10.11d

8   Slide the clamps and boot onto the axleshaft. It's a good idea to wrap the axleshaft splines with tape to prevent damaging the boot (see illustration). Place the tripod on the shaft (see illustration) and install the snap-ring. Apply grease to the tripod assembly, the inside of the joint housing and the inside of the boot.

9   Install the housing on the joint, then install the retaining ring, making sure it seats in its groove in the housing.

10 Slide the boot into place, making sure both ends seat in their grooves.

10.8a Wrap the splined area of the axleshaft with tape to prevent damage to the boots when installing them

10.8b Install the tripod with the chamfered (tapered) ends of the splines facing toward the axleshaft

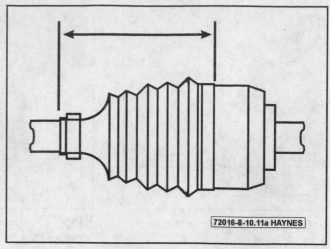

72016-8-10.11a HAYNES

10.11a Adjust the joint to the length indicated in this Chapter's Specifications, making sure the boot isn't distorted

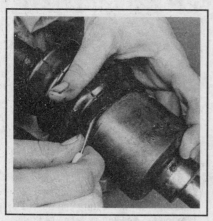

10.11b Equalize the pressure inside the boot by inserting a small, DULL screwdriver between the boot and the CV joint housing

10.11c To install the new clamps, bend the tang down . . .

10.11d . . . and tap the tabs down to hold it in place

11 Adjust the length of the joint (see illustration), equalize the pressure in the boot (see illustration), then tighten and secure the boot clamps (see illustrations).

12 Install a new circlip on the inner CV joint stub axle.

13 Install the driveaxle (see Section 9).

OUTER CV JOINT

♦ **Refer to illustrations 10.15a through 10.15k**

14 Remove the driveaxle (see Section 9), then remove the boot clamps (see illustration 10.2).

15 Refer to the accompanying illustrations and perform the outer CV joint boot replacement procedure (see illustrations).

10.15a Outer CV joints can be removed with a slide hammer; you'll need an adapter and a slide hammer setup such as the one shown here

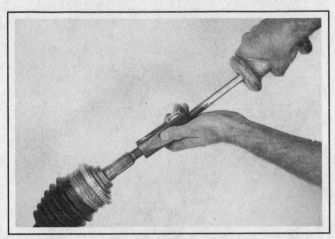

10.15b With the axleshaft firmly clamped down in a bench vise and the adapter gripping the driveaxle/hub nut, carefully extract the outer CV joint from the axleshaft. If it won't come off after five or six attempts, replace the driveaxle assembly

10.15c After the old grease has been rinsed away, move the inner race through its full range of motion and inspect the bearing surfaces for wear or damage

10.15d Apply CV joint grease through the splined hole, then insert a wooden dowel (slightly smaller in diameter than the hole) into the hole and push down - the dowel will force the grease into the joint. Repeat this until the joint is packed

10.15e Wrap the splined area of the axleshaft with tape to prevent damage to the boot when installing it

10.15f Install the small clamp and the boot on the driveaxle and apply grease to the inside of the axle boot . . .

10.15g . . . until the level is up to the end of the axle

10.15h Install a new circlip into the groove at the end of the driveaxle. Position the CV joint assembly on the driveaxle, aligning the splines . . .

10.15i . . . then use a hammer and brass punch to carefully drive the joint onto the driveaxle

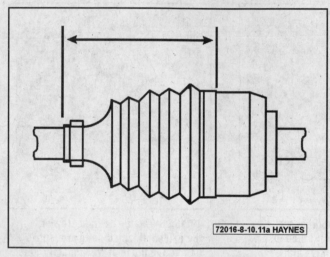

72016-8-10.11a HAYNES

10.15j Seat the boot in its grooves and adjust the joint to the length listed in this Chapter's Specifications . . .

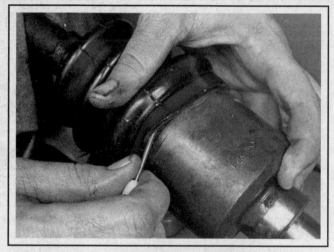

10.15k . . . equalize the pressure inside the boot by inserting a small, dull screwdriver between the boot and the outer race, then tighten the clamps (see illustrations 10.11c and 10.11d)

Specifications

Clutch

Clutch fluid type	See Chapter 1
ASCD switch-to-clutch pedal clearance, pedal released	0.03 to 0.08 inch
Clutch interlock switch-to-pedal clearance, pedal depressed	0.03 to 0.08 inch

Driveaxles

Driveaxle boot length	
Wheel end	6.42 inches
Transaxle end	
Left driveaxle	6.61 inches
Right driveaxle	7.45 inches

Torque specifications   Ft-lbs (unless otherwise indicated)

➡ **Note: One foot-pound of torque is equivalent to 12 inch-pounds of torque. Torque values below approximately 15-ft-lbs. are expressed in inch-pounds, since most foot pound torque wrenches are not accurate at these smaller values.**

Clutch release cylinder retaining bolts	15
Clutch pressure plate-to-flywheel bolts	
Four-cylinder models	
Step 1	132 in-lbs
Step 2	19
V6 models	
Step 1	132 in-lbs
Step 2	29
Driveaxle/hub nut	
2007 models	92
2008 and later models	129
Driveaxle support bearing retainer bolts	
Four-cylinder models	
2008 and earlier models	18
2009 and later models	35
Flat plate design	18
Driveaxle support bearing bracket-to-engine block bolts	
2009 and earlier models	22
2010 models	35

Notes

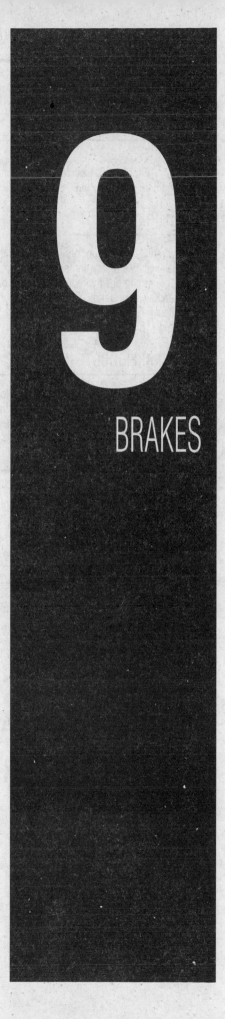

9

BRAKES

Section

Reference to other Chapters

1 General information

GENERAL

The vehicles covered by this manual are equipped with hydraulically operated front and rear brake systems. Both front and rear brakes are disc-type and are self-adjusting.

HYDRAULIC SYSTEM

The hydraulic system consists of two separate circuits. The master cylinder has separate reservoirs for the two circuits, and, in the event of a leak or failure in one hydraulic circuit, the other circuit will remain operative and a warning indicator will light up on the instrument panel when a substantial amount of brake fluid is lost, showing that a failure has occurred.

POWER BRAKE BOOSTER

The power brake booster uses engine manifold vacuum to provide assistance to the brakes. It is mounted on the firewall in the engine compartment, directly behind the master cylinder.

PARKING BRAKE

Control cables are routed to the rear axle, where they operate small drum brake shoes that apply pressure to the inner diameter of the rear brake discs.

SERVICE

After completing any operation involving disassembly of any part of the brake system, always test drive the vehicle to check for proper braking performance before resuming normal driving. When testing the brakes, perform the tests on a clean, dry, flat surface. Conditions other than these can lead to inaccurate test results.

Test the brakes at various speeds with both light and heavy pedal pressure. The vehicle should stop evenly without pulling to one side or the other. Under hard braking, the ABS system may engage, resulting in brake pedal pulsation. This is considered normal operation.

Tires, vehicle load and wheel alignment are factors which also affect braking performance.

PRECAUTIONS

There are some general cautions and warnings involving the brake system on this vehicle:

a) *Use only brake fluid conforming to DOT 3 specifications.*
b) *The brake pads and linings contain fibers which are hazardous to your health if inhaled. Whenever you work on brake system components, clean all parts with brake system cleaner. Do not allow the fine dust to become airborne. Also, wear an approved filtering mask.*
c) *Safety should be paramount whenever any servicing of the brake components is performed. Do not use parts or fasteners which are not in perfect condition, and be sure that all clearances and torque specifications are adhered to. If you are at all unsure about a certain procedure, seek professional advice. Upon completion of any brake system work, test the brakes carefully in a controlled area before putting the vehicle into normal service. If a problem is suspected in the brake system, don't drive the vehicle until it's fixed.*
d) *Used brake fluid is considered a hazardous waste and it must be disposed of in accordance with federal, state and local laws. DO NOT pour it down the sink, into septic tanks or storm drains, or on the ground.*
e) *Clean up any spilled brake fluid immediately and then wash the area with large amounts of water. This is especially true for any finished or painted surfaces.*

2 Troubleshooting

PROBABLE CAUSE	CORRECTIVE ACTION
No brakes - pedal travels to floor	
1 Low fluid level 2 Air in system	1 and 2 Low fluid level and air in the system are symptoms of another problem a leak somewhere in the hydraulic system. Locate and repair the leak
3 Defective seals in master cylinder	3 Replace master cylinder
4 Fluid overheated and vaporized due to heavy braking	4 Bleed hydraulic system (temporary fix). Replace brake fluid (proper fix)
Brake pedal slowly travels to floor under braking or at a stop	
1 Defective seals in master cylinder	1 Replace master cylinder
2 Leak in a hose, line, caliper or wheel cylinder	2 Locate and repair leak
3 Air in hydraulic system	3 Bleed the system, inspect system for a leak

PROBABLE CAUSE	CORRECTIVE ACTION

Brake pedal feels spongy when depressed

1 Air in hydraulic system	1 Bleed the system, inspect system for a leak
2 Master cylinder or power booster loose	2 Tighten fasteners
3 Brake fluid overheated (beginning to boil)	3 Bleed the system (temporary fix). Replace the brake fluid (proper fix)
4 Deteriorated brake hoses (ballooning under pressure)	4 Inspect hoses, replace as necessary (it's a good idea to replace all of them if one hose shows signs of deterioration)

Brake pedal feels hard when depressed and/or excessive effort required to stop vehicle

1 Power booster faulty	1 Replace booster
2 Engine not producing sufficient vacuum, or hose to booster clogged, collapsed or cracked	2 Check vacuum to booster with a vacuum gauge. Replace hose if cracked or clogged, repair engine if vacuum is extremely low
3 Brake linings contaminated by grease or brake fluid	3 Locate and repair source of contamination, replace brake pads or shoes
4 Brake linings glazed	4 Replace brake pads or shoes, check discs and drums for glazing, service as necessary
5 Caliper piston(s) or wheel cylinder(s) binding or frozen	5 Replace calipers or wheel cylinders
6 Brakes wet	6 Apply pedal to boil-off water (this should only be a momentary problem)
7 Kinked, clogged or internally split brake hose or line	7 Inspect lines and hoses, replace as necessary

Excessive brake pedal travel (but will pump up)

1 Drum brakes out of adjustment	1 Adjust brakes
2 Air in hydraulic system	2 Bleed system, inspect system for a leak

Excessive brake pedal travel (but will not pump up)

1 Master cylinder pushrod misadjusted	1 Adjust pushrod
2 Master cylinder seals defective	2 Replace master cylinder
3 Brake linings worn out	3 Inspect brakes, replace pads and/or shoes
4 Hydraulic system leak	4 Locate and repair leak

Brake pedal doesn't return

1 Brake pedal binding	1 Inspect pivot bushing and pushrod, repair or lubricate
2 Defective master cylinder	2 Replace master cylinder

Brake pedal pulsates during brake application

1 Brake drums out-of-round	1 Have drums machined by an automotive machine shop
2 Excessive brake disc runout or disc surfaces out-of-parallel	2 Have discs machined by an automotive machine shop
3 Loose or worn wheel bearings	3 Adjust or replace wheel bearings
4 Loose lug nuts	4 Tighten lug nuts

Brakes slow to release

1 Malfunctioning power booster	1 Replace booster
2 Pedal linkage binding	2 Inspect pedal pivot bushing and pushrod, repair/lubricate
3 Malfunctioning proportioning valve	3 Replace proportioning valve
4 Sticking caliper or wheel cylinder	4 Repair or replace calipers or wheel cylinders
5 Kinked or internally split brake hose	5 Locate and replace faulty brake hose

PROBABLE CAUSE	CORRECTIVE ACTION

Brakes grab (one or more wheels)

PROBABLE CAUSE	CORRECTIVE ACTION
1 Grease or brake fluid on brake lining	1 Locate and repair cause of contamination, replace lining
2 Brake lining glazed	2 Replace lining, deglaze disc or drum

Vehicle pulls to one side during braking

PROBABLE CAUSE	CORRECTIVE ACTION
1 Grease or brake fluid on brake lining	1 Locate and repair cause of contamination, replace lining
2 Brake lining glazed	2 Deglaze or replace lining, deglaze disc or drum
3 Restricted brake line or hose	3 Repair line or replace hose
4 Tire pressures incorrect	4 Adjust tire pressures
5 Caliper or wheel cylinder sticking	5 Repair or replace calipers or wheel cylinders
6 Wheels out of alignment	6 Have wheels aligned
7 Weak suspension spring	7 Replace springs
8 Weak or broken shock absorber	8 Replace shock absorbers

Brakes drag (indicated by sluggish engine performance or wheels being very hot after driving)

PROBABLE CAUSE	CORRECTIVE ACTION
1 Brake pedal pushrod incorrectly adjusted	1 Adjust pushrod
2 Master cylinder pushrod (between booster and master cylinder)	2 Adjust pushrod incorrectly adjusted
3 Obstructed compensating port in master cylinder	3 Replace master cylinder
4 Master cylinder piston seized in bore	4 Replace master cylinder
5 Contaminated fluid causing swollen seals throughout system	5 Flush system, replace all hydraulic components
6 Clogged brake lines or internally split brake hose(s)	6 Flush hydraulic system, replace defective hose(s)
7 Sticking caliper(s) or wheel cylinder(s)	7 Replace calipers or wheel cylinders
8 Parking brake not releasing	8 Inspect parking brake linkage and parking brake mechanism, repair as required
9 Improper shoe-to-drum clearance	9 Adjust brake shoes
10 Faulty proportioning valve	10 Replace proportioning valve

Brakes fade (due to excessive heat)

PROBABLE CAUSE	CORRECTIVE ACTION
1 Brake linings excessively worn or glazed	1 Deglaze or replace brake pads and/or shoes
2 Excessive use of brakes	2 Downshift into a lower gear, maintain a constant slower speed (going down hills)
3 Vehicle overloaded	3 Reduce load
4 Brake drums or discs worn too thin	4 Measure drum diameter and disc thickness, replace drums or discs as required
5 Contaminated brake fluid	5 Flush system, replace fluid
6 Brakes drag	6 Repair cause of dragging brakes
7 Driver resting left foot on brake pedal	7 Don't ride the brakes

Brakes noisy (high-pitched squeal)

PROBABLE CAUSE	CORRECTIVE ACTION
1 Glazed lining	1 Deglaze or replace lining
2 Contaminated lining (brake fluid, grease, etc.)	2 Repair source of contamination, replace linings
3 Weak or broken brake shoe hold-down or return spring	3 Replace springs
4 Rivets securing lining to shoe or backing plate loose	4 Replace shoes or pads
5 Excessive dust buildup on brake linings	5 Wash brakes off with brake system cleaner
6 Brake drums worn too thin	6 Measure diameter of drums, replace if necessary
7 Wear indicator on disc brake pads contacting disc	7 Replace brake pads

PROBABLE CAUSE	CORRECTIVE ACTION

Brakes noisy (high-pitched squeal) (continued)

8 Anti-squeal shims missing or installed improperly	8 Install shims correctly

➡Note: Other remedies for quieting squealing brakes include the application of an anti-squeal compound to the backing plates of the brake pads, and lightly chamfering the edges of the brake pads with a file. The latter method should only be performed with the brake pads thoroughly wetted with brake system cleaner, so as not to allow any brake dust to become airborne.

Brakes noisy (scraping sound)

1 Brake pads or shoes worn out; rivets, backing plate or brake shoe metal contacting disc or drum	1 Replace linings, have discs and/or drums machined (or replace)

Brakes chatter

1 Worn brake lining	1 Inspect brakes, replace shoes or pads as necessary
2 Glazed or scored discs or drums	2 Deglaze discs or drums with sandpaper (if glazing is severe, machining will be required)
3 Drums or discs heat checked	3 Check discs and/or drums for hard spots, heat checking, etc. Have discs/drums machined or replace them
4 Disc runout or drum out-of-round excessive	4 Measure disc runout and/or drum out-of-round, have discs or drums machined or replace them
5 Loose or worn wheel bearings	5 Adjust or replace wheel bearings
6 Loose or bent brake backing plate (drum brakes)	6 Tighten or replace backing plate
7 Grooves worn in discs or drums	7 Have discs or drums machined, if within limits (if not, replace them)
8 Brake linings contaminated (brake fluid, grease, etc.)	8 Locate and repair source of contamination, replace pads or shoes
9 Excessive dust buildup on linings	9 Wash brakes with brake system cleaner
10 Surface finish on discs or drums too rough after machining (especially on vehicles with sliding calipers)	10 Have discs or drums properly machined
11 Brake pads or shoes glazed	11 Deglaze or replace brake pads or shoes

Brake pads or shoes click

1 Shoe support pads on brake backing plate grooved or	1 Replace brake backing plate excessively worn
2 Brake pads loose in caliper	2 Loose pad retainers or anti-rattle clips
3 Also see items listed under Brakes chatter	

Brakes make groaning noise at end of stop

1 Brake pads and/or shoes worn out	1 Replace pads and/or shoes
2 Brake linings contaminated (brake fluid, grease, etc.)	2 Locate and repair cause of contamination, replace brake pads or shoes
3 Brake linings glazed	3 Deglaze or replace brake pads or shoes
4 Excessive dust buildup on linings	4 Wash brakes with brake system cleaner
5 Scored or heat-checked discs or drums	5 Inspect discs/drums, have machined if within limits (if not, replace discs or drums)
6 Broken or missing brake shoe attaching hardware	6 Inspect drum brakes, replace missing hardware

Rear brakes lock up under light brake application

1 Tire pressures too high	1 Adjust tire pressures
2 Tires excessively worn	2 Replace tires
3 Defective proportioning valve	3 Replace proportioning valve

PROBABLE CAUSE	CORRECTIVE ACTION

Brake warning light on instrument panel comes on (or stays on)

1 Low fluid level in master cylinder reservoir (reservoirs with fluid level sensor)	1 Add fluid, inspect system for leak, check the thickness of the brake pads and shoes
2 Failure in one half of the hydraulic system	2 Inspect hydraulic system for a leak
3 Piston in pressure differential warning valve not centered	3 Center piston by bleeding one circuit or the other (close bleeder valve as soon as the light goes out)
4 Defective pressure differential valve or warning switch	4 Replace valve or switch
5 Air in the hydraulic system	5 Bleed the system, check for leaks
6 Brake pads worn out (vehicles with electric wear sensors - small probes that fit into the brake pads and ground out on the disc when the pads get thin)	6 Replace brake pads (and sensors)

Brakes do not self adjust

Disc brakes

1 Defective caliper piston seals	1 Replace calipers. Also, possible contaminated fluid causing soft or swollen seals (flush system and fill with new fluid if in doubt)
2 Corroded caliper piston(s)	2 Same as above

Drum brakes

1 Adjuster screw frozen	1 Remove adjuster, disassemble, clean and lubricate with high-temperature grease
2 Adjuster lever does not contact star wheel or is binding	2 Inspect drum brakes, assemble correctly or clean or replace parts as required
3 Adjusters mixed up (installed on wrong wheels after brake job)	3 Reassemble correctly
4 Adjuster cable broken or installed incorrectly (cable-type adjusters)	4 Install new cable or assemble correctly

Rapid brake lining wear

1 Driver resting left foot on brake pedal	1 Don't ride the brakes
2 Surface finish on discs or drums too rough	2 Have discs or drums properly machined
3 Also see Brakes drag	

3   Anti-lock Brake System (ABS) - general information

1   The Anti-lock Brake System (ABS) is designed to maintain vehicle steerability, directional stability and optimum deceleration under severe braking conditions and on most road surfaces. It does so by monitoring the rotational speed of each wheel and controlling the brake line pressure to each wheel during braking. This prevents the wheels from locking up.

COMPONENTS

Actuator assembly

▶ **Refer to illustration 3.2**

2   The actuator assembly consists of an electric hydraulic pump and a pair of solenoid valves for each wheel. The electric pump provides hydraulic pressure to charge the reservoirs in the actuator, which supplies pressure to the braking system during ABS operation. The solenoid valves modulate brake line pressure during ABS operation. The body contains four valves - one for each wheel. The pump, the reservoirs and the solenoid valves are all housed in the actuator assembly (see illustration).

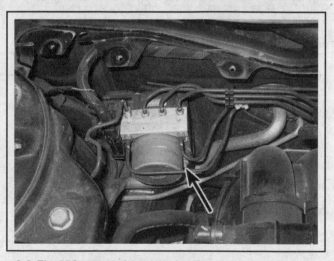

3.2 The ABS actuator is mounted at the passenger side of the firewall - the cowl panel and suspension strut braces have been removed here for clarity

Speed sensors

3   The speed sensors, which are located at each wheel, generate a sine wave current when the sensor rotors are turning. This analog voltage signal is monitored by the ABS control unit, which converts it to a digital signal from which it can determine wheel rotational speed.

4   The wheel speed sensors are integral with the wheel hub/bearing assemblies.

ABS computer

5   The ABS control unit is the brain of the ABS system. The function of the control unit is to monitor and process information received from

the wheel speed sensors to control the hydraulic line pressure, avoiding wheel lock up. The control unit also monitors the system for malfunctions, even when the ABS system is inactive during normal driving conditions.

6   Each time you start the engine, the system turns on the ABS warning light on the instrument cluster for about a second. As soon as the engine is running, the light should go off. The system then performs a self-test the first time the vehicle speed exceeds four mph. You may hear a mechanical noise during the test; this is normal. If the system detects a problem, the ABS light will come on and remain on. A diagnostic code will also be stored in the control unit, which indicates the problem area or component.

---

4   Disc brake pads - replacement

▶ **Refer to illustrations 4.5 and 4.6a through 4.6u**

❄❄ WARNING:

Disc brake pads must be replaced on both front wheels at the same time - never replace the pads on only one wheel. Also, the dust created by the brake system is harmful to your health. Never blow it out with compressed air and don't inhale any of it. An approved filtering mask should be worn when working on the brakes. Do not, under any circumstances, use petroleum-based solvents to clean brake parts. Use brake system cleaner only!

1   Remove the cap from the brake fluid reservoir.

2   Loosen the front or rear wheel lug nuts, raise the front or rear of the vehicle and support it securely on jackstands. Block the wheels at the opposite end.

3   Remove the wheels. Work on one brake assembly at a time, using the assembled brake for reference if necessary.

4   Inspect the brake disc carefully as outlined in Section 6. If

machining is necessary, follow the information in that Section to remove the disc.

5   Push the piston back into its bore to provide room for the new brake pads. A C-clamp can be used to accomplish this (see illustration). As the piston is depressed to the bottom of the caliper bore, the fluid in the master cylinder will rise. Make sure that it doesn't overflow. If necessary, siphon off some of the fluid.

6   Follow the accompanying photos (see illustrations 4.6a through 4.6u) for the front or rear pad replacement procedure. Be sure to stay in order and read the caption under each illustration.

➡**Note: The illustrations show a front brake job, but the rear is almost identical.**

7   When reinstalling the caliper, be sure to tighten the mounting bolts to the torque listed in this Chapter's Specifications. Tighten the wheel lug nuts to the torque listed in the Chapter 1 Specifications.

8   After the job has been completed, firmly depress the brake pedal a few times to bring the pads into contact with the disc. Check the level of the brake fluid, adding some if necessary. Check the operation of the brakes carefully before placing the vehicle into normal service.

4.5 Use a C-clamp to depress the piston into the caliper before removing the caliper and pads

4.6a Before disassembling the brake, wash it thoroughly with brake system cleaner and allow it to dry - position a drain pan under the brake to catch the residue - DO NOT use compressed air to blow off brake dust!

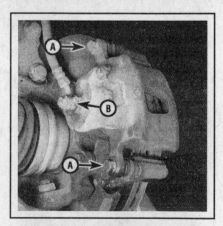

4.6b Remove the caliper mounting bolts (A) to detach the caliper from the caliper mounting bracket; the brake hose banjo bolt (B) shouldn't be removed unless the caliper or hose requires service

4.6c Lift the caliper off the pads

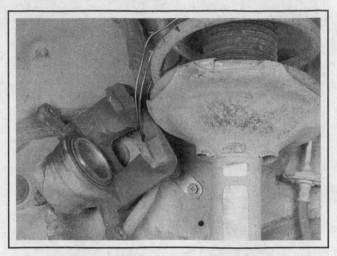

4.6d Hang the caliper out of the way with a piece of coat hanger or wire

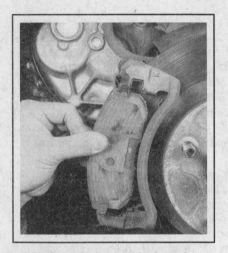

4.6e Remove the outer brake pad

4.6f Remove the inner brake pad

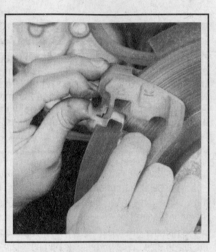

4.6g Remove the upper pad retainer

4.6h Remove the lower pad retainer

4.6i Remove the shim (or shim cover and shim) from the brake pads

4.6j Remove the caliper pins and the dust boots

4.6k Inspect the boots for cracks and tears and replace them if they're damaged

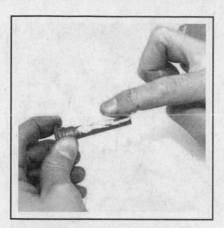

4.6l Clean the caliper pins, inspect them for scoring and corrosion, and replace them if necessary; coat the pins with high-temperature grease . . .

4.6m . . . and install them in the caliper mounting bracket

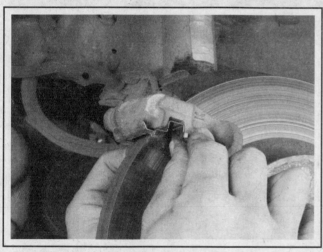

4.6n Install the upper pad retainer

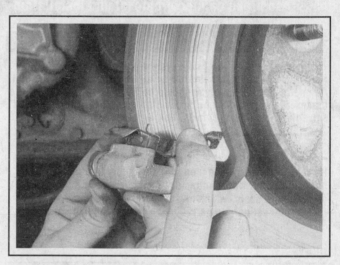

4.6o Install the lower pad retainer

4.6p Make sure the upper and lower pad retainers are properly seated as shown

4.6q Install the shim (or shim and shim cover) on the pads

4.6r Apply anti-squeal compound to the back of both pads (let the compound set up a few minutes before installing them)

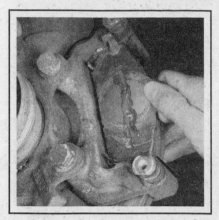

4.6s Install the inner brake pad

4.6t Install the outer brake pad

4.6u Install the caliper and the caliper bolts, tightening the caliper bolts to the torque listed in this Chapter's Specifications. Note: If the caliper won't fit over the pads, use a C-clamp to push the piston into the caliper a little farther

5   Disc brake caliper - removal and installation

✳✳ WARNING:

The dust created by the brake system is harmful to your health. Never blow it out with compressed air and don't inhale any of it. An approved filtering mask should be worn when working on the brakes. Do not, under any circumstances, use petroleum-based solvents to clean brake parts. Use brake system cleaner only!

➡ Note: If replacement is indicated (usually because of fluid leakage), it is recommended that the calipers be replaced, not overhauled. New and factory rebuilt units are available on an exchange basis, which makes this job quite easy. Always replace the calipers in pairs - never replace just one of them.

REMOVAL

◆ Refer to illustration 5.2

1   Loosen the front or rear wheel lug nuts, raise the front or rear of the vehicle and place it securely on jackstands. Block the wheels at the opposite end. Remove the front or rear wheel.

2   Remove the banjo bolt (see illustration 4.6b). Disconnect the brake hose from the caliper and discard the sealing washers (new ones should be used on installation). Plug the brake hose to keep contaminants out of the brake system and to prevent losing any more brake fluid than is necessary (see illustration).

3   Remove the caliper mounting bolts and lift the caliper from its bracket.

➡ Note: See Section 4 for additional information (it's part of brake pad replacement).

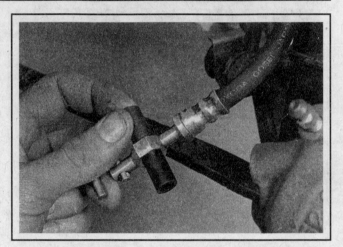

5.2 Using a piece of rubber hose of the appropriate size, plug the brake line

INSTALLATION

4   Installation is the reverse of removal, tightening the caliper mounting bolt to the torque listed in this Chapter's Specifications and the wheel lug nuts to the torque in the Chapter 1 Specifications. Don't forget to use new sealing washers for the brake hose-to-caliper banjo bolt.

5   Bleed the brake system (see Section 9). Make sure there are no leaks from the hose connections. Test the brakes carefully before returning the vehicle to normal service.

6   Brake disc - inspection, removal and installation

INSPECTION

◆ Refer to illustrations 6.3, 6.4a, 6.4b and 6.5

1   Loosen the wheel lug nuts, raise the vehicle and support it securely on jackstands. Remove the wheel and install the lug nuts to hold the disc in place.

➡ Note: If the lug nuts don't contact the disc when screwed on all the way, install washers under them.

2   Remove the brake caliper (see Section 5). It isn't necessary to

disconnect the brake hose. After removing the caliper bolts, suspend the caliper out of the way with a piece of wire.

3   Visually inspect the disc surface for score marks and other damage. Light scratches and shallow grooves are normal after use and may not always be detrimental to brake operation, but deep scoring - over 0.039-inch (1.0 mm) - requires disc removal and refinishing by an automotive machine shop. Be sure to check both sides of the disc (see illustration). If pulsating has been noticed during application of the brakes, suspect disc runout.

4   To check disc runout, place a dial indicator at a point about 1/2-inch from the outer edge of the disc (see illustration). Set the indicator to zero and turn the disc. The indicator reading should not exceed the specified allowable runout limit. If it does, the disc should be refinished by an automotive machine shop.

➡Note: When replacing the brake pads, it's a good idea to resurface the discs regardless of the dial indicator reading, as this will impart a smooth finish and ensure a perfectly flat surface, eliminating any brake pedal pulsation or other undesirable symptoms related to questionable discs. At the very least, if you elect not to have the discs resurfaced, remove the glaze

from the surface with emery cloth using a swirling motion (see illustration).

5   It's absolutely critical that the disc not be machined to a thickness under the specified minimum allowable disc refinish thickness. The minimum wear (or discard) thickness is cast into the disc. The disc thickness can be checked with a micrometer (see illustration).

REMOVAL

➡ Refer to illustrations 6.6a and 6.6b

6   Remove the two caliper mounting bracket bolts (see illustrations) and detach the caliper mounting bracket. On rear discs, fully release the parking brake.

7   Remove the lug nuts which you installed to hold the disc in place and remove the disc from the hub.

➡Note: If a rear disc won't come off, remove the rubber plug from the parking brake adjuster hole. Use a small screwdriver to turn the star wheel and retract the parking brake shoes (see Section 12).

6.3 The brake pads on this vehicle were obviously neglected, as they wore down completely and cut deep grooves into the disc - wear this severe means the disc must be replaced

6.4a To check disc runout, mount a dial indicator as shown and rotate the disc

6.4b Using a swirling motion, remove the glaze from the disc surface with sandpaper or emery cloth

6.5 Use a micrometer to measure disc thickness

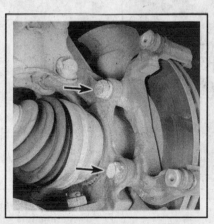

6.6a To remove the front caliper mounting bracket, remove these bolts

6.6b To remove the rear caliper mounting bracket, remove these bolts

INSTALLATION

8   Place the disc in position over the threaded studs.

9   Install the caliper mounting bracket over the disc and tighten the bolts to the torque listed in this Chapter's Specifications.

10 Install the caliper and tighten the bolts to the torque listed in this Chapter's Specifications.

11 Install the wheel, then lower the vehicle to the ground. Tighten the lug nuts to the torque listed in the Chapter 1 Specifications. Depress the brake pedal a few times to bring the brake pads into contact with the disc. Bleeding won't be necessary unless the brake hose was disconnected from the caliper. Check the operation of the brakes carefully before driving the vehicle.

7   Master cylinder - removal and installation

REMOVAL

▶ **Refer to illustration 7.2**

1   Disconnect the cable from the negative terminal of the battery (see Chapter 5).

2   Unplug the electrical connector for the fluid level warning switch (see illustration). On manual transmission vehicles, disconnect and plug the clutch fluid hose.

3   Remove as much fluid as possible from the reservoir with a syringe.

4   Place rags under the fittings and prepare caps or plastic bags to cover the ends of the lines once they're disconnected.

❊❊ CAUTION:

Brake fluid will damage paint. Cover all body parts and be careful not to spill fluid during this procedure.

Loosen the fittings at the ends of the brake lines where they enter the master cylinder. To prevent rounding off the flats, use a flare-nut wrench, which wraps around the fitting hex.

5   Pull the brake lines away from the master cylinder and plug the ends to prevent contamination.

6   Remove the nuts attaching the master cylinder to the power booster. Pull the master cylinder off the studs to remove it. Again, be careful not to spill any remaining fluid as this is done.

INSTALLATION

▶ **Refer to illustrations 7.8 and 7.16**

7   Bench bleed the new master cylinder before installing it. Mount the master cylinder in a vise, with the jaws of the vise clamping on the mounting flange.

8   Attach a pair of master cylinder bleeder tubes to the outlet ports of the master cylinder (see illustration).

9   Fill the reservoir with brake fluid of the recommended type (see Chapter 1).

10 Slowly push the pistons into the master cylinder (a large Phillips screwdriver can be used for this) - air will be expelled from the pressure chambers and into the reservoir. Because the tubes are submerged in fluid, air can't be drawn back into the master cylinder when you release the pistons. Repeat the procedure until no more air bubbles are present.

11 Remove the bleed tubes, one at a time, and install plugs in the open ports to prevent fluid leakage and air from entering. Install the reservoir cap.

12 Install a new O-ring seal in the groove on the end of the master cylinder and coat it with silicone grease. Also coat the bore of the power brake booster.

13 Install the master cylinder over the studs on the power brake booster and tighten the nuts only finger-tight at this time.

14 Thread the brake line fittings into the master cylinder. Since the master cylinder is still a bit loose, it can be moved slightly so the fittings thread in easily. Don't strip the threads as the fittings are tightened.

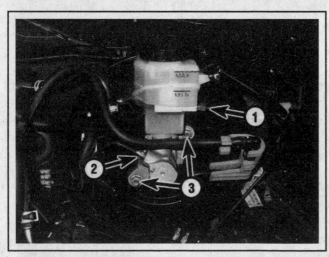

7.2 Master cylinder details

1   Electrical connector   3   Mounting nuts
2   Fluid lines

7.8 The best way to bleed the master cylinder before installing it is with a pair of bleeder tubes

15 Tighten the mounting nuts to the torque listed in this Chapter's Specifications. Tighten the brake line fittings securely.

16 Fill the master cylinder reservoir with fluid, then bleed the lines at the master cylinder, followed by bleeding the remainder of the brake system (see Section 9). To bleed the lines at the master cylinder, have an assistant depress the brake pedal and hold it down. Loosen the fitting to allow air and fluid to escape (see illustration). Tighten the fitting, then allow your assistant to return the pedal to its rest position. Repeat this procedure on both fittings until the fluid is free of air bubbles, then bleed the rest of the system. Check the operation of the brake system carefully before driving the vehicle.

> ❊❊❊ **WARNING:**
>
> **If you do not have a firm brake pedal at the end of the bleeding procedure, or have any doubts as to the effectiveness of the brake system, DO NOT drive the vehicle. Have it towed to a dealer service department or other qualified repair shop for diagnosis.**

17 Reconnect the battery and perform the necessary re-learn procedures (see Chapter 5).

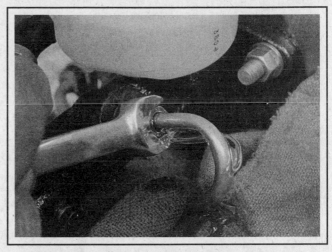

7.16 Have an assistant depress the brake pedal and hold it down, then loosen the fitting nut, allowing the air and fluid to escape; repeat this procedure on both fittings until the fluid is clear of air bubbles

8   Brake hoses and lines - inspection and replacement

INSPECTION

1   About every six months, with the vehicle raised and supported securely on jackstands, the flexible hoses which connect the steel brake lines with the front and rear brake assemblies should be inspected for cracks, chafing of the outer cover, leaks, blisters and other damage. These are important and vulnerable parts of the brake system and inspection should be complete. A light and mirror will be helpful for a thorough check. If a hose exhibits any of the above conditions, replace it with a new one.

REPLACEMENT

Brake hoses

▶ **Refer to illustrations 8.3 and 8.4**

2   Loosen the wheel lug nuts, raise the vehicle and support it securely on jackstands. Remove the wheel.

3   At the bracket, unscrew the brake line fitting from the hose (see illustration). Use a flare-nut wrench to prevent rounding off the corners.

4   Remove the U-clip from the female fitting at the bracket with a pair of pliers (see illustration), then pass the hose through the bracket.

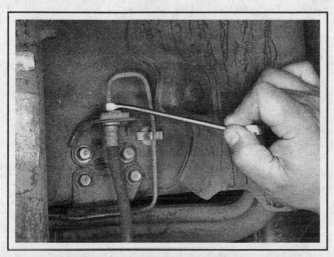

8.3 Loosen the threaded fitting on the brake line; use a flare-nut wrench to protect the corners of the nut

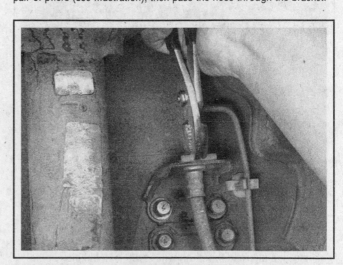

8.4 Pull off the U-clip with a pair of pliers

5   At the caliper end of the hose, remove the banjo bolt, then separate the hose from the caliper. Note that there are two sealing washers on either side of the banjo fitting - they should be replaced with new ones during installation.

6   If you're replacing a front brake hose, remove the U-clip from the strut bracket, then detach the hose from the bracket.

7   To install the hose, pass the caliper fitting end through the strut bracket (front hose only), then connect the fitting to the caliper with the banjo bolt and new sealing washers.

8   Make sure the hose isn't twisted between the caliper and the strut bracket (or the chassis on rear brake hoses).

9   Route the hose into the frame bracket, again making sure it isn't twisted, then connect the brake line fitting, starting the threads by hand. Install the U-clip, then tighten the fitting securely.

10   Bleed the caliper (see Section 9).

11   Install the wheel and lug nuts, lower the vehicle and tighten the lug nuts to the torque listed in the Chapter 1 Specifications.

Metal brake lines

12   When replacing brake lines, be sure to use the correct parts. Don't use copper tubing for any brake system components. Purchase steel brake lines from a dealer or auto parts store.

13   Prefabricated brake line, with the tube ends already flared and fittings installed, is available at auto parts stores and dealer parts departments.

14   When installing the new line, make sure it's securely supported in the brackets and has plenty of clearance between moving or hot components.

15   After installation, check the master cylinder fluid level and add fluid as necessary. Bleed the brake system (see Section 9) and test the brakes carefully before driving the vehicle in traffic.

9   Brake hydraulic system - bleeding

▶ **Refer to illustration 9.8**

※※ WARNING:

Wear eye protection when bleeding the brake system. If the fluid comes in contact with your eyes, immediately rinse them with water and seek medical attention.

→Note: Bleeding the hydraulic system is necessary to remove any air that manages to find its way into the system when it's been opened during removal and installation of a hose, line, caliper or master cylinder.

1   You'll probably have to bleed the system at all four brakes if air has entered it due to low fluid level, or if the brake lines have been disconnected at the master cylinder.

2   If a brake line was disconnected only at a wheel, then only that caliper or wheel cylinder must be bled.

3   If a brake line is disconnected at a fitting located between the master cylinder and any of the brakes, that part of the system served by the disconnected line must be bled.

4   Remove any residual vacuum from the brake power booster by applying the brake several times with the engine off.

5   Remove the master cylinder reservoir cover and fill the reservoir with brake fluid. Reinstall the cover. Check the fluid level often during the bleeding operation and add fluid as necessary to prevent the fluid level from falling low enough to allow air bubbles into the master cylinder.

※※ CAUTION:

Turn the ignition switch off and disconnect the electrical connectors for the ABS actuator or detach the battery ground cable.

6   Have an assistant on hand, as well as a supply of new brake fluid, a clear plastic container partially filled with clean brake fluid, a length of 3/16-inch plastic, rubber or vinyl tubing to fit over the bleeder valve and a wrench to open and close the bleeder valve.

7   Beginning at the right rear wheel, loosen the bleeder valve slightly, then tighten it to a point where it's snug but can still be loosened quickly and easily.

8   Place one end of the tubing over the bleeder valve and submerge the other end in brake fluid in the container (see illustration).

9   Have the assistant pump the brakes slowly a few times to get pressure in the system, then hold the pedal down firmly.

10   While the pedal is held down, open the bleeder valve just enough to allow a flow of fluid to leave the valve. Watch for air bubbles to exit the submerged end of the tube. When the fluid flow slows after a couple of seconds, close the valve and have your assistant release the pedal.

11   Repeat Steps 9 and 10 until no more air is seen leaving the tube, then tighten the bleeder valve and proceed to the left front wheel, the left rear wheel and the right front wheel, in that order, and perform the same procedure. Be sure to check the fluid in the master cylinder reservoir frequently.

12   Never use old brake fluid. It contains moisture which will deteriorate the brake system components and could cause the fluid to boil,

9.8 When bleeding the brakes, a hose is connected to the bleed screw at the caliper or wheel cylinder and then submerged in brake fluid - air will be seen as bubbles in the tube and container (all air must be expelled before moving to the next wheel)

which could render the brake system inoperative.

13 Refill the master cylinder with fluid at the end of the operation. If you're working on a model with ABS, be sure to reconnect the electrical connectors to the ABS actuator or reconnect the battery.

14 Check the operation of the brakes. The pedal should feel solid when depressed, with no sponginess. If necessary, repeat the entire process.

---

10 Power brake booster - check, replacement and adjustment

CHECK

Operating check

1 Depress the brake pedal several times with the engine off and make sure there's no change in the pedal reserve distance.

2 Depress the pedal and start the engine. If the pedal goes down slightly, operation is normal.

Airtightness check

3 Start the engine and turn it off after one or two minutes. Depress the brake pedal slowly several times. If the pedal depresses less each time, the booster is airtight.

4 Depress the brake pedal while the engine is running, then stop the engine with the pedal depressed. If there's no change in the pedal reserve travel after holding the pedal for 30 seconds, the booster is airtight.

REPLACEMENT

⬧ **Refer to illustrations 10.11a and 10.11b**

➡**Note: Power brake booster units shouldn't be disassembled. They require special tools not normally found in most automotive repair stations or shops. They're fairly complex and, because of their critical relationship to brake performance, should be replaced with a new or rebuilt one.**

5 Remove the air filter housing for clearance (see Chapter 4).

6 Remove the master cylinder (see Section 7).

7 Relieve the fuel pressure, then disconnect the fuel line (see Chapter 4).

8 Remove the cowl cover (see Chapter 11) and the strut brace.

9 Disconnect the vacuum hose from the booster.

10 On V6 models, remove the accelerator pedal and the brake pedal.

11 Pull out the safety clip, then remove the pin from the clevis to detach it from the brake pedal (see illustrations).

12 Remove the four mounting nuts securing the booster to the firewall, then remove the booster from the engine compartment.

13 Before installing the new booster, measure the booster input rod length and adjust it if necessary.

14 Installation is the reverse of removal. Be sure to use a new gasket between the booster and the firewall.

ADJUSTMENT

⬧ **Refer to illustration 10.15**

15 Measure the distance between the power brake booster and the hole in the input rod clevis (see illustration) and compare it to the dimension listed in this Chapter's Specifications. If necessary, loosen the adjusting nut and turn the clevis in or out to the specified length, then install the booster, connect the clevis to the brake pedal, and tighten the nut securely.

**10.11a Brake booster
mounting details**

1   Clevis pin retaining clip
2   Clevis lock nut (loosen to adjust
     input rod length)
3   Left-side mounting nuts

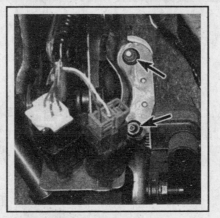

**10.11b Booster right-side
mounting nuts**

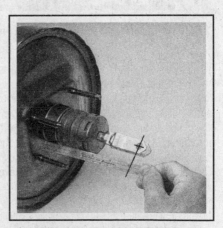

**10.15 Measure the distance between
the power brake booster and the
hole in the clevis and compare your
measurement to the dimension listed
in this Chapter's Specifications; if
necessary, adjust the clevis before
installing the power brake booster**

11 Parking brake - check and adjustment

CHECK

1   The parking brake pedal or lever, when properly adjusted, should travel the correct number of clicks when a 45 pound force is applied. See the Specifications in this Chapter.

2   If the parking brake pedal or lever travels less than the specified minimum number of clicks, it might not be releasing completely and the shoes could even be dragging against the drum. If it moves more than the specified maximum number of clicks, the parking brake may not hold adequately on an incline, allowing the car to roll.

ADJUSTMENT

▶ **Refer to illustration 11.4**

3   Loosen the rear wheel lug nuts. Raise the vehicle and support it securely on jackstands. Remove the rear wheels.

4   On pedal-equipped vehicles, loosen the cable adjusting nut under the instrument panel, then release the parking brake (see illustration).

5   On lever-equipped models, loosen the cable adjusting nut under the front of the lever using a ratchet and socket with a long extension. Release the parking brake.

6   Install three lug nuts snugly to each rear disc to support it against the hub flange.

7   Remove the rubber adjuster hole plugs from the discs (see illustration 12.4a).

8   Turn the star wheel downward until it locks the disc, then back it off five or six notches.

9   Turn the disc and make sure there is no drag. Readjust it if nec-

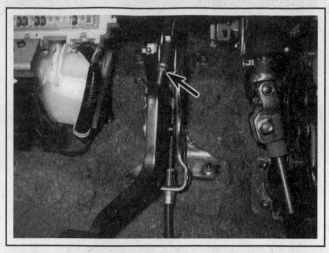

11.4 Parking brake cable adjusting nut - pedal-actuated type (trim panels removed for clarity)

essary to obtain a close adjustment with zero drag. Replace the hole plugs.

10   Tighten the adjusting nut (see Step 4 or 5) so you get the proper number of clicks when you apply a 45 pound force to the lever or pedal.

11   Release the parking brake and turn the rear discs again to verify that there is no drag. If drag exists, go over the adjustment procedure until it's correct.

12   Reinstall the wheels, lower the vehicle and tighten the lug nuts to the torque listed in Chapter 1.

12 Parking brake shoes - replacement

▶ **Refer to illustrations 12.4a through 12.4r**

1   Loosen the rear wheel lug nuts. Raise the vehicle and support it securely on jackstands. Remove the rear wheels.

2   Release the parking brake. Remove the discs (see Section 6).

3   Inspect the parking brake surfaces of each disc for wear or damage. Replace the discs if necessary.

4   Follow the accompanying photos (see illustrations 12.4a through 12.4r) for the actual parking brake shoe replacement procedure. Be sure to stay in order and read the caption under each illustration. Work on only one side at a time to avoid confusion.

5   Adjust the shoes (see Section 11).

6   When reinstalling the calipers, be sure to tighten the mounting bolts to the torque listed in this Chapter's Specifications.

7   The rest of the replacement procedure is the reverse of removal.

8   The parking brake pedal or lever may need adjustment in a few weeks after the parking brake shoes become seated.

12.4a If the disc can't be removed when the parking brake is fully released, you'll have to remove this rubber plug and use a screwdriver to turn the star wheel to retract the parking brake shoes

12.4b Wash the assembly with brake system cleaner; DO NOT blow off the brake dust with compressed air

12.4c Remove the upper spring . . .

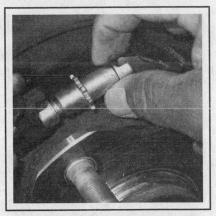

12.4d . . . then take out the adjuster

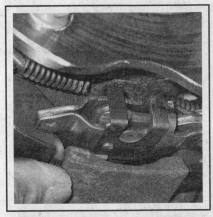

12.4e Use pliers to remove the lower spring

12.4f Turn the shoe hold-down springs to release them . . .

12.4g . . . then lift the shoe off

12.4h Do the same to the remaining shoe

12.4i After cleaning the backing plates, apply brake grease to the raised contact surfaces around the perimeter

12.4j Check the actuator assembly for wear or damage

12.4k Set the actuator assembly into place

12.4l Install the new parking brake shoes . . .

12.4m . . . and secure them with their hold-down springs

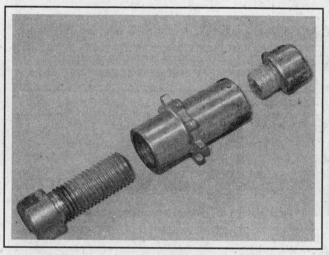

12.4n Disassemble the adjuster, clean it and lightly lubricate the threads with high-temperature brake grease

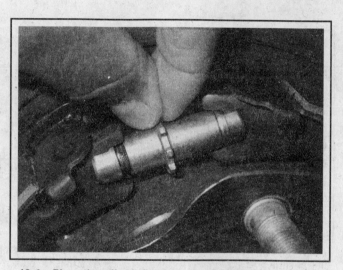

12.4o Place the adjuster between the shoes

12.4p Install the top spring . . .

12.4q . . . so that it engages the star wheel

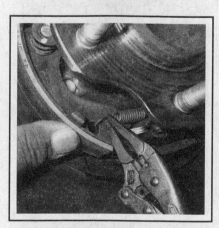

12.4r Attach the lower spring, then reinstall the disc and adjust the shoes as described in Section 11

13 Parking brake cables - replacement

PEDAL TYPE

Front cable

▶ Refer to illustrations 13.2 and 13.5

1   Loosen the rear wheel lug nuts. Raise the vehicle and support it securely on jackstands. Remove the rear wheels.
2   Remove the trim panels that cover the parking brake pedal (see Chapter 11). Remove the adjusting nut from the cable at the pedal (see illustration).
3   Remove the pedal assembly if necessary and detach the cable from it.
4   Remove the console (see Chapter 11).
5   Detach the front cable from the rear cables (see illustration).
6   Remove the front cable mounting fasteners and remove it.
7   Installation is the reverse of removal. Adjust the parking brakes (see Section 11).

Rear cables

▶ Refer to illustrations 13.10, 13.11 and 13.12

8   Raise the vehicle and support it securely on jackstands.
9   Disconnect the front cable from the rear cables at the center console (see Step 5).
10 Remove the heat shield from the center exhaust pipe (see illustration).
11 Remove the parking brake shoes (see Section 12), then disconnect the parking brake cables from the toggle levers (see illustration).
12 Remove the rear cable mounting bolts and detach them from the rear knuckles (see illustration).
13 Installation is the reverse of removal. Adjust the parking brakes (see Section 11).

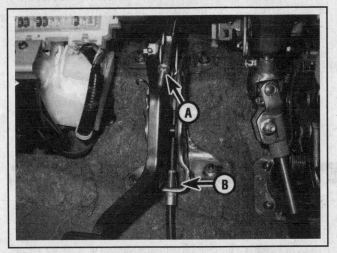

13.2 Remove the parking brake cable adjusting nut (A), then use pliers to pinch the tangs of the cable housing (B) to detach the cable from the pedal bracket

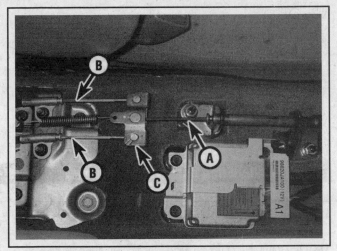

13.5 On models with a parking brake pedal, the front cable (A) connects to the rear cables (B) under the console at the equalizer (C)

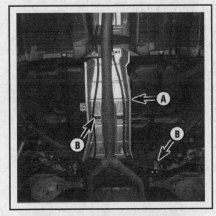

13.10 Heat shield (A) and typical parking brake cable retainers (B)

13.11 Remove this pin to disconnect the parking brake cable from the rear brake assembly

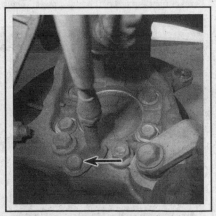

13.12 Parking brake cable-to-rear brake mounting bolt

LEVER TYPE

14 Loosen the rear wheel lug nuts. Raise the vehicle and support it securely on jackstands. Remove the rear wheels.

15 Remove the center console (see Chapter 11).

16 Disconnect the parking brake switch wiring.

17 Remove the two cable housing nuts just behind the equalizer and disengage the cables from the equalizer.

18 Remove the heat shield from the center exhaust pipe.

19 Remove the parking brake shoes (see Section 12), then disconnect the parking brake cables from the toggle levers (see illustration 13.11).

20 Remove the rear cable mounting bolts and detach them from the rear knuckles (see illustration 13.12).

21 Installation is the reverse of removal. Adjust the parking brakes (see Section 11).

14 Brake pedal - adjustment

1 With the brake pedal fully released, measure the distance from the top of the pad to the floor with the carpet and padding removed. Measure at a right angle to the floor.

2 If the height is not as listed in this Chapter's Specifications, it must be adjusted.

3 Release the brake light and cruise control cancel switches by turning them counterclockwise 45 degrees.

4 Loosen the lock nut just in front of the power brake booster clevis

(see illustration 10.11a).

5 Turn the booster input rod until the pedal height is correct.

6 Tighten the lock nut.

7 With the threaded portion of the brake light and cruise control cancel switches contacting the bracket, turn the switches 45 degrees clockwise to lock them in place.

8 Adjust the brake light and cruise control switches if necessary (see Section 15).

15 Brake light and cruise control cancel switches - adjustment and replacement

➡ Note: The cruise control cancel switch is also known as the ASCD (Automatic Speed Control Device) switch.

ADJUSTMENT

▸ Refer to illustration 15.6

1 The brake light and cruise control cancel switches are located on a bracket near the top of the brake pedal. The switches activate the brake

lights at the rear of the vehicle when the pedal is depressed and cancel the cruise control operation.

2 To check the brake light switch, simply note whether the brake lights come on when the pedal is depressed and go off when the pedal is released.

3 If the brake lights don't come on or the cruise control doesn't cancel when the brake pedal is depressed, make sure the brake pedal is correctly adjusted (see Section 14), then try adjusting the switch as follows.

4 Release the switch by turning it counterclockwise 45-degrees.

5 Pull the brake pedal back and hold it there, then push the switch into its bracket until the body of the switch (threaded portion) touches its stop.

6 Turn the switch 45-degrees clockwise to lock it in place. The distance from the pedal and the threaded part of the switch should be as listed in this Chapter's Specifications (see illustration).

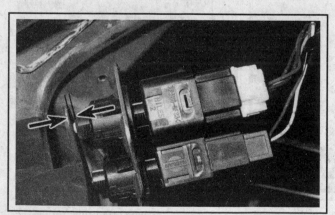

15.6 The clearance between the threaded body of the switch and the pedal bracket must be as shown in the Specifications

REPLACEMENT

7 Unplug the electrical connector from the switch.

8 Turn the switch 45-degrees counterclockwise, pull the switch to the rear and remove it.

9 Installation is the reverse of removal.

10 Adjust the brake pedal height (see Section 14), then adjust the switch (see Steps 4 through 6).

Specifications

General

Brake fluid type	See Chapter 1

Disc brakes

Minimum pad thickness	See Chapter 1
Brake disc minimum thickness*	
Front	0.945 inch
Rear	0.315 inch
Maximum disc runout	
Front	0.0016 inch
Rear	0.002 inch
Maximum disc thickness variation	0.0006 inch

*If different specifications are cast into the disc, they supersede information printed here

Power brake booster

Booster-to-clevis hole center dimension	4.92 (+/- 0.02) inches

Brake pedal dimensions

Free height from steel floor to top of pedal	
Manual transaxle models	7.14 to 7.61 inches
Automatic transaxle models	7.51 to 7.98 inches

Parking brake

Parking brake adjustment	
Foot pedal design	4 to 5 clicks
Hand lever design	5 to 7 clicks
Minimum lining thickness	0.059 inch

Brake light and cruise control cancel switches

Clearance between pedal bracket and threaded part of switch	0.03 to 0.08 inch

Torque specifications   Ft-lbs (unless otherwise indicated)

➡ Note: One foot-pound (ft-lb) of torque is equivalent to 12 inch-pounds (in-lbs) of torque. Torque values below approximately 15 foot-pounds are expressed in inch-pounds, since most foot-pound torque wrenches are not accurate at these smaller values.

Brake caliper	
Caliper mounting bolts	
Front	20
Rear	32
Caliper mounting bracket bolts	
Front	98
Rear	62
Brake hose-to-caliper banjo bolt	156 in-lbs
Master cylinder-to-brake booster retaining nuts	132 in-lbs
Power brake booster mounting nuts	120 in-lbs

Notes

Section

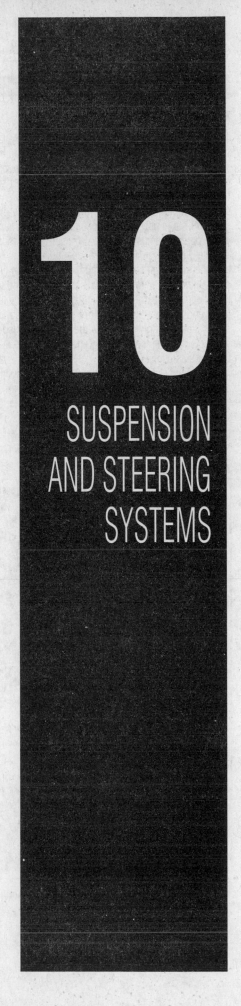

Reference to other Chapters

10

SUSPENSION
AND STEERING
SYSTEMS

1   General information

▶ **Refer to illustrations 1.1, 1.2a and 1.2b**

The front suspension system (see illustration) is a strut/coil spring design. The upper end of each strut is attached to the vehicle body. The lower end of the strut is connected to the upper end of the steering knuckle. The steering knuckle is attached to a balljoint mounted on the outer end of the control arm. The balljoint is an integral part of the control arm; if the balljoint is worn, the control arm must be replaced. A stabilizer bar is used on all models. The bar is attached to the subframe with a pair of clamps and to the struts with link rods.

The rear suspension system (see illustrations) uses separate shock absorbers and coil springs, an upper suspension arm and two lower suspension arms (front and rear) and a radius rod at each corner. The upper ends of the shocks are attached to the vehicle body and their lower ends are attached to the upper ends of the rear knuckles. The coil springs are positioned between the lower rear suspension arm and the vehicle body. The lower ends of the knuckles are attached to the outer ends of the suspension arms. A stabilizer bar is attached to the subframe by a pair of brackets and to the upper suspension arms by link rods.

The rack-and-pinion steering gear is bolted to the rear part of the subframe. The steering gear actuates the tie-rods, which are attached to the steering knuckles. The inner ends of the tie-rods are protected by rubber boots which should be inspected periodically for secure attachment, tears and leaking lubricant (which would indicate failed rack seals).

The power assist system consists of a belt-driven pump and associated lines and hoses. The fluid level in the power steering pump reservoir should be checked periodically (see Chapter 1).

The steering wheel operates the steering shaft, which actuates the steering gear through universal joints. Looseness in the steering can be caused by wear in the steering shaft universal joints, the steering gear, the tie-rod ends and loose retaining bolts.

Frequently, when working on the suspension or steering system components, you may come across fasteners which seem impossible to loosen. These fasteners on the underside of the vehicle are continually subjected to water, road grime, mud, etc., and can become rusted or frozen, making them extremely difficult to remove. In order to unscrew these stubborn fasteners without damaging them (or other components), be sure to use lots of penetrating oil and allow it to soak in for a while. Using a wire brush to clean exposed threads will also ease removal of the nut or bolt and prevent damage to the threads. Sometimes a sharp blow with a hammer and punch will break the bond between a nut and bolt threads, but care must be taken to prevent the punch from slipping off the fastener and ruining the threads. Heating the stuck fastener and surrounding area with a torch sometimes helps too, but isn't recommended because of the obvious dangers associated with fire. Long

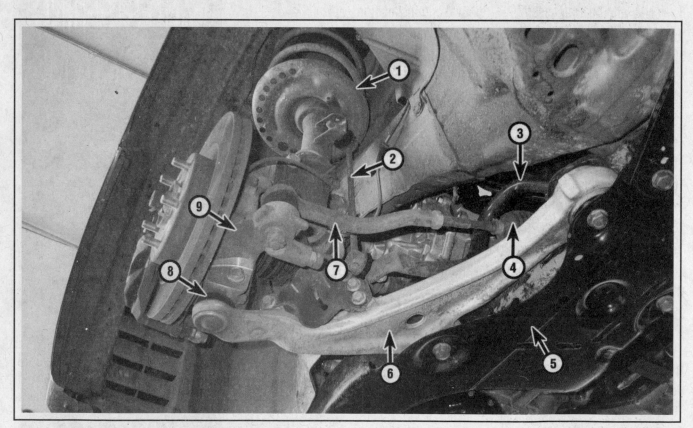

1.1 Front suspension and steering components

1	Strut/coil spring assembly	4	Steering gear boot	7	Tie-rod end
2	Stabilizer bar link	5	Subframe	8	Balljoint
3	Stabilizer bar	6	Control arm	9	Steering knuckle

1.2a Typical rear suspension components

1	Stabilizer bar	3	Lower front suspension arm
2	Lower rear suspension arm and coil spring seat	4	Radius rod

5   Subframe

breaker bars and extension, or cheater, pipes will increase leverage, but never use an extension pipe on a ratchet - the ratcheting mechanism could be damaged. Sometimes tightening the nut or bolt first will help to break it loose. Fasteners that require drastic measures to remove should always be replaced with new ones.

Since most of the procedures dealt with in this Chapter involve jacking up the vehicle and working underneath it, a good pair of jackstands will be needed. A hydraulic floor jack is the preferred type of jack to lift the vehicle, and it can also be used to support certain components during various operations.

❋❋ WARNING:

Never, under any circumstances, rely on a jack to support the vehicle while working on it. Whenever any of the suspension or steering fasteners are loosened or removed they must be inspected and, if necessary, replaced with new ones of the same part number or of original equipment quality and design. Torque specifications must be followed for proper reassembly and component retention. Never attempt to heat or straighten any suspension or steering components. Instead, replace any bent or damaged part with a new one.

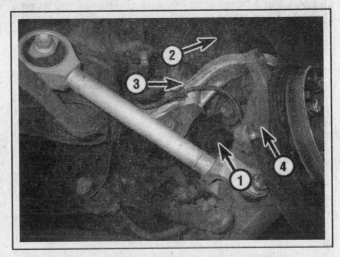

1.2b Typical rear suspension components - side view

1	Coil spring	3	Upper suspension arm
2	Shock absorber	4	Knuckle and hub assembly

2 Strut/coil spring assembly (front) - removal, inspection and installation

REMOVAL

▶ **Refer to illustrations 2.2, 2.4 and 2.7**

1   Loosen the front wheel lug nuts, raise the front of the vehicle and support it securely on jackstands. Remove the wheels.

2   If the vehicle is equipped with ABS, detach the speed sensor wiring harness from the strut (see illustration).

3   Remove the clip retaining the brake hose to the strut and detach the hose from the bracket.

4   Disconnect the stabilizer bar link from the strut (see illustration).

5   Remove the strut-to-knuckle nuts and knock the bolts out with a hammer and punch.

6   Separate the strut from the steering knuckle. Be careful not to overextend the inner CV joint and don't let the knuckle fall outward, as this could damage the brake hose and the ABS speed sensor wiring (if equipped).

7   Support the strut and spring assembly with one hand and remove the three strut upper mounting bolts (see illustration). Remove the assembly out from the fenderwell.

INSPECTION

8   Check the strut body for leaking fluid, dents, cracks and other obvious damage which would warrant repair or replacement.

9   Check the coil spring for chips or cracks in the spring coating (this will cause premature spring failure due to corrosion). Inspect the spring seat for cuts, hardness and general deterioration.

10 If any undesirable conditions exist, proceed to the strut disassembly procedure (see Section 3).

INSTALLATION

11 Guide the strut assembly up into the fenderwell and install the upper mounting bolts, tightening them to the torque listed in this Chapter's Specifications. This is most easily accomplished with the help of an assistant, as the strut is quite heavy and awkward.

12 Slide the steering knuckle into the strut flange and insert the bolts. Install the nuts and tighten them to the torque listed in this Chapter's Specifications.

13 The remainder of the installation procedure is the reverse of removal. Tighten the stabilizer bar link nut to the torque listed in this Chapter's Specifications. Tighten the wheel lug nuts to the torque listed in the Chapter 1 Specifications.

14 Have the front end alignment checked and, if necessary, adjusted.

2.2 Strut lower mounting details

1   ABS wheel speed sensor harness brackets
2   Brake hose retaining clip
3   Strut-to-steering knuckle nuts/bolts

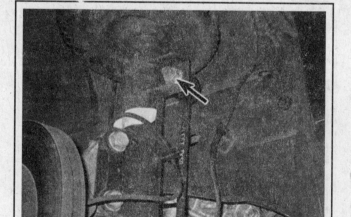

2.4 Stabilizer bar link-to-strut nut

2.7 Strut upper mounting bolts. Warning: Don't unscrew the piston rod nut (the nut in the center of the strut tower)

3 Strut/coil spring assembly (front) - replacement

1   If the struts or coil springs exhibit the telltale signs of wear (leaking fluid, loss of damping capability, chipped, sagging or cracked coil springs) explore all options before beginning any work. The strut/shock absorber assemblies are not serviceable and must be replaced if a problem develops. However, strut assemblies complete with springs may be available on an exchange basis, which eliminates much time and work. Whichever route you choose to take, check on the cost and availability of parts before disassembling your vehicle.

✳✳ WARNING:

Disassembling a strut is a potentially dangerous undertaking and utmost attention must be directed to the job, or serious injury may result. Use only a high-quality spring compressor and carefully follow the manufacturer's instructions furnished with the tool. After removing the coil spring from the strut assembly, set it aside in a safe, isolated area.

DISASSEMBLY

▶ **Refer to illustrations 3.3, 3.4, 3.5 and 3.7**

2   Remove the strut and spring assembly (see Section 2). Mount the strut assembly in a vise. Line the vise jaws with wood or rags to prevent damage to the unit and don't tighten the vise excessively.

3   Following the tool manufacturer's instructions, install the spring compressor (which can be obtained at most auto parts stores or equipment yards on a daily rental basis) on the spring and compress it sufficiently to relieve all pressure from the upper spring seat (see illustration). This can be verified by wiggling the spring.

4   Remove the piston rod nut (see illustration).

5   Remove the upper suspension support (see illustration). Inspect the bearing in the suspension support for smooth operation. If it does not turn smoothly, replace the suspension support. Check the rubber portion of the suspension support for cracking and general deterioration. If there is any separation of the rubber, replace it.

6   Lift the spring seat and upper insulator from the piston rod. Check the rubber spring seat for cracking and hardness, replacing it if necessary.

7   Carefully lift the compressed spring from the assembly (see illustration) and set it in a safe place.

✳✳ WARNING:

Carry the spring carefully and never place any part of your body near the end of the spring!

8   Slide the dust boot off the piston rod.

9   Check the lower insulator (if equipped) for wear, cracking and hardness and replace it if necessary.

3.3 Install the spring compressor according to the tool manufacturer's instructions and compress the spring until all pressure is relieved from the upper spring seat

3.4 Remove the piston rod nut

3.5 Remove the upper suspension support mount and spring seat

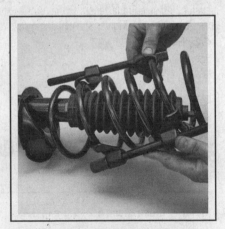

3.7 Remove the compressed spring assembly. Warning: Keep the ends of the spring pointed away from your body

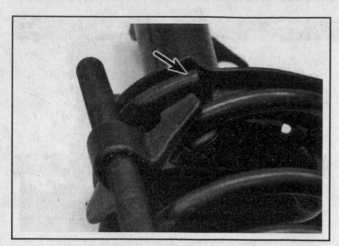

3.11 When installing the spring, make sure the end fits into the recessed portion of the lower seat

REASSEMBLY

▶ **Refer to illustration 3.11**

10 If the lower insulator is being replaced, set it into position with the dropped portion seated in the lowest part of the seat. Extend the damper rod to its full length and install the dust boot.

11 Place the coil spring onto the lower insulator, with the end of the spring resting in the lowest part of the insulator (see illustration).

12 Install the upper insulator and the spring seat. Make sure the marks or arrow on the spring seat and mount insulator are facing out (away from the vehicle), in line with the strut-to-knuckle flange.

13 Install the dust seal and suspension support to the piston rod.

14 Install the nut and tighten it to the torque listed in this Chapter's Specifications.

15 Install the strut/shock absorber and coil spring assembly (see Section 2).

4 Stabilizer bar (front) - removal and installation

▶ **Refer to illustration 4.4**

1 Loosen the wheel lug nuts, raise the front of the vehicle, support it securely on jackstands and remove the wheels.

2 Remove the steering gear (see Section 19).

3 Detach the stabilizer bar links from the struts (see illustration 2.4).

4 Remove the bolts from the stabilizer bar clamps (see illustration) and remove the stabilizer bar.

5 Inspect the clamp bushings and the link bushings. If they're cracked or torn, replace them.

➡ **Note: When installing new bushings, the slit in the bushing should face the rear of the vehicle. Also, be sure to install the clamps in the original positions.**

6 Installation is the reverse of removal. Be sure to tighten all suspension and steering fasteners to the torque values listed in this Chapter's Specifications. Tighten the wheel lug nuts to the torque listed in the Chapter 1 Specifications.

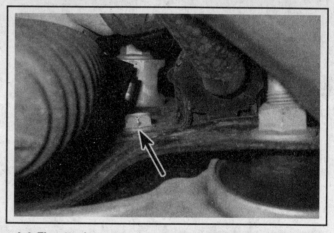

4.4 The steering gear must be removed in order to access the stabilizer bar - front clamp bolt shown

5 Control arm (front) - removal, inspection and installation

REMOVAL

▶ **Refer to illustrations 5.2, 5.3 and 5.4**

1 Loosen the wheel lug nuts, raise the front of the vehicle, support it securely on jackstands and remove the wheel.

2 Remove the balljoint pinch bolt (see illustration).

3 Separate the balljoint stud from the steering knuckle (see illustration).

4 Remove the control arm bushing bolt nuts and bolts (see illustra-

tion). Remove the control arm.

INSPECTION

5 Inspect the front and rear bushings for cracks and tears. If either bushing is damaged or worn, replace the control arm; the bushings are not replaceable.

6 Inspect the control arm for straightness. If it's bent, replace it. Do not attempt to straighten a bent control arm.

5.2 Remove this balljoint pinch bolt . . .

5.3 . . . then pry the balljoint out of the steering knuckle, taking care to avoid damaging the rubber boot

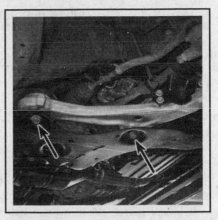

5.4 Control arm bushing bolts

INSTALLATION

7   Installation is the reverse of removal. Tighten all of the fasteners to the torque listed in this Chapter's Specifications.

8   Install the wheel and lug nuts, lower the vehicle and tighten the lug nuts to the torque listed in the Chapter 1 Specifications.

9   It's a good idea to have the front wheel alignment checked and, if necessary, adjusted after this job has been performed.

6   Balljoints - replacement

The balljoint is an integral part of the control arm. If it's worn or damaged, the control arm must be replaced (see Section 5).

7   Steering knuckle - removal and installation

✳ WARNING:

Dust created by the brake system is harmful to your health. Never blow it out with compressed air and don't inhale any of it. Do not, under any circumstances, use petroleum-based solvents to clean brake parts. Use brake system cleaner only.

REMOVAL

1   Remove the cotter pin, then loosen the driveaxle/hub nut (see Chapter 8).

2   Loosen the wheel lug nuts, raise the vehicle and support it securely on jackstands. Remove the wheel.

3   Remove the brake disc (see Chapter 9).

4   Remove the wheel speed sensor from the knuckle.

5   Remove the driveaxle/hub nut.

6   Separate the tie-rod end from the steering knuckle (see Section 17).

7   Remove the strut-to-steering knuckle nuts, but don't remove the bolts yet (see Section 2).

8   Separate the control arm balljoint from the steering knuckle (see Section 5).

9   Separate the driveaxle from the steering knuckle (see Chapter 8). Support the end of the driveaxle with a length of wire so the CV joints aren't overextended.

10   Remove the strut-to-knuckle bolts and separate the knuckle from the strut.

11   Remove the hub-to-steering knuckle bolts, then detach the two components and remove the brake disc splash shield.

INSTALLATION

12   Assemble the hub, knuckle and splash shield. Tighten the bolts to the torque listed in this Chapter's Specifications.

13   Lubricate the splines of the driveaxle with multi-purpose grease. Guide the knuckle and hub assembly into position, inserting the driveaxle into the hub.

14   Push the knuckle into the strut flange and install the bolts and nuts, but don't tighten them yet.

15   Attach the control arm balljoint to the steering knuckle (see Section 5).

16   Attach the tie-rod end to the steering knuckle arm (see Section 17). Tighten the tie-rod end nut and the strut-to-knuckle nuts to the torque listed in this Chapter's Specifications. Install a new cotter pin through the tie-rod end ballstud.

17   Place the brake disc on the hub and install the caliper (see Chapter 9).

18   Install the driveaxle/hub nut and tighten it to the torque listed in the Chapter 8 Specifications.

19   Install the wheel and lug nuts. Lower the vehicle and tighten the lug nuts to the torque listed in the Chapter 1 Specifications.

8 Hub and bearing assembly - removal and installation

FRONT

▶ **Refer to illustration 8.5**

1 Loosen the driveaxle/hub nut (see Chapter 8).

2 Loosen the wheel lug nuts, raise the front of the vehicle and support it securely on jackstands. Remove the wheel.

3 Remove the brake disc (see Chapter 9).

4 Remove the driveaxle/hub nut.

5 Remove the hub/bearing assembly mounting bolts from the rear of the steering knuckle (see illustration).

6 Remove the hub/bearing assembly from the steering knuckle.

➡**Note: If the driveaxle splines stick in the hub, push the driveaxle out of the hub with a two-jaw puller.**

Once the driveaxle has been freed from the hub, support it with a length of wire to prevent overextension of the inner CV joint.

7 Installation is the reverse of removal. Be sure to tighten all fasteners to the proper torque values.

REAR

▶ **Refer to illustration 8.11**

8 Loosen the wheel lug nuts. Raise the rear of the vehicle and support it securely on jackstands. Remove the wheel.

9 Remove the brake disc (see Chapter 9).

10 Remove the wheel speed sensor (see Chapter 9).

11 Remove the hub and bearing assembly mounting bolts (see illustration).

12 Remove the hub and bearing assembly.

13 Installation is the reverse of removal. Be sure to tighten all fasteners to the proper torque values.

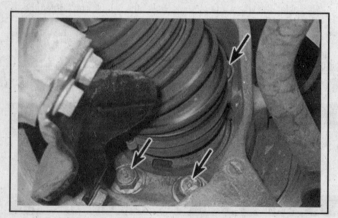

8.5 Front hub and bearing mounting bolts (fourth bolt not visible in this photo)

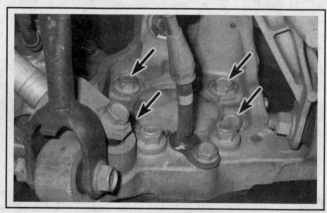

8.11 Rear hub and bearing mounting bolts

9 Stabilizer bar (rear) - removal and installation

▶ **Refer to illustrations 9.2 and 9.3**

1 Raise the vehicle and support it securely on jackstands.

2 Remove the nuts from the link rods at the stabilizer bar ends (see illustration).

3 Remove the bushing clamp nuts (see illustration) and remove the stabilizer.

4 Inspect all clamp bushings. If they're cracked or torn, replace them.

5 Installation is the reverse of removal. Be sure to tighten all fasteners to the torques listed in this Chapter's Specifications.

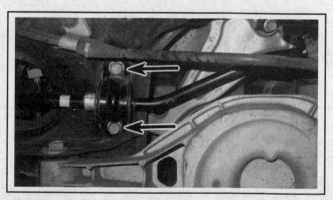

9.2 Rear stabilizer bar link nuts

9.3 Rear stabilizer bar clamp bolts

10 Knuckle (rear) - removal and installation

◆ **Refer to illustrations 10.5, 10.7 and 10.8**

1   Loosen the rear wheel lug nuts. Raise the rear of the vehicle and support it securely on jackstands. Block the front wheels to prevent the vehicle from rolling. Remove the wheel.

2   Remove the caliper and disc (see Chapter 9).

3   Remove the hub and bearing assembly (see Section 9).

4   Remove the brake backing plate.

5   Support the lower control arm with a floor jack positioned under the coil spring pocket (see illustration).

※※ WARNING:

The jack must remain in this position throughout the entire procedure.

6   Detach the radius rod from the knuckle (see Section 14).

7   Disconnect the front and rear lower suspension arms from the knuckle (see illustration).

8   Disconnect the upper suspension arm from the knuckle (see Section 13) (see illustration).

9   Disconnect the lower shock mounting bolt and nut from the knuckle (see Section 12).

10 Remove the knuckle from the vehicle.

11 Installation is the reverse of removal. Be sure to tighten all fasteners to the torque listed in this Chapter's Specifications.

➡**Note: Before tightening the radius arm fasteners, the lower arm-to-knuckle fasteners and the shock absorber lower mounting fasteners, raise the rear lower arm with the floor jack to simulate normal ride height.**

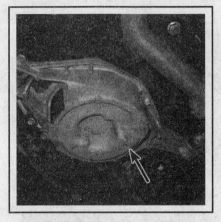

10.5 Support the rear lower control arm with a floor jack positioned under the spring pocket

10.7 With the rear lower arm supported by a floor jack, remove these fasteners and detach both lower control arms from the knuckle

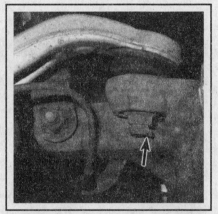

10.8 Remove the cotter pin, then use a balljoint separator to release the upper arm balljoint stud from the knuckle

11 Coil springs (rear) - removal and installation

◆ **Refer to illustration 11.3**

1   Loosen the rear wheel lug nuts, raise the rear of the vehicle, support it securely on jackstands and remove the wheels.

2   Position a floor jack under the lower rear suspension arm and raise the suspension arm slightly (see illustration 10.5).

3   Mark the relationship of the adjusting cam to the subframe (see illustration), then remove the bolt for the rear lower suspension arm at the subframe.

4   Loosen the bolt and nut for the lower rear suspension arm at the knuckle (see illustration 10.7).

5   Carefully lower the suspension arm using the floor jack until the coil spring is fully extended.

6   Remove the coil spring, the rubber mount and the rubber seal.

7   Installation is the reverse of removal, noting the following points:

a) *Raise the lower suspension arm with a floor jack until it is at normal ride height, then tighten the suspension arm bolt/nuts to the torque listed in this Chapter's Specifications. Be sure to align the marks on the adjusting cam and the subframe before tightening the fasteners.*

11.3 Mark the position of the cam to the subframe before loosening the bolt

b) *Tighten the wheel lug nuts to the torque listed in the Chapter 1 Specifications.*

12 Shock absorbers (rear) - removal and installation

▶ Refer to illustrations 12.3 and 12.4

❈❈ WARNING:

Always replace the shock absorbers in pairs - never replace just one of them.

1 Loosen the rear wheel lug nuts. Raise the rear of the vehicle and support it securely on jackstands. Block the front wheels to prevent the vehicle from rolling. Remove the wheel.

2 Support the lower rear suspension arm with a floor jack placed under the coil spring pocket.

❈❈ WARNING:

The jack must remain in this position until the shock absorber is reinstalled.

3 Remove the shock absorber upper mounting nuts (see illustration).

4 Remove the shock absorber lower mounting bolt and nut and remove the shock absorber (see illustration).

5 To install the shock absorber, reverse the removal procedure.

6 Raise the lower suspension arm with the jack to simulate normal ride height, then tighten the mounting fasteners to the torque listed in this Chapter's Specifications.

7 Install the wheel and lug nuts. Lower the vehicle and tighten the lug nuts to the torque listed in the Chapter 1 Specifications.

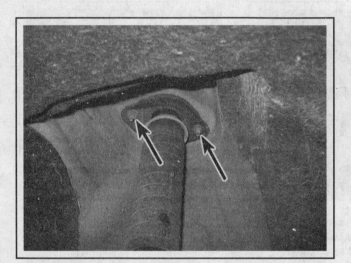

12.3 Remove these nuts from the top of the rear shock absorber

12.4 Lower rear shock absorber mounting bolt

13 Rear suspension arms and rear subframe - removal and installation

1 Loosen the rear wheel lug nuts. Raise the rear of the vehicle and support it securely on jackstands. Remove the wheel.

REAR LOWER SUSPENSION ARM

2 Remove the coil spring (see Section 11).

3 Remove the lower arm-to-knuckle mounting bolt/nut.

4 Remove the lower rear suspension arm from the vehicle.

5 Installation is the reverse of removal, noting the following points:

a) Raise the lower suspension arm with a floor jack until it is at normal ride height, then tighten the suspension arm bolt/nuts to the torque listed in this Chapter's Specifications. Be sure to align the marks on the adjusting cam and the subframe before tightening the bolt/nut.

b) Tighten the wheel lug nuts to the torque listed in the Chapter 1 Specifications.

FRONT LOWER SUSPENSION ARM

▶ Refer to illustration 13.7

6 Support the rear lower suspension arm with a floor jack placed under the coil spring pocket.

❈❈ WARNING:

The jack must remain in this position until the arm is reinstalled.

7 Mark the relationship of the adjusting cam to the subframe (see illustration). Remove the lower front suspension arm-to-subframe mounting bolt/nut and the lower front suspension arm-to-knuckle mounting bolt/nut.

8 Remove the arm from the vehicle.

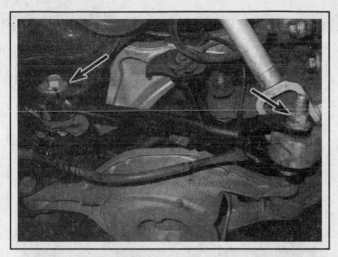

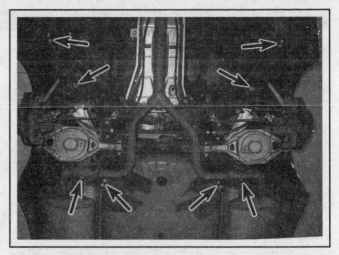

13.7 Front lower suspension arm fasteners. Mark the position of the cam to the subframe before loosening the inner pivot bolt

13.23 Rear subframe mounting points

9   Installation is the reverse of removal, noting the following points:

a) *Raise the lower suspension arm with a floor jack until it is at normal ride height, then tighten the suspension arm bolt/nuts to the torque listed in this Chapter's Specifications. Be sure to align the marks on the adjusting cam and the subframe before tightening the bolt/nut.*

b) *Tighten the wheel lug nuts to the torque listed in the Chapter 1 Specifications.*

UPPER SUSPENSION ARM AND REAR SUBFRAME

▶ **Refer to illustrations 13.23 and 13.25**

10 Raise the vehicle and support it securely on jackstands.

11 Remove the rear wheel speed sensors.

12 Remove the rear wheel brake calipers (see Chapter 9). Hang them out of the way with wire so the hoses aren't under stress. Remove the brake discs.

13 Disconnect the parking brake cables from the knuckles (see Chapter 9).

14 Remove the nuts from the lower shock absorber mounts.

15 Remove the lower rear suspension arms (see Steps 2 through 4).

16 Remove the cotter pins and nuts from the upper suspension arm balljoint.

17 Disconnect the radius rods from the subframe (see Section 14).

18 Remove the front lower suspension arms (see Steps 6 through 8).

19 Remove the knuckles (see Section 10).

20 Remove the stabilizer bar (see Section 8).

21 Disconnect the wiring harness from the rear subframe and upper arms.

22 Place two floor jacks under the rear subframe so it is securely supported.

23 Remove the subframe mounting bolts, then carefully lower the rear subframe a little at a time until it is clear of the body of the vehicle (see illustration).

13.25 Upper suspension arm pivot bolts

24 Remove the stabilizer bar brackets from the upper suspension arms.

25 Remove the upper suspension arm mounting nuts and bolts (see illustration). Remove the upper suspension arms.

26 Installation is the reverse of removal, noting the following points:

a) *Tighten the balljoint stud nut to the torque figure listed in this Chapter's Specifications, then install a new cotter pin.*

b) *With the rear suspension supported by jackstands, raise the lower suspension arm with a floor jack until it is at normal ride height, then tighten the pivot bolt nuts to the torque listed in this Chapter's Specifications.*

c) *Tighten all other fasteners to the torques listed in this Chapter's Specifications.*

14 Radius rod (rear) - removal and installation

▶ **Refer to illustration 14.2**

1   Loosen the rear wheel lug nuts. Raise the rear of the vehicle and support it securely on jackstands. Block the front wheels to prevent the vehicle from rolling. Remove the wheel.

2   Remove the radius rod-to-subframe mounting bolt/nut and the radius rod-to-knuckle mounting bolt/nut (see illustration).

3   Remove the radius rod from the vehicle.

4   Installation is the reverse of removal, noting the following points:

   a) *Raise the rear lower suspension arm with a floor jack until it is at normal ride height, then tighten the radius rod fasteners to the torque listed in this Chapter's Specifications.*

   b) *Tighten the wheel lug nuts to the torque listed in the Chapter 1 Specifications.*

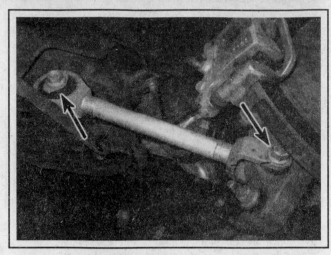

14.2 Rear radius rod mounting fasteners

15 Subframe (front) - removal and installation

▶ **Refer to illustration 15.13**

➡ **Note: This procedure applies only to four-cylinder models and V6 manual transmission models. On V6 models with automatic transmissions, the front subframe can only be removed together with the engine and transmission as a complete assembly.**

1   Disconnect the cable from the negative terminal of the battery (see Chapter 5).

2   Loosen the front wheel lug nuts, raise the front of the vehicle and support it securely on jackstands. Remove both front wheels.

➡ **Note: The jackstands must be behind the front suspension subframe, not supporting the vehicle by the subframe.**

3   Remove the engine splash shield and the wheel wells

4   On V6 models, remove the air filter housing and the inlet air duct.

5   Detach the stabilizer bar links from the struts.

6   Remove the front exhaust pipe.

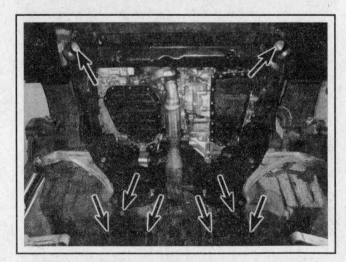

15.13 Front subframe mounting fasteners

7   Roll an engine hoist into position and attach it to the engine with a couple pieces of heavy-duty chain (an engine support fixture could be used instead). If the engine is equipped with lifting brackets, use them. If not, you'll have to fasten the chain to some substantial part of the engine - one that is strong enough to take the weight, but in a location that will provide good balance. If you're attaching the chain to a stud on the engine, or are using a bolt passing through the chain and into a threaded hole, place a washer between the nut or bolt head and the chain, and tighten the nut or bolt securely. Take up the slack in the chain, but don't lift the engine.

❋❋ **WARNING:**

DO NOT place any part of your body under the engine when it's supported only by a hoist or other lifting device.

8   Disconnect the wiring from the power steering gear.

9   Remove the steering gear mounting bolts, then remove the steering gear and the bracket from the subframe. Hang the gear out of the way with wire.

10   Unbolt the front and rear engine mounts. On V6 models, disconnect the vacuum hoses from the mounts.

11   Remove the bolts that secure the subframe braces to the body.

12   Using two floor jacks, support the subframe. Position one jack on each side of the subframe, midway between the front and rear mounting points.

13   With the floor jacks sufficiently supporting the subframe, remove the four subframe-to-chassis mounting bolts (see illustration).

14   Lower the jacks until the subframe is sufficiently resting on blocks.

15   Installation is the reverse of removal.

16   Reconnect the battery and perform the necessary re-learn procedures (see Chapter 5).

17   Have the front wheel alignment checked, and, if necessary, adjusted.

16 Steering wheel - removal and installation

✷✷ WARNING:

The models covered by this manual are equipped with Supplemental Restraint Systems (SRS), more commonly known as airbags. Always disarm the airbag system before working in the vicinity of any airbag system component to avoid the possibility of accidental deployment of the airbag, which could cause personal injury (see Chapter 12). Do not use a memory saving device to preserve the PCM's memory when working on or near airbag system components.

REMOVAL

◆ Refer to illustrations 16.2a, 16.2b, 16.3, 16.5, 16.6 and 16.7

1   Disconnect the cable from the negative terminal of the battery (see Chapter 5).
2   Pry off the steering wheel side covers, then remove the airbag bolts (see illustrations).

✷✷ WARNING:

The manufacturer recommends replacing these bolts with new ones (of original part number) whenever they are removed.

3   Lift the airbag module and disconnect the electrical connectors (see illustration).
➡Note: Use a small screwdriver to lift the lock button on each connector before trying to disconnect them.
4   Set the airbag module out of the way.

✷✷ WARNING:

Handle the airbag module with care, carry the module with the trim cover side facing away from your body and store it in a safe location with the trim side facing up. See the precautions in Chapter 12.

5   Unplug the remaining electrical connector (see illustration).
6   Remove the steering wheel retaining nut, then mark the relationship of the steering wheel to the steering shaft (see illustration).

16.2a Pop off these plastic covers . . .

16.2b . . . then unscrew the airbag bolts

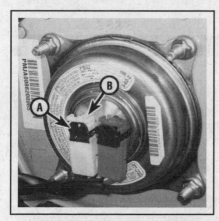

16.3 Pry up the locking clip (A), detach the electrical connector (B) from each terminal . . .

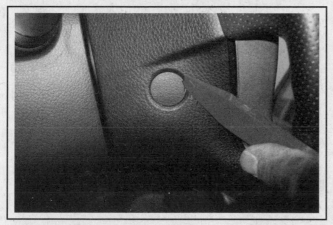

16.5 . . . then unplug this electrical connector

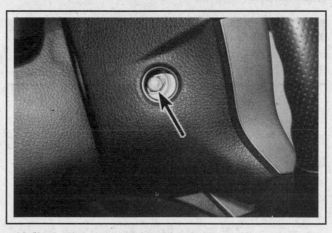

16.6 If your vehicle doesn't have steering wheel alignment marks like these, make your own

16.7 Use a steering wheel puller to break it loose from the steering shaft. Caution: Do not hammer on the steering wheel or shaft to break it loose

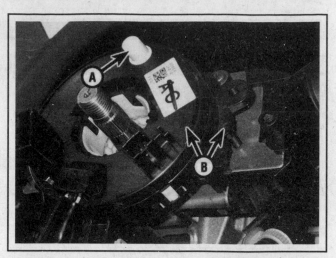

16.8 These two arrows (A) on the surface of the spiral cable housing will be aligned when it's centered; the white locating pin (B) must be at the top

7   Use a steering wheel puller to separate the steering wheel from the steering shaft (see illustration). When removing the wheel, make sure the electrical leads for the airbag module and the cruise control system don't snag on the wheel.

✳✳ WARNING:

Do not turn the steering shaft while the steering wheel is removed.

INSTALLATION

▶ **Refer to illustration 16.8**

8   Verify that the front wheels are pointing straight ahead. If the spiral cable for the airbag has been removed and/or its center position lost, turn the spiral cable clockwise by hand until it becomes hard to turn (don't apply too much force), then rotate it about two turns counter-clockwise until the marks align and the location pin is straight up at the 12 o'clock position (see illustration).

9   Pull the electrical leads for the airbag module and the cruise control system through the steering wheel and install the wheel. Make sure the spiral cable pin is properly engaged with the corresponding hole in the back of the steering wheel and pull the spiral cable through.

10 Install the steering wheel retaining nut and tighten it to the torque listed in this Chapter's Specifications.

11 Install the airbag module, tightening the bolts to the torque listed in this Chapter's Specifications. Install the covers.

12 Reconnect the battery and perform the necessary re-learn procedures (see Chapter 5).

13 Verify that the airbag circuit is operational by turning the ignition key to the On or Start position. The "AIR BAG" warning light should illuminate for a few seconds, then turn off.

17   Tie-rod ends - removal and installation

REMOVAL

▶ **Refer to illustrations 17.2, 17.3 and 17.4**

1   Loosen the wheel lug nuts. Raise the front of the vehicle, support it securely on jackstands, then remove the front wheel.

2   Loosen the jam nut enough to mark the position of the tie-rod end in relation to the threads (see illustration).

3   Remove the cotter pin and loosen, but don't remove, the nut on the tie-rod end stud (see illustration).

4   Disconnect the tie-rod end from the steering knuckle arm with a puller (see illustration). Remove the nut and separate the tie-rod.

5   Unscrew the tie-rod end from the steering rod.

INSTALLATION

6   Thread the tie-rod end on to the marked position and insert the tie-rod stud into the steering knuckle arm. Tighten the jam nut securely.

7   Install the nut on the ballstud and tighten it to the torque listed in this Chapter's Specifications. Install a new cotter pin.

8   Install the wheel and lug nuts. Lower the vehicle and tighten the lug nuts to the torque listed in the Chapter 1 Specifications.

9   Have the wheel alignment checked by a dealer service department or an alignment shop.

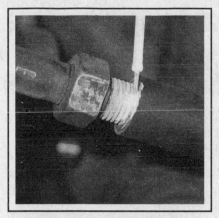

17.2 Loosen the jam nut, then mark the position of the tie-rod end on the threaded part of the tie-rod

17.3 Remove the cotter pin and loosen (but don't remove) the tie-rod end nut

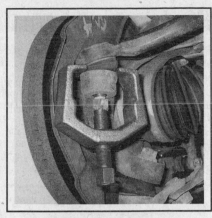

17.4 Install a small puller to separate the tie-rod end from the steering knuckle

18 Steering gear boots - replacement

▶ **Refer to illustrations 18.3a and 18.3b**

1   Loosen the lug nuts, raise the vehicle and support it securely on jackstands. Remove the wheel.

2   Remove the tie-rod end and jam nut (see Section 17).

3   Remove the outer steering gear boot clamp (see illustration) with a pair of pliers. Cut off the inner boot clamp (see illustration) with a pair of diagonal cutters. Slide the boot off.

4   Before installing the new boot, wrap the threads on the end of the steering rod with a layer of tape so the small end of the new boot isn't damaged.

5   Slide the new boot into position on the steering gear until it seats in the groove in the steering rod and install new clamps.

6   Remove the tape and install the tie-rod end (see Section 17).

7   Install the wheel and lug nuts. Lower the vehicle and tighten the lug nuts to the torque listed in the Chapter 1 Specifications.

8   Have the wheel alignment checked by a dealer service department or an alignment shop.

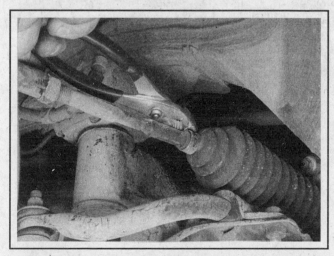

18.3a The outer end of the boot is secured by a spring clamp that can be slid off by pinching the ends together

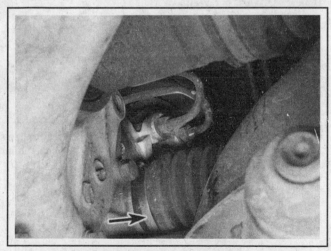

18.3b The inner end of the boot is retained by a clamp that must be cut off and discarded

19 Steering gear - removal and installation

❊❊ WARNING:

The models covered by this manual are equipped with Supplemental Restraint Systems (SRS), more commonly known as airbags. Always disarm the airbag system before working in the vicinity of any airbag system component to avoid the possibility of accidental deployment of the airbag, which could cause personal injury (see Chapter 12). Do not use a memory saving device to preserve the PCM's memory when working on or near airbag system components.

REMOVAL

▶ **Refer to illustrations 19.3, 19.6a and 19.6b**

1   Loosen the front wheel lug nuts, raise the front of the vehicle and support it securely on jackstands. Make sure the wheels are pointed straight ahead. Apply the parking brake and remove the wheels. Remove the engine splash shields.

2   Separate the tie-rod ends from the steering knuckle arms (see Section 17).

3   Remove the lower pinch bolt from the lower steering column U-joint (see illustration). Keep the steering wheel pointed straight ahead and keep the steering gear centered in its travel

4   Place a drain pan under the steering gear, then disconnect the fluid lines. Plug the ends to prevent contamination.

5   Remove the tubing support bracket. Disconnect the steering gear wiring harness.

6   Remove the steering gear mounting bolts (see illustrations).

7   Separate the intermediate shaft from the steering gear input shaft

and remove the steering gear assembly.

❊❊ WARNING:

Do not turn the steering wheel while the steering gear is removed. If the steering wheel is inadvertently turned, remove the steering wheel and center the spiral cable (see Section 16). To prevent the steering wheel from turning, loop the seat belt through the steering wheel and fasten it into its latch.

INSTALLATION

➡ **Note: Make sure the steering gear is centered from side to side before installing it.**

8   Maneuver the steering gear into position and connect the U-joint. The steering gear should be centered in its travel and the front wheels should still be pointed straight ahead.

9   Install the bolts and tighten them to the torque listed in this Chapter's Specifications.

10   Connect the tie-rod ends to the steering knuckle arms (see Section 17).

11   Install the U-joint pinch bolt and tighten it to the torque listed in this Chapter's Specifications.

12   Connect the power steering pressure and return hoses to the steering gear and fill the power steering pump reservoir with the recommended fluid (see Chapter 1).

13   Install the wheels and lug nuts, then lower the vehicle and tighten the lug nuts to the torque listed in the Chapter 1 Specifications. Bleed the steering system (see Section 21).

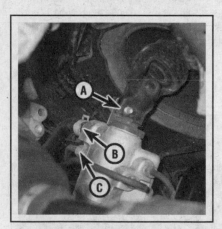

19.3   Remove this pinch bolt (A) from the lower steering shaft U-joint, then detach the return hose (B) and the pressure line (C)

19.6a   Left-side steering gear mounting bolt/nut

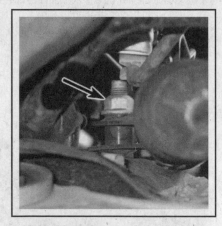

19.6b   Right-side steering gear mounting bolt/nut

20 Power steering pump - removal and installation

REMOVAL

▶ **Refer to illustrations 20.4 and 20.7**

1   Disconnect the cable from the negative terminal of the battery (see Chapter 5).

2   Loosen the right front wheel lug nuts. Raise the vehicle and support it securely on jackstands, then remove the wheel. Remove the engine lower splash shield and the right inner fender panel (see Chapter 11).

3   Using a large syringe or suction gun, suck as much fluid out of the power steering fluid reservoir as possible. Place a drain pan under the vehicle to catch any fluid that spills out when the hoses are disconnected.

4   Loosen the clamp and disconnect the fluid return hose from the pump (see illustration).

5   Remove the pressure line-to-pump banjo bolt, then detach the line from the pump. Remove and discard the sealing washers. They should be replaced when installing the pump.

6   Remove the drivebelt from the pump (see Chapter 1).

7   Remove the pump mounting bolts (see illustration 20.4 and the accompanying illustration), then remove the pump from the vehicle.

INSTALLATION

8   Installation is the reverse of removal. Be sure to use new sealing washers and tighten the banjo bolt to the torque listed in this Chapter's Specifications. Reconnect the battery and perform the necessary re-learn procedures (see Chapter 5).

9   Top up the fluid level in the reservoir (see Chapter 1) and bleed the system (see Section 21).

20.4 Power steering pressure (A) and return (B) lines; remove the lower mounting bolt (C), then remove the bracket-to-pump bolts (D, only one is visible here) (four-cylinder model shown)

20.7 Power steering pump upper mounting bolt

21 Power steering system - bleeding

1   Following any operation in which the power steering fluid lines have been disconnected, the power steering system must be bled to remove all air and obtain proper steering performance.

2   With the front wheels in the straight ahead position, check the power steering fluid level and, if low, add fluid until it reaches the Cold mark.

3   Turn the steering wheel from lock to lock several times with the engine Off.

4   Start the engine, then hold the steering wheel against each lock for no more than three seconds. Repeat this until air has been removed from the system and bubbles stop appearing in the reservoir.

5   Recheck the fluid level and add more if necessary to reach the Cold mark on the reservoir.

6   When the air is worked out of the system, return the wheels to the straight ahead position and leave the vehicle running for several more minutes before shutting it off.

7   Road test the vehicle to be sure the steering system is functioning normally and quietly.

8   Recheck the fluid level to be sure it is up to the Hot mark while the engine is at normal operating temperature. Add fluid if necessary (see Chapter 1).

22 Wheels and tires - general information

▶ **Refer to illustration 22.1**

1 All vehicles covered by this manual are equipped with metric-sized steel belted radial tires (see illustration). Use of other size or type of tires may affect the ride and handling of the vehicle. Don't mix different types of tires, such as radials and bias belted, on the same vehicle as handling may be seriously affected. It's recommended that tires be replaced in pairs on the same axle, but if only one tire is being replaced, be sure it's the same size, structure and tread design as the other.

2 Because tire pressure has a substantial effect on handling and wear, the pressure on all tires should be checked at least once a month or before any extended trips (see Chapter 1).

3 Wheels must be replaced if they are bent, dented, leak air, have elongated bolt holes, are heavily rusted, out of vertical symmetry or if the lug nuts won't stay tight. Wheel repairs that use welding or peening are not recommended.

4 Tire and wheel balance is important in the overall handling, braking and performance of the vehicle. Unbalanced wheels can adversely affect handling and ride characteristics as well as tire life. Whenever a tire is installed on a wheel, the tire and wheel should be balanced by a shop with the proper equipment.

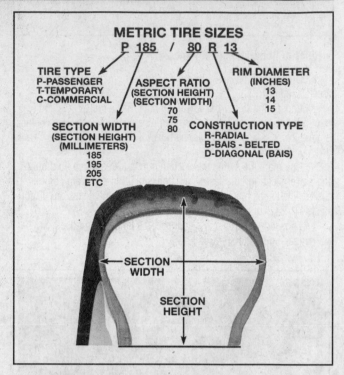

22.1 Metric tire size code

23 Wheel alignment - general information

▶ **Refer to illustration 23.1**

A wheel alignment refers to the adjustments made to the wheels so they are in proper angular relationship to the suspension and the ground. Wheels that are out of proper alignment not only affect vehicle control, but also increase tire wear. The front end angles normally measured are camber, caster and toe-in (see illustration). Camber and caster are preset at the factory on the vehicles covered by this manual; toe-in is the only adjustable angle on these vehicles (however, camber and caster are usually measured to check for bent or worn suspension parts). Toe-in and camber are both adjustable at the rear.

Getting the proper wheel alignment is an exacting process, one in which complicated and expensive machines are necessary to perform the job properly. Because of this, you should have a technician with the proper equipment perform these tasks. We will, however, use this space to give you a basic idea of what is involved with a wheel alignment so you can better understand the process and deal intelligently with the shop that does the work.

Toe-in is the turning in of the wheels. The purpose of a toe specification is to ensure parallel rolling of the wheels. In a vehicle with zero toe-in, the distance between the front edges of the wheels will be the same as the distance between the rear edges of the wheels. The actual amount of toe-in is normally only a fraction of an inch. Incorrect toe-in will cause the tires to wear improperly by making them scrub against the road surface.

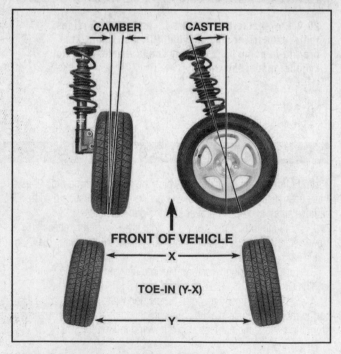

23.1 Camber, caster and toe-in angles

Camber is the tilting of the wheels from vertical when viewed from one end of the vehicle. When the wheels tilt out at the top, the camber is said to be positive (+). When the wheels tilt in at the top the camber is negative (-). The amount of tilt is measured in degrees from vertical and this measurement is called the camber angle. This angle affects the amount of tire tread which contacts the road and compensates for changes in the suspension geometry when the vehicle is cornering or traveling over an undulating surface.

Caster is the tilting of the front steering axis from the vertical. A tilt toward the rear is positive caster and a tilt toward the front is negative caster.

Torque specifications	Ft-lbs (unless otherwise indicated)

➡ **Note: One foot-pound (ft-lb) of torque is equivalent to 12 inch-pounds (in-lbs) of torque. Torque values below approximately 15-ft-lbs. are expressed in inch-pounds, since most foot-pound torque wrenches are not accurate at these smaller values.**

Front suspension

Control arm pivot bolts/nuts	114
Control arm balljoint-to-steering knuckle pinch bolt	46
Hub and bearing-to-knuckle bolts	65
Stabilizer bar	
Bushing clamp bolts	37
Link nuts	58
Strut/coil spring assembly	
Strut-to-knuckle bolts/nuts	103
Strut upper mounting bolts	26
Piston rod nut	54
Strut tower brace bolts	22
Wheel lug nuts	See Chapter 1

Subframe (front)

Subframe mounting bolts	107
Subframe brace bolts	41

Rear suspension

Hub and bearing-to-knuckle bolts	65
Radius rod-to-subframe bolt	
2007 models	72
2008 models	75
2009 and later models	
Sedan	75
Coupe	69
Radius rod-to-knuckle bolt/nut	
2007 models	72
2008 and later models	75
Suspension arms	
Upper suspension arm pivot bolt nuts	
2007 models	72
2008 models	75
2009 and later models	69
Upper suspension arm-to-rear knuckle nut	
2007 models	82
2008 and later models	70

Torque specifications (continued)   Ft-lbs (unless otherwise indicated)

➡ **Note:** One foot-pound (ft-lb) of torque is equivalent to 12 inch-pounds (in-lbs) of torque. Torque values below approximately 15-ft-lbs. are expressed in inch-pounds, since most foot-pound torque wrenches are not accurate at these smaller values.

Rear suspension (continued)

Suspension arms (continued)

Lower rear suspension arm-to-subframe nut

2007 models	72
2008 models	75
2009 and later models	69

Lower rear suspension arm-to-knuckle bolt/nut

2007 models	72
2008 models	75
2009 and later models	69

Lower front suspension arm-to-knuckle nut/bolt

2007 models	72
2008 models	75
2009 and later models	96

Lower front suspension arm-to-subframe nut/bolt

2007 models	72
2008 and later models	75

Shock absorber

Shock absorber mount-to-body nuts   20

Shock absorber-to-knuckle bolt/nut

2007 models	95
2008 and later models	66

Shock absorber piston rod-to-mount nut

2007 models	26
2008 and later models	22

Stabilizer bar

Bushing clamp nuts

2007 models	43
2008 models	22
2009 and later models	37

Link nuts

2007 models	54
2008 models	41
2009 and later models	33

Wheel lug nuts   See Chapter 1

Steering

Airbag module bolts	96 in-lbs
Power steering pump pressure line banjo bolt	44
Steering gear mounting bolts/nuts	114
Steering wheel nut	25

Steering shaft upper U-joint pinch bolt

Upper bolt	20
Lower bolt/nut	33
Steering shaft lower U-joint pinch bolt	20
Steering column mounting nuts	144 in-lbs
Tie-rod end-to-steering knuckle nut	25
Wheel lug nuts	See Chapter 1

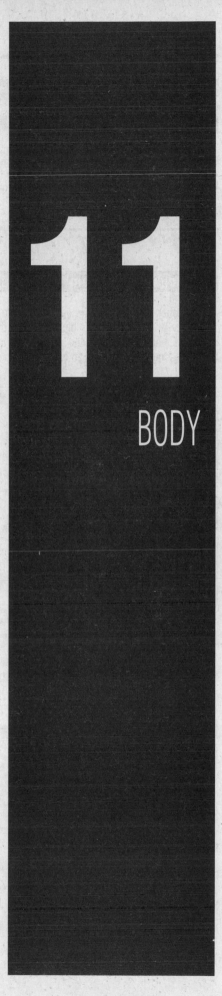

11

BODY

Section

1   General information

The models covered by this manual are equipped with Supplemental Restraint Systems (SRS), more commonly known as airbags. Always disable the airbag system before working in the vicinity of any airbag system components to avoid the possibility of accidental deployment of the airbags, which could cause personal injury (see Chapter 12).

Certain body components are particularly vulnerable to accident damage and can be unbolted and repaired or replaced. Among these parts are the hood, doors, tailgate, liftgate, bumpers and front fenders.

Only general body maintenance practices and body panel repair procedures within the scope of the do-it-yourselfer are included in this Chapter.

2   Repair minor paint scratches

No matter how hard you try to keep your vehicle looking like new, it will inevitably be scratched, chipped or dented at some point. If the metal is actually dented, seek the advice of a professional. But you can fix minor scratches and chips yourself. Buy a touch-up paint kit from a dealer service department or an auto parts store. To ensure that you get the right color, you'll need to have the specific make, model and year of your vehicle and, ideally, the paint code, which is located on a special metal plate under the hood or in the door jamb.

Make sure the damaged area is perfectly clean and rust free. If the touch-up kit has a wire brush, use it to clean the scratch or chip. Or use fine steel wool wrapped around the end of a pencil. Clean the scratched or chipped surface only, not the good paint surrounding it. Rinse the area with water and allow it to dry thoroughly

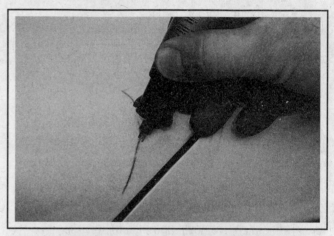

Thoroughly mix the paint, then apply a small amount with the touch-up kit brush or a very fine artist's brush. Brush in one direction as you fill the scratch area. Do not build up the paint higher than the surrounding paint

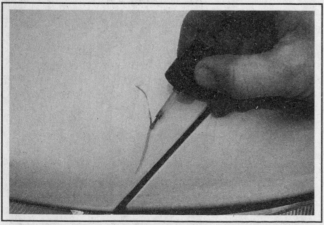

If the vehicle has a two-coat finish, apply the clear coat after the color coat has dried

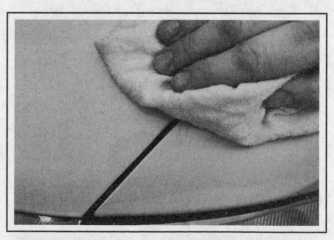

Wait a few days for the paint to dry thoroughly, then rub out the repainted area with a polishing compound to blend the new paint with the surrounding area. When you're happy with your work, wash and polish the area

3   Body repair - minor damage

PLASTIC BODY PANELS

The following repair procedures are for minor scratches and gouges. Repair of more serious damage should be left to a dealer service department or qualified auto body shop. Below is a list of the equipment and materials necessary to perform the following repair procedures on plastic body panels.

> Wax, grease and silicone removing solvent
> Cloth-backed body tape
> Sanding discs
> Drill motor with three-inch disc holder
> Hand sanding block
> Rubber squeegees
> Sandpaper
> Non-porous mixing palette
> Wood paddle or putty knife
> Curved-tooth body file
> Flexible parts repair material

Flexible panels (bumper trim)

1   Remove the damaged panel, if necessary or desirable. In most cases, repairs can be carried out with the panel installed.

2   Clean the area(s) to be repaired with a wax, grease and silicone removing solvent applied with a water-dampened cloth.

3   If the damage is structural, that is, if it extends through the panel, clean the backside of the panel area to be repaired as well. Wipe dry.

4   Sand the rear surface about 1-1/2 inches beyond the break.

5   Cut two pieces of fiberglass cloth large enough to overlap the break by about 1-1/2 inches. Cut only to the required length.

6   Mix the adhesive from the repair kit according to the instructions included with the kit, and apply a layer of the mixture approximately 1/8-inch thick on the backside of the panel. Overlap the break by at least 1-1/2 inches.

7   Apply one piece of fiberglass cloth to the adhesive and cover the cloth with additional adhesive. Apply a second piece of fiberglass cloth to the adhesive and immediately cover the cloth with additional adhesive in sufficient quantity to fill the weave.

8   Allow the repair to cure for 20 to 30 minutes at 60-degrees to 80-degrees F.

9   If necessary, trim the excess repair material at the edge.

10   Remove all of the paint film over and around the area(s) to be repaired. The repair material should not overlap the painted surface.

11   With a drill motor and a sanding disc (or a rotary file), cut a "V" along the break line approximately 1/2-inch wide. Remove all dust and loose particles from the repair area.

12   Mix and apply the repair material. Apply a light coat first over the damaged area; then continue applying material until it reaches a level slightly higher than the surrounding finish.

13   Cure the mixture for 20 to 30 minutes at 60-degrees to 80-degrees F.

14   Roughly establish the contour of the area being repaired with a body file. If low areas or pits remain, mix and apply additional adhesive.

15   Block sand the damaged area with sandpaper to establish the actual contour of the surrounding surface.

16   If desired, the repaired area can be temporarily protected with several light coats of primer. Because of the special paints and techniques required for flexible body panels, it is recommended that the vehicle be taken to a paint shop for completion of the body repair.

STEEL BODY PANELS

▶ **See photo sequence**

Repair of dents

17   When repairing dents, the first job is to pull the dent out until the affected area is as close as possible to its original shape. There is no point in trying to restore the original shape completely as the metal in the damaged area will have stretched on impact and cannot be restored to its original contours. It is better to bring the level of the dent up to a point that is about 1/8-inch below the level of the surrounding metal. In cases where the dent is very shallow, it is not worth trying to pull it out at all.

18   If the backside of the dent is accessible, it can be hammered out gently from behind using a soft-face hammer. While doing this, hold a block of wood firmly against the opposite side of the metal to absorb the hammer blows and prevent the metal from being stretched.

19   If the dent is in a section of the body which has double layers, or some other factor makes it inaccessible from behind, a different technique is required. Drill several small holes through the metal inside the damaged area, particularly in the deeper sections. Screw long, self-tapping screws into the holes just enough for them to get a good grip in the metal. Now pulling on the protruding heads of the screws with locking pliers can pull out the dent.

20   The next stage of repair is the removal of paint from the damaged area and from an inch or so of the surrounding metal. This is easily done with a wire brush or sanding disk in a drill motor, although it can be done just as effectively by hand with sandpaper. To complete the preparation for filling, score the surface of the bare metal with a screwdriver or the tang of a file or drill small holes in the affected area. This will provide a good grip for the filler material. To complete the repair, see the Section on filling and painting.

Repair of rust holes or gashes

21   Remove all paint from the affected area and from an inch or so of the surrounding metal using a sanding disk or wire brush mounted in a drill motor. If these are not available, a few sheets of sandpaper will do the job just as effectively.

22   With the paint removed, you will be able to determine the severity of the corrosion and decide whether to replace the whole panel, if possible, or repair the affected area. New body panels are not as expensive as most people think and it is often quicker to install a new panel than to repair large areas of rust.

23   Remove all trim pieces from the affected area except those which will act as a guide to the original shape of the damaged body, such as headlight shells, etc. Using metal snips or a hacksaw blade, remove all loose metal and any other metal that is badly affected by rust. Hammer the edges of the hole in to create a slight depression for the filler material.

24   Wire-brush the affected area to remove the powdery rust from the surface of the metal. If the back of the rusted area is accessible, treat it with rust inhibiting paint.

25   Before filling is done, block the hole in some way. This can be done with sheet metal riveted or screwed into place, or by stuffing the hole with wire mesh.

26   Once the hole is blocked off, the affected area can be filled and painted. See the following subsection on filling and painting.

These photos illustrate a method of repairing simple dents. They are intended to supplement Body repair - minor damage in this Chapter and should not be used as the sole instructions for body repair on these vehicles.

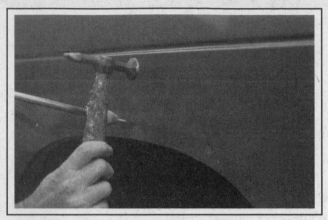

1 If you can't access the backside of the body panel to hammer out the dent, pull it out with a slide-hammer-type dent puller. Tap with a hammer near the edge of the dent to help 'pop' the metal back to its original shape, about 1/8-inch below the surface of the surrounding metal

2 Using coarse-grit sandpaper, remove the paint down to the bare metal. Clean the repair area with wax/silicone remover.

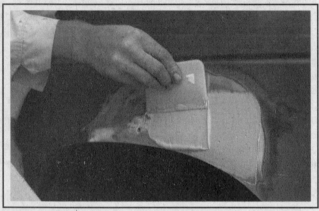

3 Following label instructions, mix up a batch of plastic filler and hardener, then quickly press it into the metal with a plastic applicator. Work the filler until it matches the original contour and is slightly above the surrounding metal

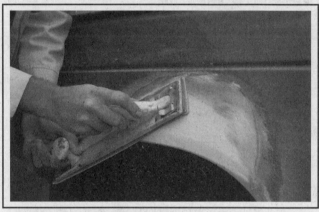

4 Let the filler harden until you can just dent it with your fingernail. File, then sand the filler down until it's smooth and even. Work down to finer grits of sandpaper - always using a board or block - ending up with 360 or 400 grit

5 When the area is smooth to the touch, clean the area and mask around it. Apply several layers of primer to the area. A professional-type spray gun is being used here, but aerosol spray primer works fine

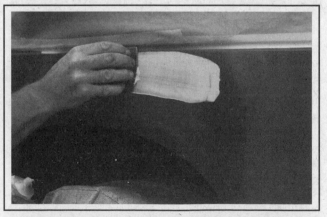

6 Fill imperfections or scratches with glazing compound. Sand with 360 or 400-grit and re-spray. Finish sand the primer with 600 grit, clean thoroughly, then apply the finish coat. Don't attempt to rub out or wax the repair area until the paint has dried completely (at least two weeks)

Filling and painting

27 Many types of body fillers are available, but generally speaking, body repair kits which contain filler paste and a tube of resin hardener are best for this type of repair work. A wide, flexible plastic or nylon applicator will be necessary for imparting a smooth and contoured finish to the surface of the filler material. Mix up a small amount of filler on a clean piece of wood or cardboard (use the hardener sparingly). Follow the manufacturer's instructions on the package, otherwise the filler will set incorrectly.

28 Using the applicator, apply the filler paste to the prepared area. Draw the applicator across the surface of the filler to achieve the desired contour and to level the filler surface. As soon as a contour that approximates the original one is achieved, stop working the paste. If you continue, the paste will begin to stick to the applicator. Continue to add thin layers of paste at 20-minute intervals until the level of the filler is just above the surrounding metal.

29 Once the filler has hardened, the excess can be removed with a body file. From then on, progressively finer grades of sandpaper should be used, starting with a 180-grit paper and finishing with 600-grit wet-or-dry paper. Always wrap the sandpaper around a flat rubber or wooden block, otherwise the surface of the filler will not be completely flat. During the sanding of the filler surface, the wet-or-dry paper should be periodically rinsed in water. This will ensure that a very smooth finish is produced in the final stage.

30 At this point, the repair area should be surrounded by a ring of bare metal, which in turn should be encircled by the finely feathered edge of good paint. Rinse the repair area with clean water until all of the dust produced by the sanding operation is gone.

31 Spray the entire area with a light coat of primer. This will reveal any imperfections in the surface of the filler. Repair the imperfections with fresh filler paste or glaze filler and once more smooth the surface with sandpaper. Repeat this spray-and-repair procedure until you are satisfied that the surface of the filler and the feathered edge of the paint are perfect. Rinse the area with clean water and allow it to dry completely.

32 The repair area is now ready for painting. Spray painting must be carried out in a warm, dry, windless and dust free atmosphere. These conditions can be created if you have access to a large indoor work area, but if you are forced to work in the open, you will have to pick the day very carefully. If you are working indoors, dousing the floor in the work area with water will help settle the dust that would otherwise be in the air. If the repair area is confined to one body panel, mask off the surrounding panels. This will help minimize the effects of a slight mismatch in paint color. Trim pieces such as chrome strips, door handles, etc., will also need to be masked off or removed. Use masking tape and several thickness of newspaper for the masking operations.

33 Before spraying, shake the paint can thoroughly, then spray a test area until the spray painting technique is mastered. Cover the repair area with a thick coat of primer. The thickness should be built up using several thin layers of primer rather than one thick one. Using 600-grit wet-or-dry sandpaper, rub down the surface of the primer until it is very smooth. While doing this, the work area should be thoroughly rinsed with water and the wet-or-dry sandpaper periodically rinsed as well. Allow the primer to dry before spraying additional coats.

34 Spray on the top coat, again building up the thickness by using several thin layers of paint. Begin spraying in the center of the repair area and then, using a circular motion, work out until the whole repair area and about two inches of the surrounding original paint is covered. Remove all masking material 10 to 15 minutes after spraying on the final coat of paint. Allow the new paint at least two weeks to harden, then use a very fine rubbing compound to blend the edges of the new paint into the existing paint. Finally, apply a coat of wax

4 Body repair - major damage

1 Major damage must be repaired by an auto body shop specifically equipped to perform body and frame repairs. These shops have the specialized equipment required to do the job properly.

2 If the damage is extensive, the frame must be checked for proper alignment or the vehicle's handling characteristics may be adversely affected and other components may wear at an accelerated rate.

3 Due to the fact that all of the major body components (hood, fenders, etc.) are separate and replaceable units, any seriously damaged components should be replaced rather than repaired. Sometimes the components can be found in a wrecking yard that specializes in used vehicle components, often at considerable savings over the cost of new parts.

5 Upholstery, carpets and vinyl trim - maintenance

UPHOLSTERY AND CARPETS

1 Every three months remove the floormats and clean the interior of the vehicle (more frequently if necessary). Use a stiff whiskbroom to brush the carpeting and loosen dirt and dust, then vacuum the upholstery and carpets thoroughly, especially along seams and crevices.

2 Dirt and stains can be removed from carpeting with basic household or automotive carpet shampoos available in spray cans. Follow the directions and vacuum again, then use a stiff brush to bring back the "nap" of the carpet.

3 Most interiors have cloth or vinyl upholstery, either of which can be cleaned and maintained with a number of material-specific cleaners or shampoos available in auto supply stores. Follow the directions on the product for usage, and always spot-test any upholstery cleaner on an inconspicuous area (bottom edge of a backseat cushion) to ensure that it doesn't cause a color shift in the material.

4 After cleaning, vinyl upholstery should be treated with a protectant.

➡ **Note: Make sure the protectant container indicates the product can be used on seats - some products may make a seat too slippery.**

❊❊ **CAUTION:**

Do not use protectant on vinyl-covered steering wheels.

5   Leather upholstery requires special care. It should be cleaned regularly with saddlesoap or leather cleaner. Never use alcohol, gasoline, nail polish remover or thinner to clean leather upholstery.

6   After cleaning, regularly treat leather upholstery with a leather conditioner, rubbed in with a soft cotton cloth. Never use car wax on leather upholstery.

7   In areas where the interior of the vehicle is subject to bright sunlight, cover leather seating areas of the seats with a sheet if the vehicle is to be left out for any length of time.

VINYL TRIM

8   Don't clean vinyl trim with detergents, caustic soap or petroleum-based cleaners. Plain soap and water works just fine, with a soft brush to clean dirt that may be ingrained. Wash the vinyl as frequently as the rest of the vehicle.

9   After cleaning, application of a high-quality rubber and vinyl protectant will help prevent oxidation and cracks. The protectant can also be applied to weather-stripping, vacuum lines and rubber hoses, which often fail as a result of chemical degradation, and to the tires.

---

6   Fastener and trim removal

▶ **Refer to illustration 6.4**

1   There is a variety of plastic fasteners used to hold trim panels, splash shields and other parts in place in addition to typical screws, nuts and bolts. Once you are familiar with them, they can usually be removed without too much difficulty.

2   The proper tools and approach can prevent added time and expense to a project by minimizing the number of broken fasteners and/or parts.

3   The following illustration shows various types of fasteners that are typically used on most vehicles and how to remove and install them (see illustration). Replacement fasteners are commonly found at most auto parts stores, if necessary.

Fasteners

This tool is designed to remove special fasteners. A small pry tool used for removing nails will also work well in place of this tool

A Phillips head screwdriver can be used to release the center portion, but light pressure must be used because the plastic is easily damaged. Once the center is up, the fastener can easily be pried from its hole

Here is a view with the center portion fully released. Install the fastener as shown, then press the center in to set it

This fastener is used for exterior panels and shields. The center portion must be pried up to release the fastener. Install the fastener with the center up, then press the center in to set it

This type of fastener is used commonly for interior panels. Use a small blunt tool to press the small pin at the center in to release it . . .

. . . the pin will stay with the fastener in the released position

Reset the fastener for installation by moving the pin out. Install the fastener, then press the pin flush with the fastener to set it

This fastener is used for exterior and interior panels. It has no moving parts. Simply pry the fastener from its hole like the claw of a hammer removes a nail. Without a tool that can get under the top of the fastener, it can be very difficult to remove

4   Trim panels are typically made of plastic and their flexibility can help during removal. The key to their removal is to use a tool to pry the panel near its retainers to release it without damaging surrounding areas or breaking-off any retainers. The retainers will usually snap out of their designated slot or hole after force is applied to them. Stiff plastic tools designed for prying on trim panels are available at most auto parts stores (see illustration). Tools that are tapered and wrapped in protective tape, such as a screwdriver or small pry tool, are also very effective when used with care.

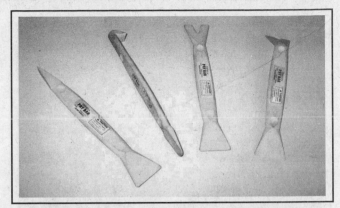

6.4 These small plastic pry tools are ideal for prying off trim panels

7   Hinges and locks - maintenance

Once every 3000 miles, or every three months, the hinges and latch assemblies on the doors, hood and trunk should be given a few drops of light oil or lock lubricant. The door latch strikers should also be lubricated with a thin coat of grease to reduce wear and ensure free movement. Lubricate the door and trunk locks with spray-on graphite lubricant.

8   Windshield and fixed glass - replacement

Replacement of the windshield and fixed glass requires the use of special fast-setting adhesive/caulk materials and some specialized tools. It is recommended that these operations be left to a dealer or a shop specializing in glass work.

9   Hood - removal, installation and adjustment

➡**Note: The hood is heavy and somewhat awkward to remove and install - at least two people should perform this procedure.**

REMOVAL AND INSTALLATION

▶ **Refer to illustrations 9.2 and 9.4**

1   Use blankets or pads to cover the cowl area of the body and fenders. This will protect the body and paint as the hood is lifted off.

2   Make marks or scribe a line around the hood hinge to ensure proper alignment during installation (see illustration).

3   Disconnect any cables or wires that will interfere with removal.

4   Have an assistant support one side of the hood while you support the other. Remove the hinge-to-hood nuts (see illustration).

5   Lift off the hood.

6   Installation is the reverse of removal.

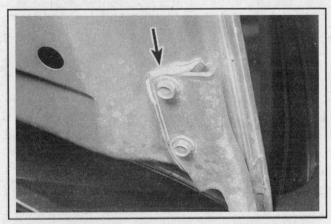

9.2 Before removing the hood, draw a mark around the hinge plate

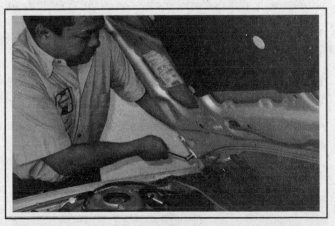

9.4 Support the hood with your shoulder while removing the hood nuts

9.10 To adjust the hood latch, loosen the retaining bolts (arrows), move the latch and retighten bolts, then close the hood to check the fit

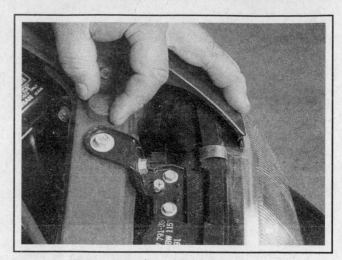

9.11 Adjust the hood closing height by turning the hood bumpers in or out

ADJUSTMENT

▶ **Refer to illustrations 9.10 and 9.11**

7   Fore-and-aft and side-to-side adjustment of the hood is done by moving the hinge plate slot after loosening the bolts or nuts.

8   Scribe a line around the entire hinge plate so you can determine the amount of movement (see illustration 9.2).

9   Loosen the bolts or nuts and move the hood into correct alignment. Move it only a little at a time. Tighten the hinge bolts and carefully lower the hood to check the position.

10 If necessary after installation, the entire hood latch assembly can be adjusted up-and-down as well as from side-to-side on the radiator support so the hood closes securely and flush with the fenders. To make the adjustment, scribe a line or mark around the hood latch mounting bolts to provide a reference point, then loosen them and reposition the latch assembly, as necessary (see illustration). Following adjustment, retighten the mounting bolts.

11 Finally, adjust the hood bumpers on the radiator support so the hood, when closed, is flush with the fenders (see illustration).

12 The hood latch assembly, as well as the hinges, should be periodically lubricated with white, lithium-base grease to prevent binding and wear.

10 Hood release latch and cable - removal and installation

LATCH

▶ **Refer to illustration 10.3**

1   Remove the radiator grille (see Section 11).

2   Scribe a line around the latch to aid alignment when installing, then remove the latch retaining bolts (see illustration 9.10) and remove the latch.

3   Disconnect the hood release cable by disengaging the cable from the latch assembly (see illustration).

4   Installation is the reverse of the removal procedure.

➡**Note: Adjust the latch so the hood engages securely when closed and the hood bumpers are slightly compressed.**

CABLE

▶ **Refer to illustrations 10.7, 10.8 and 10.9**

5   Disconnect the hood release cable from the latch assembly as described above.

6   Remove the left inner fender well liner (see Section 19).

7   Detach the cable from the clips along its length (see illustration).

8   Remove the inside hood release handle and disconnect the cable from it (see illustration).

9   Pull the cable grommet into the passenger compartment, the pull the cable through the hole (see illustration).

10 Installation is the reverse of the removal

➡**Note: Push on the grommet with your fingers from the passenger compartment to seat the grommet in the firewall correctly.**

10.3 Pry out the cable retainer from the rear of the hood latch assembly, then disengage the cable

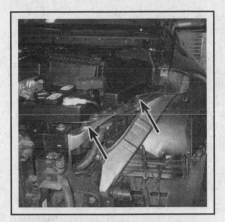

10.7 The hood release cable is secured along its length with clips

10.8 Release the end of the cable from the handle, then snap the cable housing from its retainer (instrument panel removed for clarity)

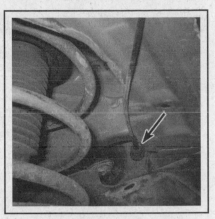

10.9 When the cable is free, push this grommet into the cabin and remove the cable

11 Radiator grille - removal and installation

♦ Refer to illustrations 11.2 and 11.3

✳✳ WARNING:

The models covered by this manual are equipped with a Supplemental Restraint System (SRS), more commonly known as airbags. Always disarm the airbag system before working in the vicinity of any airbag system component to avoid the possibility of accidental deployment of the airbag, which could cause personal injury (see Chapter 12). Do not use a memory saving device to preserve the PCM's memory when working on or near airbag system components.

1   On coupe models, remove the front bumper cover (see Section 20).

2   On sedan models, remove the four clips from the top of the grille (see illustration).

3   Unclip the bottom of the grille from the front bumper cover and remove it (see illustration).

4   Installation is the reverse of removal.

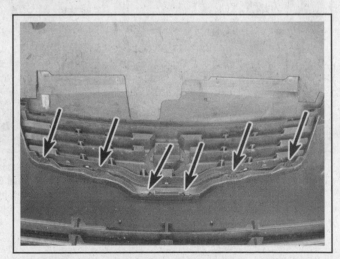

11.2 On sedan models, remove these plastic clips to remove the grille

11.3 These clips secure the grille to the bumper cover on sedans

12 Trunk lid - removal, installation and adjustment

➡ Note: The trunk lid is heavy and somewhat awkward to remove and install - at least two people should perform this procedure.

REMOVAL AND INSTALLATION

▶ **Refer to illustrations 12.2, 12.4 and 12.5**

1   Open the trunk lid and cover the edges of the trunk compartment with pads or cloths to protect the painted surfaces when the lid is removed.

2   Remove the trunk lid finish cover (see illustration).

12.2 Pry out the plastic clips to remove the trunk inner trim panel for access to the latch assembly

3   Disconnect the wiring and pull the wiring harness out.

4   Make alignment marks around the hinge mounting bolts with a marking pen (see illustration).

5   While an assistant supports the trunk lid, remove the lid-to-hinge bolts (see illustration) on both sides and lift it off.

6   Installation is the reverse of removal.

➡ Note: When reinstalling the trunk lid, align the lid-to-hinge bolts with the marks made during removal.

ADJUSTMENT

▶ **Refer to illustration 12.10**

7   Fore-and-aft and side-to-side adjustments of the trunk lid are accomplished by moving the lid in relation to the hinge after loosening the bolts or nuts.

8   Scribe a line around the entire hinge plate so you can determine the amount of movement.

9   Loosen the bolts or nuts and move the trunk lid into correct alignment. Move it only a little at a time. Tighten the hinge bolts or nuts and carefully lower the trunk lid to check the alignment.

10 If necessary after installation, the entire trunk lid striker assembly can be adjusted up and down as well as from side to side on the trunk lid, so the lid closes securely and is flush with the rear quarter panels. To do this, scribe a line around the trunk lid striker assembly to provide a reference point. Loosen the bolts and reposition the striker as necessary (see illustration). Following adjustment, retighten the mounting bolts.

11 The trunk lid latch assembly, as well as the hinges, should be periodically lubricated with white lithium-base grease to prevent sticking and wear.

12.4 Scribe a mark around the hinge plate for realignment of the trunk lid on installation

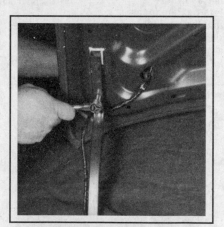

12.5 With an assistant holding the trunk lid, remove the four retaining bolts and lift off the trunk lid

12.10 The trunk lid striker can be adjusted by first loosening these bolts

13 Trunk latch - removal and installation

♦ **Refer to illustration 13.3**

1 Remove the trunk lid finish cover (see illustration 12.2).
2 Open the trunk and scribe a line around the trunk lid latch assembly for a reference point to aid the installation procedure.
3 Disconnect the electrical connector and the emergency release handle cable (see illustration).
4 Remove the mounting bolts and remove the latch.
5 Installation is the reverse of removal.

13.3 Trunk latch details

A	Electrical connector
B	Mounting bolts
C	Inside emergency release cable

14 Door trim panel - removal and installation

✳✳ CAUTION:

Plastic trim tools must be used on all operations in this Section to avoid damage to the soft plastic interior parts (see Section 6).

SEDAN MODELS

♦ **Refer to illustrations 14.2, 14.3, 14.6a, 14.6b and 14.7**

1 Use a plastic trim tool or a screwdriver wrapped with tape to carefully pry off the lens of the step light. Disconnect the wiring from it.
2 Release the claws at the rear of the inside handle trim, then lift it off. Remove the screw from the handle assembly (see illustration).
3 Lift up at the rear of the armrest pad while prying the pad away from the door panel with a plastic trim tool. This will release the clips that secure it to the door panel (see illustration).
4 Lift the rear of the armrest to release the clips along the inside edge. Lift up the pad at the front to release the front inside clips.
5 Lift the armrest pad straight upward to detach it from the clips at the front outer edge. Remove the armrest pad.
6 Gently lift the door lock switch trim panel and remove it (see illustrations). Disconnect the electrical connectors.

14.2 Remove the handle screw cover by prying it up from the rear, then remove this screw

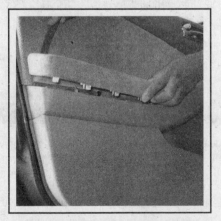

14.3 The armrest is retained by clips that must be removed in a specific order - gently pry it up at the rear while releasing the clips

14.6a Carefully, pry up the switch panel while releasing the clips

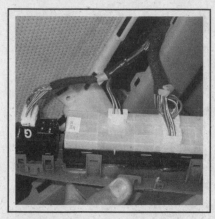

14.6b Disconnect the electrical connectors to remove the panel - it can be reconnected if you need to operate the window later

14.7 These screws secure the center of the door trim panel

14.14a Carefully pry around the edge of the panel with a flat-blade tool

14.14b Detach the cables from the door handle

7   Remove the screws under the removed panels (see illustration).

COUPE MODELS

8   Release the claws at the rear of the inside handle trim, then lift it

off. Remove the screw from the handle assembly.

9   Gently lift the door lock switch trim panel and remove it. Disconnect the wiring.

10 Use a plastic trim tool or a screwdriver wrapped with tape to disengage the bottom clips under the rear corner of the armrest trim strip.

11 Slide the tool upward along the trim strip to release the three clips. Don't try to pull on the trim strip.

12 Keep working the tool to the top of the trim strip and release the upper clip. Remove the trim strip.

13 Remove the screw under the lower part of the trim strip.

ALL MODELS

▶ **Refer to illustrations 14.14a and 14.14b**

14 Use a trim tool or a putty knife to carefully release the clips around the perimeter of the door panel (see illustration). When all clips are detached, lift the door panel off, then disconnect the two cables from its rear side (see illustration). Set the panel where it won't be damaged.

15 Installation is the reverse of removal.

16 Peel back the watershield for access to the inner door. Add more sealant to the watershield as necessary when replacing it.

15 Door - removal, installation and adjustment

➡**Note: The door is heavy and somewhat awkward to remove and install - at least two people should perform this procedure.**

REMOVAL AND INSTALLATION

▶ **Refer to illustrations 15.4, 15.6a and 15.6b**

1   Lower the window completely in the door.
2   Open the door all the way and support it on jacks or blocks cov-

ered with rags to prevent damaging the paint.

3   Pull the grommet and wiring harness out of the front door jamb until the connectors are exposed, then disconnect the electrical connectors.

4   Unbolt the door stop (see illustration).

5   Mark around the door hinges with a pen or a scribe to facilitate realignment during reassembly.

6   With an assistant holding the door, remove the hinge-to-door nuts (see illustrations) and lift the door off.

7   Installation is the reverse of removal.

15.4 Unbolt the door check strut . . .

15.6a . . . the lower front door hinge (unbolt the lower hinge first and allow the door to rest on its support while removing the upper nuts) . . .

15.6b . . . and the upper hinge

ADJUSTMENT

▶ **Refer to illustration 15.12**

8   Having proper door-to-body alignment is a critical part of a well functioning door assembly. First check the door hinge pins for excessive play. Fully open the door and lift up and down on the door without lifting the body. If a door has 1/16-inch or more excessive play, the hinges should be replaced.

9   Door-to-body alignment adjustments are made by loosening the hinge-to-body bolts or hinge-to-door bolts and moving the door. Proper body alignment is achieved when the top of the doors are parallel with the roof section, the front door is flush with the fender, the rear door is flush with the rear quarter panel and the bottom of the doors are aligned with the lower rocker panel. If these goals can't be reached by adjusting the hinge-to-body or hinge-to-door fasteners, body alignment shims may have to be purchased and inserted behind the hinges to achieve correct alignment.

10   To adjust the door closed position, scribe a line or mark around the striker plate to provide a reference point, then check that the door latch is contacting the center of the latch striker. If not, adjust the up and down position first.

11   Finally, adjust the latch striker sideways position, so that the door panel is flush with the center pillar or rear quarter panel and provides positive engagement with the latch mechanism (see illustration).

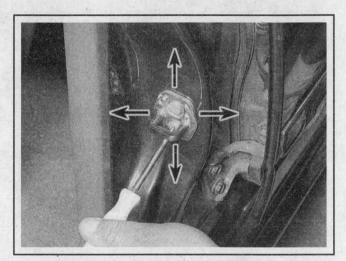

15.12 Adjust the door lock striker by loosening the mounting screws and gently tapping the striker in the desired direction

16   Door latch, lock cylinder and handles - removal and installation

▶ **Refer to illustrations 16.3, 16.5a, 16.5b, 16.6, 16.8, 16.9, 16.10 and 16.11**

1   Raise the window, then remove the door trim panel and watershield as described in Section 14.

2   Remove the door glass and the door module (this includes the large panel with the electric motor) (see Section 17).

3   Remove the rubber plug from the edge of the door (see illustra-tion), then remove the bolts from the door lock cylinder (from the driver's door) or the handle trim (passenger's side).

4   On vehicles with the Intelligent Key system, disconnect the door antenna and the door request switch electrical connectors. Remove the wiring harness clamp.

5   Disconnect the cable, the lock cylinder rod and the electrical connector (see illustrations).

16.3 Remove this plug in the door edge to reach the door handle bolt under it

16.5a Detach the plastic clip from the lock rod, then pull the rod out of the hole in the clip

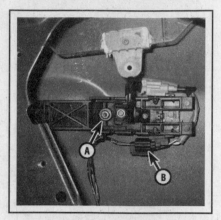

16.5b Door handle mounting bolt (A) and electrical connector (B)

16.6 Pull the door handle to release the lock

16.8 Slide the handle rearward to remove it - don't lose the gaskets under it

16.9 The latch mounting bolts are in the door edge

16.10 Unscrew the mounting bolt, then slide the bracket to the rear to remove it

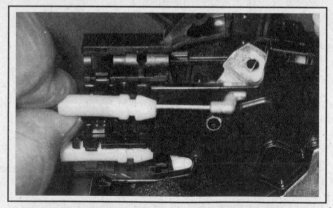

16.11 Disconnect the cables from the latch

6   Pull the outside door handle, then remove the lock cylinder assembly (driver's side) or the handle trim (passenger's side) (see illustration).

7   Disconnect the electrical connector of the door request switch.

8   Pull the outside handle and slide it to the rear to remove it and the gaskets (see illustration).

9   Remove the bolts from the door edge and remove the lock assem-bly (see illustration).

10 Remove the bolt from the outside handle bracket. Slide the bracket to the rear to remove it (see illustration).

11 Disconnect the door lock actuator connector and remove the lock assembly (see illustration).

12 Installation is the reverse of removal.

17 Door window glass - removal and installation

REMOVAL AND INSTALLATION

▶ **Refer to illustration 17.3**

1 Remove the door trim panel and the plastic watershield (see Section 14).

2 Remove the covers from the bolt access holes in the door module.

3 Connect the window switch temporarily and adjust the window so the bolts can be reached through the access holes (see illustration).

4 Remove the glass mounting bolts.

5 Pull the rear of the glass up and tilt it to the outside of the door as you remove it.

6 Installation is the reverse of removal. Check the alignment of the glass and adjust the regulator if necessary.

RESETTING THE LIMIT SWITCH

7 After installing the glass, reset the window switch reset switch by first carefully raising the glass to the top position manually.

8 There is a reset button accessible through a hole in the door panel. Hold this switch in while lowering the glass all the way.

9 Release the switch.

10 Raise the door glass all the way.

INITIALIZATION OF THE SYSTEM

➥**Note: This procedure must be done whenever any window component has been removed or when an electrical component of the system has been removed or disconnected. These parts include the battery, switches, glass, regulator, etc.**

11 Disconnect the power window switch electrical connector or dis-

17.3 Door glass bolts can be removed through these access holes

connect the battery (see Chapter 5).

12 Wait at least 1 minute.

13 Reconnect the power window switch electrical connector or reconnect the battery (see Chapter 5).

14 Turn the ignition On.

15 Open the window completely.

16 Select Auto Up and hold the switch for at least 4 seconds after the window has stopped in the fully up position.

17 Check the anti-pinch system by opening the window fully. Put a piece of plastic or wood (such as a hammer handle) into the opening.

18 Raise the window using the Auto Up button. Make sure that the window reverses itself after it contacts the object.

18 Door window glass regulator - removal and installation

▶ **Refer to illustrations 18.2 and 18.4**

1 Remove the door trim panel and the plastic watershield (see Section 14).

2 Remove the window glass assembly (see Section 17).

➥**Note: The glass need not be removed completely. It can be held in the top position and out of the way with tape (see illustration).**

3 Disconnect the electrical connector from the window regulator motor.

18.2 You can use heavy tape to secure the glass out of the way when working on the window regulator

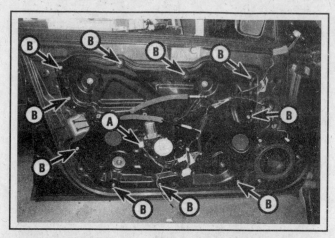

18.4 Disconnect the electrical connector from the window motor (A), then remove the door module panel mounting fasteners (B)

4 Remove the fasteners securing the door module panel, then remove the door module panel (see illustration).

5 Remove the fasteners securing the window regulator to the door module panel, then remove the window regulator from the door module panel.

6 Installation is the reverse of removal. Apply light grease to all moving parts.

7 See Section 17 for the initialization procedure.

19 Fenders - removal and installation

♦ **Refer to illustrations 19.2, 19.3, 19.4a, 19.4b and 19.4c**

1 Remove the front bumper cover (see Section 20) and the headlight housing (see Chapter 12).

2 Remove the push-pin retainers from the body side lower molding (see illustration). Remove the screw from each end, then remove the molding.

3 Remove the fenderwell liner (see illustration).

4 Remove the fender mounting bolts (see illustrations) and remove the fender.

※※ CAUTION:

The fender is glued to the body with foam. Use care when separating the fender from the body to avoid bending the fender.

5 Installation is the reverse of removal.

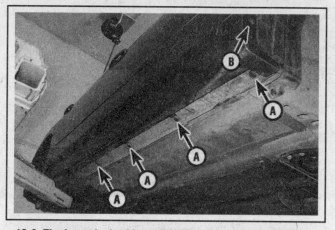

19.2 The lower body side molding is held on with clips (A) and a screw at each end (B); it must be removed for access to the fender bolts behind it

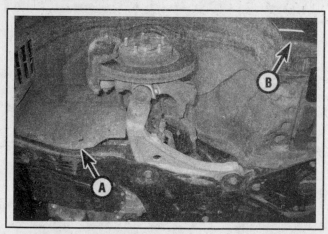

19.3 The front fender well liner and its removable panel (A) are secured with clips and screws - there are lower fender bolts behind the lower body side molding (B)

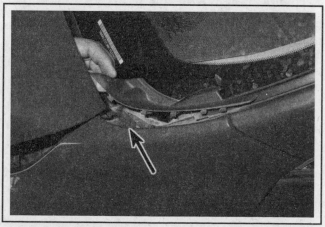

19.4a Remove this plastic cover to reach the fender bolt under it

19.4b There is an upper rear fender bolt (A), two concealed under the lower body side molding (B) and several along the top edge in the engine compartment (C)

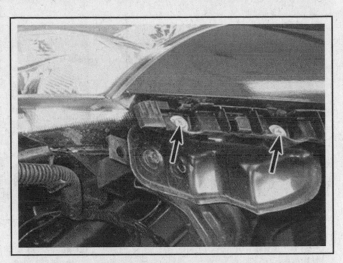

19.4c Remove the front bumper cover to access these fender bolts

20 Bumper covers - removal and installation

❈❈ WARNING:

The models covered by this manual are equipped with a Supplemental Restraint System (SRS), more commonly known as airbags. Always disarm the airbag system before working in the vicinity of any airbag system component to avoid the possibility of accidental deployment of the airbag, which could cause personal injury (see Chapter 12). Do not use a memory saving device to preserve the PCM's memory when working on or near airbag system components.

FRONT BUMPER COVER

▶ **Refer to illustrations 20.3, 20.6a and 20.6b**

1   Apply the parking brake, raise the front of the vehicle and support it securely on jackstands.

2   Remove the fenderwell liners (see Section 19).

➥**Note: They may be simply loosened and not completely removed on coupe models.**

3   Remove the lower engine splash shields (see illustration).

4   Remove the grille on sedan models (see Section 11). On coupes, the grille will be removed along with the bumper cover.

5   Remove the fog lamps or the fog lamp hole covers (see Chapter 12).

6   Remove the bumper cover clips and screws (see illustration). Separate the bumper cover from the fender (see illustration). Remove the bumper cover.

7   Installation is the reverse of removal.

REAR BUMPER COVER

▶ **Refer to illustrations 20.9, 20.11 and 20.12**

8   Apply the parking brake, raise the rear of the vehicle and support

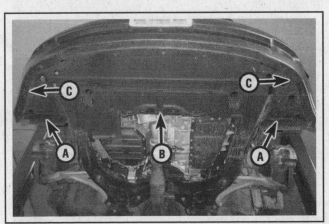

20.3 Remove the engine side splash shields (A) and the main engine splash shield (B) - there are also three screws at each end of the bumper cover (C)

20.6a This bolt secures the tip of the bumper cover to the fender bracket

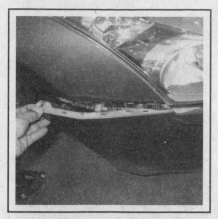

20.6b Release the bumper cover clips from the front of the fender by hand

20.9 Remove the taillight housings for access to these two rear bumper cover fasteners

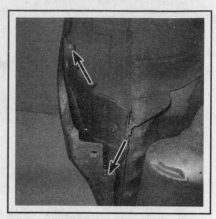

20.11 With the splash shields removed, you'll be able to reach the fasteners at the ends of the bumper cover (sedan model)

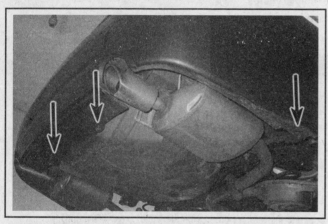

20.12 Lower rear clips of the bumper cover

it securely on jackstands.

9 Remove the taillight assemblies (see illustration) (see Chapter 12).

10 On coupe models, unclip the rear fender well liners and pull them aside for access.

11 On sedan models, remove the rear wheels, then remove the bumper splash shield from each end of the bumper (see illustration).

12 Remove the bumper clips and screws (see illustration). Remove the bumper.

13 Installation is the reverse of removal.

21 Outside mirrors - removal and installation

▶ Refer to illustrations 21.2 and 21.4

1 Remove the door trim panel and the plastic watershield (see Section 14).

2 Pry off the plastic mirror trim panel (see illustration).

3 Disconnect the electrical connector from the mirror.

4 Remove the mirror retaining fasteners and detach the mirror from the door (see illustration).

5 Installation is the reverse of removal.

21.2 Carefully pry off the mirror trim panel

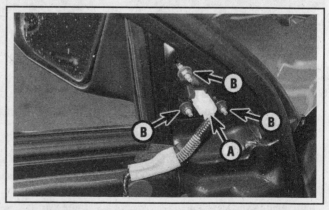

21.4 Disconnect the electrical connector from the mirror (A) before removing the mounting fasteners (B)

22 Center console - removal and installation

▶ Refer to illustrations 22.2a, 22.2b, 22.3, 22.4a, 22.4b, 22.5, 22.8, 22.9, 22.10 and 22.11

✴✴ WARNING:

The models covered by this manual are equipped with a Supplemental Restraint System (SRS), more commonly known as airbags. Always disarm the airbag system before working in the vicinity of any airbag system component to avoid the possibility of accidental deployment of the airbag, which could cause personal injury (see Chapter 12). Do not use a memory saving device to preserve the PCM's memory when working on or near airbag system components.

1   Shift into Drive (automatic transaxle) or Neutral (manual transaxle).
2   Remove the shift lever handle. On automatic transaxle models, the handle is secured by a spring clip under the handle cover (see illustrations).
3   Remove the center cluster lid by prying it off (see illustration).
4   Use a plastic trim tool or a screwdriver wrapped with tape to carefully pry up and remove the shifter trim panel (see illustrations).
5   Remove the console storage compartment (see illustration).
6   Remove the instrument panel end caps and the lower steering column trim panel (see Section 24).
7   Disconnect the aspirator tube and the wiring under the cover.

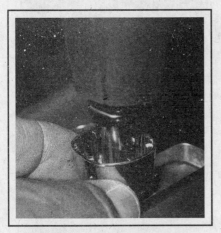

22.2a Pull down the automatic transaxle trim ring . . .

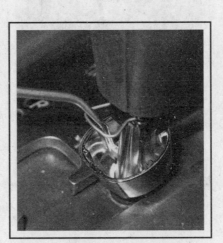

22.2b . . . then pull out the retaining clip to remove the knob

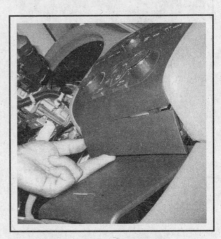

22.3 Remove the cluster lid

22.4a Use a non-marring tool to pry up the shifter trim panel . . .

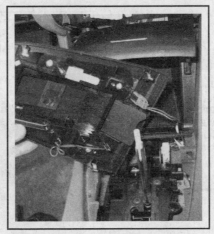

22.4b . . . then lift it off and disconnect the electrical connectors

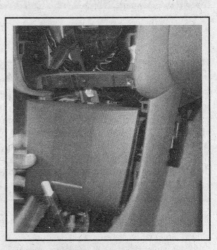

22.5 Carefully pry out the storage compartment

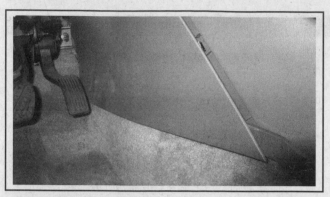

22.8 Remove the console side panels to access the mounting screws under them

8   Remove the side panels from the console (see illustration).
9   Remove the two screws from the front top of the console (see illustration).
10   Remove the two screws from the front sides of the console (see illustration).
11   Slide the seats fully forward, then remove the screws from the rear of the console (see illustration). Remove the console.
12   Installation is the reverse of removal.

22.9 The console is retained at the front by these screws at the top . . .

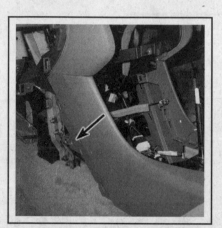

22.10 . . . and these at the sides

22.11 Center console rear mounting screws

23   Instrument cluster bezel - removal and installation

▶ Refer to illustration 23.4

✳✳ WARNING:

The models covered by this manual are equipped with a Supplemental Restraint System (SRS), more commonly known as airbags. Always disarm the airbag system before working in the vicinity of any airbag system component to avoid the possibility of accidental deployment of the airbag, which could cause personal injury (see Chapter 12). Do not use a memory saving device to preserve the PCM's memory when working on or near airbag system components.

1   Disconnect the cable from the negative terminal of the battery (see Chapter 5).
2   Remove the lower steering column trim panel (see Section 24).
3   Remove the steering column covers (see Section 25).
4   Use a plastic trim tool or a screwdriver wrapped with tape to pry the instrument cluster bezel off (see illustration). Disconnect the wiring as you remove it.
5   Installation is the reverse of removal. Reconnect the battery and perform the necessary re-learn procedures (see Chapter 5).

23.4 With the steering column covers and lower trim panel removed, the instrument cluster bezel can be pried off using a non-marring plastic tool

24 Dashboard trim panels - removal and installation

⁑⁑ WARNING:

The models covered by this manual are equipped with a Supplemental Restraint System (SRS), more commonly known as airbags. Always disarm the airbag system before working in the vicinity of any airbag system component to avoid the possibility of accidental deployment of the airbag, which could cause personal injury (see Chapter 12). Do not use a memory saving device to preserve the PCM's memory when working on or near airbag system components.

⁑⁑ CAUTION:

Plastic trim tools must be used on all operations in this Section to avoid damage to the soft plastic interior parts (see Section 6).

1   Disconnect the cable from the negative terminal of the battery (see Chapter 5).

LOWER STEERING COLUMN TRIM PANEL

▸ **Refer to illustrations 24.2 and 24.3**

2   Use a plastic trim tool or a screwdriver wrapped with tape to pry off the left instrument panel end cap (see Step 14). Remove the cover

from the fuse box (see illustration), then remove the screw under the fuse box cover.

3   Pull the trim panel away from the instrument panel (see illustration).

4   Disconnect the electrical connectors from the rear of the panel.

5   Installation is the reverse of removal. Reconnect the battery and perform the necessary re-learn procedures (see Chapter 5).

CENTER VENT GRILLES

▸ **Refer to illustration 24.6**

6   Use a plastic trim tool or a screwdriver wrapped with tape to carefully pry out the grille assembly (see illustration).

7   Installation is the reverse of removal. Reconnect the battery and perform the necessary re-learn procedures (see Chapter 5).

CENTER CLUSTER TRIM PANEL

▸ **Refer to illustrations 24.9, 24.10 and 24.11**

8   Refer to Step 6 and remove the center vent grilles.

9   Carefully pry off the lower trim panel above the console storage compartment assembly (see illustration).

24.2 Remove the fuse box cover

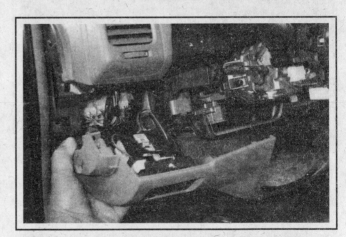

24.3 Pull the trim panel away from the instrument panel

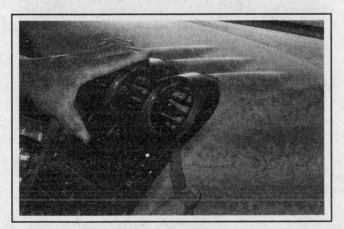

24.6 Carefully pry out the grille assembly

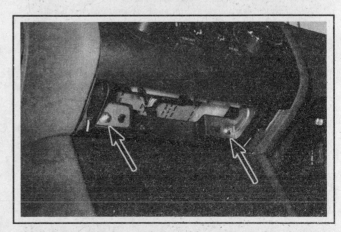

24.9 Remove the lower trim panel for access to these screws

24.10 The upper screws are accessible through the vent grille opening

24.11 Pull the assembly out, then support it while disconnecting the electrical connectors

24.14 Carefully pry the instrument panel end caps off

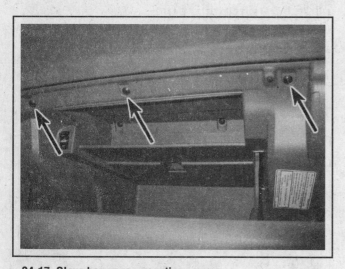

24.17 Glove box upper mounting screws

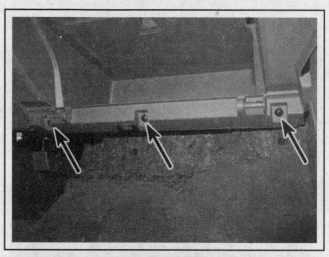

24.18 Glove box lower mounting screws

10 Remove the screws from under the vent grille and from under the lower trim panel (see illustration).

11 Remove the bezel assembly (see illustration).

12 Disconnect the electrical connectors and remove the bezel.

13 Installation is the reverse of removal. Reconnect the battery and perform the necessary re-learn procedures (see Chapter 5).

INSTRUMENT PANEL END CAPS

▶ **Refer to illustration 24.14**

14 Use a plastic trim tool or a screwdriver wrapped with tape to pry the end caps off (see illustration).

15 Align the clips with the holes while pressing it back into place.

16 Reconnect the battery and perform the necessary re-learn procedures (see Chapter 5).

GLOVE BOX

▶ **Refer to illustrations 24.17 and 24.18**

17 Open the glove box door, then remove the three screws from the top of the glove box (see illustration).

18 Remove the three screws from the lower edge of the glove box, then remove the glove box (see illustration).

19 Installation is the reverse of removal. Reconnect the battery and perform the necessary re-learn procedures (see Chapter 5).

25 Steering column covers - removal and installation

▶ Refer to illustrations 25.3 and 25.4

1   Disconnect the cable from the negative terminal of the battery (see Chapter 5).

2   Remove the lower steering column trim panel (see Section 24).

3   Remove the screw from the bottom of the lower steering column cover (see illustration).

4   Turn the steering wheel for access to the rear cover screws, then remove them (see illustration).

5   Unclip the covers from each other and remove them.

6   Installation is the reverse of removal. Reconnect the battery and perform the necessary re-learn procedures (see Chapter 5).

25.3 A single screw secures the column lower cover

25.4 Two column upper cover screws (steering wheel removed for clarity); the screws are accessed by turning the steering wheel

26 Instrument panel - removal and installation

▶ Refer to illustrations 26.11, 26.12a and 26.12b

✳ **WARNING:**

The models covered by this manual are equipped with a Supplemental Restraint System (SRS), more commonly known as airbags. Always disarm the airbag system before working in the vicinity of any airbag system component to avoid the possibility of accidental deployment of the airbag, which could cause personal injury (see Chapter 12). Do not use a memory saving device to preserve the PCM's memory when working on or near airbag system components.

1   Disconnect the cable from the negative terminal of the battery (see Chapter 5).

2   Remove the center console (see Section 22).

3   Pull off the front door weatherstrips from around the windshield pillars.

4   Use a plastic trim tool or a screwdriver wrapped with tape to pry off the windshield pillar trim panels. Be sure to insert the prying tool between the steel frame and the plastic clip.

5   Remove the steering wheel (see Chapter 10).

6   Remove the instrument cluster bezel (see Section 23), then remove the instrument cluster (see Chapter 12).

7   Remove the steering column covers (see Section 25) and the steering column switches (see Chapter 12).

8   Remove the spiral cable from the steering column (see Chapter 10).

9   Remove the instrument panel trim panels and the glove box (see Section 24).

10 Remove the small speaker grille at each end of the upper instrument panel, then remove the speakers and disconnect the electrical connectors. Remove the center speaker grille.

11 Remove the mounting bolt from the passenger's airbag (see illustration).

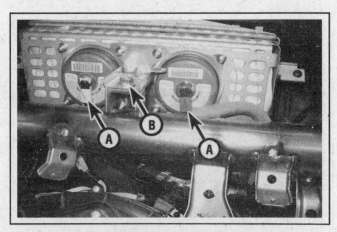

26.11 Disconnect the passenger airbag electrical connectors (A), then remove the bolt (B) and lift it out

26.12a Left side instrument panel mounting fasteners

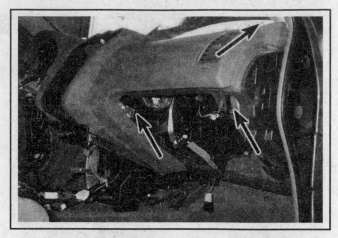

26.12b Right side mounting fasteners

12 Remove the instrument panel mounting screws (see illustrations).

13 Disconnect the sound system wiring harness from the passenger's side of the instrument panel.

14 With the help of an assistant, lift the instrument panel enough to access and disconnect all of the wiring harnesses.

15 Remove the instrument panel through the passenger's door opening.

16 Installation is the reverse of removal. Reconnect the battery and perform the necessary re-learn procedures (see Chapter 5).

27 Cowl cover - removal and installation

◆ **Refer to illustrations 27.2, 27.3, 27.4a and 27.4b**

1 Pry off the plastic trim cap on the windshield wiper arms, then detach the wiper arm retaining nuts and remove the wiper arms (see Chapter 12).

2 Remove the small end covers from the cowl (see illustration).

3 Remove the foam sealing blocks (see illustration).

4 Remove the cowl mounting clips, detach the washer hose, then remove the cowl top (see illustrations).

5 Installation is the reverse of removal.

27.2 Pull off the small cowl end covers

27.3 Peel off the foam air seals

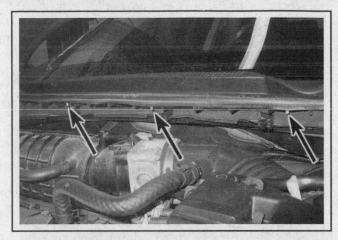

27.4a Pry these clips out to release the cowl

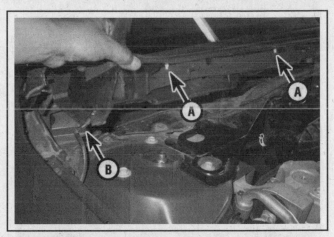

27.4b Cowl clips (A) - detach the washer hose (B) from the cowl before removing it

28 Seats - removal and installation

✳✳ WARNING:

The models covered by this manual are equipped with a Supplemental Restraint System (SRS), more commonly known as airbags. Always disarm the airbag system before working in the vicinity of any airbag system component to avoid the possibility of accidental deployment of the airbag, which could cause personal injury (see Chapter 12). Do not use a memory saving device to preserve the PCM's memory when working on or near airbag system components.

FRONT SEAT

▶ Refer to illustration 28.2, 28.3a and 28.3b

1 Disconnect the cable from the negative terminal of the battery (see Chapter 5). Position the seat in the middle of its travel to access all of the seat mounting bolts.

2 Remove the trim covers from the seat bolts (see illustration).

3 Remove the mounting bolts, then tilt the seat back (see illustration). Disconnect the airbag wiring harness and any other wiring attached to the seat (see illustration).

4 Installation is the reverse of removal. Reconnect the battery and perform the necessary re-learn procedures (see Chapter 5).

28.2 With the covers removed from the back of the front seat tracks, the bolts are accessible

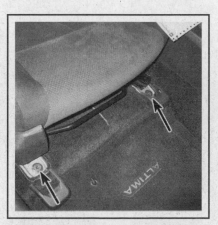

28.3a Front seat mounting bolts with the covers removed

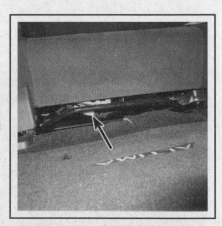

28.3b Carefully tilt the seat to the rear to reach and disconnect the wiring

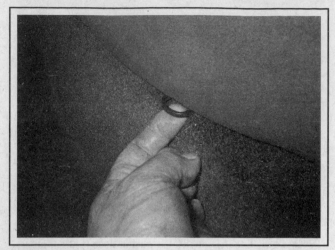

28.5 These rings show the locations of the retainers of the rear seat cushion - pull up the front of the cushion to release it; position the seat belts in their recesses when installing the seat cushion

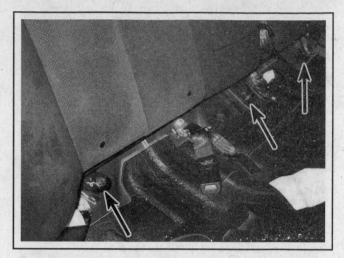

28.8 Seat back mounting bolts

REAR SEAT

▶ **Refer to illustrations 28.5 and 28.8**

5 Pull on the seat cushion rings to release it from its retainers (see illustration).

6 Pull the seat cushion forward and remove it.

7 Detach the seat belts from their guides and secure them out of the way.

8 Remove the fasteners that mount the seat back hinges to the floor (see illustration).

9 Remove the seat backs.

10 Installation is the reverse of removal. Turn each seat belt so that it's facing the correct direction when installing the cushion.

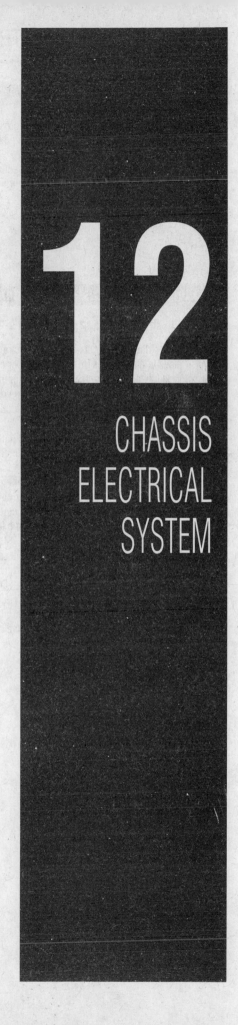

12

CHASSIS
ELECTRICAL
SYSTEM

Section

1 General information

The electrical system is a 12-volt, negative ground type. Power for the lights and all electrical accessories is supplied by a lead/acid-type battery that is charged by the alternator.

This Chapter covers repair and service procedures for the various electrical components not associated with the engine. Information on the battery, alternator, ignition system and starter motor can be found in Chapter 5.

It should be noted that when portions of the electrical system are serviced, the negative cable should be disconnected from the battery to prevent electrical shorts and/or fires.

2 Electrical troubleshooting - general information

♦ **Refer to illustrations 2.5a, 2.5b, 2.6 and 2.9**

A typical electrical circuit consists of an electrical component, any switches, relays, motors, fuses, fusible links or circuit breakers related to that component and the wiring and connectors that link the component to both the battery and the chassis. To help you pinpoint an electrical circuit problem, wiring diagrams are included at the end of this Chapter.

Before tackling any troublesome electrical circuit, first study the appropriate wiring diagrams to get a complete understanding of what makes up that individual circuit. Trouble spots, for instance, can often be narrowed down by noting if other components related to the circuit are operating properly. If several components or circuits fail at one time, chances are the problem is in a fuse or ground connection, because several circuits are often routed through the same fuse and ground connections.

Electrical problems usually stem from simple causes, such as loose or corroded connections, a blown fuse, a melted fusible link or a failed relay. Visually inspect the condition of all fuses, wires and connections in a problem circuit before troubleshooting the circuit.

If test equipment and instruments are going to be utilized, use the diagrams to plan ahead of time where you will make the necessary connections in order to accurately pinpoint the trouble spot.

The basic tools needed for electrical troubleshooting include a circuit tester or voltmeter (a 12-volt bulb with a set of test leads can also be used), a continuity tester, which includes a bulb, battery and set of test leads, and a jumper wire, preferably with a circuit breaker incorporated, which can be used to bypass electrical components (see illustrations). Before attempting to locate a problem with test instruments, use the wiring diagram(s) to decide where to make the connections.

VOLTAGE CHECKS

Voltage checks should be performed if a circuit is not functioning properly. Connect one lead of a circuit tester to either the negative battery terminal or a known good ground. Connect the other lead to a connector in the circuit being tested, preferably nearest to the battery or fuse (see illustration). If the bulb of the tester lights, voltage is present, which means that the part of the circuit between the connector and the battery is problem free. Continue checking the rest of the circuit in the same fashion. When you reach a point at which no voltage is present, the problem lies between that point and the last test point with voltage. Most of the time the problem can be traced to a loose connection.

➡**Note: Keep in mind that some circuits receive voltage only when the ignition key is in the Accessory or Run position.**

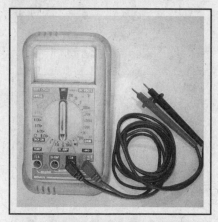

2.5a The most useful tool for electrical troubleshooting is a digital multimeter that can check volts, amps, and test continuity

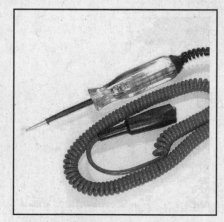

2.5b A test light is a very handy tool for checking voltage

2.6 In use, a basic test light's lead is clipped to a known good ground, then the pointed probe can test connectors, wires or electrical sockets - if the bulb lights, the part being tested has battery voltage

FINDING A SHORT

One method of finding shorts in a circuit is to remove the fuse and connect a test light or voltmeter in place of the fuse terminals. There should be no voltage present in the circuit. Move the wiring harness from side-to-side while watching the test light. If the bulb goes on, there is a short to ground somewhere in that area, probably where the insulation has rubbed through. The same test can be performed on each component in the circuit, even a switch.

GROUND CHECK

Perform a ground test to check whether a component is properly grounded. Disconnect the battery and connect one lead of a continuity tester or multimeter (set to the ohms scale), to a known good ground. Connect the other lead to the wire or ground connection being tested. If the resistance is low (less than 5 ohms), the ground is good. If the bulb on a self-powered test light does not go on, the ground is not good.

CONTINUITY CHECK

A continuity check is done to determine if there are any breaks in a circuit - if it is passing electricity properly. With the circuit off (no power in the circuit), a self-powered continuity tester or multimeter can be used to check the circuit. Connect the test leads to both ends of the circuit (or to the power end and a good ground), and if the test light comes on the circuit is passing current properly (see illustration). If the resistance is low (less than 5 ohms), there is continuity; if the reading is 10,000 ohms or higher, there is a break somewhere in the circuit. The same procedure can be used to test a switch, by connecting the continuity tester to the switch terminals. With the switch turned On, the test light should come on (or low resistance should be indicated on a meter).

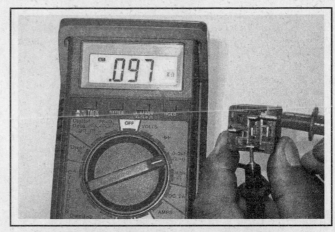

2.9 With a multimeter set to the ohms scale, resistance can be checked across two terminals - when checking for continuity, a low reading indicates continuity, a high reading indicates lack of continuity

FINDING AN OPEN CIRCUIT

When diagnosing for possible open circuits, it is often difficult to locate them by sight because the connectors hide oxidation or terminal misalignment. Merely wiggling a connector on a sensor or in the wiring harness may correct the open circuit condition. Remember this when an open circuit is indicated when troubleshooting a circuit. Intermittent problems may also be caused by oxidized or loose connections.

Electrical troubleshooting is simple if you keep in mind that all electrical circuits are basically electricity running from the battery, through the wires, switches, relays, fuses and fusible links to each electrical component (light bulb, motor, etc.) and to ground, from which it is passed back to the battery. Any electrical problem is an interruption in the flow of electricity to and from the battery.

---

3   Fuses and fusible links - general information

FUSES

▶ **Refer to illustrations 3.1a, 3.1b and 3.3**

The electrical circuits of the vehicle are protected by a combination of fuses, circuit breakers and fusible links. The main fuse/relay panel is in the engine compartment (see illustration), while the interior fuse/relay panel is located inside the passenger compartment (see illustration). Each of the fuses is designed to protect a specific circuit, and the various circuits are identified on the fuse panel itself.

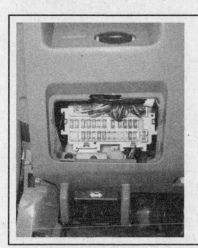

3.1a The Interior fuse box is located at the left side of the instrument panel, behind the fuse panel cover

3.1b The engine compartment fuse/ relay box is located along the left side of the engine compartment. To release the cover, depress the tab at the rear and lift up

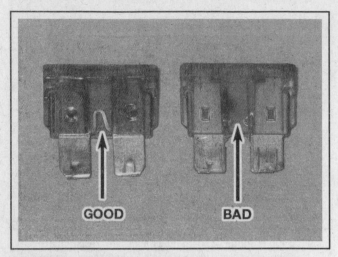

3.3 When a fuse blows, the element between the terminals melts - the fuse on the left is blown, the fuse on the right is good

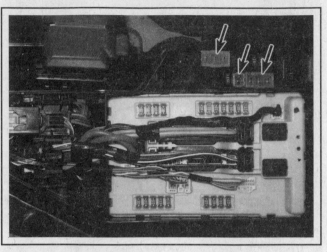

3.7 Location of the fusible links in the underhood fuse/relay box

Several sizes of fuses are employed in the fuse blocks. There are small, medium and large sizes of the same design, all with the same blade terminal design. The medium and large fuses can be removed with your fingers, but the small fuses require the use of pliers or the small plastic fuse-puller tool found in most fuse boxes.

If an electrical component fails, always check the fuse first. The best way to check the fuses is with a test light. Check for power at the exposed terminal tips of each fuse. If power is present at one side of the fuse but not the other, the fuse is blown. A blown fuse can also be identified by visually inspecting it (see illustration).

Be sure to replace blown fuses with the correct type. Fuses (of the same physical size) of different ratings may be physically interchangeable, but only fuses of the proper rating should be used. Replacing a fuse with one of a higher or lower value than specified is not recommended. Each electrical circuit needs a specific amount of protection. The amperage value of each fuse is molded into the top of the fuse body.

If the replacement fuse immediately fails, don't replace it again until the cause of the problem is isolated and corrected. In most cases, this will be a short circuit in the wiring caused by a broken or deteriorated wire.

FUSIBLE LINKS

▶ **Refer to illustration 3.7**

Some circuits are protected by fusible links. The links are used in circuits which are not ordinarily fused, or which carry high current, such as the circuit between the alternator and the starter motor. Cartridge-type fusible links are located in the engine compartment fuse/relay box and are similar to a large fuse (see illustration). After disconnecting the negative battery cable, simply unplug the fusible link and replace it with a fusible link of the same amperage. If you have to replace a blown fusible link, make sure that you replace it with one of the same rating. If the replacement fusible link blows in the same circuit, make sure that you troubleshoot the circuit in which the fusible link melted BEFORE installing another fusible link.

4   Circuit breakers - general information

Circuit breakers protect certain circuits, such as the power windows or heated seats. Depending on the vehicle's accessories, there may be one or two circuit breakers, located in the fuse/relay box in the engine compartment.

Because the circuit breakers reset automatically, an electrical overload in a circuit breaker-protected system will cause the circuit to fail momentarily, then come back on. If the circuit does not come back on, check it immediately.

For a basic check, pull the circuit breaker up out of its socket on the fuse panel, but just far enough to probe with a voltmeter. The breaker should still contact the sockets. With the voltmeter negative lead on a good chassis ground, touch each end prong of the circuit breaker with the positive meter probe. There should be battery voltage at each end. If there is battery voltage only at one end, the circuit breaker must be replaced.

Some circuit breakers must be reset manually.

5   Relays - general information

Several electrical accessories in the vehicle, such as the fuel injection system, horns, starter, and fog lamps use relays to transmit the electrical signal to the component. Relays use a low-current circuit (the control circuit) to open and close a high-current circuit (the power cir-

cuit). If the relay is defective, that component will not operate properly. Most relays are mounted in the engine compartment and interior fuse/relay boxes (see illustrations 3.1a and 3.1b).

6 Electrical connectors - general information

Most electrical connections on these vehicles are made with multiwire plastic connectors. The mating halves of many connectors are secured with locking clips molded into the plastic connector shells. The mating halves of some large connectors, such as some of those under the instrument panel, are held together by a bolt through the center of the connector.

To separate a connector with locking clips, use a small screwdriver to pry the clips apart carefully, then separate the connector halves. Pull only on the shell, never pull on the wiring harness as you may damage the individual wires and terminals inside the connectors. Look at the connector closely before trying to separate the halves. Often the locking clips are engaged in a way that is not immediately clear. Additionally, many connectors have more than one set of clips.

Each pair of connector terminals has a male half and a female half.

When you look at the end view of a connector in a diagram, be sure to understand whether the view shows the harness side or the component side of the connector. Connector halves are mirror images of each other, and a terminal shown on the right side end-view of one half will be on the left side end-view of the other half.

It is often necessary to take circuit voltage measurements with a connector connected. Whenever possible, carefully insert a small straight pin (not your meter probe) into the rear of the connector shell to contact the terminal inside, then clip your meter lead to the pin. This kind of connection is called "backprobing." When inserting a test probe into a terminal, be careful not to distort the terminal opening. Doing so can lead to a poor connection and corrosion at that terminal later. Using the small straight pin instead of a meter probe results in less chance of deforming the terminal connector.

Electrical connectors

Most electrical connectors have a single release tab that you depress to release the connector

Some electrical connectors have a retaining tab which must be pried up to free the connector

Some connectors have two release tabs that you must squeeze to release the connector

Some connectors use wire retainers that you squeeze to release the connector

Critical connectors often employ a sliding lock (1) that you must pull out before you can depress the release tab (2)

Here's another sliding-lock style connector, with the lock (1) and the release tab (2) on the side of the connector

On some connectors the lock (1) must be pulled out to the side and removed before you can lift the release tab (2)

Some critical connectors, like the multi-pin connectors at the Powertrain Control Module employ pivoting locks that must be flipped open

7 Remote keyless entry fob - battery replacement

▶ **Refer to illustrations 7.1, 7.2 and 7.3**

1   To replace the transmitter battery, remove the key from the fob, then carefully pry open the keyless entry fob by inserting a small screwdriver into the notch in the body of the transmitter (see illustration).

2   Carefully pry out the old battery with a small screwdriver (see illustration).

✳✳ CAUTION:

Do not touch the circuit board or battery terminal contacts inside the key fob.

3   Install the new battery, making sure the positive (+) terminal faces the bottom of the case, then reassemble the two halves (see illustration).

✳✳ CAUTION:

Handle the battery by its edges only; holding it like a coin (touching both sides) can reduce the battery's life by partially discharging it.

7.1 Remove the key and pry the remote keyless fob apart . . .

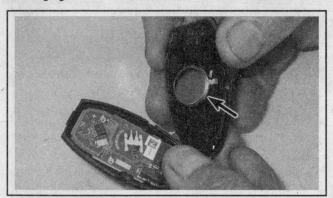

7.2 . . . then carefully remove the battery without touching any other components

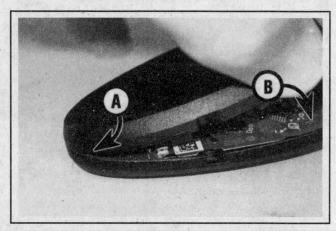

7.3 To assemble the halves, engage the lip of the back half of the cover (A) into the end of the other half of the fob, then swing the other end down and snap it into place (B)

8 Body Control Module (BCM) - general information

▶ **Refer to illustration 8.2**

The Body Control Module (BCM) receives inputs from various switches and sensors and sends commands, some in the form of multiplex voltage signals, to corresponding components to operate them. Some circuits are controlled by the BCM in conjunction with the IPDM (see Section 26) and/or the Powertrain Control Module (PCM) (see Chapter 6). The circuits under BCM control include the:

Combination switch system
Signal buffer system
Power consumption control system
Auto light system
Turn signal and hazard warning light system
Headlight system
Fog light system
Daytime running lights system
Interior illumination system
Interior illumination battery saver system
Windshield wiper/washer system
Warning chime system
Power door lock system
Power window system
Air conditioning compressor clutch
Nissan Anti-Theft System (NATS)
Vehicle security system
Rear window defogger system
Remote keyless entry system
Trunk release system
Intelligent Key system
Ignition push switch system
Electronic steering column lock
Tire pressure monitor system
Retained accessory power (RAP) system

The BCM is located under the driver's side of the instrument panel (see illustration). Removal and installation of the BCM is not covered in this manual because special equipment is required to diagnose it and the systems it controls. Additionally, if the BCM requires replacement, it must be programmed with the same special equipment before it will work. So, diagnosis and replacement of the BCM must be performed at a dealer service department or other qualified repair shop equipped with the necessary tool.

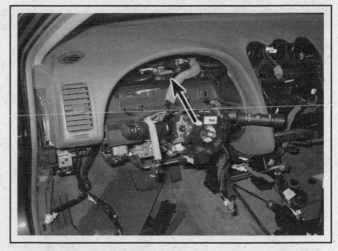

8.2 The Body Control Module is mounted under the left side of the instrument panel

9   Steering column switches - replacement

▶ **Refer to illustrations 9.3a and 9.3b**

✷✷ WARNING:

The models covered by this manual are equipped with Supplemental Restraint Systems (SRS), more commonly known as airbags. Always disable the airbag system before working in the vicinity of any airbag system components to avoid the possibility of accidental deployment of the airbags, which could cause personal injury (see Section 25).

1   Disconnect the cable from the negative terminal of the battery (see Chapter 5).

2   Remove the steering column covers (see Chapter 11).

3   Rotate the steering wheel for access to the two switch mounting screws (see illustrations).

4   Disconnect the wiring harnesses from the switch and remove it by sliding it upward.

5   Installation is the reverse of removal. Reconnect the battery and perform the necessary re-learn procedures (see Chapter 5).

9.3a The combination switch can be removed without having to first remove the steering wheel (it has been removed for clarity); the left mounting screw . . .

9.3b . . . and the right mounting screw can be reached by turning the steering wheel

10 Dashboard switches - replacement

⁕⁕ **WARNING:**

The models covered by this manual are equipped with Supplemental Restraint Systems (SRS), more commonly known as airbags. Always disable the airbag system before working in the vicinity of any airbag system components to avoid the possibility of accidental deployment of the airbags, which could cause personal injury (see Section 25).

1   Disconnect the cable from the negative terminal of the battery (see Chapter 5).

2   On driver's side switches, remove the driver's knee bolster (see Chapter 11).

3   On center dash switches, remove the center trim panel (see Chapter 11).

4   Disconnect the electrical connector from the switch being replaced.

5   Use a small screwdriver to release the clips and pull out the switch.

6   Installation is the reverse of removal. Reconnect the battery and perform the necessary re-learn procedures (see Chapter 5).

11 Instrument cluster - removal and installation

▶ **Refer to illustrations 11.3 and 11.4**

⁕⁕ **WARNING:**

The models covered by this manual are equipped with Supplemental Restraint Systems (SRS), more commonly known as airbags. Always disable the airbag system before working in the vicinity of any airbag system components to avoid the possibility of accidental deployment of the airbags, which could cause personal injury (see Section 25).

1   Disconnect the cable from the negative terminal of the battery (see Chapter 5).

2   Remove the instrument cluster bezel (see Chapter 11).

3   Remove the retaining screws and pull the cluster out (see illustration).

4   Unplug the electrical connectors and remove the cluster from the vehicle (see illustration).

5   Installation is the reverse of removal. Reconnect the battery and perform the necessary re-learn procedures (see Chapter 5).

11.3 Remove these screws to pull back the instrument cluster . . .

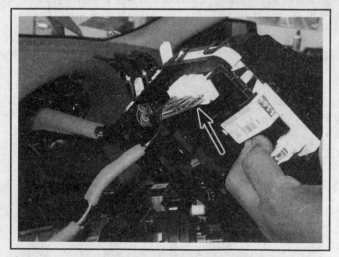

11.4 . . . then disconnect the instrument cluster wiring

12 Radio and speakers - removal and installation

❊❊ WARNING:

The models covered by this manual are equipped with Supplemental Restraint Systems (SRS), more commonly known as airbags. Always disable the airbag system before working in the vicinity of any airbag system components to avoid the possibility of accidental deployment of the airbags, which could cause personal injury (see Section 25).

RADIO

▶ **Refer to illustrations 12.3, 12.4a and 12.4b**

1 Disconnect the cable from the negative terminal of the battery (see Chapter 5).

2 Remove the center vent grilles from the instrument panel (see Chapter 11).

3 Remove the small trim panel below the radio (see illustration).

4 Remove the radio mounting screws from the top and bottom of the assembly (see illustrations).

5 Slide the radio assembly to the rear and disconnect the electrical connectors from the radio and the heater/air conditioning control panel.

6 Remove the screws that attach the radio bezel, then remove the radio mounting screws. Remove the radio.

7 Remove the radio bracket screws and the front air control unit screws. Remove the brackets if necessary.

8 Installation is the reverse of removal. Reconnect the battery and perform the necessary re-learn procedures (see Chapter 5).

INSTRUMENT PANEL SPEAKERS

9 Disconnect the cable from the negative terminal of the battery (see Chapter 5). Remove the windshield pillar trim panels (see Chapter 11, Section 26).

10 Use a plastic trim tool or a screwdriver wrapped with tape to pry up the speaker grilles.

11 Remove the four speaker mounting screws, then disconnect the electrical connector and remove the speakers.

12 Installation is the reverse of removal. Reconnect the battery and perform the necessary re-learn procedures (see Chapter 5).

DOOR SPEAKERS

▶ **Refer to illustration 12.14**

13 Remove the door trim panels (see Chapter 11).

14 Remove the speaker mounting screws, disconnect the electrical connector and remove the speakers (see illustration).

15 Installation is the reverse of removal.

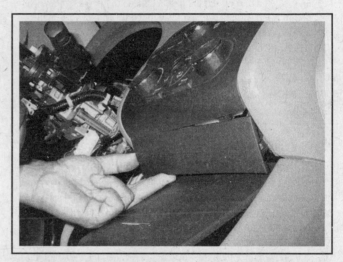

12.3 Remove the panel below the radio and heater/air conditioning control unit . . .

12.4a . . . then remove the lower . . .

12.4b . . . and upper mounting screws

12.14 Door speaker mounting screws and electrical connector

REAR SPEAKERS

Coupe models

16 Fold down the rear seat back.

17 Remove the trim panel from the upper part of the trunk compartment.

18 Remove the speaker mounting screws, disconnect the electrical connector and remove the speakers.

19 Installation is the reverse of removal.

Sedan models

20 Fold the rear seat backs forward.

21 Remove the clips from the seat back latch cover panel. Remove the panel.

22 Remove the seat back release handle trim cover.

23 Remove the high-mounted center stop light, if so equipped.

24 Remove the screws from the rear pillar trim covers, then release the clips and remove the covers.

25 Detach the seat belts from the rear parcel shelf.

26 Release the clips, then remove the rear parcel shelf.

27 Remove the speaker mounting screws, disconnect the electrical connector and remove the speakers.

28 Installation is the reverse of removal.

13 Rear window defogger - check and repair

1 The rear window defogger consists of a number of horizontal heating elements baked onto the inside surface of the glass. Power is supplied through two fuses and a relay in the IPDM relay box in the engine compartment. A defogger switch on the instrument panel controls the defogger grid.

2 Small breaks in the element can be repaired without removing the rear window.

CHECK

vRefer to illustrations 13.5, 13.6 and 13.8

3 Turn the ignition and defogger switches to the ON position.

4 Using a voltmeter, place the positive probe against the defogger grid positive side and the negative probe against the ground side. If battery voltage is not indicated, check that the ignition switch is On and that the feed and ground wires are properly connected. Check the two fuses, defogger switch, defogger relay and related wiring. A dealer can scan the body control module if necessary. If voltage is indicated, but all or part of the defogger doesn't heat, proceed with the following tests.

5 When measuring voltage during the next two tests, wrap a piece of aluminum foil around the tip of the voltmeter positive probe and press the foil against the heating element with your finger (see illustration). Place the negative probe on the defogger grid ground terminal.

6 Check the voltage at the center of each heating element (see illustration). If the voltage is 5 to 6 volts, the element is okay (there is no break). If the voltage is 0 volts, the element is broken between the center of the element and the positive end. If the voltage is 10 to 12 volts, the element is broken between the center of the element and the ground side. Check each heating element.

7 If none of the elements are broken, connect the negative probe to a good chassis ground. The voltage reading should stay the same; if it doesn't, the ground connection is bad.

8 To find the break, place the voltmeter negative probe against the defogger ground terminal. Place the voltmeter positive probe with the foil strip against the heating element at the positive side and slide it toward the negative side. The point at which the voltmeter deflects from several volts to zero is the point where the heating element is broken (see illustration).

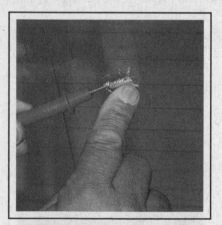

13.5 When measuring the voltage at the rear window defogger grid, wrap a piece of aluminum foil around the negative probe of the voltmeter and press the foil against the wire with your finger

13.6 To determine if a heating element has broken, check the voltage at the center of each element - if the voltage is approximately 6-volts, the element is unbroken

13.8 To find the break, place the voltmeter negative lead against the defogger ground terminal, place the voltmeter positive lead with the foil strip against the heat wire at the positive terminal end and slide it toward the negative terminal end. The point at which the voltmeter deflects from several volts to zero volts is the point at which the wire is broken

REPAIR

▶ **Refer to illustration 13.14**

9   Repair the break in the element using a repair kit specifically for this purpose, such as DuPont paste No. 4817 (or equivalent). The kit includes conductive plastic epoxy.

10   Before repairing a break, turn off the system and allow it to cool for a few minutes.

11   Lightly buff the element area with fine steel wool, then clean it thoroughly with rubbing alcohol.

12   Use masking tape to mask off the area being repaired.

13   Thoroughly mix the epoxy, following the kit instructions.

14   Apply the epoxy material to the slit in the masking tape, overlapping the undamaged area about 3/4-inch on either end (see illustration).

15   Allow the repair to cure for 24 hours before removing the tape and using the system.

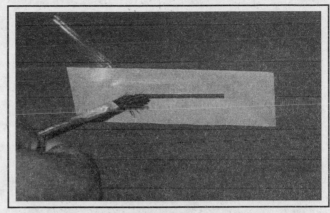

13.14 To use a defogger repair kit, apply masking tape to the inside of the window at the damaged area, then brush on the special conductive coating

14 Antenna - removal and installation

The grid-type radio antenna is an integral component of the rear window. To replace these antennas, the rear window must be replaced.

15 Headlight housing - removal and installation

✳✳ WARNING:

The models covered by this manual are equipped with Supplemental Restraint Systems (SRS), more commonly known as airbags. Always disable the airbag system before working in the vicinity of any airbag system components to avoid the possibility of accidental deployment of the airbags, which could cause personal injury (see Section 25).

MODELS EQUIPPED WITH HALOGEN BULBS

▶ **Refer to illustrations 15.3a and 15.3b**

1   Remove the front bumper cover (see Chapter 11).

2   Make sure that the light switch is Off.

3   Remove the three headlight housing mounting bolts (see illustrations).

4   Pull the headlight toward the front and disconnect the wiring.

5   Installation is the reverse of removal.

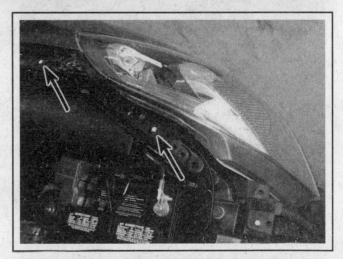

15.3a The two top headlight housing mounting bolts are accessible from the engine compartment . . .

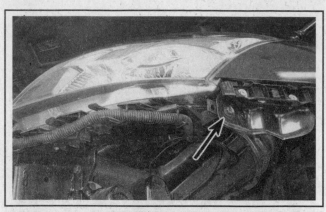

15.3b . . . but the front bumper cover must be removed for access to the lower bolt

MODELS EQUIPPED WITH XENON BULBS

☀☀ WARNING:

Some models use xenon bulbs (also known as High Intensity Discharge [HID] bulbs) instead of halogen bulbs. These can be identified by the high-voltage warning sticker on the headlight housing or under the hood. According to the manufacturer, the high voltages produced by this system can be fatal in the event of a shock. Also, the voltage can remain in the circuit even after the headlight switch has been turned to OFF and the ignition key has been removed. Therefore, for your safety, we don't recommend that you try to remove the headlight housing(s) on a vehicle equipped with xenon bulbs. Instead, have this service performed by a dealer service department or other qualified repair shop.

16 Headlight bulb - replacement

MODELS EQUIPPED WITH HALOGEN BULBS

▶ Refer to illustration 16.2

☀☀ WARNING:

Halogen gas-filled bulbs, which are under pressure, may shatter if the surface is scratched or the bulb is dropped. Wear eye protection and handle the bulbs carefully, grasping only the base whenever possible. Do not touch the surface of the bulb

with your fingers because the oil from your skin could cause it to overheat and fail prematurely. If you do touch the bulb surface, clean it with rubbing alcohol.

➡Note: There are separate headlight bulbs for the high and low beams.

1 Detach the plastic inner fender liner at the front edge, then pull the liner back to access the headlight bulbs (see Chapter 11).
2 Twist the bulb holder counterclockwise and pull it out (see illustration).
3 Unplug the electrical connector from the bulb holder.
4 Installation is the reverse of removal.

MODELS EQUIPPED WITH XENON BULBS

☀☀ WARNING:

Some models use xenon bulbs (also known as High Intensity Discharge [HID] bulbs) instead of halogen bulbs. These can be identified by the high-voltage warning sticker on the headlight housing or under the hood. According to the manufacturer, the high voltages produced by this system can be fatal in the event of a shock. Also, the voltage can remain in the circuit even after the headlight switch has been turned to OFF and the ignition key has been removed. Therefore, for your safety, we don't recommend that you try to replace one of these bulbs yourself. Instead, have this service performed by a dealer service department or other qualified repair shop.

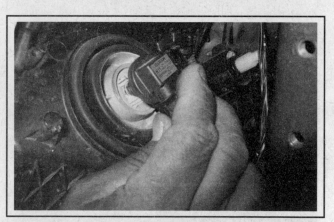

16.2 The headlight bulbs can be reached when the inner fender liner is detached and pulled back - twist the headlight bulb holder counterclockwise to remove it (low beam bulb shown)

17 Headlights - adjustment

▶ Refer to illustrations 17.2 and 17.7

➡Note: It is important that the headlights are aimed correctly. If adjusted incorrectly they could blind the driver of an oncoming vehicle and cause a serious accident or seriously reduce your ability to see the road. The headlights should be checked for proper aim every 12 months and any time a new headlight

is installed or front end body work is performed. It should be emphasized that the following procedure is only an interim step that will provide temporary adjustment until the headlights can be adjusted by a properly equipped shop.

1 Adjustment should be made with the vehicle sitting level, the gas tank half-full and no unusually heavy load in the vehicle.

2   All models are equipped with one adjustment screw in each headlight housing (see illustration). The headlights are only adjustable vertically.

3   If headlight housing has been replaced or the vehicle has suffered front end damage refer to following procedure.

4   This method requires a blank wall, masking tape and a level floor.

5   Position masking tape vertically on the wall in reference to the vehicle centerline and the centerlines of both headlights.

6   Position a horizontal tape line in reference to the centerline of all the headlights.

➡Note: It may be easier to position the tape on the wall with the vehicle parked only a few inches away.

7   Adjustment should be made with the vehicle parked 25 feet from the wall, sitting level, the gas tank half-full and no unusually heavy load in the vehicle (see illustration).

8   Starting with the low beam adjustment, position the high intensity zone so it is two inches below the horizontal line and two inches to the side of the headlight vertical line away from oncoming traffic.

9   With the high beams on, the high intensity zone should be vertically centered with the exact center just below the horizontal line. Note: It may not be possible to position the headlight aim exactly for both high and low beams. If a compromise must be made, keep in mind that the low beams are the most used and have the greatest effect on safety.

10 Have the headlights adjusted by a dealer service department or service station at the earliest opportunity.

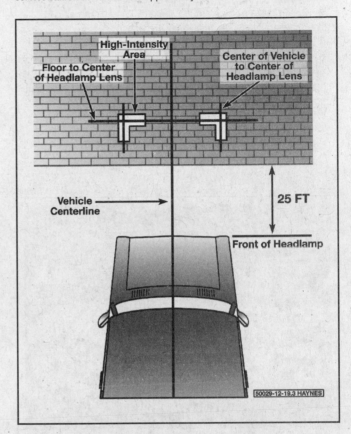

17.7 Headlight adjustment details

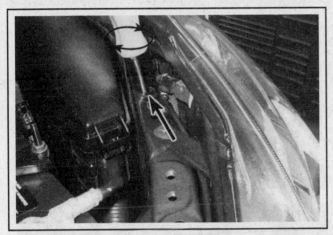

17.2 Headlight housing adjustment screw

18 Bulb replacement

FRONT PARKING/TURN SIGNAL AND SIDE MARKER LIGHTS

▸ **Refer to illustration 18.2**

1   If you're removing a park/turn signal bulb, detach the plastic inner fender liner at the front edge, then pull the liner back to access the bulbs (see Chapter 11). The side marker bulb is accessible from under the hood.

2   Turn the bulb sockets counterclockwise and pull them out of the housing (see illustration).

3   Remove the bulb from the bulb holder (see "Bulb removal").

4   Installation is the reverse of removal.

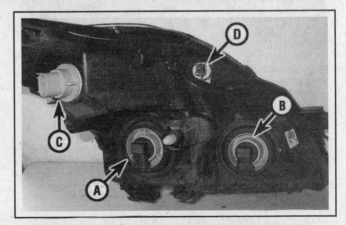

18.2 Headlight housing bulb locations (left side shown)

A   Low beam bulb
B   High beam bulb
C   Park/turn signal bulb
D   Side marker bulb

REAR TURN SIGNAL, BRAKE, TAIL, SIDE MARKER AND BACK-UP LIGHTS

♦ **Refer to illustrations 18.5, 18.6, 18.7, 18.8 and 18.9**

5 Remove the rear trim panel from the trunk interior (see illustration).

6 Unclip the trunk interior liner and pull it back far enough to access the rear taillight assembly (see illustration).

7 Remove the nuts from the studs (see illustration).

8 Remove the taillight assembly (see illustration).

9 Twist the bulb holder counterclockwise and pull it from the housing (see illustration). Remove the bulb from the bulb holder (see "Bulb removal").

10 Installation is the reverse of removal.

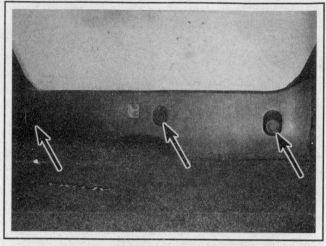

18.5 Remove these plastic fasteners and the trunk trim panel . . .

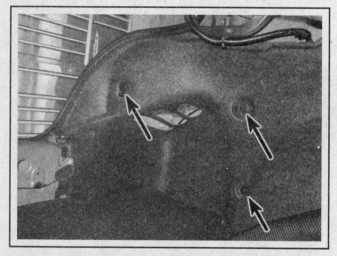

18.6 . . . then remove these fasteners and pull back the side trim

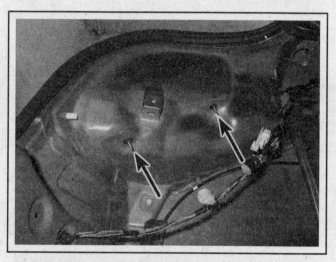

18.7 Taillight housing mounting nuts

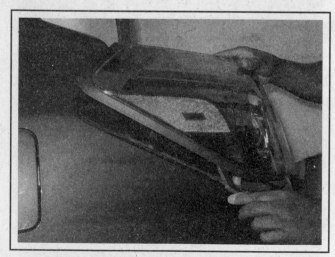

18.8 Pry the taillight housing rearward to pop the studs out of the mounting holes

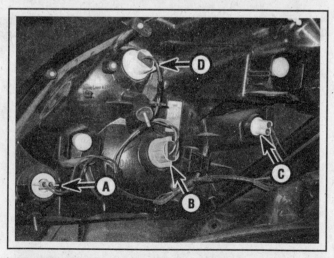

18.9 Taillight bulb details (left side shown)

A Back-up light bulb   C Side marker light bulb
B Stop/taillight bulb   D Turn signal bulb

Bulb removal

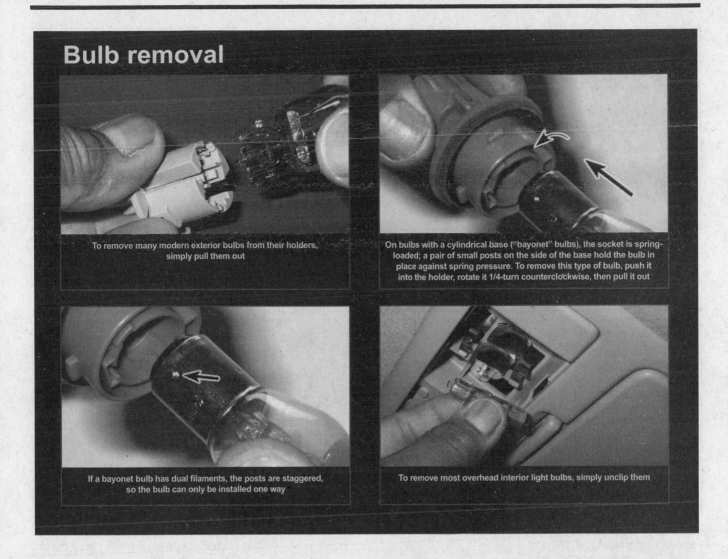

To remove many modern exterior bulbs from their holders, simply pull them out

On bulbs with a cylindrical base ("bayonet" bulbs), the socket is spring-loaded; a pair of small posts on the side of the base hold the bulb in place against spring pressure. To remove this type of bulb, push it into the holder, rotate it 1/4-turn counterclockwise, then pull it out

If a bayonet bulb has dual filaments, the posts are staggered, so the bulb can only be installed one way

To remove most overhead interior light bulbs, simply unclip them

FOG LIGHTS

☀☀ WARNING:

Wear eye protection and handle the bulbs carefully, grasping only the base whenever possible. Do not touch the surface of the bulb with your fingers because the oil from your skin could cause it to overheat and fail prematurely. If you do touch the bulb surface, clean it with rubbing alcohol.

11 Detach the plastic inner fender liner at the front edge, then pull the liner back to access the bulb (see Chapter 11).
12 Disconnect the electrical connector from the bulb holder.
13 Turn the bulb holder counterclockwise and pull it out of the housing.
14 Installation is the reverse of removal.

LICENSE PLATE LIGHT

▶ Refer to illustration 18.16

15 Loosen the trunk lid finish panel and move it out of the way.

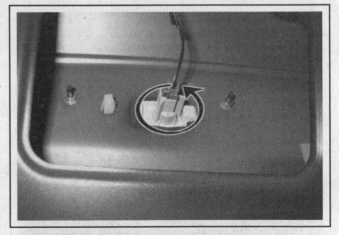

18.16 Twist the license plate light bulb holder counterclockwise to remove it from the housing

16 Twist the bulb socket counterclockwise and pull it out (see illustration).
17 Pull the bulb out of the socket to replace it.
18 Installation is the reverse of removal.

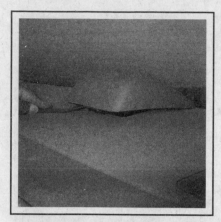

18.19 Push the high-mounted stop light to the rear . . .

18.20 . . . then lift it up for access to the bulb holder

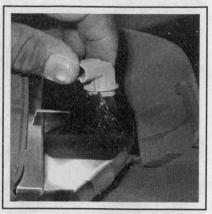

18.21 Twist the bulb socket to remove it from the housing

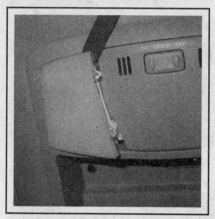

18.24a Use a plastic trim tool or a screwdriver wrapped with tape to carefully pry the lens off . . .

18.24b . . . then remove the bulb

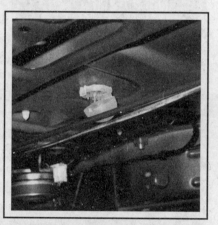

18.24c The trunk light bulb is covered by a plastic lens - pry it open to remove the bulb

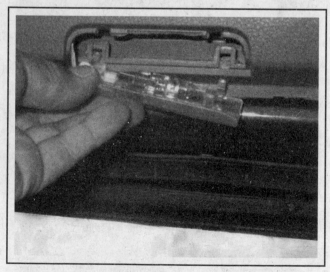

18.24d The door courtesy lights are serviced by prying off the lens, then pulling the bulb out of its holder

HIGH-MOUNTED BRAKE LIGHT

◆ **Refer to illustrations 18.19, 18.20 and 18.21**

➡**Note: This procedure applies only to models without a rear spoiler. On models with spoilers, LEDs are used instead of replaceable bulbs.**

19 Push the brake light housing to the rear, then release the front mounting tabs (see illustration).

20 Slide it to the front and release the rear tabs (see illustration).

21 Lift the housing and twist the bulb socket counterclockwise to remove it (see illustration).

22 Pull the bulb out of the socket to replace it.

23 Installation is the reverse of removal.

INTERIOR LIGHTS

◆ **Refer to illustrations 18.24a, 18.24b, 18.24c and 18.24d**

24 All interior light bulbs are replaced in the same general way. Use a small screwdriver or trim tool to carefully pry off the lens (see illustrations).

25 Pull the bulb straight out of its socket to remove it.

26 Replace the bulb, then snap the lens back in place.

27 To replace the trunk light bulb, release the tab on the side of the lens, then pivot the lens open. The bulb can then be replaced as above.

INSTRUMENT CLUSTER ILLUMINATION

28 Instrument cluster illumination is contained within the cluster. Replace the cluster (see Section 11) as a complete unit if there is a problem with any of its individual components.

19 Horn - replacement

▶ **Refer to illustration 19.4**

1 Loosen the lug nuts of the left front wheel. Raise the vehicle and support it securely on jackstands. Remove the left front wheel.

2 Remove the fasteners at the forward end of the left inner fender splash shield so that it can be pulled back for access to the horns (see Chapter 11).

3 Remove the lower splash shield from the engine compartment.

4 To replace the horn(s), disconnect the electrical connector and remove the bracket bolt (see illustration).

5 Installation is the reverse of removal.

19.4 The horns can be reached through the left wheel well - bumper cover removed for clarity

20 Wiper motor - replacement

▶ **Refer to illustrations 20.3, 20.6, 20.7 and 20.8**

1 Turn the wiper ON then OFF, making sure that the blades are at the proper park position.

2 Mark the positions of the blades on the windshield with tape so they can be installed in the same alignment.

3 Pry off the wiper arm pivot caps, then remove the nuts (see illustration).

4 Remove the wiper arms from the drive studs.

5 Remove the cowl cover (see Chapter 11).

6 Remove any components attached to the strut brace (see illustration).

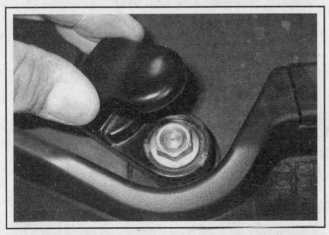

20.3 Pry open the cap, then remove the wiper arm nut - lock the wiper arm and use its leverage to wiggle the arm from the stud

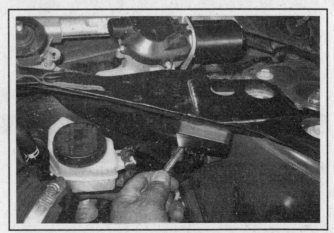

20.6 Detach all components from the strut brace and lay them aside

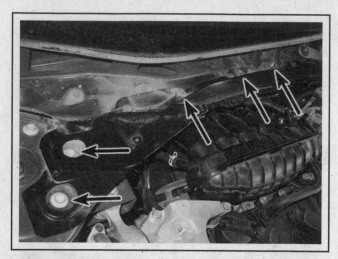

20.7 Remove all of the mounting bolts from the suspension strut brace

20.8 Wiper assembly mounting bolts

7   Detach the wiring harness from the wiper frame and the strut brace, then unbolt and remove the brace (see illustration).

8   Remove the cover from the left wiper drive stud, then remove the three mounting bolts and remove the wiper assembly (see illustration).

9   When installing the wiper motor assembly, turn it ON and then OFF to place the unit in the PARK position before attaching the wiper arms.

21   Cruise control system - description and check

All models have an electronically-controlled throttle body - there is no accelerator cable (or cruise control cable). When you select the speed that you want to maintain, the PCM controls vehicle speed by opening and closing the throttle plate by means of a computer-controlled solenoid (motor) inside the throttle body.

The diagnostic procedures for troubleshooting the cruise control system are beyond the scope of this manual, but if the system can't be set, or the set speed doesn't cancel when the brake pedal is depressed, check the fuses. Start with the fuses in the engine compartment fuse and relay box, then check the fuses in the under-dash fuse and relay box. If the set speed doesn't cancel when the CANCEL button is depressed, check the fuse for that circuit. Also check the operation and adjustment of the cruise control cancel switch (see Chapter 9) and, on manual transaxle models, the ASCD switch (see Chapter 8).

22   Power window system - general information

The power window system operates electric motors, mounted on the doors, which lower and raise the windows. The system consists of the control switches, the motors, regulators, glass mechanisms, the Body Control Module (BCM) and associated wiring.

The power windows can be lowered and raised from the master control switch by the driver or by the switch located at the passenger window. Each window has a separate motor that is reversible. The position of the control switch determines the polarity and therefore the direction of operation.

The circuit is protected by fuses and a circuit breaker. Check the fuses in the fuse panel. Each motor is equipped with an internal circuit breaker; this prevents one stuck window from disabling the whole system. Refer to the wiring diagrams at the end of this Chapter. Problems within this system can only be diagnosed with a factory scan tool. If you have eliminated the obvious causes of a problem, have the vehicle checked at a dealership service department or other properly equipped repair shop.

23 Power door lock system - general information

1   The power door lock system operates the power door motors, which are integral components of the door latch units in each door. The system consists of a fuse (in the engine compartment fuse and relay box), the Body Control Module (BCM), the control switches (in each of the front doors), the power door motors and the electrical wiring harnesses connecting all of these components.

2   The lock mechanisms in the door latch units are actuated by a reversible electric motor in each door. When you push the door lock switch to LOCK, the motor operates one way and locks the latch mechanism. When you push the door lock switch the other way, to the UNLOCK position, the motor operates in the other direction, unlocking the latch mechanism. Because the motors and lock mechanisms are an integral part of the door latch units, they cannot be repaired. If a door lock motor or lock mechanism fails, replace the door latch unit (see Chapter 11).

3   Some vehicles have an optional Intelligent Key system that allows you to lock and unlock the doors from outside the vehicle. The intelligent key system consists of the transmitter (the electronic push-button "key") and a remote keyless entry receiver mounted behind the glove box.

4   Some features of the door lock system on these vehicles rely on resources that they share with other electronic modules through the Programmable Communications Interface (PCI) data bus network. Professional diagnosis of these modules and the PCI data bus network requires the use of a CONSULT-III (proprietary factory) scan tool and factory diagnostic information. At-home repairs are therefore limited to inspecting the wiring for bad connections and for minor faults that can be easily repaired. If you are unable to locate the trouble using the following general steps, consult your dealer service department.

5   Always check the circuit fuses first. Refer to the wiring diagrams at the end of this Chapter. Problems within this system can only be diagnosed with a factory scan tool. If you have eliminated the obvious causes of a problem, have the vehicle checked at a dealership service department or other properly equipped repair shop.

➡**Note: It is not uncommon for wires to break in the harness between the body and the door because repeatedly opening and closing the door fatigues and eventually breaks the wires.**

24 Sunroof - general information

1   The sunroof is powered by a single motor located in the roof.

2   The sunroof switch (tilt and slide) sends an operation signal to the sunroof motor CPU encoder when the switches are pressed. Power is supplied to the motor from the Body Control Module (BCM) located under the instrument panel. The front door switch detects the open/close condition and sends an operating signal to the BCM. The sunroof will retain power for 45 seconds after the key has been turned off to operate the system. The retained power can be cancelled by opening the front door, turning the ignition switch to ON again or allowing the 45 seconds to elapse.

3   With the ignition On but the engine Off, operate the sunroof control switch through the tilt and slide functions.

4   Listen carefully for the sound of the sunroof motor running in the roof.

5   If the motor can be heard but the sunroof glass doesn't move, there's probably a problem with the drive mechanism.

6   If the sunroof does not operate and no sound comes from the motor, check the fuses (in the interior fuse panel and in the engine compartment power distribution center).

7   If there's voltage at the switch, disconnect it. Check the switch for continuity in all its operating positions. If the switch does not have continuity, replace it. If you have eliminated the obvious causes of a problem, have the vehicle checked at a dealership service department or other properly equipped repair shop.

25 Airbag system - general information

1   These models are equipped with a Supplemental Restraint System (SRS), more commonly known as airbags, designed to protect the driver and the passenger from serious injury in the event of a head-on collision. Some models are also equipped with side impact airbags in the front seats and along the roof rail. All models have a diagnostic control unit, located on the floor under the center console.

✳✳ WARNING:

If your vehicle is ever involved in a flood, or the interior carpeting is soaked for any reason, disconnect the battery and do not start the vehicle until the airbag system can be checked by a dealer service department or other repair facility equipped with the proper tool. If the SRS system is subjected to flooding, the airbags could go off upon starting the vehicle, even without an accident taking place.

AIRBAG MODULES

2   The airbag modules consist of a housing incorporating the cushion (airbag) and inflator unit. The inflator assembly is mounted on the back of the housing over a hole through which gas is expelled, inflating the bag almost instantaneously when an electrical signal is sent from the system. The specially wound wire on the driver's side that carries this signal to the module is called a spiral cable. The spiral cable is a flat, ribbon-like electrically conductive tape that is wound many times so that it can transmit an electrical signal regardless of steering wheel position. Airbag modules are located in the steering wheel, on the passenger side above the glove box and, on some models, side-impact airbags located in the seat backs and head-level airbags located along the roof rails (side curtain airbags).

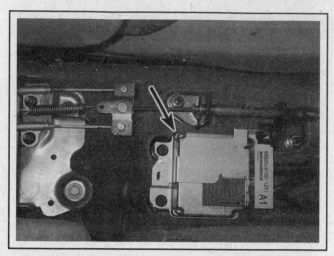

25.3a The airbag diagnosis sensor unit is mounted under the center console

25.3b The front crash zone sensor is mounted to the rear of the radiator support panel

CONTROL UNIT AND SENSORS

♦ **Refer to illustrations 25.3a and 25.3b**

3   The diagnosis/sensor unit contains an on-board microprocessor which monitors the operation of the system, and also contains a crash sensor. It checks this system every time the vehicle is started, causing the "AIRBAG" light to go on then off, if the system is operating properly. If there is a fault in the system, the light will go on and stay on and the unit will store fault codes indicating the nature of the fault. If the AIRBAG light goes on and stays on, the vehicle should be taken to your dealer immediately for service. The diagnosis/sensor unit is located under the center console (see illustration). The crash zone sensor is located on the radiator support (see illustration) and the side airbags sensor (satellite crash sensor) is in each door "B" pillar.

OPERATION

4   For the airbag(s) to deploy, the impact sensor(s) must be activated. When this condition occurs, the circuit to the airbag inflator is closed and the airbag inflates.

SELF-DIAGNOSIS SYSTEM

5   A self-diagnosis circuit in the SRS unit displays a light on the instrument panel when the ignition switch is turned to the On position. If the system is operating normally, the light should go out after about five seconds. If the light doesn't come on, or doesn't go out after a short time, or if it comes on while you're driving the vehicle, or if it blinks at any time, there's a malfunction in the SRS system. Have it inspected and repaired as soon as possible. Do not attempt to troubleshoot or service the SRS system yourself. Even a small mistake could cause the SRS system to malfunction when you need it.

SERVICING COMPONENTS NEAR THE SRS SYSTEM

6   Nevertheless, there are times when you need to remove the steering wheel, radio or service other components on or near the dashboard.

At these times, you'll be working around components and wire harnesses for the SRS system.

⁂ WARNING:

Do not use electrical test equipment on airbag system wires; it could cause the airbag(s) to deploy. ALWAYS DISABLE THE SRS SYSTEM BEFORE WORKING NEAR THE SRS SYSTEM COMPONENTS OR RELATED WIRING.

DISABLING THE SRS SYSTEM

⁂ WARNING:

Any time you are working in the vicinity of airbag wiring or components, DISABLE THE SRS SYSTEM.

⁂ WARNING:

An auxiliary voltage input device (memory saver) must not be used when working near airbag system components.

7   To disable the airbag system, perform the following steps:
  a) *Turn the steering wheel to the straight-ahead position and turn the ignition switch to the Lock position, then remove the key.*
  b) *Disconnect the battery negative and positive cables, then wait ten minutes before proceeding with any work.*
  c) *Before touching any airbag system component, ground yourself to a metal part of the vehicle to discharge any static electricity built up in your body.*

ENABLING THE SYSTEM

8   After you've disabled the airbag and performed the necessary service, reconnect the two-pin airbag connector into the two-pin spiral

cable connector (driver's side), the SRS main harness (passenger's side) or the side-impact airbag. Reinstall the lid to the underside of the steering wheel or reinstall the glove box/trim panel or upper trim panels.

9 To enable the airbag system, perform the following steps:

a) Turn the ignition switch to the On position.

b) Make sure nobody is inside the vehicle.

c) Connect the battery cables.

d) Turn the ignition to the Off position, then with your body out of the path of the airbag, turn the ignition switch to the On position. Confirm that the airbag warning light is functioning properly.

e) Perform the necessary re-learn procedures (see Chapter 5).

f) Take the vehicle to a dealer service department or other qualified repair facility and have the airbag system checked and the warning light canceled if it remains lit.

REMOVAL AND INSTALLATION

✳✳ WARNING:

The bolts used throughout the airbag system to mount the airbag modules, diagnosis sensor unit, crash zone sensor and satellite sensors have a special coating. These bolts are designed to be used once. Replace them with new factory bolts, and never use a substitute fastener.

Driver's side airbag and spiral cable

10 Refer to Chapter 10, Section 16, for removal and installation of the driver's side airbag and steering wheel (which will give you access to the spiral cable).

✳✳ WARNING:

When installing the spiral cable, be sure to follow the centering instructions carefully.

Passenger side airbag and other airbag modules

11 Even if you ever have to remove the instrument panel, it's not necessary to remove the passenger airbag module to do so; it can simply remain installed in the instrument panel. We don't recommend removing any of the other airbag modules either. These jobs are best left to a professional.

Impact seat belt retractors

12 All models are equipped with pyrotechnic (explosive) units in the front seat belt retracting mechanisms for both the lap and shoulder belts. During an impact that would trigger the airbag system, the airbag control unit also triggers the seat belt retractors. When the pyrotechnic charges go off, they accelerate the retractors to instantly take up any slack in the seat belt system to more fully prepare the driver and front seat passenger for impact. The airbag system should be disabled any time work is done to or around the seats.

✳✳ WARNING:

Never strike the pillars or floor pan with a hammer or use an impact-driver tool in these areas unless the system is disabled.

26 Intelligent Power Distribution Module (IPDM) - description, check and replacement

DESCRIPTION

1 The Intelligent Power Distribution Module (IPDM) is a solid state device that controls controls various relays and circuits when commands are received from the Powertrain Control Module (PCM) and/or the Body Control Module (BCM). The circuits under its control are:

Headlights
Parking and side marker lights
Tail lights/license plate lights
Fog lights
Windshield wipers
Electronic steering column lock
Air conditioning compressor clutch
Starter relay
Fuel pump relay
Cooling fan relay
Horn relay
Rear window defogger relay

CHECK

2 Although the IPDM is usually very reliable, it must always be factored in to any diagnosis of the circuits under its control. Thorough testing of the unit requires a proprietary Nissan scan tool, but a simple test, called the Auto Active Test, can help you determine the possible source of a problem with some of the circuits under its control. The circuits checked in this test include the:

Windshield wiper circuit
Tail/parking/license plate light circuits
Fog light circuit
Headlight circuit
Air conditioning compressor clutch circuit
Engine cooling fan circuit
Oil pressure warning light

3 Lift the windshield wipers from the windshield and close the right front door. Make sure the ignition switch is in the Off position.

4 To initiate the Auto Active Test, turn the ignition switch to the On position and depress the left front door switch 10 times within 20 seconds, then turn the ignition switch to the Off position.

5 Within 10 seconds, turn the ignition switch back to the On position. The horn should beep once, signifying the start of the test.

6 When the test begins, the following sequence of events should happen (and the sequence of events should repeat three times):

The oil pressure light should blink continuously for the duration of the test.

The windshield wiper should operate on low speed for 5 seconds, then high speed for 5 seconds

The parking lights/tail lights/license plate lights/fog lights should come on for 10 seconds

The headlights should turn on and switch from low-beam to high-beam five times

The air conditioning compressor clutch should engage (click on and off) 5 times

The engine cooling fan should come on for 10 seconds (mid-speed for five seconds, high-speed for five seconds)

DIAGNOSIS

Wipers, parking lights/daytime running lights (if equipped)/tail lights/license plate lights/fog lights

7   If any of these systems do not operate during the Auto Active Test, the problem could be caused by:

a) *Wiper motor or the circuit between IPDM and wiper motor faulty*

b) *Wiper motor ground problem*

c) *Light bulb or the circuit between IPDM and light faulty*

d) *Light bulb/housing ground problem*

e) *Faulty IPDM*

8   If the system in question does operate during the Auto Active Test but doesn't operate under normal conditions, the problem could be a faulty switch, a faulty Body Control Module (BCM), or the circuit between the two.

Air conditioning compressor clutch

9   If the compressor clutch doesn't operate during the Auto Active Test, the problem could be caused by:

a) *Compressor clutch or the circuit between IPDM and compressor clutch faulty*

b) *Faulty IPDM*

10   If the compressor clutch does operate during the Auto Active Test but doesn't operate under normal conditions, the problem could be a faulty switch, a faulty Body Control Module (BCM), a faulty PCM, a fault in the circuit between the PCM and the BCM, or a fault in the circuit between the PCM and the IPDM.

Electric engine cooling fan

11   If the engine cooling fan doesn't operate during the Auto Active Test, the problem could be caused by:

a) *Cooling fan motor or the circuit between cooling fan motor and IPDM faulty*

b) *Faulty IPDM*

12   If the engine cooling fan does operate during the Auto Active Test but doesn't operate under normal conditions, the problem could be a faulty PCM, a faulty coolant temperature sensor, the circuit between the coolant temperature sensor and the PCM, or the circuit between the PCM and the IPDM.

Oil pressure warning light

13   If the oil pressure warning light doesn't blink during the Auto

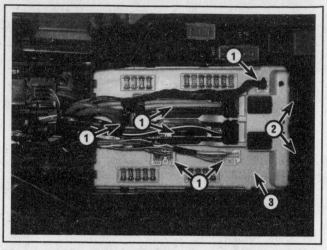

26.17 Intelligent Power Distribution Module (IPDM) details

1	*Electrical connectors*	3	*IPDM*
2	*Release tabs*		

Active Test, the problem could be caused by:

a) *Problem in the CAN communication circuit between the BCM and the IPDM*

b) *Problem in the CAN communication circuit between the BCM and the instrument cluster*

c) *Faulty instrument cluster*

14   If the oil pressure warning light does blink during the Auto Active Test but doesn't operate when it should (during the bulb check when the ignition is turned On), the problem could be a faulty oil pressure sending unit, a faulty IPDM, or the circuit between the two.

REPLACEMENT

♦ **Refer to illustration 26.17**

➡**Note: The IPDM is located in the left rear corner of the engine compartment.**

15   Disconnect the cable from the negative terminal of the battery (see Chapter 5).

16   Remove the cover from the IPDM.

17   Disconnect the electrical connectors, push back the two retainers at the rear end of the IPDM (see illustration), pull the IPDM up and remove it from the vehicle.

18   Installation is the reverse of removal.

27 Wiring diagrams - general information

Since it isn't possible to include all wiring diagrams for every year and model covered by this manual, the following diagrams are those that are typical and most commonly needed.

Prior to troubleshooting any circuits, check the fuses and circuit breakers (if equipped) to make sure they are in good condition. Make sure the battery is properly charged and has clean, tight cable connec-

tions (see Chapter 1).

When checking the wiring system, make sure that all electrical connectors are clean, with no broken or loose pins. When unplugging an electrical connector, do not pull on the wires, only on the connector housings themselves.

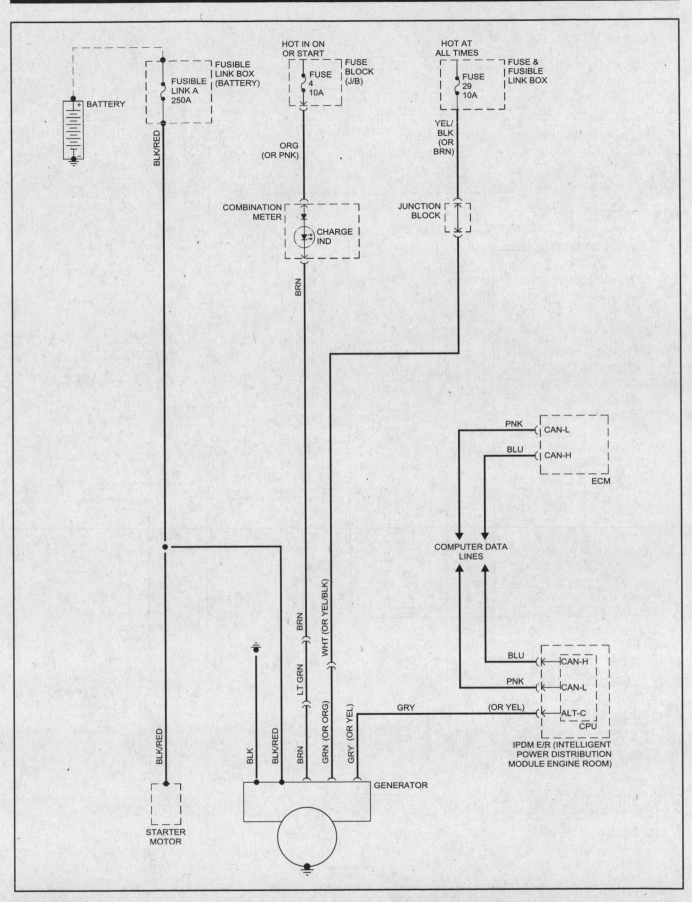

Charging system

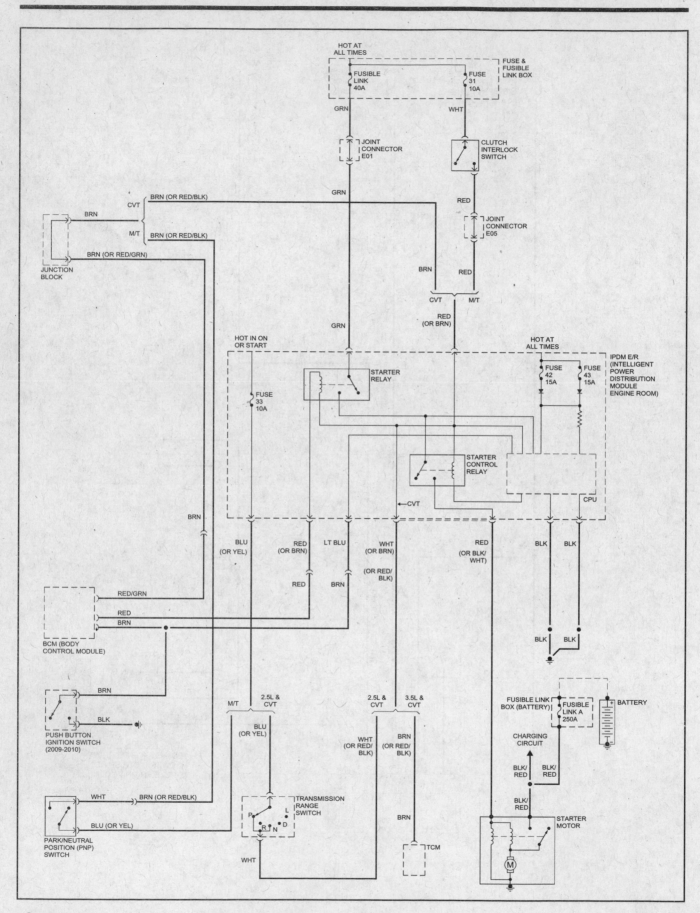

Starting system

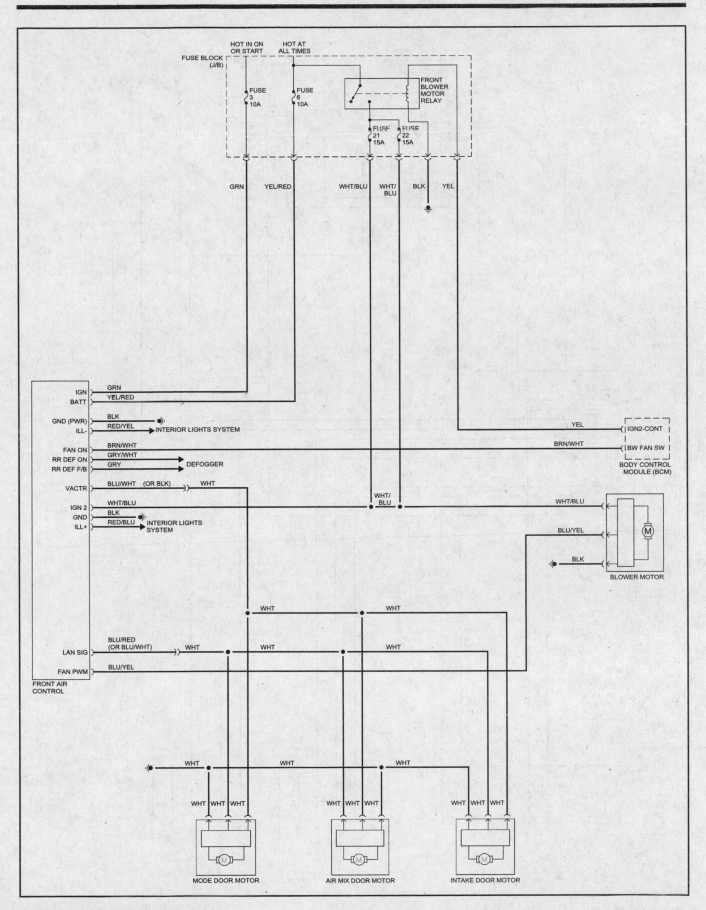

Heater system - 2007 and 2008 models

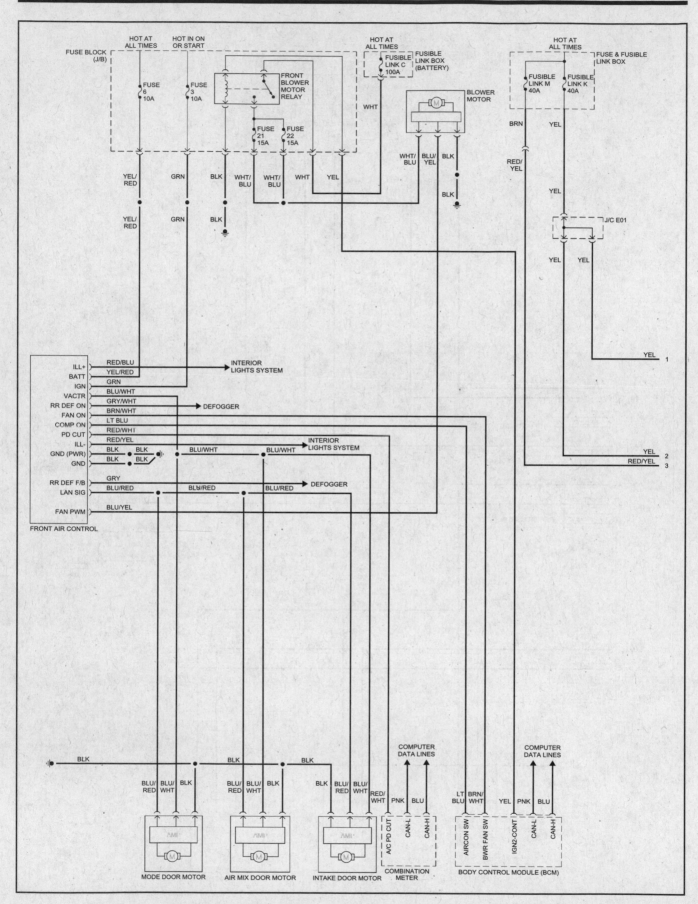

Air conditioning system (manual) - 2010 models (1 of 2)

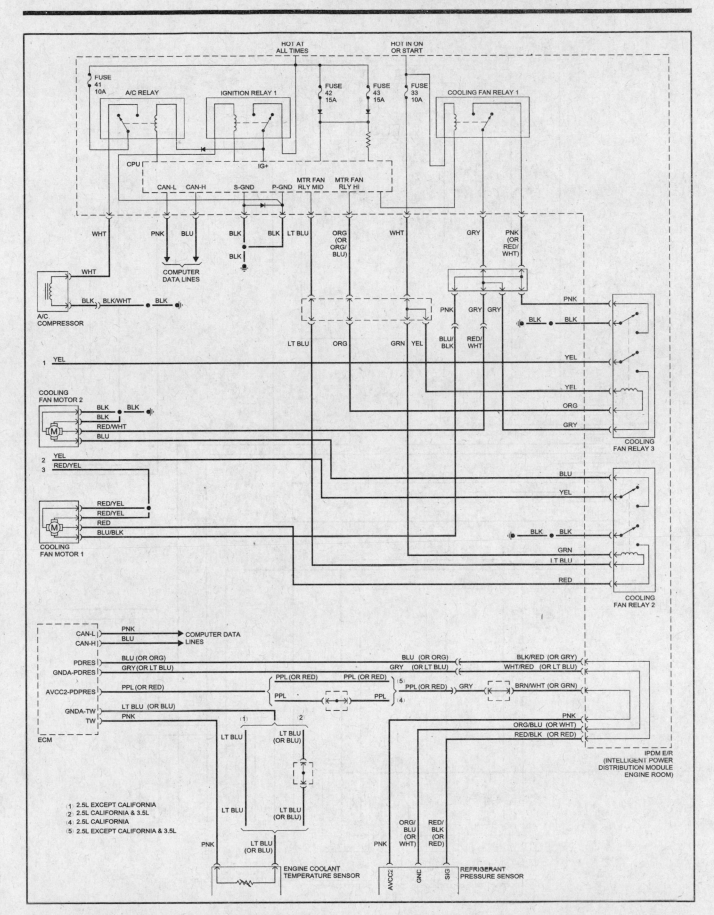

Air conditioning system (manual) - 2010 models (2 of 2)

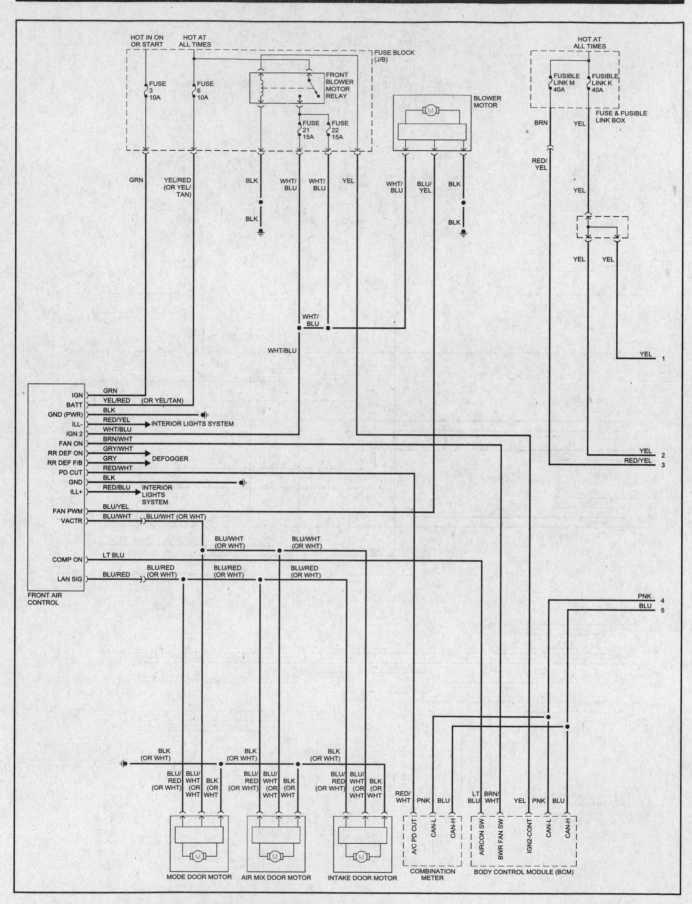

Air conditioning system (manual) - 2007 through 2009 models (1 of 2)

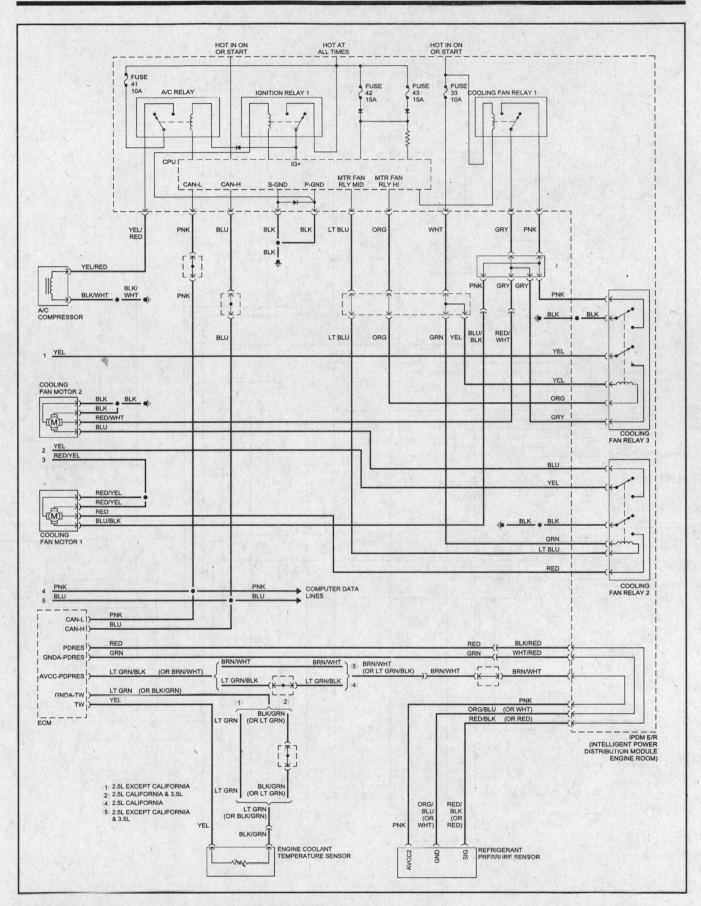

Air conditioning system (manual) - 2007 through 2009 models (2 of 2)

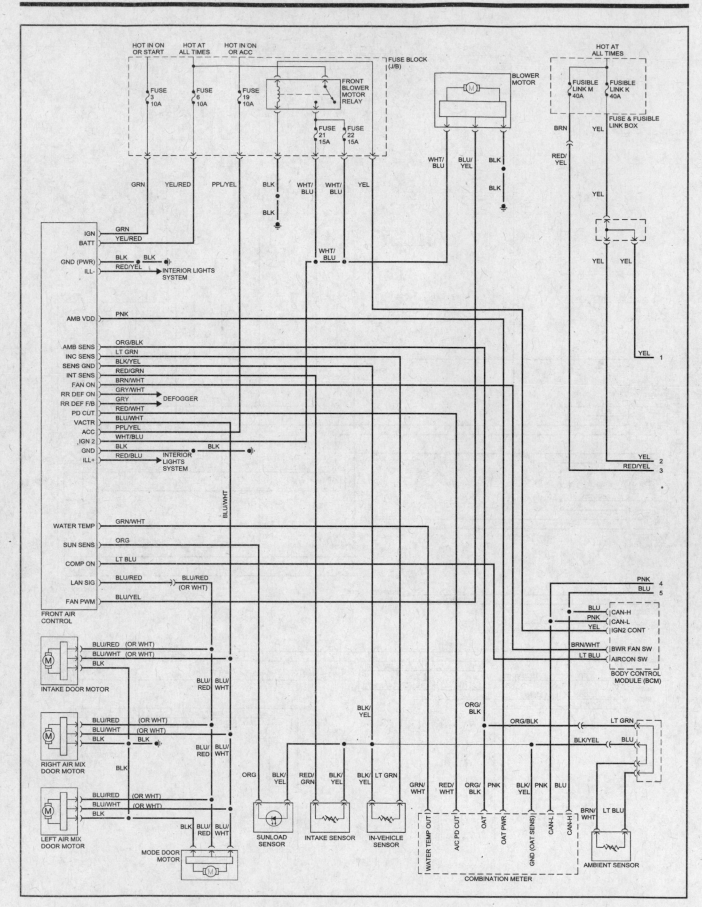

Air conditioning system (automatic) (1 of 2)

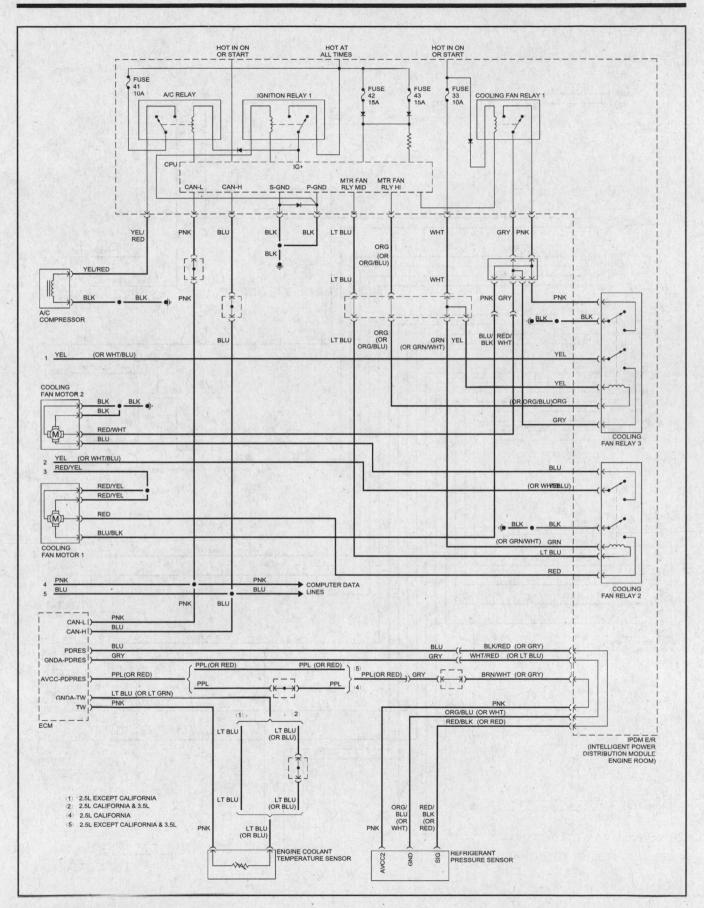

Air conditioning system (automatic) (2 of 2)

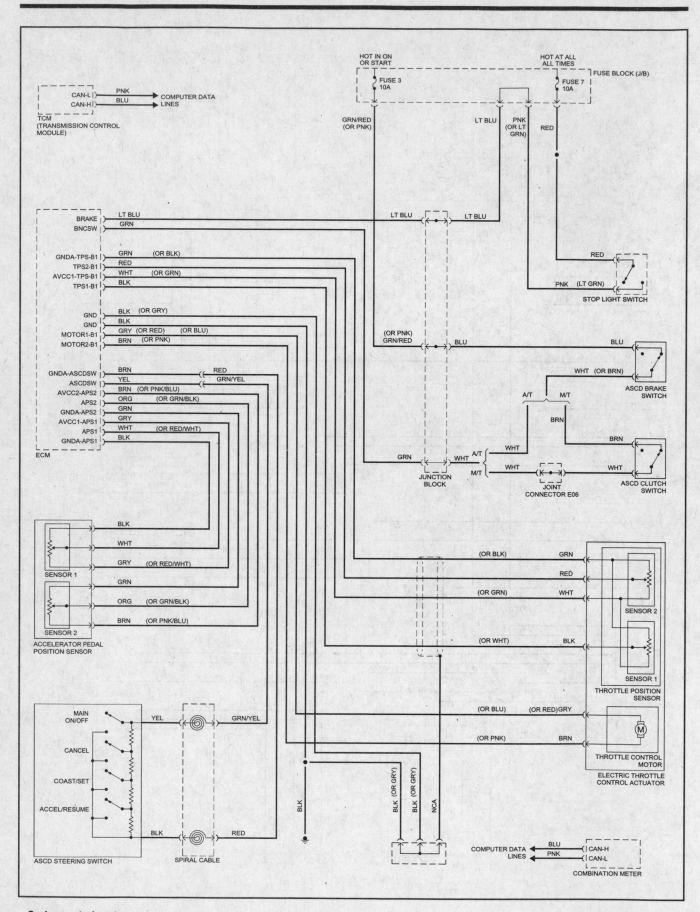

Cruise control system

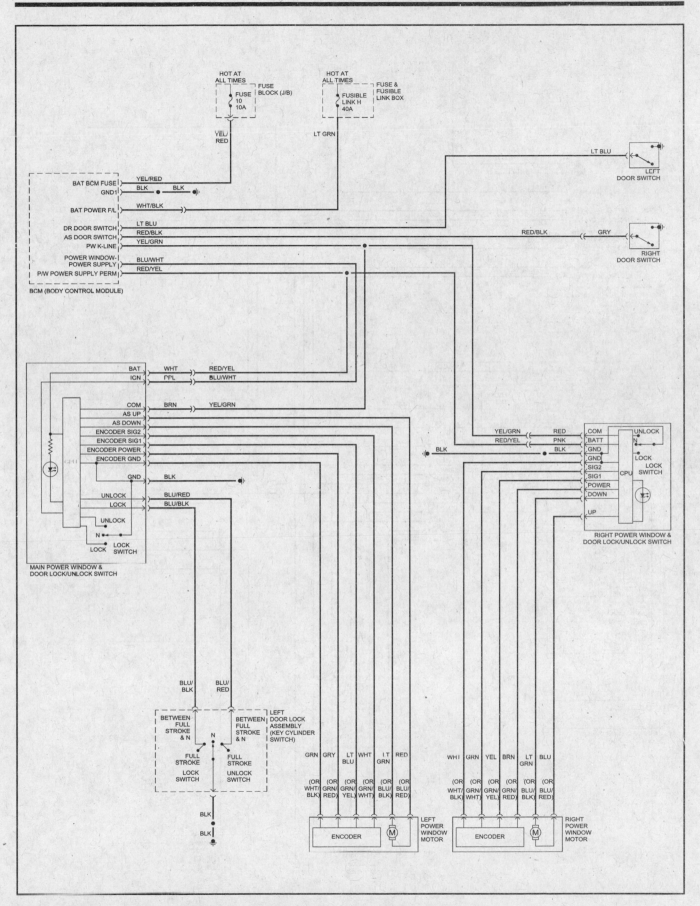

Power window system - 2008 and later coupe models with driver and passenger anti-pinch system

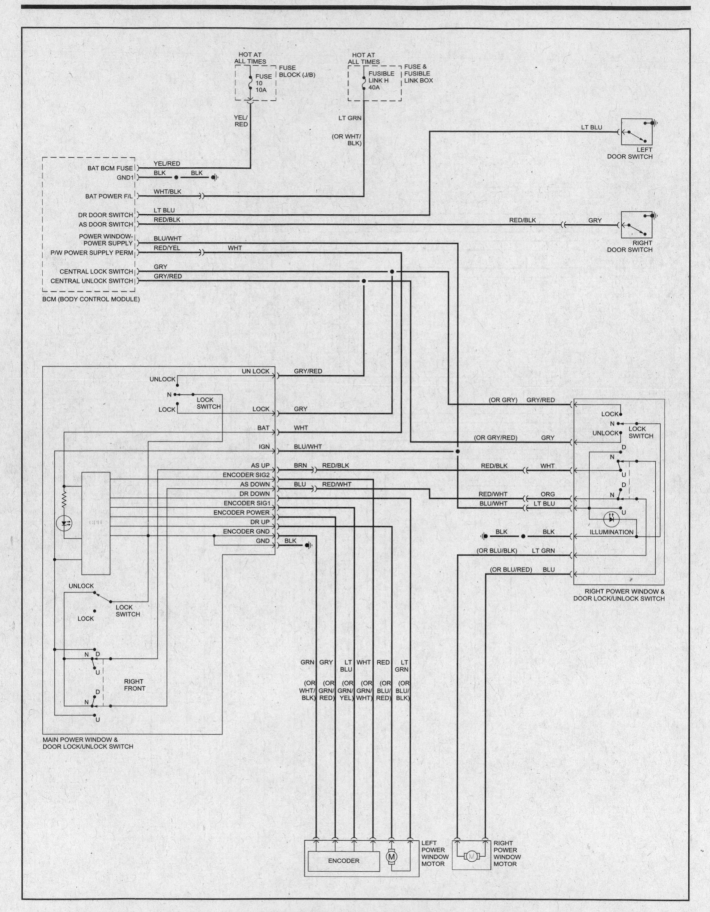

Power window system - 2008 and later coupe models with driver anti-pinch system

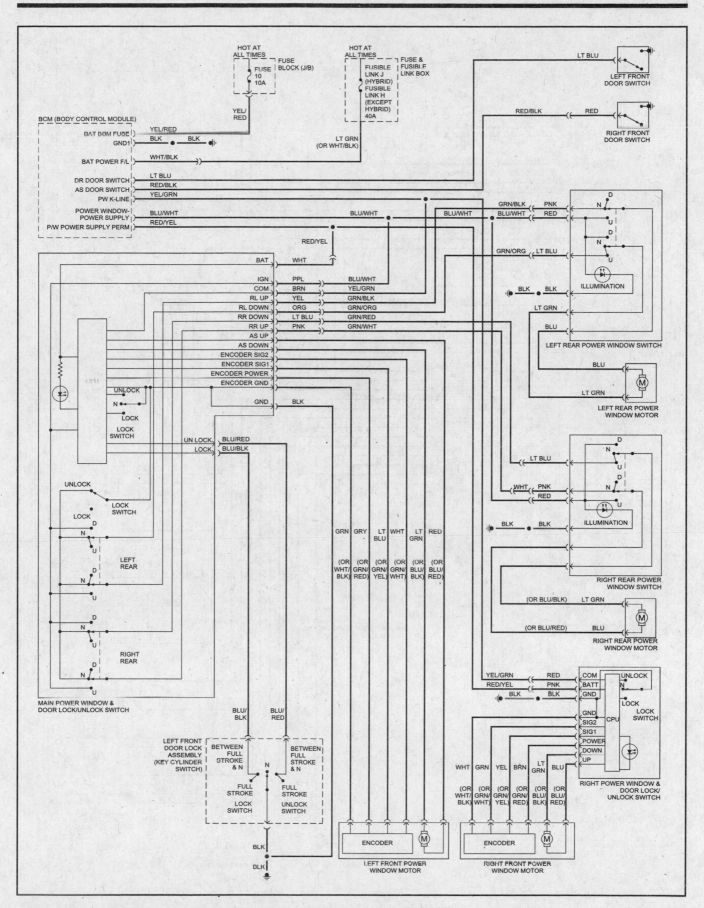

Power window system - sedan models with driver and passenger anti-pinch system

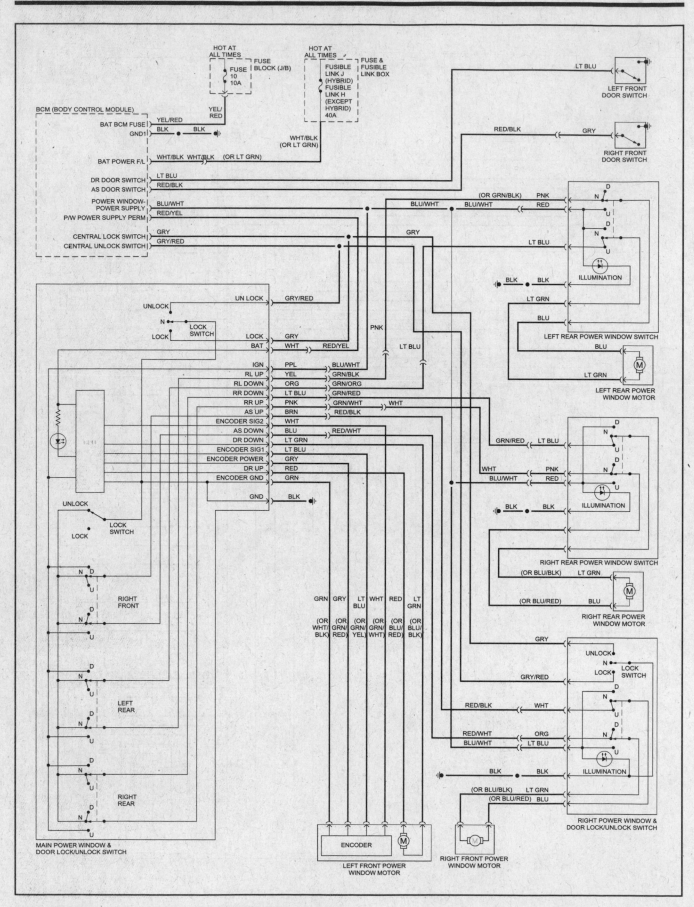

Power window system - sedan models with driver anti-pinch system

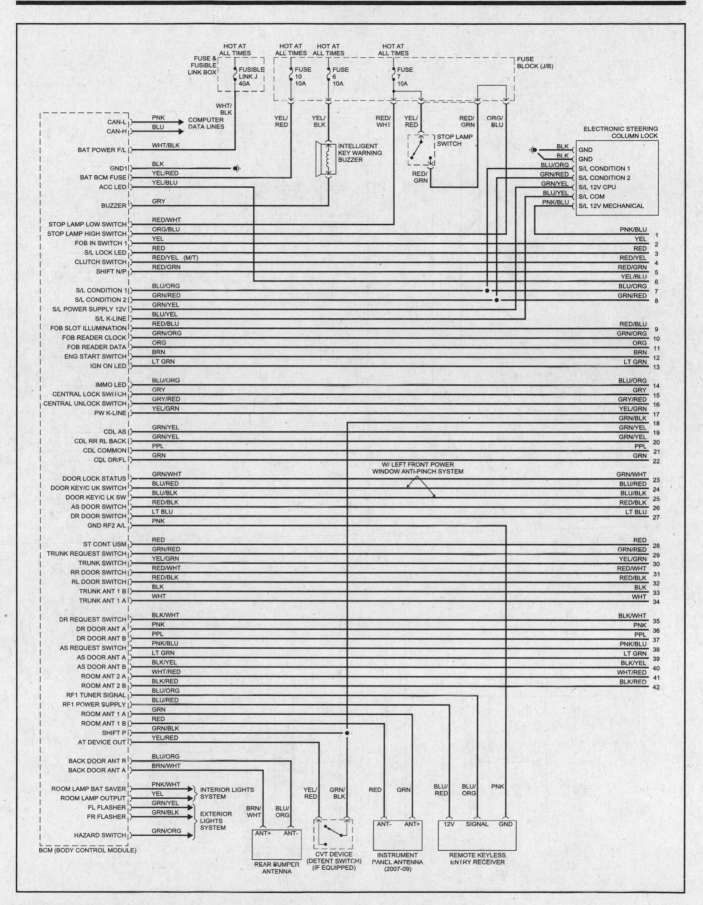

Power door lock system - models with intelligent key (1 of 4)

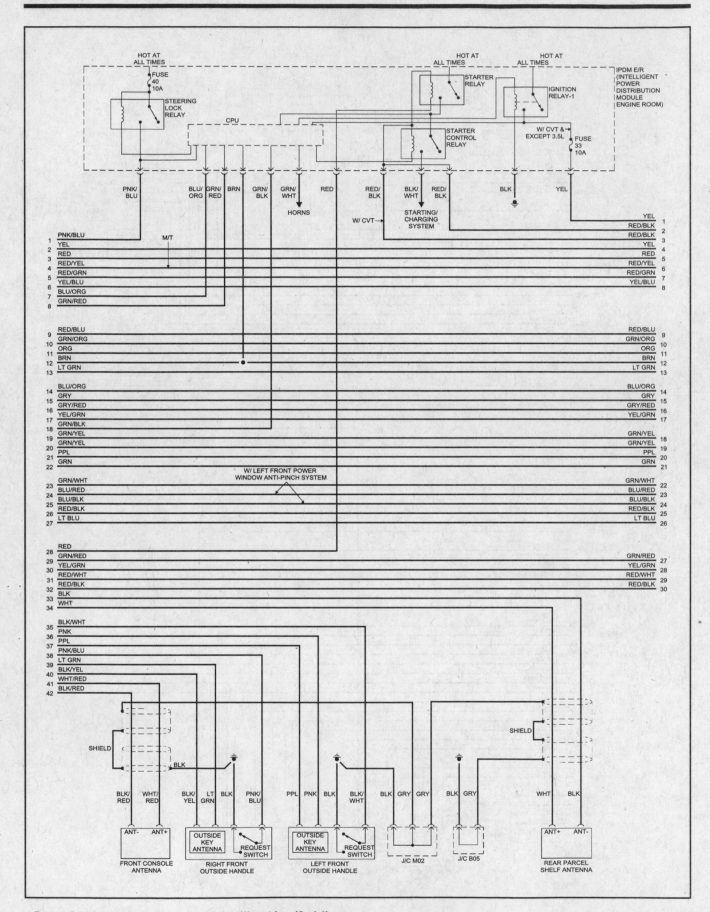

Power door lock system - models with intelligent key (2 of 4)

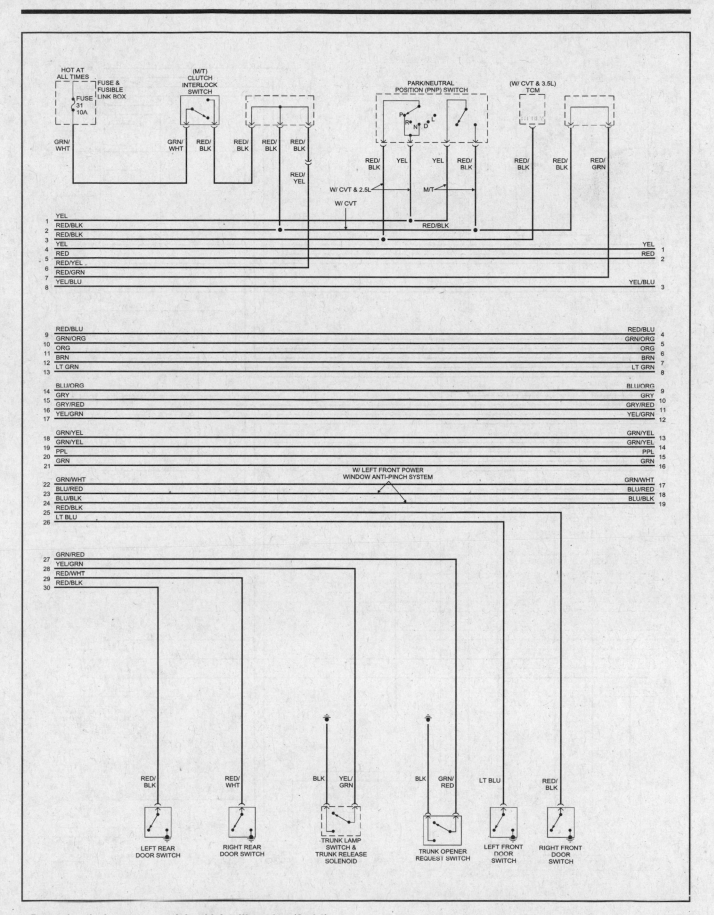

Power door lock system - models with intelligent key (3 of 4)

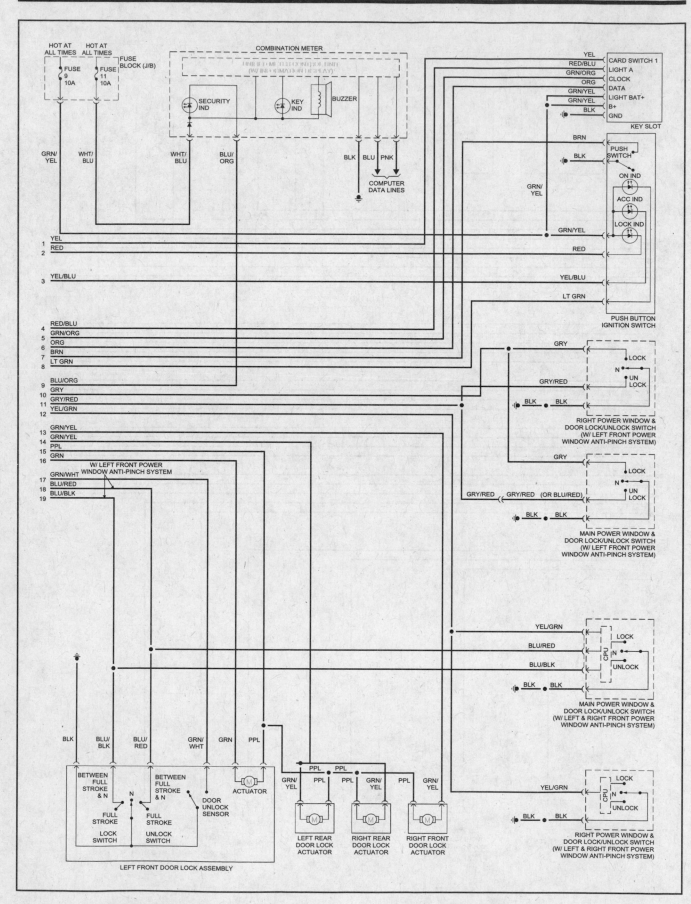

Power door lock system - models with intelligent key (4 of 4)

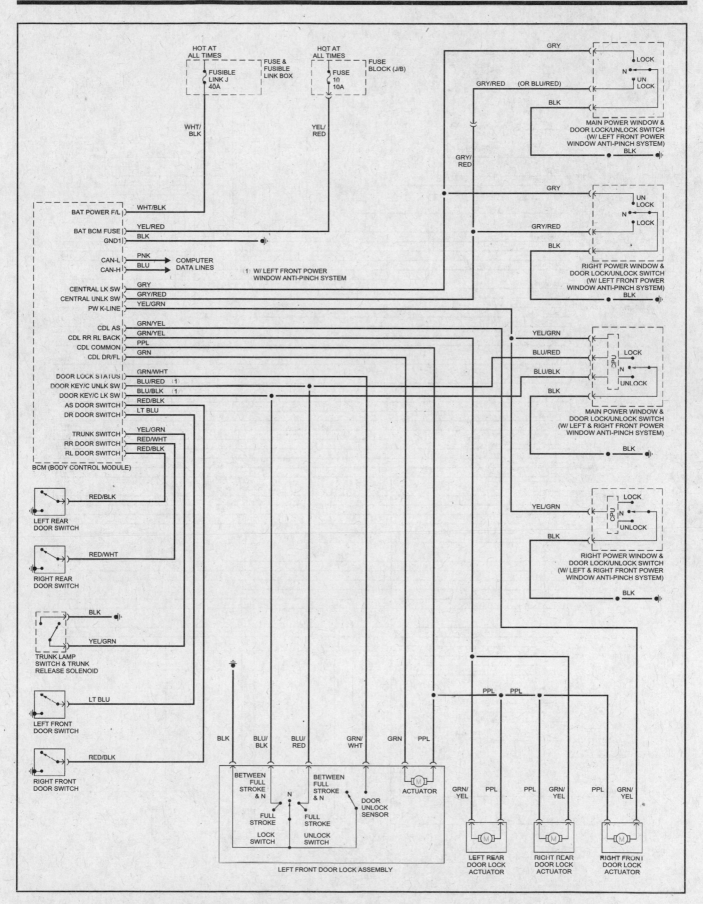

Power door lock system - 2007 and 2008 models without intelligent key

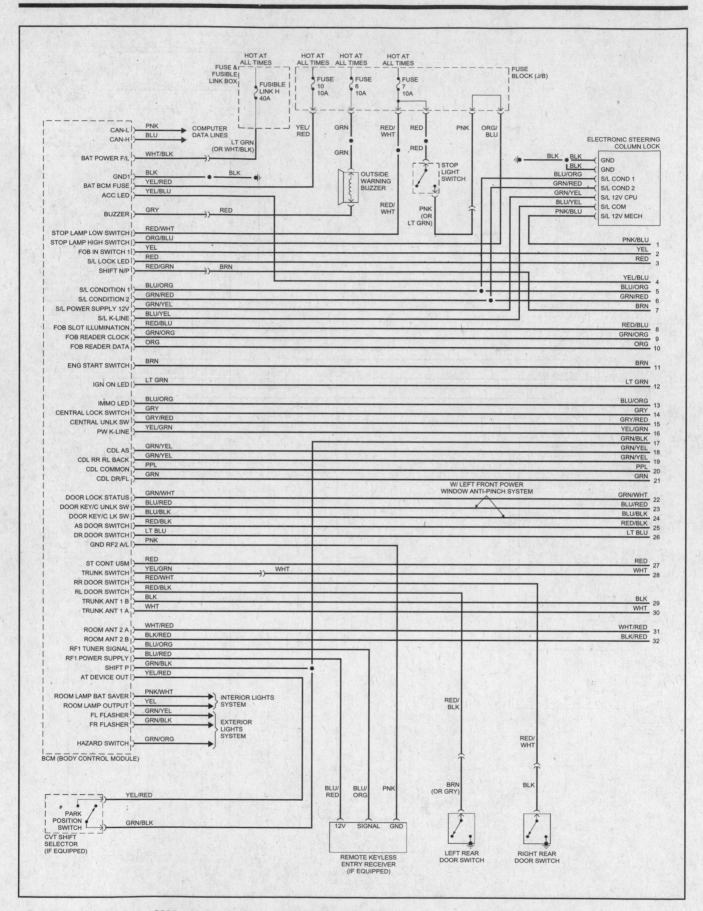

Power door lock system - 2009 and later models without intelligent key (1 of 3)

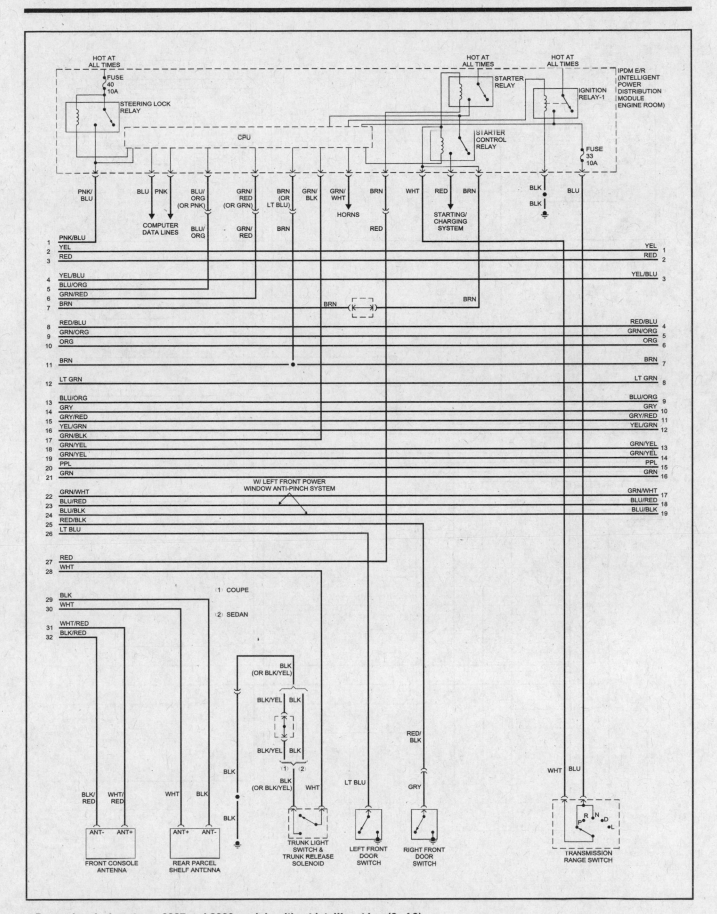

Power door lock system - 2007 and 2008 models without intelligent key (2 of 3)

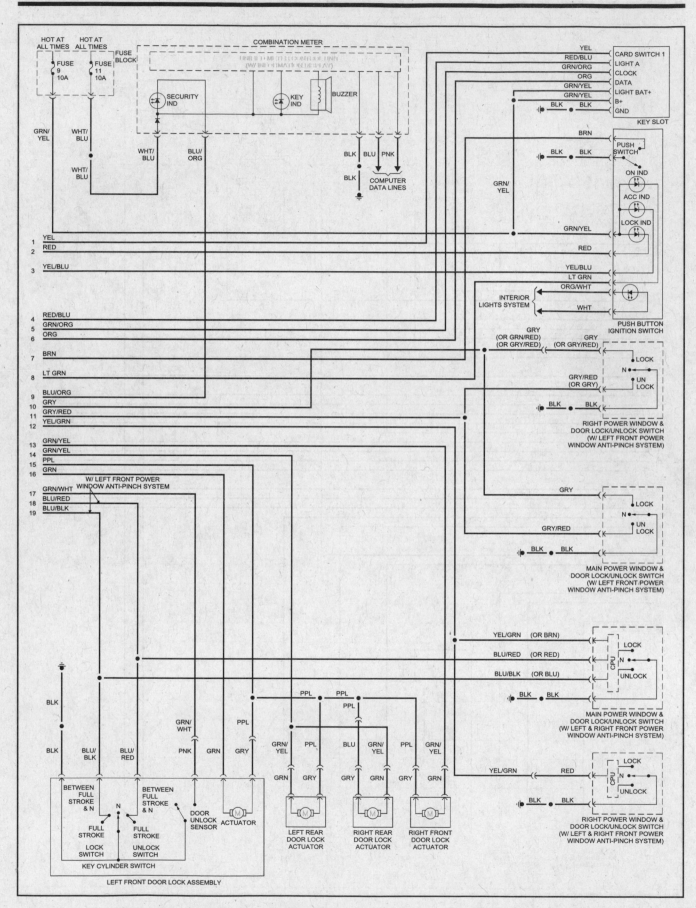

Power door lock system - 2007 and 2008 models without intelligent key (3 of 3)

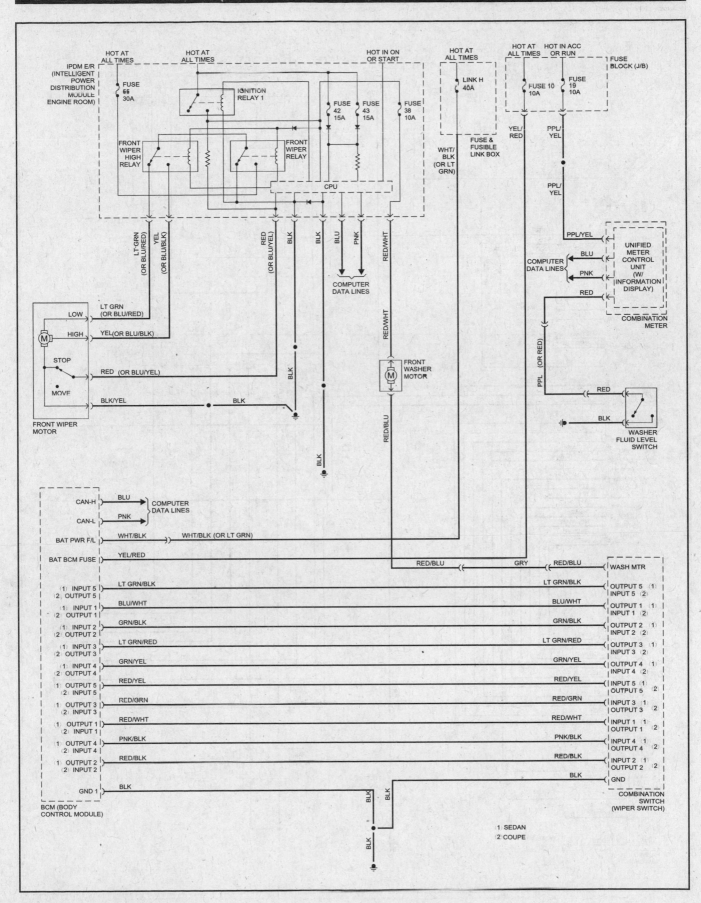

Windshield wiper/washer system

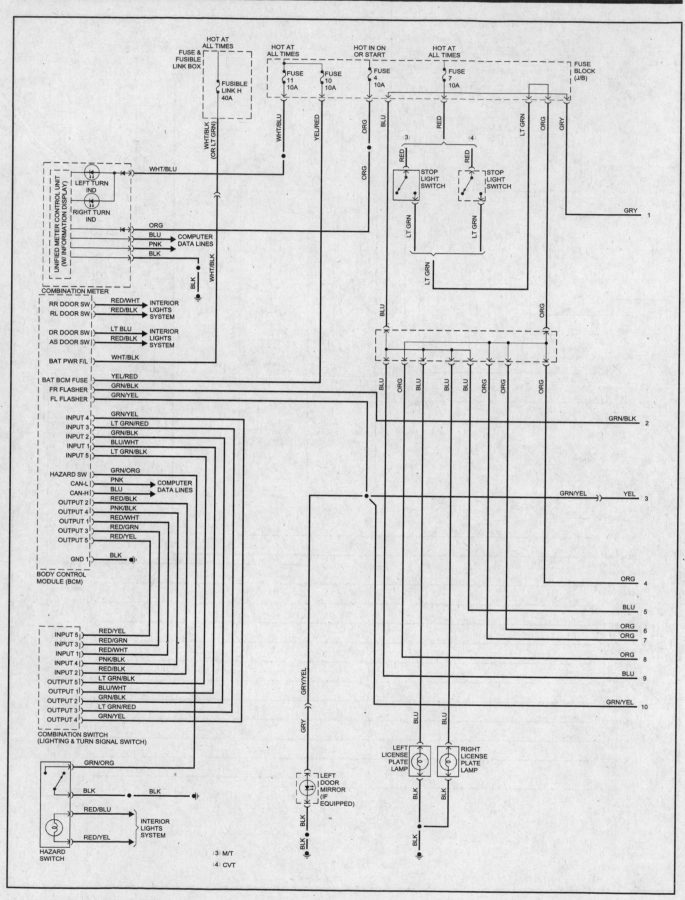

Exterior lighting system - sedan models (1 of 2)

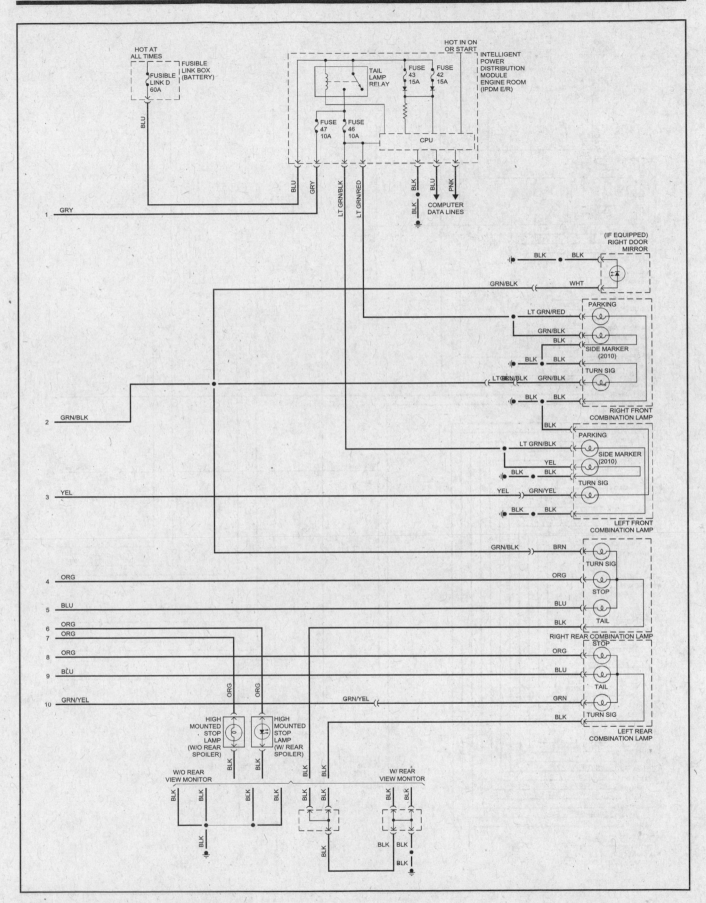

Exterior lighting system - sedan models (2 of 2)

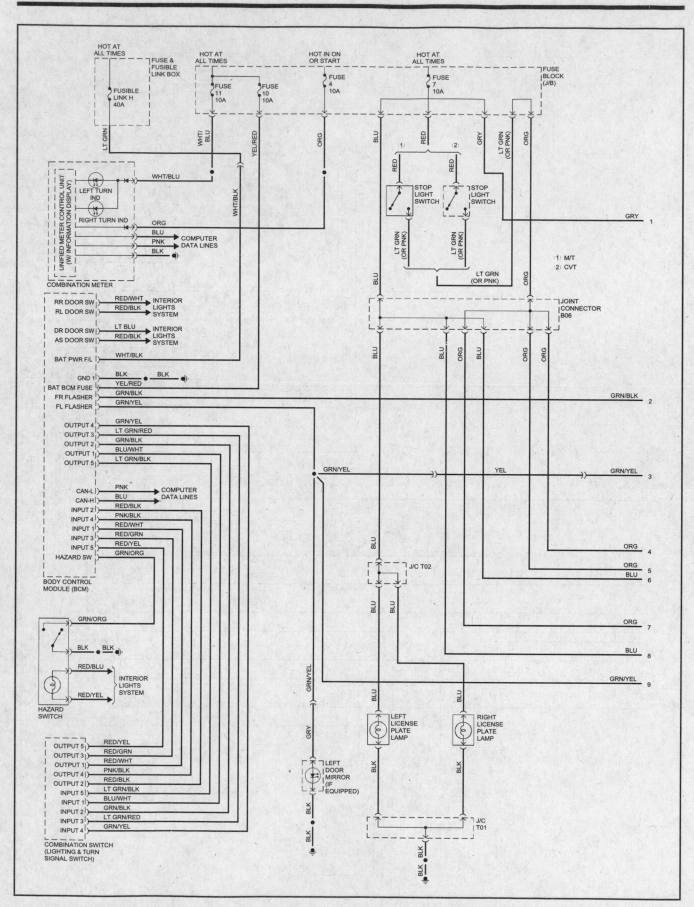

Exterior lighting system - coupe models (1 of 2)

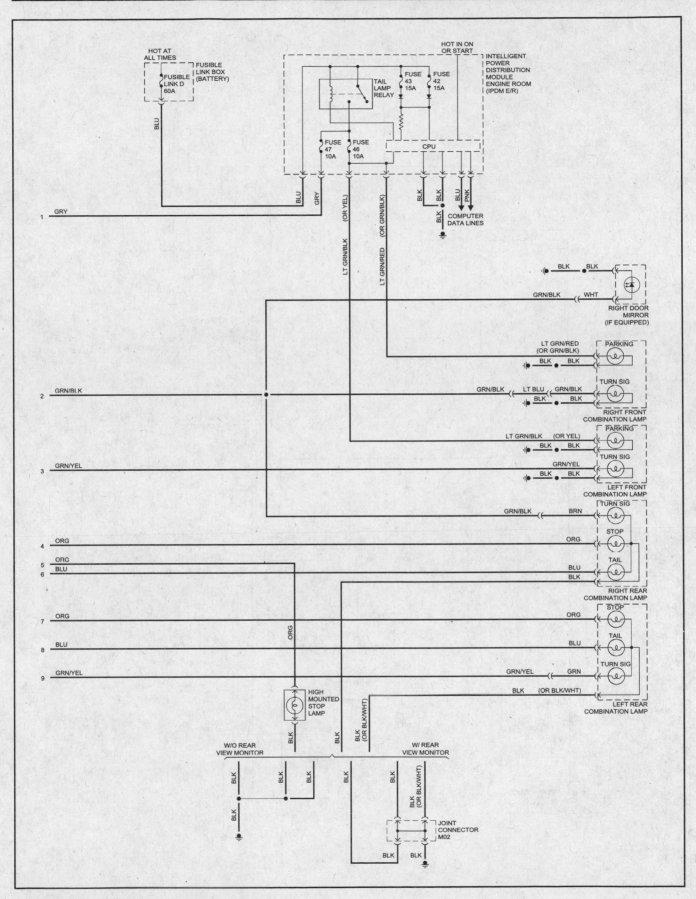

Exterior lighting system - coupe models (2 of 2)

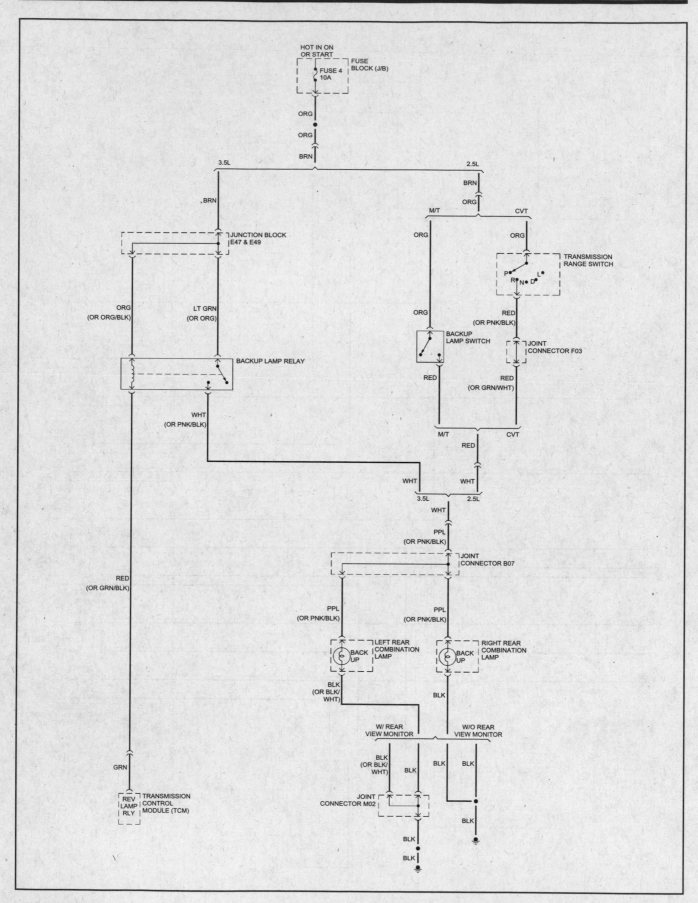

Back-up light system

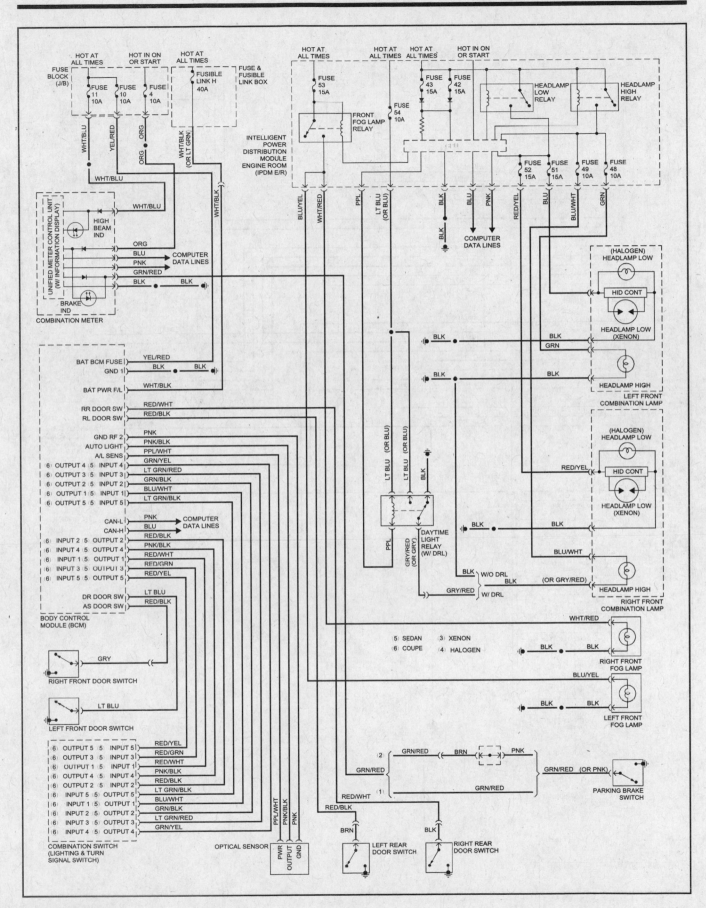

Headlight system

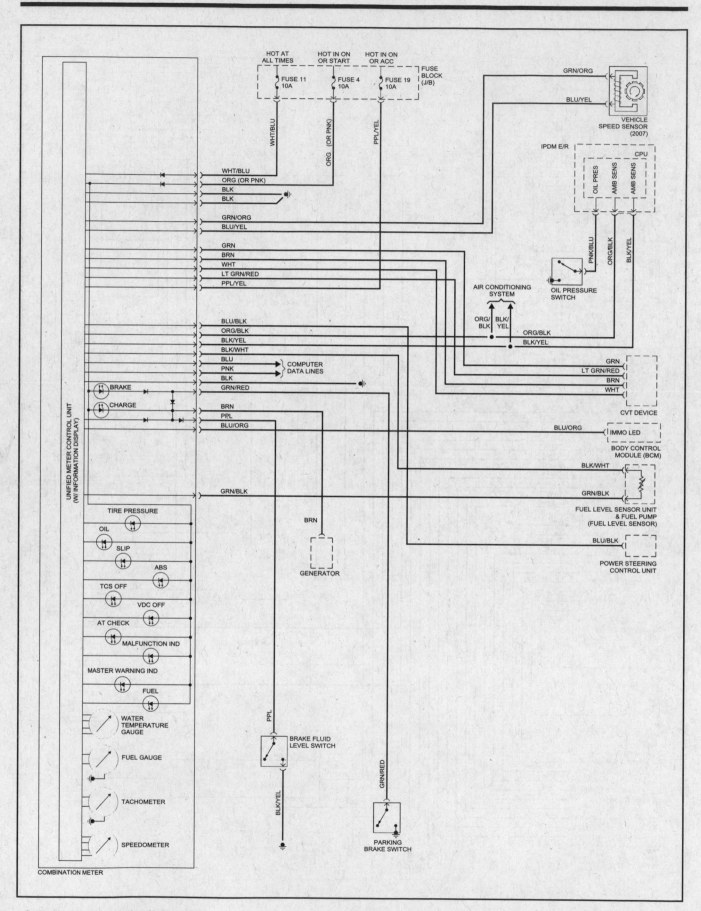

Instruments and warning lights system

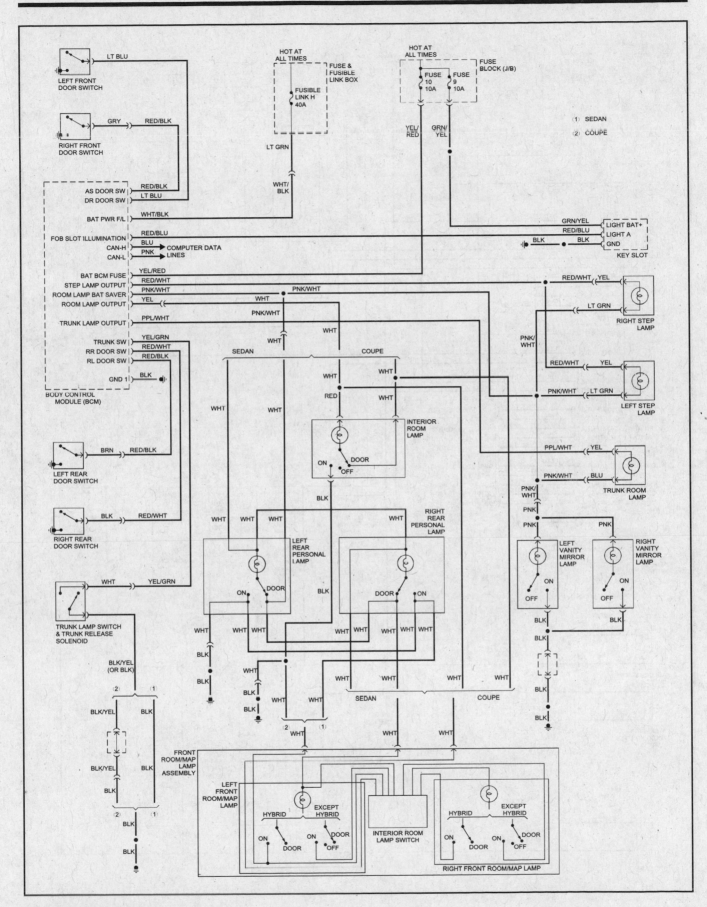

Courtesy lights system

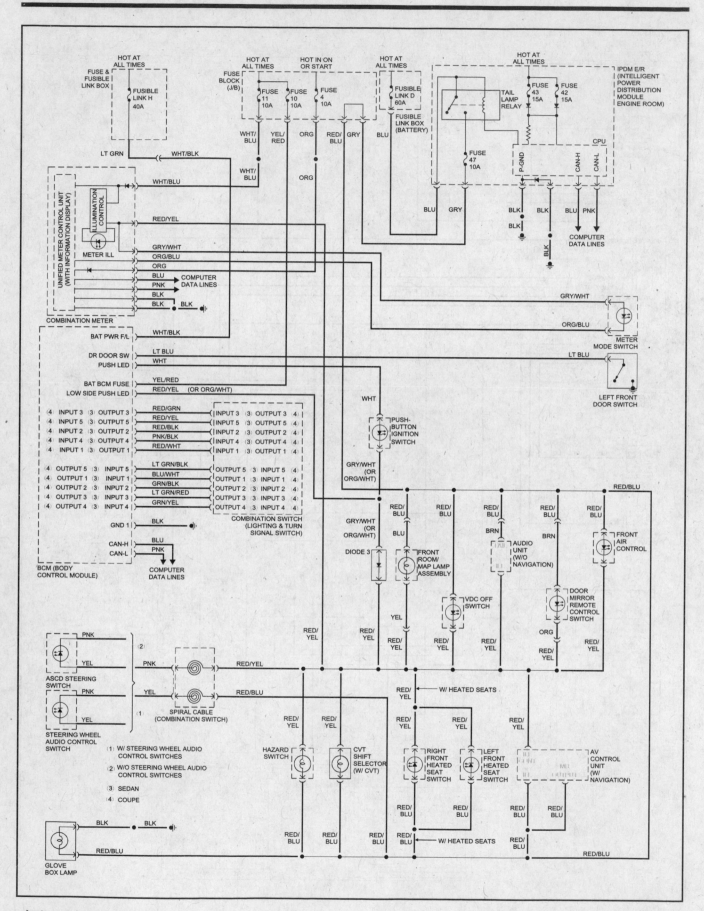

Insturment panel and switch illumination

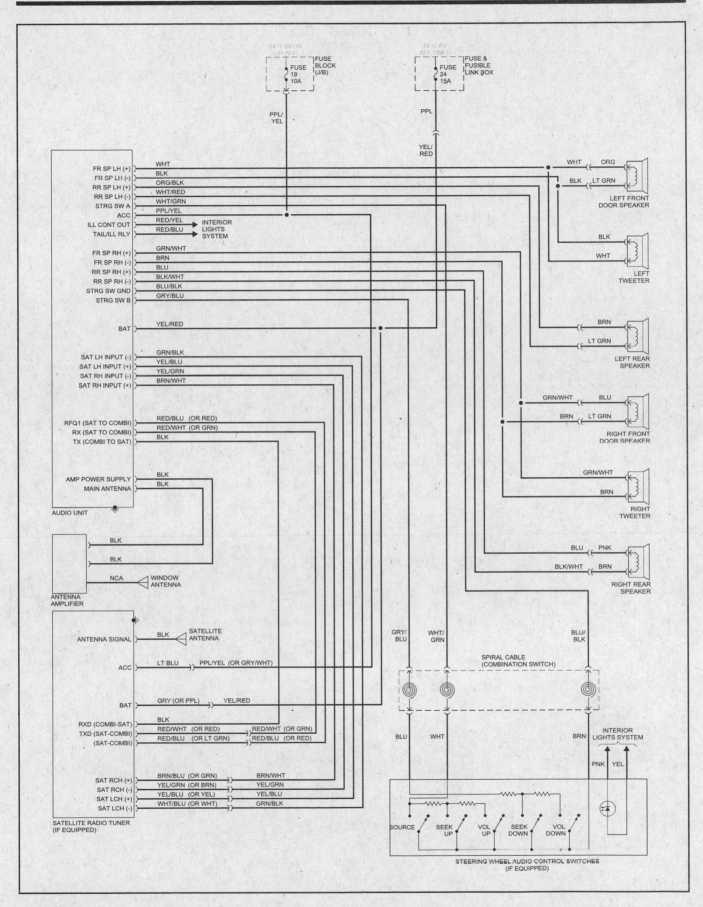

Audio system

Notes

GLOSSARY

AIR/FUEL RATIO: The ratio of air-to-gasoline by weight in the fuel mixture drawn into the engine.

AIR INJECTION: One method of reducing harmful exhaust emissions by injecting air into each of the exhaust ports of an engine. The fresh air entering the hot exhaust manifold causes any remaining fuel to be burned before it can exit the tailpipe.

ALTERNATOR: A device used for converting mechanical energy into electrical energy.

AMMETER: An instrument, calibrated in amperes, used to measure the flow of an electrical current in a circuit. Ammeters are always connected in series with the circuit being tested.

AMPERE: The rate of flow of electrical current present when one volt of electrical pressure is applied against one ohm of electrical resistance.

ANALOG COMPUTER: Any microprocessor that uses similar (analogous) electrical signals to make its calculations.

ARMATURE: A laminated, soft iron core wrapped by a wire that converts electrical energy to mechanical energy as in a motor or relay. When rotated in a magnetic field, it changes mechanical energy into electrical energy as in a generator.

ATMOSPHERIC PRESSURE: The pressure on the Earth's surface caused by the weight of the air in the atmosphere. At sea level, this pressure is 14.7 psi at 32°F (101 kPa at 0°C).

ATOMIZATION: The breaking down of a liquid into a fine mist that can be suspended in air.

AXIAL PLAY: Movement parallel to a shaft or bearing bore.

BACKFIRE: The sudden combustion of gases in the intake or exhaust system that results in a loud explosion.

BACKLASH: The clearance or play between two parts, such as meshed gears.

BACKPRESSURE: Restrictions in the exhaust system that slow the exit of exhaust gases from the combustion chamber.

BAKELITE: A heat resistant, plastic insulator material commonly used in printed circuit boards and transistorized components.

BALL BEARING: A bearing made up of hardened inner and outer races between which hardened steel balls roll.

BALLAST RESISTOR: A resistor in the primary ignition circuit that lowers voltage after the engine is started to reduce wear on ignition components.

BEARING: A friction reducing, supportive device usually located between a stationary part and a moving part.

BIMETAL TEMPERATURE SENSOR: Any sensor or switch made of two dissimilar types of metal that bend when heated or cooled due to the different expansion rates of the alloys. These types of sensors usually function as an on/off switch.

BLOWBY: Combustion gases, composed of water vapor and unburned fuel, that leak past the piston rings into the crankcase during normal engine operation. These gases are removed by the PCV system to prevent the buildup of harmful acids in the crankcase.

BRAKE PAD: A brake shoe and lining assembly used with disc brakes.

BRAKE SHOE: The backing for the brake lining. The term is, however, usually applied to the assembly of the brake backing and lining.

BUSHING: A liner, usually removable, for a bearing; an anti-friction liner used in place of a bearing.

CALIPER: A hydraulically activated device in a disc brake system, which is mounted straddling the brake rotor (disc). The caliper contains at least one piston and two brake pads. Hydraulic pressure on the piston(s) forces the pads against the rotor.

CAMSHAFT: A shaft in the engine on which are the lobes (cams) which operate the valves. The camshaft is driven by the crankshaft, via a belt, chain or gears, at one half the crankshaft speed.

CAPACITOR: A device which stores an electrical charge.

CARBON MONOXIDE (CO): A colorless, odorless gas given off as a normal byproduct of combustion. It is poisonous and extremely dangerous in confined areas, building up slowly to toxic levels without warning if adequate ventilation is not available.

CARBURETOR: A device, usually mounted on the intake manifold of an engine, which mixes the air and fuel in the proper proportion to allow even combustion.

CATALYTIC CONVERTER: A device installed in the exhaust system, like a muffler, that converts harmful byproducts of combustion into carbon dioxide and water vapor by means of a heat-producing chemical reaction.

CENTRIFUGAL ADVANCE: A mechanical method of advancing the spark timing by using flyweights in the distributor that react to centrifugal force generated by the distributor shaft rotation.

CHECK VALVE: Any one-way valve installed to permit the flow of air, fuel or vacuum in one direction only.

CHOKE: A device, usually a moveable valve, placed in the intake path of a carburetor to restrict the flow of air.

CIRCUIT: Any unbroken path through which an electrical current can flow. Also used to describe fuel flow in some instances.

CIRCUIT BREAKER: A switch which protects an electrical circuit from overload by opening the circuit when the current flow exceeds a predetermined level. Some circuit breakers must be reset manually, while most reset automatically.

COIL (IGNITION): A transformer in the ignition circuit which steps up the voltage provided to the spark plugs.

COMBINATION MANIFOLD: An assembly which includes both the intake and exhaust manifolds in one casting.

COMBINATION VALVE: A device used in some fuel systems that routes fuel vapors to a charcoal storage canister instead of venting them into the atmosphere. The valve relieves fuel tank pressure and allows fresh air into the tank as the fuel level drops to prevent a vapor lock situation.

COMPRESSION RATIO: The comparison of the total volume of the cylinder and combustion chamber with the piston at BDC and the piston at TDC.

CONDENSER: 1. An electrical device which acts to store an electrical charge, preventing voltage surges. 2. A radiator-like device in the air conditioning system in which refrigerant gas condenses into a liquid, giving off heat.

CONDUCTOR: Any material through which an electrical current can be transmitted easily.

CONTINUITY: Continuous or complete circuit. Can be checked with ah ohmmeter.

COUNTERSHAFT: An intermediate shaft which is rotated by a mainshaft and transmits, in turn, that rotation to a working part.

CRANKCASE: The lower part of an engine in which the crankshaft and related parts operate.

CRANKSHAFT: The main driving shaft of an engine which receives reciprocating motion from the pistons and converts it to rotary motion.

CYLINDER: In an engine, the round hole in the engine block in which the piston(s) ride.

CYLINDER BLOCK: The main structural member of an engine in which is found the cylinders, crankshaft and other principal parts.

CYLINDER HEAD: The detachable portion of the engine, usually fastened to the top of the cylinder block and containing all or most of the combustion chambers. On overhead valve engines, it contains the valves and their operating parts. On overhead cam engines, it contains the camshaft as well.

DEAD CENTER: The extreme top or bottom of the piston stroke.

DETONATION: An unwanted explosion of the air/fuel mixture in the combustion chamber caused by excess heat and compression, advanced timing, or an overly lean mixture. Also referred to as "ping".

DIAPHRAGM: A thin, flexible wall separating two cavities, such as in a vacuum advance unit.

DIESELING: A condition in which hot spots in the combustion chamber cause the engine to run on after the key is turned off.

DIFFERENTIAL: A geared assembly which allows the transmission of motion between drive axles, giving one axle the ability to turn faster than the other.

DIODE: An electrical device that will allow current to flow in one direction only.

DISC BRAKE: A hydraulic braking assembly consisting of a brake disc, or rotor, mounted on an axle, and a caliper assembly containing, usually two brake pads which are activated by hydraulic pressure. The pads are forced against the sides of the disc, creating friction which slows the vehicle.

DISTRIBUTOR: A mechanically driven device on an engine which is responsible for electrically firing the spark plug at a predetermined point of the piston stroke.

DOWEL PIN: A pin, inserted in mating holes in two different parts allowing those parts to maintain a fixed relationship.

DRUM BRAKE: A braking system which consists of two brake shoes and one or two wheel cylinders, mounted on a fixed backing plate, and a brake drum, mounted on an axle, which revolves around the assembly.

DWELL: The rate, measured in degrees of shaft rotation, at which an electrical circuit cycles on and off.

ELECTRONIC CONTROL UNIT (ECU): Ignition module, module, amplifier or igniter. See Module for definition.

ELECTRONIC IGNITION: A system in which the timing and firing of the spark plugs is controlled by an electronic control unit, usually called a module. These systems have no points or condenser.

END-PLAY: The measured amount of axial movement in a shaft.

ENGINE: A device that converts heat into mechanical energy.

EXHAUST MANIFOLD: A set of cast passages or pipes which conduct exhaust gases from the engine.

FEELER GAUGE: A blade, usually metal, or precisely, predetermined thickness, used to measure the clearance between two parts.

FIRING ORDER: The order in which combustion occurs in the cylinders of an engine. Also the order in which spark is distributed to the plugs by the distributor.

FLOODING: The presence of too much fuel in the intake manifold and combustion chamber which prevents the air/fuel mixture from firing, thereby causing a no-start situation.

FLYWHEEL: A disc shaped part bolted to the rear end of the crankshaft. Around the outer perimeter is affixed the ring gear. The starter drive engages the ring gear, turning the flywheel, which rotates the crankshaft, imparting the initial starting motion to the engine.

FOOT POUND (ft. lbs. or sometimes, ft.lb.): The amount of energy or work needed to raise an item weighing one pound, a distance of one foot.

FUSE: A protective device in a circuit which prevents circuit overload by breaking the circuit when a specific amperage is present. The device is constructed around a strip or wire of a lower amperage rating than the circuit it is designed to protect. When an amperage higher than that stamped on the fuse is present in the circuit, the strip or wire melts, opening the circuit.

GEAR RATIO: The ratio between the number of teeth on meshing gears.

GENERATOR: A device which converts mechanical energy into electrical energy.

HEAT RANGE: The measure of a spark plug's ability to dissipate heat from its firing end. The higher the heat range, the hotter the plug fires.

HUB: The center part of a wheel or gear.

HYDROCARBON (HC): Any chemical compound made up of hydrogen and carbon. A major pollutant formed by the engine as a byproduct of combustion.

HYDROMETER: An instrument used to measure the specific gravity of a solution.

INCH POUND (inch lbs.; sometimes in.lb. or in. lbs.): One twelfth of a foot pound.

INDUCTION: A means of transferring electrical energy in the form of a magnetic field. Principle used in the ignition coil to increase voltage.

INJECTOR: A device which receives metered fuel under relatively low pressure and is activated to inject the fuel into the engine under relatively high pressure at a predetermined time.

INPUT SHAFT: The shaft to which torque is applied, usually carrying the driving gear or gears.

INTAKE MANIFOLD: A casting of passages or pipes used to conduct air or a fuel/air mixture to the cylinders.

JOURNAL: The bearing surface within which a shaft operates.

KEY: A small block usually fitted in a notch between a shaft and a hub to prevent slippage of the two parts.

MANIFOLD: A casting of passages or set of pipes which connect the cylinders to an inlet or outlet source.

MANIFOLD VACUUM: Low pressure in an engine intake manifold formed just below the throttle plates. Manifold vacuum is highest at idle and drops under acceleration.

MASTER CYLINDER: The primary fluid pressurizing device in a hydraulic system. In automotive use, it is found in brake and hydraulic clutch systems and is pedal activated, either directly or, in a power brake system, through the power booster.

MODULE: Electronic control unit, amplifier or igniter of solid state or integrated design which controls the current flow in the ignition primary circuit based on input from the pick-up coil. When the module opens the primary circuit, high secondary voltage is induced in the coil.

NEEDLE BEARING: A bearing which consists of a number (usually a large number) of long, thin rollers.

OHM: (Ω) The unit used to measure the resistance of conductor-to-electrical flow. One ohm is the amount of resistance that limits current flow to one ampere in a circuit with one volt of pressure.

OHMMETER: An instrument used for measuring the resistance, in ohms, in an electrical circuit.

OUTPUT SHAFT: The shaft which transmits torque from a device, such as a transmission.

OVERDRIVE: A gear assembly which produces more shaft revolutions than that transmitted to it.

OVERHEAD CAMSHAFT (OHC): An engine configuration in which the camshaft is mounted on top of the cylinder head and operates the valve either directly or by means of rocker arms.

OVERHEAD VALVE (OHV): An engine configuration in which all of the valves are located in the cylinder head and the camshaft is located in the cylinder block. The camshaft operates the valves via lifters and pushrods.

OXIDES OF NITROGEN (NOx): Chemical compounds of nitrogen produced as a byproduct of combustion. They combine with hydrocarbons to produce smog.

OXYGEN SENSOR: Use with the feedback system to sense the presence of oxygen in the exhaust gas and signal the computer which can reference the voltage signal to an air/fuel ratio.

PINION: The smaller of two meshing gears.

PISTON RING: An open-ended ring with fits into a groove on the outer diameter of the piston. Its chief function is to form a seal between the piston and cylinder wall. Most automotive pistons have three rings: two for compression sealing; one for oil sealing.

PRELOAD: A predetermined load placed on a bearing during assembly or by adjustment.

PRIMARY CIRCUIT: the low voltage side of the ignition system which consists of the ignition switch, ballast resistor or resistance wire, bypass, coil, electronic control unit and pick-up coil as well as the connecting wires and harnesses.

PRESS FIT: The mating of two parts under pressure, due to the inner diameter of one being smaller than the outer diameter of the other, or vice versa; an interference fit.

RACE: The surface on the inner or outer ring of a bearing on which the balls, needles or rollers move.

REGULATOR: A device which maintains the amperage and/or voltage levels of a circuit at predetermined values.

RELAY: A switch which automatically opens and/or closes a circuit.

RESISTANCE: The opposition to the flow of current through a circuit or electrical device, and is measured in ohms. Resistance is equal to the voltage divided by the amperage.

RESISTOR: A device, usually made of wire, which offers a preset amount of resistance in an electrical circuit.

RING GEAR: The name given to a ring-shaped gear attached to a differential case, or affixed to a flywheel or as part of a planetary gear set.

ROLLER BEARING: A bearing made up of hardened inner and outer races between which hardened steel rollers move.

ROTOR: 1. The disc-shaped part of a disc brake assembly, upon which the brake pads bear; also called, brake disc. 2. The device mounted atop the distributor shaft, which passes current to the distributor cap tower contacts.

SECONDARY CIRCUIT: The high voltage side of the ignition system, usually above 20,000 volts. The secondary includes the ignition coil, coil wire, distributor cap and rotor, spark plug wires and spark plugs.

SENDING UNIT: A mechanical, electrical, hydraulic or electromagnetic device which transmits information to a gauge.

SENSOR: Any device designed to measure engine operating conditions or ambient pressures and temperatures. Usually electronic in nature and designed to send a voltage signal to an on-board computer, some sensors may operate as a simple on/off switch or they may provide a variable voltage signal (like a potentiometer) as conditions or measured parameters change.

SHIM: Spacers of precise, predetermined thickness used between parts to establish a proper working relationship.

SLAVE CYLINDER: In automotive use, a device in the hydraulic clutch system which is activated by hydraulic force, disengaging the clutch.

SOLENOID: A coil used to produce a magnetic field, the effect of which is to produce work.

SPARK PLUG: A device screwed into the combustion chamber of a spark ignition engine. The basic construction is a conductive core inside of a ceramic insulator, mounted in an outer conductive base. An electrical charge from the spark plug wire travels along the conductive core and jumps a preset air gap to a grounding point or points at the end of the conductive base. The resultant spark ignites the fuel/air mixture in the combustion chamber.

SPLINES: Ridges machined or cast onto the outer diameter of a shaft or inner diameter of a bore to enable parts to mate without rotation.

TACHOMETER: A device used to measure the rotary speed of an engine, shaft, gear, etc., usually in rotations per minute.

THERMOSTAT: A valve, located in the cooling system of an engine, which is closed when cold and opens gradually in response to engine heating, controlling the temperature of the coolant and rate of coolant flow.

TOP DEAD CENTER (TDC): The point at which the piston reaches the top of its travel on the compression stroke.

TORQUE: The twisting force applied to an object.

TORQUE CONVERTER: A turbine used to transmit power from a driving member to a driven member via hydraulic action, providing changes in drive ratio and torque. In automotive use, it links the driveplate at the rear of the engine to the automatic transmission.

TRANSDUCER: A device used to change a force into an electrical signal.

TRANSISTOR: A semi-conductor component which can be actuated by a small voltage to perform an electrical switching function.

TUNE-UP: A regular maintenance function, usually associated with the replacement and adjustment of parts and components in the electrical and fuel systems of a vehicle for the purpose of attaining optimum performance.

TURBOCHARGER: An exhaust driven pump which compresses intake air and forces it into the combustion chambers at higher than atmospheric pressures. The increased air pressure allows more fuel to be burned and results in increased horsepower being produced.

VACUUM ADVANCE: A device which advances the ignition timing in response to increased engine vacuum.

VACUUM GAUGE: An instrument used to measure the presence of vacuum in a chamber.

VALVE: A device which control the pressure, direction of flow or rate of flow of a liquid or gas.

VALVE CLEARANCE: The measured gap between the end of the valve stem and the rocker arm, cam lobe or follower that activates the valve.

VISCOSITY: The rating of a liquid's internal resistance to flow.

VOLTMETER: An instrument used for measuring electrical force in units called volts. Voltmeters are always connected parallel with the circuit being tested.

WHEEL CYLINDER: Found in the automotive drum brake assembly, it is a device, actuated by hydraulic pressure, which, through internal pistons, pushes the brake shoes outward against the drums.

MASTER INDEX

NOTES